AS level

SOCIOLOGY

a Coursebook for the AQA Specification

ROB WEBB and H[illegible]RD

with LIZ STEEL

Published by Napier Press, PO Box 6383, Brentwood CM13 2NQ
First edition © Napier Press 2004
First published 2004
ISBN 0-9540079-0-5

ish Library Cataloguing in Publication Data

gue record for this book is available from the British Library.

ited by Steve Attmore
Design by Deborah Matthews
Cover design by Deborah Matthews
Picture research by Hal Westergaard
Printed and bound by Fuller-Davies Limited

ACKNOWLEDGEMENTS
George Mann and Barbara Large for commenting on earlier drafts of the text

Every effort has been made to contact the holders of copyright material, but if any have been inadvertently overlooked the publishers will be pleased to make the necessary arrangements at the first opportunity.

Guardian Newspapers Ltd for the extract from *The Observer*, 30 August 1978; from the article 'Today's Special' by Rebecca Smithers in *The Guardian*, 19 July 2001; and for the league table (data supplied by DfES).

Extract by David Morgan 'Risk and Family Practices' reprinted by permission of Sage Publications Ltd from E. Silva et al, *The New Family* (1999) (© David Morgan 1997). Extract from *The Family* by William J. Goode. Copyright 1964 Prentice-Hall Inc. Used with the permission of Pearson Education In., Upper Saddle River, NJ. Extract from Stephen Wagg, *I Blame the Parents* (1992), Blackwell Publishing Ltd. Extracts from Liz Steel and Warren Kidd, *The Family*, 2001, Palgrave Macmillan. Sharon Gewirtz for extract from S. Gewirtz et al, *Markets, Choice and Equity in Education*, Open University (1995). Extract from Karen Chapman, *The Sociology of Schools*, Tavistock (1986) by Thomson Publishing Services. Extract from Debbie Esptein's 'Boys' Under-achievement in Context' in D. Epstein et al, *Failing Boys?* (1998) Open University Press is reproduced by kind permission of the Open University Press/McGraw-Hill Publishing Company. Extract from *Social Trends* vol. 32 (2002) by kind permission of the Office for National Statistics. Extract from Sarah Thornton, *Club Cultures*, Polity Press, Cambridge (1995).

The publishers would like to thank the following for permission to reproduce pictures on these pages. (L=Left, R=Right).
Alamy Images pages 2, 4, 6, 28, 43, 49, 50, 52, 60, 61, 66, 73, 77, 93, 98, 104, 128 L+R, 134, 139 L+R, 149, 157, 164, 166 and 210; Associated Press pages 16 and 41; Corbis page 145; Diana Blofeld page 120; Don Rutledge page 185; Hulton Archive pages 20, 32, 34, 36, 64, 86, 87, 167 and 197; Mirrorpix pages 9, 70, 84, 195 and 213; Photofusion pages 18, 19, 21, 27, 39, 47, 56, 58, 78, 89, 96, 103, 107, 109, 112, 113, 118, 121, 125, 127, 132, 147, 154, 160, 169, 174, 178, 183, 192, 194, 200, 206 and 222.

Cover photograph: Les Polders, Alamy Images

Contents

Chapter 1

Introduction to Sociology

What is sociology?

Sociology is the study of society and of people and their behaviour.

Sociologists study a wide range of topics. For example, the AQA AS and A level specification includes topics such as those in Box 1.

Box 1: Key topics in sociology

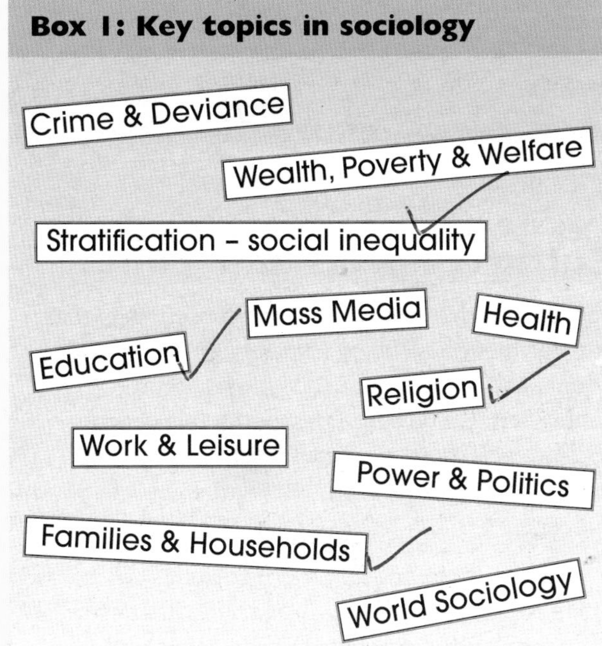

In studying topics like these, sociologists create **theories** to explain human behaviour and the workings of society. Theories are explanations of the patterns we find in society. For example, we may have a theory as to why there are differences in girls' and boys' achievement levels in school.

A theory tries to make **generalisations**; that is, it tries to explain all similar cases, not just a single case. For example, it tries to say why boys in general do less well at school than girls, rather than why simply this or that individual boy does less well.

Sociology is an **evidence-based** subject. This means it is not just about the sociologist's personal opinion or pet theory: our opinions and theories must be backed up by facts about society. Sociologists therefore collect evidence methodically by carrying out research to establish whether their theories are correct. A good theory is one that explains the available evidence.

As well as producing theories about society, sociology has practical applications. For example, if we know the causes of social problems such as educational under-achievement, we may be able to use this knowledge to design social policies to improve children's educational opportunities. A **social policy** is a programme or plan introduced by government that aims to achieve a particular goal, such as raising educational standards or reducing crime rates. Governments may use the findings of sociological research to develop more effective policies.

question

Suggest three social problems apart from educational under-achievement and crime rates that sociologists might usefully investigate. (You could look at the list of topics in Box 1 for ideas.)

Nature or nurture?

People disagree about whether our behaviour is somehow 'natural' or innate (inborn), or whether it is the result of nurture; that is, our upbringing in society.

Some biologists argue that behaviour is mainly shaped by natural **instincts**. An instinct is an innate, fixed, pre-programmed pattern of behaviour shared by all members of a given species. For example, all blackbirds are 'programmed' to produce the same song patterns, and a blackbird reared in isolation from others will still produce the same song.

In other words, instinctive behaviour doesn't have to be learnt. Many instincts are an automatic response to particular stimuli in the environment, such as birds migrating as the seasons change. These behaviours are not learnt and the animal apparently has no control over them.

Many biologists argue that, like animal behaviour, our behaviour too is governed by instinct. For example, they claim that humans have natural instincts for reproduction and self-preservation, and women have a maternal instinct for childbearing and rearing.

Much of our learning occurs in our early years.

However, sociologists question whether human behaviour really is governed by instincts. They point out that on the whole our behaviour is not fixed biologically. Although we may all possess the same biological urges or drives, the way we satisfy these *varies* between individuals and societies. For example:

- Although we all have a sex drive, the way we satisfy it can vary: from promiscuity to monogamy, polygamy etc – or we may choose to remain celibate.
- We have a drive for self-preservation, yet some people choose to commit suicide or risk their lives in war.
- Women are said to have a maternal instinct, yet some choose to abandon or abuse their children, while today over a fifth of all women in Britain choose not to have children.

If our behaviour really was determined by instincts, we would not expect to find such enormous variations in behaviour between individuals and societies.

Sociologists argue that the reason for these variations is that our behaviour is **learnt** rather than instinctive. Much of this learning occurs in our early years through contact with others and this has an enormous influence on our behaviour and development. For example, language, knowledge of right and wrong, practical skills such as dressing oneself, table manners and so on all have to be learnt from other members of society. The effects on human development of a lack of social contact are shown in Box 2.

Sociologists therefore argue that biology and instinct cannot explain our behaviour, because most of it is learnt not inborn, and because it is not fixed for all members of our species, but varies between societies. As an alternative way of explaining human behaviour, therefore, sociologists use the two related ideas of culture and socialisation.

Culture, norms and values

Sociologists define **culture** as all those things that are learnt and shared by a society or group of people and transmitted from generation to generation. Culture includes all the things that a society regards as important, such as customs, traditions, language, skills, knowledge, beliefs, norms and values.

For example, the culture of societies whose way of life is based on hunting will include hunting skills and techniques, knowledge of the habits and movements of game animals and so on. Similarly, such cultures often contain shared *beliefs* about the spirits of the animals they hunt and how they should be treated.

Members of a society also share norms and values. **Values** are general principles or goals. They tell us what is good and what we should aim for. For example, modern American society places a high value on individual achievement and the accumulation of personal wealth. By contrast, societies such as those of American Indians place a high value on individuals fulfilling their duties to the group, including the duty to share their wealth rather than keep it for themselves.

While values lay down general principles or guidelines, **norms** are the specific rules that govern behaviour in particular situations. For example, cultures that place a high value on respect for elders usually have specific rules on how they are to be approached or addressed. It may not be permissible

Box 2: The effects of extreme isolation

Over the years there have been several cases of 'feral' (wild) children found in forests and elsewhere who had apparently been reared by wolves or other animals. There is no way of knowing for sure if such children really had been nurtured by animals, but it is certain they had had little contact with other humans. One case was that of Shamdev, an Indian boy aged about five found in a forest playing with wolf cubs. When first found:

> 'Shamdev cowered from people and would only play with dogs. He hated the sun and used to curl up in shadowy places. After dark he grew restless and they had to tie him up to stop him following the jackals which howled around the village at night. If anyone cut themselves, he could smell the scent of blood and would scamper towards it. He caught chickens and ate them alive, including the entrails. Later, when he had evolved a sign language of his own, he would cross his thumbs and flap his hands: this meant "chicken" or "food".' (*The Observer*, 30 August 1978)

Of course, it is possible that parents abandon children like Shamdev precisely because they are abnormal, and such children may not have developed normally even if they had been raised in human company. However, the case of Isabelle suggests otherwise. Discovered at the age of six, Isabelle was the child of a deaf mute single mother, both of whom had been kept shut up by the family in a darkened room for most of the time. According to Kingsley Davis (1970):

> 'Her behaviour towards strangers, especially men, was almost that of a wild animal, manifesting much fear and hostility. In place of speech she made a strange croaking sound. In many ways she acted like an infant... At first it was even hard to tell whether or not she could hear, so unused were her senses. Many of her actions resembled those of deaf children.'

She was also unable to walk properly, and at first it was thought she might have severe learning difficulties. However, in two years of intensive training, Isabelle was able to cover the stages of learning that normally take six years and went on to develop normally. These examples show that basic human social characteristics are not inborn or instinctive. We have to *learn* to be 'normal human beings' through contact with others in our early years.

activity

Working alone or in small groups:

1 Make a list of all the characteristics of Shamdev and Isabelle that might be described as 'non-human'.

2 What 'human' characteristics, skills and abilities would you expect a normal five or six year old child to possess? Are any of these inborn?

3 What conclusions would you draw about the importance of nurture and nature in human development?

to look directly at them when speaking to them, or openly to disagree with or disobey them.

Each culture has detailed rules or norms governing every aspect of behaviour, from food and dress to how we perform our jobs or who we may marry. Some norms, such as written laws or rules, are formal. Other norms are informal, such as table manners.

If we fail to keep to a norm, others may punish us. For example, stealing may result in a fine or imprisonment. Likewise, when we uphold a norm, we may be rewarded. For example, obeying the norm that we should work hard at school may earn us a place at university. Sociologists use the term **sanctions** to describe anything that encourages people to conform to norms. Rewards are positive sanctions, while punishments are negative sanctions. Sanctions are a form of **social control**: that is, a way of ensuring that society's members behave as others expect them to.

Cultures and their norms vary greatly. What one culture considers normal or desirable, another may see as unacceptable. For example, in some cultures

Every culture has detailed norms governing all aspects of daily life.

it is permitted to have several spouses at the same time (polygamy), whereas in others only one is allowed (monogamy). Similarly, some cultures have taboos on specific foods, or rules about what foods may be eaten together.

There may also be cultural variations within a society, especially a large complex one such as Britain. Different groups may have their own **subcultures** that vary significantly from the mainstream culture. For example, different religious groups have different dietary norms as well as different beliefs about the afterlife.

Socialisation

As the examples of feral children (see Box 2) show, we are not born knowing right from wrong, how to speak a language or what type of food we should eat. That is, we are not born with a culture but must learn it from other members of society.

Sociologists refer to this process of learning one's culture as socialisation – learning all the things that are necessary for us to be accepted as full members of society. Another way of describing

activity

In small groups, discuss the following questions. Compare your answers with the other groups in the class.

Food norms

1 Are there any things that other cultures consider to be food that your culture would not and vice versa?

2 What norms do our culture and others have governing:

(a) how to eat (implements, manners etc)?

(b) what should be eaten when (time of day/year, special occasions etc)?

Bus norms

1 To get from home to school or college, you might need to take a bus. Make a list of all the norms you can think of that the passengers, the driver and other road users will have to follow if you are to get to your destination safely and on time.

2 What norms govern whether or not we should sit next to someone else?

3 What norms govern the kind of communication permitted between passengers sitting next to one another?

4 Imagine you were taking a three year old on a bus. What sort of things might they do that you would not dream of doing? What does this tell us about norms?

socialisation is to say it is a process of 'internalising' the culture, whereby society gets 'into' and becomes part of us.

Socialisation begins when we are born and continues throughout life. Sociologists distinguish between primary and secondary socialisation:

- **Primary socialisation** takes place in the early years of life and occurs largely within the family, where we learn language, basic skills and norms.
- **Secondary socialisation** takes place later, at school and in wider society.

Through primary socialisation, we learn what is expected of us as members of a family, but secondary socialisation introduces us to the more impersonal adult world. As well as the family and school, there are other agencies of socialisation, including peer groups, the mass media and religion. Each of these plays a part in transmitting the norms, values and skills that individuals need to perform their roles in society.

Status and role

A **status** is a position in society. We can think of society as made up of lots of different positions or statuses. Some statuses are **ascribed**: based on fixed characteristics that we are born with and cannot normally change, such as our sex or ethnicity. Other statuses are **achieved** through our own efforts, such as getting into university or being promoted at work.

Those who occupy a given status are expected to follow particular norms of behaviour. For example, someone occupying the status of teacher is expected to mark students' work, treat them fairly, start lessons punctually, know their subject and so on. This set of norms together makes up the **role** of teacher.

Socialisation involves not only learning the general culture of society as a whole, but also the things we need to perform our particular roles within society. For example, boys and girls may be socialised differently to prepare them for different gender roles in adulthood.

questions

1 What norms make up the role of (a) student (b) employee?

2 In what way does the socialisation of boys and girls differ?

Individual and society

So far we have assumed that individuals are shaped by the socialisation process to ensure that they perform the roles society requires of them. However, this implies we are simply the products of society and have no choice in how we act. How true is this? There are two main views:

- the structuralist view
- the social action view.

The **structuralist view** sees the individual as entirely shaped by the structure of society (the way society is organised or set up). It sees us as behaving according to society's norms and expectations, which we internalise through the socialisation process.

In this view, society determines our behaviour: we are like puppets on a string, manipulated by society. This is sometimes described as a 'macro' (large-scale) approach because it focuses on how wider society influences us. The emphasis is firmly on the power of society to shape us.

The **social action view** sees us as having free will and choice. It emphasises the power of individuals to create society through their actions and interactions. This is sometimes described as a 'micro' approach because it focuses on small-scale, face-to-face interactions between individuals. An example is the study described in Box 3, which shows how the beliefs people hold about others influence how they interact with them.

In practice, most sociologists accept that individuals do have some degree of choice, as the social action view argues, but that their choices are limited by the structure of society, as the structuralist view argues.

activity

Think about your own educational experiences and choices.

- In what ways do you have freedom of choice about your education?
- In what ways are your choices shaped by wider society (e.g. by your parents' views or income, the job market, your school or college)?

Box 3: Shoplifting in Chicago

Interactionist sociologists take a social action approach to crime. Rather than seeing crime as caused by 'society', they see it as the outcome of the labels people apply to others in their interactions with them. Mary Cameron's (1964) study of shoplifting in Chicago department stores is a good example of this approach.

Cameron found that stores didn't automatically prosecute everyone they suspected of shoplifting. They were often reluctant to prosecute because of the difficulty of proving the case and the cost of releasing employees to be witnesses. They were inclined to let suspects off with a warning, particularly if they were willing and able to pay for the goods.

However, not everyone was treated in the same way. According to Cameron, store detectives made assumptions about what the 'typical shoplifter' is like. They believed adolescents and black people were more likely to be shoplifters and kept them under surveillance when they were in the store. By contrast, the detectives were unlikely to be suspicious of people they saw as 'respectable'. These people tended to be middle-class and white. Even when the detectives witnessed an offence, they were less likely to report it if the suspect was of a similar background to themselves.

When arrests were made the stores were more likely to press charges if the suspects were black. For example, only 9% of arrested white women were charged, but 42% of black women. Furthermore, when cases went to court, not only were black women more likely to be found guilty; they were six times more likely to be jailed than white women.

Cameron's study shows how people's beliefs about others influence how they act towards them. In this case, the ideas of the store detectives and others about the 'typical shoplifter' affected which groups they chose to pursue, and this in turn criminalised more blacks than whites.

questions

1 What evidence does Cameron give of suspects being able to negotiate an outcome other than prosecution?

2 Apart from being young and black, what other characteristics do you think store detectives might see as typical of shoplifters?

3 How could you apply Cameron's ideas to explaining the fact the working class are more likely to be convicted of crimes than the middle class?

Consensus or conflict?

Although structuralists agree that society shapes our behaviour, there are disagreements among them about the *kind* of structure society has. Functionalist sociologists see society as based on value consensus; that is, harmony and agreement among its members about basic values. By contrast, Marxist sociologists see society as based on conflict.

According to **functionalists**, society is held together by a shared culture into which all its members are socialised. Sharing the same culture integrates individuals into society by giving them a sense of solidarity or 'fellow feeling' with others. It enables members of society to agree on goals and how to achieve them and so enables them to cooperate harmoniously.

Functionalists see society as like a biological organism such as the human body. Like a body whose parts (organs, cells etc) fit together and depend on one another, society too is a system of interdependent parts. Each part performs functions that contribute to the well being of society as a whole. For example, the family reproduces the population and performs the function of primary socialisation, while the education system equips us with the knowledge and skills needed for work.

Marxists disagree with the functionalist view. They see society as based on class conflict, not consensus. They argue that society is divided into two social classes:

- The minority capitalist class, or *bourgeoisie*, own the means of production such as the factories, raw materials and land.

Why do the police target some groups more than others?

- The majority working class, or *proletariat*, own nothing but their own labour, which they have to sell to the bourgeoisie in order to survive.

The bourgeoisie exploit the workers and profit from their labour. This exploitation breeds class conflict, which Karl Marx (1818–83) believed would eventually lead to the working class overthrowing capitalism and creating a classless, equal society. In the Marxist view, all social institutions – such as religion, the media and the education system – serve to maintain capitalism, for example by promoting the idea that inequality is inevitable and fair.

Feminist sociologists agree with Marxists that there are fundamental divisions and conflicts in society, but they see gender rather than class as the most important division. They see society and its institutions as *patriarchal*; that is, male-dominated. For example, they see the family as unequal, with women doing most of the housework and childcare.

Diversity and identity

According to Marxists and functionalists, in modern society the individual's identity is largely fixed. Marxists see our identity as stemming from our class position, while functionalists see it as the result of being socialised into the shared culture.

However, **postmodernist** sociologists argue that we are now living in a postmodern society (see Box 4). Unlike modern society, where individuals share a common culture or class identity, postmodern society is fragmented (splintered) into a wide variety of different groups. These are based on differences in ethnicity, age, religion, region, nationality, sexuality and so on. This diversity gives individuals greater freedom to 'pick and mix' their identities from a wide variety of sources.

Critics argue that postmodernists exaggerate how far things have really changed. In particular, postmodernists ignore the continuing importance of social inequality and the ways this limits people's choices and shapes their lives.

question

In what ways does poverty limit people's choices and shape their lives?

Inequality

Britain remains an unequal society. For example, in 2001 the wealthiest 5% of people in Britain owned 43% of the nation's total wealth, while the poorest 50% of the population owned only 5% of the wealth.

Sociologists are interested in **social stratification**; that is, inequalities between groups such as social classes, men and women, ethnic groups and age groups. They use the concept of 'life chances' to describe these inequalities. Life chances refers to the chances of enjoying the 'good things', such as educational success, a long and healthy life, high quality housing, and well paid, interesting work. Different classes, genders, ethnic groups and age groups tend to have different life chances.

Box 4: Social change and types of society

Sociology as a subject first developed in response to major changes that began to take place in society from the 18th century onwards. One key change was **urbanisation**: the shift from a largely rural society where people lived in villages, to an urban society in which they lived in towns and cities. The process of urbanisation was paralleled by one of **industrialisation**, in which the workforce increasingly moved out of agriculture and into factory production.

These changes had an enormous impact on all areas of social life and to understand them many sociologists made a distinction between traditional and modern society:

- **traditional society**: a rural-agricultural society where there was little social change, a strong sense of community and religion dominated people's view of the world
- **modern society**: an urban-industrial society with social and technological change and a belief in progress and science.

However, some sociologists argue that we now live in a new type of society:

- **postmodern society**: a post-industrial society in which change is increasingly rapid but uneven and where people have lost faith in the ability of science to bring about progress.

In postmodern society, information technology and the media play a central role. The world moves towards a single global economy and culture. Sources of individual identity become more diverse.

Critics argue that this change has been exaggerated and that we are still living in the modern rather than a postmodern era. For example, Marxists argue that society is still capitalist and class inequality remains its key feature.

Social class

Sociologists usually define a person's class in terms of their occupation. Those in non-manual jobs such as doctors, teachers and office workers are defined as middle-class, while those in manual jobs such as electricians, bus drivers and street sweepers are defined as working-class. Class has a major effect on many aspects of our lives, as the following examples show:

- Manual workers earn less than non-manual workers and are more likely to become unemployed.
- Men in class V (unskilled manual workers such as cleaners) are three times as likely to be heavy smokers and nearly five times as likely to die of lung cancer, as men in class I (professionals such as doctors).
- The infant mortality rate (deaths during the first year of life) is twice as high for children in class V as for those in class I.

Gender

Although there have been major changes in recent years, such as girls overtaking boys at school, men and women still do not occupy equal positions in society.

- More women than men are in poverty. Most low-paid workers and poor pensioners are women.
- On average, women's earnings are only about three-quarters those of men.
- Women do more housework and childcare than men.

Ethnicity

Ethnicity refers to shared culture and identity. An ethnic group is one whose members see themselves as a group with a shared heritage and cultural background, often including the same language and religion. Ethnicity doesn't just refer to minority groups – most societies also have an ethnic majority.

- Unemployment among ethnic minority men is three times higher than among whites; among women, it is four times higher.
- Minority employees tend to earn less than whites and are more likely to work shifts.
- The infant mortality rate of African Caribbean and Pakistani babies is double that of whites.

Age

Age is an important factor affecting a person's status

and age stratification is a basic feature of many societies.

- In many traditional societies, the old are accorded high status. By contrast, in today's society, they have a low status.
- Children in today's society are economically dependent on adults and legal restrictions prevent them from working. This is not the case in all societies.
- The old and the young are more likely to be poor, compared with other age groups.

These different forms of inequality often overlap. For example, gender and age inequalities may reinforce one another. Women are likely to have smaller pensions in old age because they have not worked full-time for as long, due to family responsibilities.

questions

1 Suggest two reasons for class differences in death rates.

2 Suggest two reasons why women earn less than men.

3 Suggest two reasons why members of ethnic minority groups are more likely than whites to be unemployed.

How do sociologists study society?

As we saw earlier, sociologists create theories to explain society and human behaviour. To be of any value, these theories must be based on evidence about the real world.

Sociologists have to collect this evidence. To do so, they carry out research using a variety of methods and sources of evidence. These include:

- social surveys, which involve asking a sample of people a series of questions in an interview or a written questionnaire
- participant observation, where the sociologist joins in with the group they are studying in order to gain deeper insight into their lives
- official statistics compiled by the government (e.g. on educational achievement, family size, unemployment and crime rates).

When choosing a method of research, sociologists need to be aware that every method has its particular strengths and weaknesses. For example, a social survey can usually gather information from a large cross-section of the population, but often the results will lack depth and detail, compared for example with a study using participant observation. However, research using participant observation can usually only study small numbers of people.

QuickCheck Questions

1 Explain what is meant by a social policy.

2 What do the examples of 'feral' children show about human behaviour?

3 Explain what is meant by:
(a) culture
(b) norms
(c) socialisation.

4 Explain the difference between ascribed status and achieved status.

5 True or false? The social action approach believes that individuals are like puppets on a string, manipulated and shaped by society.

6 True or false? The bourgeoisie is another name for the working class.

7 Explain what is meant by value consensus.

8 According to functionalists, what is the advantage of members of society sharing the same culture?

9 Explain what is meant by patriarchal society.

10 Explain the difference between urbanisation and industrialisation.

11 In which types of society (traditional, modern or postmodern) are the following features likely to be found:
(a) belief in progress;
(b) little social change;
(c) diverse sources of identity?

12 True or false? Conducting a social survey normally involves joining in with the group you are studying.

Answers are on page 270.

What does AS level sociology involve?

AS level sociology gives you an understanding of important aspects of society, and of how sociologists study and explain people's behaviour. Studying AS sociology will enable you to discuss social issues in a more informed and systematic way, and it will help you to make sense of your own and other people's experiences. The skills you develop will help you to think logically about the world. AS level will give you a firm foundation if you want to study sociology at A2 or degree level.

Topics and exams

If you are doing AQA AS sociology, you have to study three topics. Each one is assessed in a separate unit. The three topics you will be studying if you are using this coursebook are:

- Unit 1: Families and Households
- Unit 2: Education
- Unit 3: Sociological Methods

Units 1 and 2 are assessed by written exams. Unit 3 can be assessed either by an exam or by coursework.

What the examiners are looking for

When you sit an exam or submit your coursework, your work is assessed in terms of two aims or 'assessment objectives', each worth half the marks:

- Assessment Objective 1 (AO1): Knowledge and Understanding
- Assessment Objective 2 (AO2): Identification, Interpretation, Analysis and Evaluation

Knowledge and Understanding means you need to know and understand some of the main ideas and methods sociologists use, and what they have discovered as a result of their studies.

Identification is about being able to identify relevant facts, reasons, examples etc connected with the topics you study.

Interpretation involves selecting and applying information in ways that help you answer the question, including using examples and material from the stimulus Items on the exam paper.

Analysis involves explaining in detail, showing how ideas fit together, comparing and contrasting, organising answers logically and drawing conclusions.

Evaluation involves judging something, such as the advantages and disadvantages of different research methods, or the arguments for and against a sociologist's views.

For further details of the exams and assessment objectives, see chapter 6. For coursework, see chapter 5.

Developing your knowledge and skills

Developing your knowledge and understanding of sociology and building your skills of identification, interpretation, analysis and evaluation is a gradual process and something you will need to work at throughout your AS course. There is no quick fix. However, here are some pointers that will help you:

- **Keep up with your course**: attend regularly, do the work your teacher sets you, pay attention to the feedback you receive, keep your folder well organised.
- **Work with others**: join in class discussions, form study groups with classmates, discuss sociology topics outside class, revise together, talk to friends who have already done AS sociology.
- **When you don't understand, ask** your teacher or classmates, or look it up. Don't be shy – you're probably not the only one who doesn't get it.
- **Use your coursebook**: it contains thorough coverage of the topics you're studying and detailed guidance on coursework and exam success.
- **Apply what you learn**: sociology is about the real world, and you'll find lots of examples of sociological ideas all around you – in the news, on the street, at home, in school or college. Use examples in your writing.

- **Be critical**: when you come across new information, don't take it at face value. Look for the strengths and weaknesses of ideas; ask what evidence there is for someone's argument. This will help you develop the skill of Evaluation.
- **Take ideas apart** to see how they 'tick'. Try to make comparisons and contrasts between the different ideas, theories and methods you study. This will help you develop the skill of Analysis.
- **Answer the question**: when doing written work, keep focused on what you've actually been asked. Make a plan, and keep checking back to it and the question. Make it clear why you're including the material.

activity

Analysis: Using information from the section on 'Consensus or conflict?' on pages 8–9, state one similarity and one difference between Marxists and feminists.

Evaluation: Using information from the section on 'Diversity and identity' on page 9, state one criticism of the postmodernist view.

How this coursebook is organised

This coursebook introduces you to sociology and prepares you for success in the AS sociology exams. It has a range of features to help you succeed.

Chapters 2, 3 and 4 cover the three topics you will be studying for AS sociology: Families and Households, Education and Sociological Methods. Each chapter is divided into sections, each one covering a major sociological issue or area that you can be asked questions about in the exam.

To help you develop your knowledge and skills in tackling these issues, the coursebook contains the following features.

The AQA Specification

Each chapter starts with a box outlining the AQA Specification and what you have to study. The box also tells you which parts of the OCR Specification the chapter deals with.

questions

Throughout the text, there are short questions about what you have just read in the chapter. You can answer them on your own or with others. They are very similar to the kind of short questions you will find in the exam.

activities

In each section you will find a variety of activities. These develop your knowledge, understanding and skills by giving you a task to carry out, either on your own or with classmates. Sometimes this will involve research outside class, using libraries and the Internet, or carrying out small surveys.

synoptic links

If you continue with sociology at A2, you will take the synoptic unit. This unit assesses your understanding of the connections between different areas of sociology. In the synoptic unit, you choose to study one of two topics: Crime and Deviance, or Stratification and Differentiation.

Part of the synoptic unit involves making links between your synoptic topic and your AS topics. The synoptic links boxes point out connections you can make. They stimulate your thinking, broaden your understanding of sociology and help you prepare for further study.

Boxes

These contain additional information on a topic, such as examples of ideas in the chapter, details of important sociological issues, theories, perspectives or studies, or relevant policies and laws. Some also have questions to get you thinking further.

QuickCheck Questions

You will find QuickCheck Questions at the ends of sections. These are self-assessment questions to test your knowledge and understanding of what you have read.

You can check whether you have got the answers right by re-reading the preceding section, or by looking at the Answers to QuickCheck Questions on page 270.

Examining

Throughout this coursebook you will find practice exam questions and advice on how to tackle them under the heading ***Examining***. The questions are of two kinds:

At the end of Chapters 2, 3 and 4, you will find a full exam question covering the unit as a whole. **Chapter 6** also includes three other full questions, along with examples of student answers. All these are exactly like the six-part questions found in the exam. In each one, parts (a) to (d) are short questions, while (e) and (f) are mini-essays. Part (e) questions emphasise knowledge and understanding (AO1), whereas part (f) questions emphasise AO2 skills such as evaluation.

At the ends of sections in Chapters 2, 3 and 4, you will find a shorter, five-part question. This includes (a) to (d) questions, plus one mini-essay. The mini-essay will be *either* a type (e) *or* a type (f) question.

(In case you're wondering why it doesn't include both, this is because it's not possible to set two different mini-essays just on a single section or topic. In the exam, a six-part question tests you on the whole unit, not just one topic within it.)

These questions can be done as homework, or as exam practice under timed conditions.

The Examiner's advice

Each 'Examining' question is followed by the Examiner's advice on how to tackle it.

Chapter summaries

Each chapter concludes with a summary that picks out the most important points to give you an at-a-glance overview of the topic. This will help you consolidate what you have learnt and revise for the exam.

Coursework

For those doing coursework, chapter 5 explains clearly what is involved and guides you through the stages of preparing your coursework successfully. It contains clear dos and don'ts for tackling each section, spelling out what you need to do to produce good coursework and pointing out the pitfalls. The chapter also gives an example of a student's coursework with the Examiner's marks, comments and advice on how to improve.

Preparing for the exam

Chapter 6 is designed to help you make the most of what you know when it comes to the exams. It tells you clearly what the examiners are looking for in your answers, and gives you detailed advice on exam technique and how to tackle questions effectively.

The chapter includes exam questions for you to try, along with student answers and the Examiner's marks and comments on how to improve. The chapter also deals with how to prepare for exam success from day one, and how to revise successfully towards the end of your course.

Key concepts

The final part of the coursebook is a list of key sociological terms and concepts that you need to be familiar with. Each concept is defined briefly and clearly, with links where relevant to other concepts to help you develop your understanding.

You can refer to this section to help you understand terms when you come across them. You should also use it to learn definitions and help you prepare for exam questions that ask you to explain sociological terms.

QuickCheck Questions

1 How many Units do you have to take for AS sociology?

2 True or false? Coursework is
(a) compulsory
(b) an option in every Unit.

3 List three ways in which you can develop your sociological knowledge and skills during your course.

4 Fill in the gaps using words from the following list:

knowledge; understanding; identification; interpretation; analysis; evaluation.

(a) .... includes selecting and applying the right material to answer the question.

(b) Discussing the strengths and weaknesses of a sociological study is a way of showing ....

(c) Comparing and contrasting two ideas is an example of ....

Answers are on page 270.

Chapter summary

What is sociology?

Sociology is the study of society and human behaviour. Sociologists construct **theories** – general explanations of social patterns. They conduct research to collect **evidence** to support their theories. Governments may use sociologists' findings to develop **social policies**.

Human behaviour is not instinctive, but **learnt** through contact with others, as the examples of **feral** children show.

Culture includes all those things learnt and shared by a group, including knowledge, beliefs, norms and values. **Values** are general principles. **Norms** are specific rules of behaviour. Complex societies may contain many **subcultures**.

Socialisation is the process of learning one's culture. Sociologists distinguish between **primary** and **secondary** socialisation.

Society is made up of **statuses**, some of which are **ascribed** (fixed at birth) while others are **achieved**. A **role** is the set of norms that govern how a person in a particular status should act.

The **structuralist view** sees society as shaping the individual. The **social action view** sees individuals as having choice, creating social reality through their interactions.

Functionalists see society as based on **value consensus** and as being like an organism, with interdependent parts performing functions for the good of the whole.

Marxists see society as based on **class conflict**, in which the bourgeoisie exploit the proletariat. They believe capitalism will ultimately be replaced by a classless society. **Feminists** see society as **patriarchal** or male dominated.

Postmodernists believe we have moved to a more **fragmented** society in which there are diverse sources of identity. Critics argue that they ignore important **class, gender, ethnic and age inequalities**. These have a powerful effect on people's **life chances**.

Sociologists use a variety of **methods** and sources, such as surveys, participant observation and official statistics to gather evidence to test their theories.

What does AS level sociology involve?

AS level sociology provides you with an understanding of society and how sociologists study it; with the skills to think critically and logically about the world and with a firm foundation for further study.

Most students do the AQA AS specification. If you are using this coursebook to follow the AQA specification, your topics will be Families and Households (Unit 1), Education (Unit 2) and Sociological Methods (Unit 3).

Units 1 and 2 are assessed by written exams, Unit 3 by exam or coursework.

You are assessed in terms of two assessment objectives, AO1: knowledge and understanding, and AO2: the skills of identification, interpretation, analysis and evaluation.

If you are doing the OCR specification, chapters 2 and 4 will be relevant for AS and chapter 3 will be relevant for A2.

Your teacher will tell you whether you are doing AQA or OCR, whether you will be doing coursework, and when you will sit your exams.

You can develop your knowledge and skills by keeping up with your course, working with others, asking questions and studying your coursebook. Try to apply sociology to the world around you and to look critically at ideas. When doing written work, always make a plan to focus you on the question.

Chapter 2

Families and Households

Introduction

Almost all of us are born into a family and spend our most formative years there. This family of origin is responsible for our **primary socialisation**. That is, it equips us with the basic toolkit of social survival, teaching us essentials like language, right and wrong, how to interact with others and skills such as how to dress and eat properly.

As children and again as adults, when we form new families, we spend our lives in family relationships of one kind and another. Much of the work we do is done for other family members by cooking, cleaning and caring for them and by earning money to support them.

Family spending helps keep the wheels of the economy turning. Politicians, religious leaders and the media speak endlessly about the importance of the family for the well being of individuals and society. For these and other reasons, sociologists are very interested in the family. But what exactly do we mean by 'the family'?

What is a family? What is a household?

A household is a person living alone or a group of people living together (e.g. sharing meals, bills, housework etc). This group may or may not be related to one another. For instance, a group of students sharing a flat would be a household, but so would a husband, wife and their children living under the same roof.

Defining the family is harder. One common definition is that the family involves:

- monogamous marriage and a heterosexual relationship between a man and a woman
- the child or children of this couple (their own or adopted)
- sharing the same residence.

This of course is the **nuclear family**. This family type is often held up as the ideal in our society and frequently appears in advertisements – so much so that Edmund Leach (1967) describes it as the 'cereal packet norm'.

However, this 'cereal packet' definition rules out a lot of groups that many would see as families, such as unmarried cohabiting couples (gay or straight), childless couples, polygamous marriages (where a man has several wives or a woman has several husbands), as well as any relatives who don't live under the same roof.

The AQA Specification

The specification is the syllabus produced by the exam board, telling you what you have to study. The AQA specification (studied by the majority of students) for Families and Households requires you to examine the following:

- different conceptions of the relationships of the family to the social structure, with particular reference to the economy and to state policies
- changes in family and household structure and their relationship to industrialisation and urbanisation
- changing patterns of marriage, cohabitation, separation, divorce and child bearing, and the diversity of contemporary family and household structure
- the nature and extent of changes within the family, with reference to gender roles, domestic labour and power relationships, and to changes in the status of children and childhood.

Note on the OCR Specification

If you are studying the OCR specification, this chapter will help you if you are doing the 'Family' option in the Culture and Socialisation module at AS. This option module covers very similar issues to the AQA specification above and comprises:

- The family and recent social change
- Diversity in families and households
- Power, inequality and family policy.

If you are unsure which specification (AQA or OCR) you are studying, check with your teacher.

At the other extreme from the 'cereal packet' definition is the idea that *any* set of arrangements that those involved *see* as a family, *is* a family. This approach has the advantage that it does not require us to make any judgements about other people's lifestyles and relationships: if you define your own personal set-up as a *family* – whatever this set-up may be – then sociologists have no right to disagree.

A typical family?

However, one problem with this approach to defining the 'family' is that some would see it as too broad, since literally any group can count as a family. As a result, it may well include domestic set-ups that some people would not see as 'proper' families. For example, while gay relationships and lone-parent families are now more widely accepted than in the past, there are many who still regard them as abnormal or deviant.

Key questions about the family

Sociologists are interested in many different aspects of family life. Firstly, **are husbands and wives today equal?** In the past, men dominated both the family and society at large. However, in recent years, there have been important moves towards equality, such as laws against sex discrimination and many more women going out to work.

Sociologists are interested in how far there have been similar changes in the family. For example, do men now do their fair share of housework and childcare and do both spouses have an equal say in decision making? Feminist sociologists, for example, would argue that this is not the case.

Secondly, sociologists are also interested in how far our attitudes towards childhood have changed, and **whether the position of children today is better or worse** than in the past. For example, some sociologists argue that we now live in a 'child-centred' society where children's needs and wishes are put first.

Thirdly, sociologists are interested in **changes in the size and structure of families.** Some sociologists argue that when Britain industrialised, this brought about the decline of the large, three-generation extended family and the rise of the more compact, two-generation nuclear family.

The family continues to change today, taking a growing variety of different forms, such as lone-parent families, stepfamilies and gay families. Fourthly, therefore, sociologists seek to discover the **reasons for family diversity and changing patterns** such as the rise in divorce, cohabitation and births outside marriage.

The **laws and policies made by the government** can have an important impact on families. For example, the level of welfare benefits that the state provides affects how many children will grow up in poverty. Sociologists are interested in the reasons for these policies and how they affect families.

These are some of the important questions sociologists ask about the family, and we shall be examining their answers in this chapter. As we shall see, just like other members of society, sociologists often disagree about these issues. This is because they look at them from different standpoints or perspectives. For example, functionalist sociologists see the family as beneficial for all its members, whereas feminist sociologists see the family as exploiting women.

Couples

This section is about married and cohabiting couples. It looks at equality and inequality in families and households. Key questions are:

- Do men and women share housework and childcare equally?
- Do men and women have an equal say in family decisions and do they get equal shares of the household's income?
- Why does domestic violence occur and who commits it?

Do couples share childcare equally?

The domestic division of labour

The domestic division of labour refers to the roles that men and women play in relation to housework, childcare and paid work. Sociologists are interested in whether men and women share domestic tasks equally.

Parsons: instrumental and expressive roles

In the traditional nuclear family, the roles of husbands and wives are segregated – separate and distinct from one another. In Talcott Parsons' (1955) functionalist model of the family, for example, there is a clear division of labour between spouses:

- The husband has an **instrumental role**, geared towards achieving success at work so that he can provide for the family financially. He is the breadwinner.
- The wife has an **expressive role**, geared towards primary socialisation of the children and meeting the family's emotional needs. She is the homemaker, a full-time housewife rather than a wage earner.

Parsons argues that this division of labour is based on biological differences, with women 'naturally' suited to the nurturing role and men to that of provider. He claims that this division of labour is beneficial to both men and women, to their children and to wider society. Some conservative thinkers and politicians, known as the New Right, also hold this view.

However, other sociologists have criticised Parsons:

- Michael Young and Peter Willmott (1962) argue that men are now taking a greater share of domestic tasks and more wives are becoming wage earners.
- Feminist sociologists reject Parsons' view that the division of labour is natural. They argue that it only benefits men.

Joint and segregated conjugal roles

Elizabeth Bott (1957) distinguishes between two types of conjugal roles; that is, roles within marriage:

- **Segregated conjugal roles**, where the couple have separate roles: a male breadwinner and a female homemaker/carer, as in Parsons' instrumental and expressive roles. Their leisure activities also tend to be separate.
- **Joint conjugal roles**, where the couple share tasks such as housework and childcare and spend their leisure time together.

Young and Willmott identify a pattern of segregated conjugal roles in their study of traditional working-class extended families in Bethnal Green, east London, in the 1950s. Men were the breadwinners, most often working in the docks. They played little part in home life and spent their leisure time with workmates in pubs and working men's clubs. Women were full-time housewives with sole responsibility for housework and childcare, helped by their female relatives. What limited leisure women had was also spent with female kin.

The symmetrical family

Young and Willmott (1973) take a 'march of progress' view of the history of the family. They see family life as gradually improving for all its members, becoming more equal and democratic. They argue that there has been a long-term trend away from segregated conjugal roles and towards joint conjugal roles and the 'symmetrical family'.

By the symmetrical family they mean one in which the roles of husbands and wives, although not identical, are now much more similar:

- Women now go out to work, although this may be part-time rather than full-time.
- Men now help with housework and childcare.
- Couples now spend their leisure time together instead of separately with workmates or female relatives. They are more home-centred or 'privatised'.

In their study of families in London, Young and Willmott found that the symmetrical family was more common among younger couples, those who are geographically and socially isolated, and the more affluent (better off). For example, the young couples who had moved away from Bethnal Green and were living at a distance from the extended family and workmates were more likely to have a symmetrical relationship. Young and Wilmott see the rise of the symmetrical nuclear family as the result of major social changes that have taken place during the past century:

- changes in women's position, including married women going out to work
- geographical mobility – more couples living away from the communities in which they grew up
- new technology and labour-saving devices making the home a more pleasant place
- higher standards of living.

Many of these factors are inter-linked. For example, married women bringing a second wage into the home raises the family's standard of living. This enables the couple to make the home more attractive, and therefore encourages men to spend time at home rather than in the pub with their workmates. It also means the couple can afford more labour-saving devices. This makes housework easier and encourages men to do more.

Dockers playing cards, 1961

> **question**
>
> Explain how geographical mobility might help to give rise to symmetrical families.

A feminist view of housework

Feminist sociologists reject this 'march of progress' view. They argue that little has changed: men and women remain unequal within the family and women still do most of the housework. They see this inequality as stemming from the fact that the family and society are male-dominated or **patriarchal**. Women occupy a subordinate and dependent role within the family and in wider society.

> **synoptic link: stratification**
>
> Feminists see gender inequality as the most basic form of social inequality and the family as a crucial source of this inequality.

The feminist Ann Oakley (1974) criticises Young and Willmott's view that the family is now symmetrical. She argues that their claims are exaggerated. Although Young and Willmott found that most of the husbands they interviewed 'helped' their wives at least once a week, this could include simply taking the children for a walk or making breakfast on one occasion. For Oakley, this is hardly convincing evidence of symmetry.

In her own research on housewives, Oakley found some evidence of husbands helping in the home but no evidence of a trend towards symmetry. Only 15% of husbands had a high level of participation in housework, and only 25% had a high level of participation in childcare.

Husbands were more likely to share in childcare than in housework, but only in its more pleasurable aspects. Most couples defined the father's role as one of 'taking an interest'. A good father was one who would play with the children in the evenings and at weekends and 'take them off her hands' on Sunday morning. However, this could mean that mothers lost the rewards of childcare, such as playing with the children, and were simply left with more time for housework.

Later research supports Oakley's findings. Mary Boulton (1983) found that fewer than 20% of husbands had a major role in childcare. She argues that Young and Willmott exaggerate men's contribution by looking at the tasks involved in childcare rather than the responsibilities. A father might help with specific tasks, but it was almost always the mother who was responsible for the child's security and well-being.

Husbands are thirty times less likely than their wives to do the washing.

Similarly, research conducted in Manchester by Alan Warde and Kevin Hetherington (1993) shows that sex-typing of domestic tasks remains strong (see Table 2A). In general, they found that men would only carry out routine 'female' tasks when their partners were not around to do them. Nevertheless, Warde and Hetherington did find evidence of a slight change of attitude among younger men. They no longer assumed that women should do the housework, and were more likely to think they were doing less than their fair share.

Table 2A

How many times more likely wives were to have last done the following tasks, compared to their husbands:

Task	
Washing	30 times as likely
Ironing	14 times as likely
Tidying up	9 times as likely
Cooking	7 times as likely
Washing up	Twice as likely

How many times more likely husbands were to have last done the following tasks, compared to their wives:

Task	
Plastering	20 times as likely
Painting	4 times as likely
Car washing	4 times as likely
Cutting the lawn	3 times as likely

Source: adapted from Warde and Hetherington (1993)

Oakley: the rise of the housewife role

Rather than seeing a march of progress towards symmetry since the 19th century as Young and Willmott do, Oakley describes how the housewife role has become the dominant role for married women.

Industrialisation and the rise of factory production in the 19th century led to the separation of paid work from the home. Although women had initially been part of the industrial labour force, they were gradually excluded from the workplace and confined to the home with sole responsibility for housework and childcare, while men became the sole breadwinners.

This enforced women's subordination and economic dependence on men. In this way, the housewife role was socially constructed, rather than being women's 'natural' role, as Parsons claims.

In Oakley's view, even though the 20th century saw an increase in the number of married women working, the housewife role is still women's primary role. Also, women who work are concentrated in low-paid jobs that are often an extension of the housewife role, such as nursing, secretarial work or childcare.

activity

Many studies have attempted to measure the extent of symmetry in relationships.

1 In groups of four, devise a set of questions that you will use to ask a sample of couples about their relationship. You will need to include questions about women working, the contribution of each partner to housework and childcare, and joint and separate leisure activities.

2 Each member of the group should interview at least two couples.

3 When you have completed the interviews, get back together in your group to discuss the results. Did the answers vary a great deal? If so, why? What factors seem to be important in influencing how symmetrical the relationship is?

The impact of paid work

Most of the women in Oakley's study in the 1970s were full-time housewives, but many more households now have a second income from the wife's full- or part-time work. Today, three-quarters of married or cohabiting women in the UK are economically active, as against less than half in 1971.

Sociologists are interested in whether this trend towards both partners working is leading to a more equal division of domestic tasks, with a 'new man' doing his fair share of the housework and childcare – or whether it simply means that women now have to carry a 'dual burden' of paid work as well as domestic work.

Gershuny: the trend towards equality

Some sociologists argue that women working full-time is leading to a more equal division of labour in the home. Jonathan Gershuny (1994) found that men whose wives worked full-time did less domestic work:

- Wives who did not go to work did 83% of the housework and even wives who worked part-time still did 82%.
- Wives who worked full-time did 73% of the housework. The longer the wife had been in paid work, the more housework her husband was likely to do.
- Couples whose parents had a more equal relationship were likely to share housework more equally themselves.

Gershuny explains this trend towards greater equality in terms of a gradual change in values and parental role models. He argues that social values are gradually adapting to the fact that women are now working full-time. However, he found that even though men are now doing more housework, they still tend to take responsibility for different tasks, as Table 2A shows.

Gershuny's view is an optimistic one, similar to Young and Willmott's march of progress view that conjugal roles are becoming more symmetrical.

Rosemary Crompton (1997) accepts Gershuny's evidence. However, she explains it differently, in terms of economic factors rather than changing values or role models. As women's earning power increases relative to men's, so men do more in the home.

However, earnings remain unequal. On average, women's earnings are only about three-quarters those of men. Crompton therefore concludes that as long as earnings remain unequal, so too will the division of labour at home.

question

Why might men's higher earnings mean they are able to do less housework than women?

The commercialisation of housework

Another approach that emphasises economic factors is that of Hilary Silver (1987) and Juliet Schor (1993). They stress the importance of two major economic developments in reducing the burden of housework on women:

- Housework has become 'commercialised'. Goods and services that housewives previously had to produce themselves are now mass-produced and supplied by supermarkets, fast food outlets and so on. Freezers, microwave ovens, 'ready meals' etc all reduce the amount of domestic labour that needs to be done.
- Women working means that they can afford to buy these goods and services.

As a result, Silver and Schor argue, the burden of housework on women has decreased. Schor even goes so far as to claim that these developments have led to 'the death of the housewife role'.

However, critics argue that for many poorer women, buying in expensive goods and services is not an option. Also, even if commercialisation has reduced the amount of housework to be done, this does not prove that couples are sharing the remaining chores equally.

questions

1 What is meant by the 'commmercialisation of housework'?

2 Make a list of all the services you can think of that families can buy in instead of providing themselves.

3 Why is the disappearance of housework more likely to be a middle-class phenomenon?

The dual burden

Many feminists argue that, despite women working, there is little evidence of a 'new man' who does an equal share of domestic work. They argue that women have simply acquired a dual burden of paid work and unpaid housework. In the view of feminists, the family remains patriarchal: men benefit both from women's earnings and from their domestic labour.

Elsa Ferri and Kate Smith (1996) provide evidence of the dual burden. They found that increased employment of women outside the home has had little impact on the domestic division of labour. Based on a sample of 1,589 33-year-old fathers and mothers, they found that the father took the main responsibility for childcare in fewer than 4% of families.

Even where a woman works and her husband is unemployed, there is little evidence of husbands doing more at home. Lydia Morris (1990) found that men who had suffered a loss of their masculine role as a result of becoming unemployed saw domestic work as women's work and therefore to be avoided.

For many women access to full-day childcare is essential. While middle-class women may be able to afford this, however, as Sara Arber and Jay Ginn (1995) point out, many working-class women cannot and as a result, they remain trapped in a vicious circle of childcare responsibilities and low-paid, part-time employment.

These class differences between women are well illustrated by Nicky Gregson and Michelle Lowe's (1994) study of the employment of domestic 'help' by dual-earner middle-class families. These couples found it more economical to employ working-class women as nannies and cleaners than for the wife to stay at home doing the housework. Unlike the middle class, of course, most working-class women cannot afford to employ someone to do their housework for them and so have to carry a dual burden of paid and unpaid domestic work.

Emotion work

'Emotion work' describes work whose main feature is the management of one's own and other people's emotions. Arlie Hochschild (1983) originally used the concept to describe jobs such as airline stewardesses. She notes that women are more likely than men to be performing jobs involving emotional labour.

Other sociologists have applied this idea to the family. David Morgan (1997) illustrates this with the example of caring for a sick child. This involves:

> *'physical care and monitoring, handling the fears and frustrations experienced by the sick child, handling the adjustments required on behalf of other members of the family who may be resentful of the attention being accorded to the sick child, and drawing upon one's own emotional resources and exercising emotional control while doing all of this.'*

Emotion work is usually seen as a 'labour of love' because it involves caring for other family members. Nevertheless, it is work, and work done mainly by women. Jean Duncombe and Dennis Marsden (1995) argue that women are expected not only to do a double shift of both housework and paid work, but to work a triple shift that also includes emotion work.

question

Suggest four situations in which women might carry out emotion work within their families.

Lesbian couples and gender scripts

Why has there been so little change in the division of labour, despite the increase in the number of women working? Gillian Dunne (1999) argues that the division of labour continues because of deeply ingrained 'gender scripts'. These set out the different gender roles that men and women in heterosexual couples are expected to play.

Dunne contrasts this with the situation among lesbian couples, where gender scripts do not operate to the same degree. In her study of 37 cohabiting lesbian couples with dependent children, Dunne found evidence of symmetry in their relationships. Compared to heterosexual women, lesbians are more likely to:

- describe their relationship as equal and share housework and childcare equally
- give equal importance to both partners' careers
- view childcare positively.

Dunne argues that this is because lesbian and heterosexual partners interact in different ways. Heterosexuals are under pressure to conform to a masculine or feminine 'gender script' by performing different kinds of tasks within the home that confirm their gender identities.

In lesbian relationships, however, household tasks are not linked to particular gender scripts. This allows lesbian couples to create a more equal relationship. For example, as one of the women in Dunne's study commented, in heterosexual relationships there is always a subconscious belief that women are supposed to do the housework.

Box 5: Feminism

Feminists take a critical view of the family. They argue that the family oppresses women and that in the wider society too, women occupy a subordinate position. They do not regard this inequality as 'natural' but as created by society. However, feminism is a broad term covering several different types.

Liberal feminists are concerned with campaigning against sex discrimination and for equal rights and opportunities for women (e.g. equal pay and an end to discrimination in employment).

- They argue that women's oppression is being gradually overcome through changing people's attitudes and through changes in the law such as the Sex Discrimination Act (1975).
- They believe that we are moving towards greater equality but that full equality will depend on further reforms and changes in the attitudes and socialisation patterns of both sexes.

However, Marxist feminists and radical feminists criticise them for failing to challenge the underlying causes of women's oppression and for believing that changes in the law or attitudes will be enough to bring equality.

Marxist and radical feminists believe instead that far-reaching, revolutionary changes to deep-rooted social structures will be needed.

Marxist feminists argue that the main cause of women's oppression in the family is not men but capitalism. They see capitalist society as divided into two classes: the capitalist class, who own the means of production, and the working class, whose labour the capitalists exploit for profit. Women's oppression performs several functions for capitalism:

- Women reproduce the labour force, by socialising the next generation of workers and by maintaining and servicing the current generation.
- Women absorb the anger that would otherwise be directed at capitalism. Fran Ansley (1972) describes wives as 'takers of shit' who soak up the frustration their husbands feel because of the alienation and exploitation they suffer at work.
- Capitalism uses women as a 'reserve army' of cheap, easily disposable labour when extra workers are needed. When no longer needed, their employers can 'let them go' to return to their domestic role.

Marxist feminists see the oppression of women in the family as linked to the exploitation of the working class. They argue that the family must be abolished at the same time as a socialist revolution replaces capitalism with a classless society.

Radical feminists argue that all societies have been founded on patriarchy – rule by men. For radical feminists, the key division in society is between men and women.

- Men are the enemy: they are the source of women's oppression and exploitation.
- The family and marriage are the key institutions in patriarchal society. Men benefit from women's unpaid domestic labour and from their sexual services and they dominate women through violence or the threat of it.

For radical feminists, the patriarchal system needs to be overturned. In particular, the family, the root of women's oppression, must be abolished. To do this, they argue that women must organise themselves to live independently of men.

Black feminists argue that by regarding the family solely as a source of oppression, white feminists neglect black women's experience of racial oppression.

Instead, black feminists view the black family positively as a source of support and resistance against racism.

This supports the radical feminist view that relationships between men and women are inevitably patriarchal and that women can only achieve equality in a same-sex relationship.

Similarly, Jeffrey Weeks (1999) argues that same-sex relationships offer greater possibilities of equality because the division of labour is open to negotiation and agreement, and not based on patriarchal tradition.

However, Dunne found that where one partner did much more paid work than the other, the time that each partner spent on domestic work was likely to be unequal. This suggests that paid work exerts an important influence on the division of labour even in same-sex relationships.

The impact of paid work: summary

- There is some evidence that a woman being in paid work leads to more equality in the division of labour, though probably only if she is in full-time work.
- Many feminists argue that, in reality, the effect of this is limited: women still continue to shoulder a dual or triple burden. And even if men are doing more in the home, domestic tasks themselves remain gendered.
- Feminists argue that the root of the problem is patriarchy. Patriarchal gender scripts shape society's expectations about the domestic roles that men and women ought to perform. Patriarchy also ensures that women earn less at work and so have less bargaining power in the home. Until patriarchy is successfully challenged in the home and in the workplace, therefore, the domestic division of labour is likely to remain unequal.

synoptic link: deviance

Gender scripts are sets of expectations or norms (rules). They define what society sees as 'normal' behaviour for men and women. Going against these norms may lead to an individual being defined as deviant.

Resources and decision-making in households

As we have seen, there is inequality in who *does* what in the home. There is also inequality in who *gets* what – in how the family's resources are shared out between men and women. This is linked to who controls the family's income and who has the power to make decisions about how it is spent.

Michelle Barrett and Mary McIntosh (1991) note that:

- Men gain far more from women's domestic work than they give back in financial support.
- The financial support that husbands give to their wives is often unpredictable and comes with 'strings' attached.
- Men usually make the decisions about spending on important items.

Research shows that family members do not share resources such as money and food equally. For example, Elaine Kempson (1994) found that among low-income families, women denied their own needs, seldom going out, and eating smaller portions of food or skipping meals altogether in order to make ends meet.

Similarly, in Hilary Graham's (1984) study, over half the women who were living on benefits after separating from their husbands said that they and their children were actually better off. Although their husbands' earnings had not necessarily been low, they found that benefits were a more reliable source of income.

In many households, a woman has no entitlement to a share of household resources in her own right. As a result, she is likely to see anything she spends on herself as money that ought to be spent on essentials for the children. Even in households with apparently adequate incomes, resources may be shared unequally, leaving women in poverty.

Decision-making and paid work

One reason why men often take a greater share of the family's resources is because they usually contribute more money, due to their higher earnings. The feminist sociologists Jan Pahl and Carolyn Vogler (1993) focus on how each partner's contribution to family income affects decision-making within the family. They identify two main types of control over family income:

- pooling – where both partners have access to income and joint responsibility for expenditure; for example, a joint bank account
- allowance system – where men give their wives an allowance out of which they have to budget to meet the family's needs, with the man retaining any surplus income for himself.

Pooling is on the increase. Comparing a sample of 1,211 couples with their parents, Vogler (1994) found a large increase in pooling (from 19% to 50%), and a sharp decline in the housekeeping allowance system (from 36% to 12%).

Pahl and Vogler found that pooling was more common among couples where both partners work full-time. However, they found that even here, the men usually made the major financial decisions.

This is supported by Irene Hardill's (1997) research. In her study of 30 dual-career professional couples, she found that the important decisions were usually taken either by the man alone or jointly and that his career normally took priority when deciding whether to move house for a new job. This supports Janet Finch's (1983) observation that women's lives tend to be structured around their husbands' careers.

Similarly, Stephen Edgell's (1980) study of professional couples found that:

- Very important decisions, such as those involving finance, a change of job or moving house, were either taken by the husband alone or taken jointly but with the husband having the final say.
- Important decisions, such as those about children's education or where to go on holiday, were usually taken jointly, and seldom by the wife alone.
- Less important decisions, such as the choice of home décor, children's clothes or food purchases, were usually made by the wife.

Like Pahl and Vogler, Edgell argues that the reason men are likely to take the decisions is that they earn more. Women usually earn less than their husbands, and being dependent on them economically, have less say in decision-making.

However, other feminists argue that inequalities in decision-making are not simply the result of inequalities in earnings. They argue that in patriarchal society, the cultural definition of men as decision-makers is deeply ingrained in both men and women and instilled through gender role socialisation. Until this definition is challenged, decision-making is likely to remain unequal.

questions

1. How might employment outside the home affect power over the family's resources?
2. Why do you think 'pooling' is more likely to be found among younger couples than among their parents?
3. Pahl interviewed couples both together and separately. This was rather expensive to do, so why do you think she felt it was necessary?

House-hunting – who makes the big decisions?

Domestic violence

The Women's Aid Federation (2003) defines domestic violence as:

> *'physical, psychological, sexual or financial violence that takes place within an intimate or family-type relationship and forms a pattern of coercive and controlling behaviour. It may involve partners, ex-partners, household members or other relatives.'*

A common view of domestic violence is that it is the behaviour of a few disturbed or 'sick' individuals, and that its causes are psychological rather than social. However, sociologists have challenged this view:

- Domestic violence is far too widespread to be simply the work of a few disturbed individuals. According to the British Crime Survey (2000), domestic violence accounts for almost a quarter of all violent crime. Catriona Mirrlees-Black's (1999) survey of 16,000 people estimates that there are 6.6 million domestic assaults a year, about half involving physical injury.
- Domestic violence does not occur randomly but follows particular social patterns and these patterns have social causes. The most striking of these patterns is that it is mainly violence by men against women. Mirrlees-Black found that:
  - most victims are women
  - 99% of all incidents against women are committed by men
  - nearly one in four women has been assaulted by a partner at some time in her life, and one in eight repeatedly so.

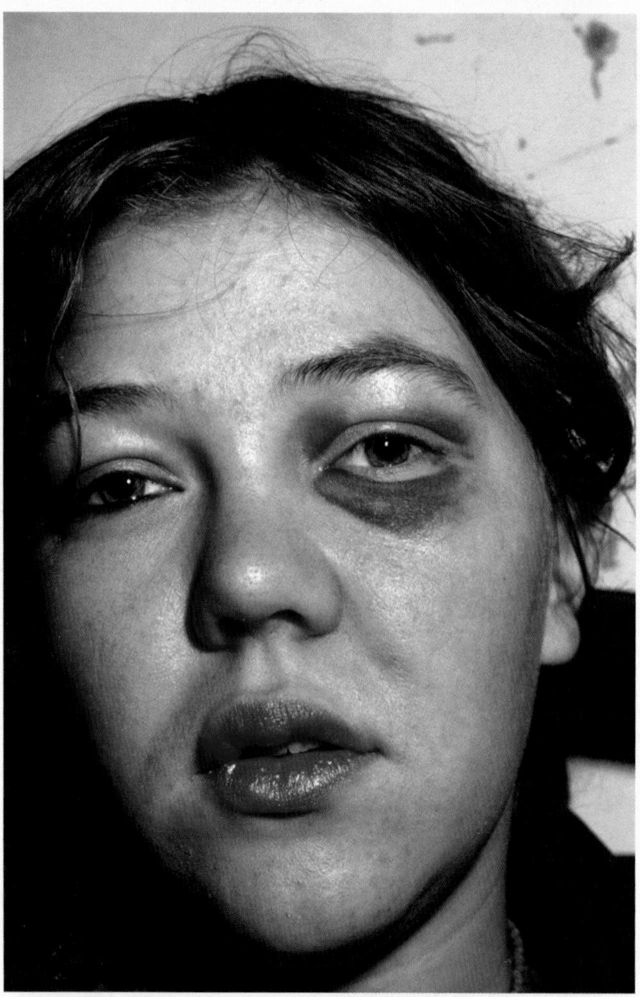

Domestic violence accounts for almost a quarter of all violent crime.

This is confirmed by Russell and Rebecca Dobash's (1979) research in Scotland, based on police and court records and interviews with women in women's refuges. They cite examples of wives being slapped, pushed about, beaten, raped or killed by their husbands. Dobash and Dobash found that violent incidents could be set off by what a husband saw as a challenge to his authority, such as his wife asking why he was late home for a meal. They argue that marriage legitimates violence against women by conferring power and authority on husbands and dependency on wives.

Official statistics

Official statistics on domestic violence understate the true extent of the problem for two main reasons. Firstly, victims may be unwilling to report it to the police. Stephanie Yearnshire (1997) found that on average a woman suffers 35 assaults before making a report. Domestic violence is the violent crime least likely to be reported.

Secondly, police and prosecutors may be reluctant to record, investigate or prosecute those cases that are reported to them. According to David Cheal (1991), this reluctance is due to the fact that police and other state agencies are not prepared to become involved in the family. They make three assumptions about family life:

- that the family is a private sphere, so access to it by state agencies should be limited

- that the family is a good thing and so agencies tend to neglect the 'darker side' of family life
- that individuals are free agents, so it is assumed that if a woman is experiencing abuse she is free to leave. However, this is not true. Male violence is often coupled with male economic power: abused women are often financially dependent on their husbands and unable to leave.

synoptic link: deviance

A major problem in studying domestic violence is the difficulty of obtaining valid information on the subject. Official police statistics rely on people reporting assaults and the police recording the complaint. However, not all assaults are reported, and not all those reported are recorded.

With other methods, such as interviews or self-completed questionnaires, people may refuse to answer, misunderstand the questions, lie, exaggerate or forget. Equally, the researchers may misunderstand or misclassify the answers given. Male researchers may receive different answers from female researchers.

There are also difficulties in defining domestic violence in the first place.

The radical feminist explanation

Radical feminists interpret findings such as those of Dobash and Dobash as evidence of patriarchy. For example, Kate Millett (1970) and Shulamith Firestone (1970) argue that all societies have been founded on patriarchy. They see the key division in society as that between men and women. Men are the enemy: they are the oppressors and exploiters of women.

Radical feminists see the family and marriage as the key institutions in patriarchal society and the main source of women's oppression. Within the family, men dominate women through domestic violence or the threat of it.

For radical feminists, widespread domestic violence is an inevitable feature of patriarchal society and serves to preserve the power that all men have over all women. Furthermore, in their view, male domination of state institutions helps to explain the reluctance of the police and courts to deal effectively with cases of domestic violence. (For more details of the radical feminist perspective, see Box 5.)

activity

Working in small groups:

1 Suggest reasons why there is such under-reporting of domestic violence.

2 What problems might there be in defining domestic violence? How would you define it? How might different definitions affect the results of research?

Radical feminists help to explain why most domestic violence is committed by men. They argue that violence against women is part of a patriarchal system that maintains men's power. They give a sociological, rather than a psychological, explanation by linking patterns of domestic violence to dominant social norms about marriage.

However, Faith Robertson Elliot (1996) rejects the radical feminist claim that all men benefit from violence against women. Not all men are aggressive and most are opposed to domestic violence. Radical feminists ignore this.

Radical feminists also fail to explain female violence, including child abuse by women and violence against male partners. For example, Mirrlees-Black found that about one in seven men has been assaulted, and one in 20 repeatedly so.

activity

In small groups, answer the following questions, then report back to the whole class and compare your answers with other groups.

1 Dobash and Dobash identified the following as common 'triggers' to domestic violence: jealousy; money; children; drunkenness; arguments over food. Explain why each of these might trigger violence, linking them where possible to ideas about gender roles.

2 Suggest reasons why many battered wives remain with their violent husbands.

3 In what ways apart from p[illegible] violence may men be ab[illegible] their wives?

4 Give examples of ways [illegible] areas of society, such [illegible] education and the la[illegible] patriarchal.

Other groups at risk

Sociologists have identified other patterns of domestic violence in addition to male violence against women. According to Mirrlees-Black, social groups at greater risk of domestic violence include:

- children and young people
- those in the lowest social classes
- those who live in rented accommodation
- those on low incomes or in financial difficulties
- those with high levels of alcohol consumption and users of illegal drugs.

Some of these groups overlap. For example, statistics show that children from lower social classes appear at higher risk of abuse and violence.

question

Suggest reasons why poorer families are more likely to end up in the child abuse statistics than better-off families.

Wilkinson: domestic violence, inequality and stress

Richard Wilkinson (1996) offers an explanation of these patterns. He sees domestic violence as the result of stress on family members caused by social inequality.

Inequality means that some families have fewer resources than others, such as income and housing. Those on low incomes or living in overcrowded accommodation are likely to experience higher levels of stress. This reduces their chances of maintaining stable, caring relationships and increases the risk of conflict and violence. For example:

- Worries about money, jobs and housing may spill over into domestic conflict as tempers become frayed.
- Lack of money and time restricts people's social circle and reduces social support for those under stress.

synoptic link: stratification

The findings of Wilkinson and Mirrlees-Black show that not all people are equally in danger of suffering domestic violence: those with less power, status, wealth or income are often at greatest risk.

Wilkinson's approach is useful in showing how social inequality produces stress and triggers conflict and violence in families. As those in lower social classes face greater hardship and thus stress, this helps to explain the class differences in the statistics on domestic violence.

However, unlike the radical feminist approach, Wilkinson does not explain why women rather than men are the main victims.

QuickCheck Questions

1. True or false? According to Parsons, women perform the instrumental role.
2. Complete the sentence: Symmetrical families involve .... conjugal roles.
3. Gershuny believes that men are more likely to do domestic labour if their wives are:
   (a) working full-time
   (b) working part-time
   (c) not working.
4. Give two examples of the commercialisation of housework.
5. What are gender scripts?
6. Explain the difference between Marxist feminism and radical feminism.
7. Name one sociologist whose findings indicate that family resources are not shared equally.
8. What reason does Edgell give for why men have more power to influence family decision-making?
9. Suggest two reasons why domestic violence is not simply the behaviour of a few psychologically disturbed individuals.
10. Name two other groups apart from women who are at risk of domestic violence.

rs are on page 270.

Examining **Couples**

Item A According to Young and Willmott, there has been a long-term trend towards the symmetrical nuclear family in Britain since around the beginning of the 20th century, with more and more families taking this form. Initially, the symmetrical family was more common among the middle class, but it has now spread to the working class too – a process that Young and Willmott call 'stratified diffusion'.

However, the view that the nuclear family is now symmetrical is widely contested by feminist and other sociologists. They argue that there is still an unequal gender division of labour in the family that disadvantages women. Not only do women remain responsible for most of the housework and childcare, but increasingly they are now also expected to go out to work as well, meaning that in effect they have to work a double shift. Others go further, arguing that women have to work not a double but a triple shift.

Short questions

(a) Explain what is meant by the term 'triple shift' (**Item A**, line 11). (2 marks)

(b) Identify **two** features of the 'symmetrical family' (**Item A**, line 3). (4 marks)

(c) Suggest **three** reasons why the symmetrical family may have become more common over the last century (**Item A**, lines 1-4). (6 marks)

(d) Identify and briefly explain **two** reasons why a 'gender division of labour' continues to exist among many couples (**Item A**, lines 7-8). (8 marks)

Mini-essay

Examine the patterns of, and reasons for, domestic violence in society. (20 marks)

This is a type (e) question of the kind found in the exam, carrying 14 AO1 marks (knowledge and understanding) and 6 AO2 marks (identification, interpretation, analysis and evaluation).

The Examiner's advice **For the mini-essay, the emphasis is on knowledge and understanding (AO1), though you must still show AO2 skills for high marks. A good start would be a definition of domestic violence (see page 28). You must deal with both 'patterns' and 'reasons'. For patterns, the main focus needs to be on gender. For reasons why women are more likely to be victims, use Dobash and Dobash and radical feminism – and Ansley's Marxist feminist view (see Box 5 on page 25). Deal with other patterns too: social class, and also non-partner violence (e.g. against children, elders), using Mirrlees-Black and Wilkinson. These can also be used to evaluate radical feminism (it only explains violence against women). Also evaluate by raising problems about the statistics. Write a conclusion summing up the patterns and reasons.**

The family and industrialisation

This section deals with changes in the structure of the family. 'Structure' refers, for example, to whether the family takes a two-generation, nuclear form or a three-generation, extended form. Sociologists are interested in the structure of the family today and in how it has changed over time. They are particularly interested in the relationship between changes in family structure and the twin processes of industrialisation and urbanisation.

The family as a unit of production: a three-generation farming family at harvest time.

- Industrialisation refers to the shift from an agricultural economy to one based on factory production.
- Urbanisation refers to a shift in population, from one living mainly in the countryside to one living in towns and cities.

Industrialisation and the nuclear family

In Britain, industrialisation and urbanisation occurred more or less together from the late 18th to the mid-19th century. They transformed British society in many important respects. These two processes have certainly had an impact on family structure, but sociologists disagree as to what this impact has been. One view is that of the functionalist sociologist Talcott Parsons (1955), who argues that industrialisation brought about the rise of the nuclear family.

question

What new problems and opportunities might industrialisation and urbanisation create for individuals, families and society?

Parsons: 'functional fit' theory

Parsons distinguishes between two types of society – industrial and pre-industrial. He argues that each of these societies contains a corresponding type of family structure that fits its needs: there is a 'functional fit' between the extended family and pre-industrial society, and the nuclear family and industrial society.

The family in pre-industrial society

According to Parsons, in pre-industrial society, the dominant family structure was the 'classic' three-generation extended family living together or very close by one another. It included grandparents, married sons or daughters and grandchildren, and sometimes other kin such as cousins, aunts and uncles.

- It was a unit of economic production. Work and home were not separated. Members of the family worked together; for example, on the family farm.

- There was a strong obligation to help other family members.
- The extended family was multi-functional, providing for its members' health and welfare, employment, protection and so on. It met most individual and social needs.

The family in industrial society

According to Parsons, in industrial society, the dominant family structure is the two-generation nuclear family of parents and their dependent children.

- The nuclear family is no longer a unit of production: work now takes place in factories. Work and home are now separate.
- The nuclear family is 'structurally isolated' from the wider family. That is, it has no binding obligations to extended family members: any ties are now a matter of choice, not duty.
- The nuclear family has lost most of its functions to other institutions such as schools and the health service and now specialises in performing just two essential ones:
    - the primary socialisation of children to equip them with basic skills and society's values
    - the stabilisation of adult personalities: the family is a place where adults can relax and release tensions, enabling them to return to the workplace refreshed and ready to meet its demands.

synoptic link: deviance

Through the primary socialisation of children into society's norms and values, the family plays an important part in preventing deviance and ensuring conformity.

Mobility and the nuclear family

Modern industry requires a mobile workforce. Work in industrial society is not fixed in one location, but moves from place to place as industries rise and fall.

The compact, two-generation nuclear family, free of binding obligations to wider kin, is small enough to move easily to where the work is and so has the *geographical mobility* that industry requires. This contrasts with pre-industrial society, where geographical mobility was rare; people often spent their whole life in the same village.

Similarly, in pre-industrial society, a person's status is largely ascribed (fixed by birth). *Social mobility* – changing one's social class position – is rare. For example, a son is likely to follow in his father's footsteps and pursue the same occupation.

By contrast, in industrial society, our status is achieved by our own efforts, not ascribed by birth. This makes social mobility possible: an individual can move from one social class to another. For example, the son of a labourer can become a lawyer through ability and hard work.

However, if the son were to remain in the extended family, this could cause conflict since within the family his father would have higher status, while in the wider society the son would command higher status. This conflict can be avoided if the son is able to leave home and set up his own nuclear family. The nuclear family therefore encourages social mobility as well as geographical mobility.

activity

Complete the following table, comparing the characteristics Parsons attributes to the pre-industrial family with those he sees as typical of the modern industrial family.

Pre-industrial family	*Industrial family*
Large and extended	
	Performs only two essential functions
Both a unit of consumption and a unit of production	
	Geographically mobile
	Socially mobile
Individuals and couples are dominated by the wider family	
Work and home are not separated	
	Status is achieved

Not everyone agrees with Parsons' views. Other sociologists and historians have examined family structure in pre-industrial and industrial societies. They have produced evidence that contradicts Parsons' claims of a fit between the extended family and pre-industrial society and between the nuclear family and industrial society. We examine their findings next.

Young and Willmott: stages of family history

Unlike Parsons' large-scale generalisations about the development of the family, Young and Willmott look specifically at the history of the family in Britain. In their view, family structure has evolved through three stages from pre-industrial times to the present day.

stage 1

This was the stable *pre-industrial* stage before 1750. Home and work were not separated. Most families were nuclear, not extended as Parsons claims. All members worked together as an inter-dependent unit of production under the authority of the father, in farming or in cottage industries such as weaving.

stage 2

This was the *early industrial* stage, from about 1750 to 1900 (but continuing until at least the 1950s in traditional working-class communities such as Bethnal Green in east London). This was a period of disruption caused by industrialisation, in which home and work became separated. Work now took place in factories, mills and mines. During the 19th century, Factory Acts excluded women and children from paid work and they became dependent on the man's wage.

This was the phase of the 'mum-centred' working-class extended family, based on mutual aid ties between a mother and her married daughters. In the face of poverty, female relatives came to rely on each other for financial, practical and emotional support.

synoptic link: stratification

Young and Willmott's work shows the importance of social class in influencing family structure. The hardships faced by working-class people encouraged them to maintain extended family ties.

stage 3

This is the *modern industrial* stage, from about 1900. The symmetrical nuclear family began to emerge as a result of social changes such as geographical mobility, higher standards of living, more married women in paid work, the welfare state, improved housing and labour-saving technology in the home. These changes made the extended family less important as a source of support and families became nuclear.

question

Young and Willmott see the stage 3 nuclear family emerging first among the middle class and then spreading downwards to the working class later (a process they call 'stratified diffusion').

Why do you think the nuclear family might be more likely to emerge in the middle class first?

Wedding reception, Bethnal Green, 1952

Unlike Parsons, therefore, Young and Willmott do not see industrialisation as replacing the extended family with the nuclear family. Instead, they see a *pre-industrial nuclear* family being replaced by an *early industrial extended* family. Only later, in the modern industrial period, does the family become nuclear again.

activity

Complete the following table comparing the characteristics of the family in each of Young and Willmott's three stages. For each stage, you should indicate whether the characteristic is present (✔) or absent (**x**).

	stage 1	stage 2	stage 3
Unit of production			
Nuclear unit			
Worked together at home			
Dependence on extended family			
Help from the state			
Geographically mobile unit			

Laslett: household structure

The historian Peter Laslett (1972) used parish records to study the make-up of households in England during the period 1564 to 1821. His findings challenge Parsons' view that pre-industrial societies are characterised by large, three-generation extended families living under one roof. Laslett found that:

- The average household size remained small (at around 4.75 persons) throughout the period.
- Households were likely to include only two generations, not three. A combination of late childbearing and short life expectancy meant that grandparents were unlikely to be alive for very long after the birth of their first grandchild.

Evidence also indicates that households elsewhere in north-west Europe were similarly small during this period.

Laslett concludes that the pre-industrial family was almost always nuclear and that the large, three-generation extended family described by Parsons is a myth. He argues that the widespread presence of the nuclear family in pre-industrial England encouraged industrialisation. If so, then Parsons is wrong to see the pre-industrial family as extended.

Laslett's findings about household size are generally accepted, but his conclusions have been questioned. He assumes that each household makes up a separate family. However, it is possible that two nuclear family households who live close to each other and whose members are related may operate as an extended family, even though they do not live under the same roof. Even a small household may not be an isolated nuclear family but part of a larger extended family.

questions

1 Explain why low life expectancy, coupled with late childbirth, meant that households were likely to contain two rather than three generations.

2 Why may household size not be a very accurate measure of family size?

Anderson and Hareven: exchange theory

'Exchange theory' is the view that people create, maintain or break off relationships depending on the costs and benefits involved in doing so. For example, William Goode (1964) shows that the younger members of upper-class families maintain ties with extended kin because they stand to inherit wealth from them. The 'role bargain' they enter into is that the younger generation will be dutiful and obedient to their elders, for example in their choice of career or marriage partner. In turn, the older generation will pass on their substantial assets to the young.

The family in early industrial Britain

Michael Anderson (1980) uses exchange theory in his study of Preston in Lancashire in the mid-19th century. He shows that during the early stages of industrialisation, working-class people formed extended family networks. At this time, life was extremely harsh. Working conditions in the factories and mines were dangerous and unhealthy; there were few laws against child labour or excessive hours of work; pay was poor and unemployment common; housing conditions were squalid and there was no welfare state to cushion the poor against misfortune. As a result, disease and disability, early death and poverty were commonplace.

In these harsh conditions, the benefits of maintaining extended family ties greatly outweighed the costs. These benefits included:

- assistance to newcomers from the countryside in finding accommodation or work in the cotton mills
- using older kin for childcare while parents went to work
- taking in an orphaned relative to produce extra income and help towards the rent.

Harsh conditions in early industrial towns encouraged people to rely on extended kin.

In many ways, this is similar to Young and Willmott's view of the stage 2 working-class extended family as a system of mutual aid. In each case, the kinship network helped its members to cope with the harsh circumstances of their lives.

As conditions began to improve later in the 19th century, the extended family began to decline. Better wages, improved housing, lower unemployment and the beginnings of a welfare state meant that there was less need to rely on the support of extended kin and so the benefits of maintaining these ties were fewer.

question

Anderson and Goode both explain the benefits of maintaining extended family ties. But what costs (e.g. financial, emotional etc) might a person face in maintaining such ties?

The family in early industrial America

Tamara Hareven (1999) also uses exchange theory in her study of kinship networks among French Canadian migrants in the textile industry in New Hampshire USA from 1880 to 1930. Like Anderson, she describes how kinship networks acted as a source of security and mutual aid to cushion the effects of poverty and unemployment. Families supported relatives at times of crisis, illness and bereavement, and parents placed infants in the care of elderly family members while they went out to work.

Like Anderson, Hareven also examines the role that family networks played in organising migration and recruiting new workers for the textile industry. Workers would recommend their relatives to the employers and introduce them to factory work.

Hareven believes that exchange theory helps us to understand these patterns of mutual aid. However, unlike Anderson, she argues that mutual aid given by relatives over the course of a lifetime is not based on a narrow calculation of costs and benefits, but on a more deeply felt and long-term sense of obligation.

Like Anderson, Hareven rejects Parsons' view that industrialisation caused the disappearance of the extended family. She shows that the extended family performed important economic functions and provided support for its members, such as organising their migration, finding them jobs and cushioning them against poverty. She concludes that the family structure best equipped to meet the needs of early industrial society is not the isolated nuclear family, as Parsons claims, but the extended family.

activity

1 Complete the table below by inserting 'E' for extended family or 'N' for nuclear family in the appropriate boxes. Don't complete the shaded boxes.
2 Working in pairs, pick one sociologist each (Young and Willmott count as one, as do Anderson and Hareven) and outline their explanation of changes in the family to your partner.
3 Check the text to see if your partner has given you an accurate explanation.

	pre-industrial society	*early industrial society*	*modern industrial society*
Parsons		(shaded)	
Young & Wilmott			
Laslett			(shaded)
Anderson & Hareven	(shaded)		

Box 6: Functionalism and the family

Functionalists believe that society is based on a value consensus (a set of norms and values) into which society socialises its members. This enables them to cooperate harmoniously to meet society's needs.

Functionalists regard society as a system made up of different parts or sub-systems that depend on each other, such as the family, education and the economy. Functionalists often compare society to a biological organism like the human body. Both society and the body can be seen as systems made up of different parts whose function is to help maintain the whole system. For example, just as the heart or lungs perform functions vital to the well-being of the body, so the family and education system meet some of society's essential needs, such as the need to socialise children.

Functionalists see the family as a particularly important sub-system – a basic building block of society. For example, George Peter Murdock (1949) argues that the family performs four essential functions to meet the needs of society and its members:

- stable satisfaction of the sex drive
- reproduction of the next generation
- socialisation of the young into society's shared norms and values
- satisfying its members' economic needs, such as food and shelter.

Murdock accepts that other institutions could perform these functions. However, he argues that the sheer practicality of the nuclear family as a way of meeting these four needs explains why it is universal (found in all societies).

The family may meet other needs too. For example, it may perform welfare, military, political or religious functions. The functions it performs will depend on the kind of society in which it is found. For example, Parsons argues that in modern industrial society the family performs only two functions (see page 33).

However, functionalism has been criticised for its rose-tinted view of society and the family: it emphasises harmony and consensus, and ignores conflict and exploitation. For example, feminists argue that the family oppresses women (see Box 5 on page 25).

questions

1 What similarities can you see between society and an organism such as the human body?

2 What other institutions apart from the family might be able to perform any of the functions that Murdock identifies? Do you think they would be as effective as the family?

The extended family today

As we saw earlier, Parsons argues that there is no place for the extended family today because it does not fit the needs of industrial society for a mobile workforce. However, research has shown evidence of the continuing importance of the extended family.

For example, British research shows the survival of extended family ties in working-class communities. Many of these communities were disrupted by slum clearance and re-housing programmes in the 1950s and 1960s that led to couples moving away to suburbs or new towns. Although these changes caused the temporary break-up of the extended family, such families have since re-established themselves.

For example, while Dagenham in the 1930s was an area of young couples separated from their kin, by the 1950s extended families had developed there. Studying Dagenham in the 1990s, Margaret O'Brien and Deborah Jones (1996) found that kinship ties remain important. For instance, 40% of people had grandparents living locally and 72% had had a visit from a relative in the last week.

The modified extended family

In America, Eugene Litwak (1960) found evidence of a 'modified extended family' of interconnected nuclear families that live separately but help each other. This family type was particularly common among ethnic minorities and the poor. Similarly, Peter Willmott (1988) found evidence in Britain of a 'dispersed extended family' whose members are geographically separated but maintain frequent contact through visits and phone calls.

The extended family continues to exist because it still performs important functions for its members. Litwak found that these included the exchange of gifts and advice, and mutual aid between ageing parents and their married children.

Similarly, Colin Bell's (1968) research in Swansea found that both working-class and middle-class families had emotional bonds with kin and relied on them for support. Among the middle class, there was more financial help from father to son, while working-class families had more frequent contact (they lived closer) and there was more domestic help from mothers to daughters.

Such evidence suggests that Parsons was wrong to claim that the extended family is no longer significant. However, Parsons rejects this. He argues that the modified or dispersed extended family is very different from the 'classic' pre-industrial extended family. This classic extended family was both a residential unit and a unit of economic production: its members lived and worked together and had binding obligations to each other. With industrialisation, however, extended kin no longer live together, production has been transferred out of the home into factories, and cooperation with relatives is no longer an obligation but a choice.

However, others argue that people do continue to feel some obligation towards at least some members of their extended family. For example, Graham Allan (1985) argues that there is a sense of obligation to support kin, but usually only at times of crisis. Even then, it is usually only children, parents and grandparents who provide such support, not wider kin.

Similarly, Janet Finch and Jennifer Mason (1993) found that people do feel a sense of obligation to extended kin. For example, over 90% of those in their study had given or received financial help and about half had cared for a sick relative. However, the strength of these obligations depended on gender: more is expected of female kin. Finch and Mason also found that the principle of balance was important: people felt that help given should be returned to avoid any feelings of indebtedness.

Ethnic minority families

Research on ethnic minority families in Britain also shows that the extended family continues to perform important functions for its members. For example, Roger Ballard (1982) found that extended family ties played an important role among Asian migrants during the 1950s and 1960s.

In this early period of migration, houses were often shared by extended rather than nuclear families. As in the early industrial period described by Anderson and Hareven, family networks provided a source of support. Ballard notes that by the 1980s, most Asian households in Britain were nuclear but relatives often lived nearby. There was frequent visiting and kinship networks continued to be a source of support.

Similarly, Mary Chamberlain's (1999) study of Caribbean families in Britain found that although they are geographically dispersed, they continue to provide support. She describes them as 'multiple nuclear families' with close and frequent contact between siblings, uncles, aunts and cousins who often make as big a contribution to childrearing as do a child's parents.

'Fictive kin' also play an important part in Caribbean families. These are people who are not related by blood or marriage but are regarded as relatives. For Caribbean families that have experienced migration, kinship networks continue to play an important role in maintaining a sense of cultural identity.

Most Asian households in Britain are nuclear but the extended family remains a source of support and identity.

synoptic link: stratification

Black feminists point to the important role of the black extended family as a haven and source of support for black people in a racist society.

Overall, evidence suggests that the extended family continues to play an important role for many people today, providing both practical and emotional support when called upon:

- during periods of migration (as studies of ethnic minority families show)
- as a cushion against poverty (as studies of working-class families show).

However, this is very different from Parsons' classic extended family, who lived and worked together and were bound by strong mutual obligations. On the other hand, the evidence also shows that nuclear families are not completely isolated from wider kin, nor completely free to choose whether to maintain ties with them: some sense of obligation remains, at least to some kin and as a last resort.

activity

In small groups, draw up a list of all the similarities you can find between the role played by the extended family in early industrial society (as described by Anderson and Hareven) and the role that it has played among ethnic minority groups in Britain today.

Are there any differences? Can you think of any other ways in which extended kin support each other?

QuickCheck Questions

1. What is meant by ascribed status?
2. True or false? According to Parsons, status in pre-industrial society is largely ascribed.
3. Explain the difference between geographical and social mobility.
4. In Young and Willmott's view, why did the nuclear family become dominant in stage 3?
5. What evidence does Laslett provide for the view that the pre-industrial family was generally nuclear?
6. According to Anderson, why did working-class people maintain extended family ties during the early industrial period?
7. Name three sociologists who argue that the extended family remains important today.

Answers are on page 271.

Examining The family and industrialisation

Item A With industrialisation, traditional extended family systems break down. On the other hand, the nuclear family fits the needs of industrial society well.

Under the industrial system, the individual worker is hired because of his competence, and in promotion the same standards are applied to everyone. Because of its emphasis on performance, such a system requires that a worker be allowed to rise or fall according to his abilities and to move to wherever the job market is best.

The nuclear family fits this need, because each couple sets up its own separate household. Because its kinship network is weak, there are fewer barriers in the way of its geographical or social mobility.

Extended families lose their functions to other agencies, such as the state, and as a result they lose the loyalty they once commanded. Individual nuclear families can thus go their own way, ignoring such extended kinship ties and performing only the two essential functions that Parsons has identified. More importantly, elders no longer control opportunities for the young, so that family authority slips from them. Industrialisation undermines the traditional systems of family control and exchange. The terms of the role bargaining between the generations have been altered.

Source: adapted from William J. Goode (1964)

Short questions

(a) Explain what is meant by 'role bargaining' (**Item A**, line 16). (2 marks)

(b) Name 'the two essential functions that Parsons has identified' the nuclear family as performing (**Item A**, lines 12-13). (4 marks)

(c) Suggest **three** functions that the family may have lost to the state or other agencies since industrialisation (**Item A**, line 10). (6 marks)

(d) Identify and briefly explain **two** reasons why the nuclear family may be more mobile than the extended family. (8 marks)

Mini-essay

Using material from **Item A** and elsewhere, assess the view that in industrial society, the extended family ceases to be important. (20 marks)

This is a type (f) question of the kind found in the exam, carrying 6 AO1 marks (knowledge and understanding) and 14 AO2 marks (identification, interpretation, analysis and evaluation).

The Examiner's advice **For the mini-essay, you should write about 400 words. You could start by identifying the view as a functionalist one, linking this to an explanation of Parsons' views on the extended family. The emphasis is on AO2 skills, so you must also evaluate (make judgements about) the view. You could do this by using the findings of other studies of the extended family in both early industrial and modern industrial society to criticise Parsons (e.g. in terms of its support functions, its assistance in mobility etc). These include Young and Willmott, Anderson, Hareven and the studies on the extended family today. Use Item A: look for points you can quote or paraphrase and then build on (e.g. by linking them to studies). Write a conclusion.**

Childhood

Sociologists are interested not only in how the family's structure has changed over time. They are also interested in changes in the status of family members. Here, we look at changes in childhood and the position of children. Again, processes such as industrialisation can be seen as playing an important role.

In this section, we examine three major issues:

- How childhood is socially constructed (created and defined by society).
- Is the position of children better today than it was in the past?
- The future of childhood.

Child soldiers armed with AK-47 rifles, the Congo.

Childhood as a social construct

Sociologists see childhood as socially constructed; in other words, as something created and defined by society. They argue that what people mean by childhood, and the position that children occupy in society, is not fixed but differs between different times, places and cultures. We can see this by comparing the western idea of childhood today with childhood in the past and in other societies.

The modern western notion of childhood

It is generally accepted in our society today that childhood is a special time of life and that children are fundamentally different from adults. They are regarded as physically and psychologically immature and not yet competent to run their own lives. There is a belief that children's lack of skills, knowledge and experience means that they need a lengthy, protected period of nurturing and socialisation before they are ready for adult society and its responsibilities.

As Jane Pilcher (1995) notes, the most important feature of the modern idea of childhood is *separateness*. Childhood is seen as a clear and distinct life stage, and children in our society occupy a separate status from adults.

This is emphasised in several ways, for instance through laws regulating what children are allowed, required or forbidden to do. Their difference from adults is also emphasised through differences in dress, especially for younger children, and through products and services specially for children, such as toys, food, books, entertainments, play areas and so on.

Related to the separateness of children's status is the idea of childhood as a 'golden age' of happiness and innocence. However, this innocence means that children are seen as vulnerable and in need of protection from the dangers of the adult world and so they must be kept 'quarantined' and separated from it. As a result, children's lives are lived largely in the sphere of the family and education, where adults provide for them and protect them from the outside world. Similarly, unlike adults, they lead lives of leisure and play and are largely excluded from paid work.

However, this view of childhood as a separate age-status is not found in all societies. It is not universal. As Stephen Wagg (1992) puts it:

> *'Childhood is socially constructed. It is, in other words, what members of particular societies, at particular times and in particular places, say it is. There is no single universal childhood, experienced by all. So, childhood isn't "natural" and should be distinguished from mere biological immaturity.'*

This means that, while all humans go through the same stages of physical development, different cultures construct or define this differently.

In western cultures today, children are defined as vulnerable and unable to fend for themselves. However, other cultures do not necessarily see such a great difference between children and adults. We can see this by looking at examples both from other cultures today and from European societies of the past.

questions

1. Explain in your own words the meaning of the statement that childhood is a 'social construct'.
2. Suggest three examples of ways in which childhood today 'is seen as a clear and distinct life stage'.

Cross-cultural differences in childhood

A good way to illustrate the social construction of childhood is to take a comparative approach; that is, to look at how children are seen and treated in other times and places than our own. The anthropologist Ruth Benedict (1934) argues that children in simpler, non-industrial societies are generally treated differently from their modern western counterparts in three ways:

- They take responsibility at an early age. For example, Lowell Holmes' (1974) study of a Samoan village found that 'too young' was never given as a reason for not permitting a child to undertake a particular task: 'Whether it be the handling of dangerous tools or the carrying of extremely heavy loads... if a child thinks he can handle the activity, parents do not object.'
- Less value is placed on children showing obedience to adult authority. For example, Raymond Firth (1970) found that among the Tikopia of the western Pacific, doing as you are told by a grown-up is regarded as a concession to be granted by the child, not as a right to be expected by the adult.
- Children's sexual behaviour is often viewed differently. For example, among the Trobriand Islanders of the south-west Pacific, Bronislaw Malinowski (1957) found that adults took an attitude of 'tolerance and amused interest' towards children's sexual explorations and activities.

Benedict argues that in many non-industrial cultures, there is much less of a dividing line between the behaviour expected of children and that expected of adults. Such evidence illustrates the key idea that childhood is not a fixed thing found universally in the same form in all human societies, but is socially constructed and so differs from culture to culture.

Historical differences in childhood

The position of children differs over time as well as between societies. Many sociologists and historians argue that childhood as we understand it today is a relatively recent 'invention'. The historian Philippe Ariès (1960) argues that in the Middle Ages (from about the 10th to the 13th centuries), 'the idea of childhood did not exist'. Children were not seen as having a different 'nature' or needs from adults – at least, not once they had passed the stage of physical dependency during infancy.

In the Middle Ages, childhood as a separate age-stage was also short. Soon after being weaned, the child entered wider society on much the same terms as an adult, beginning work from an early age, often in the household of another family. Children were in effect 'mini-adults' with the same rights, duties and skills as adults. For example, the law often made no distinction between children and adults, and children often faced the same severe punishments as those meted out to adults.

As evidence of his view, Ariès uses works of art from the period. In these, children appear without 'any of the characteristics of childhood: they have simply been depicted on a smaller scale'. The paintings show children and adults dressed in the same clothing and working and playing together.

question

What problems might there be in using evidence such as paintings and diaries, as Ariès does, to understand childhood or family life in the past?

Parental attitudes towards children in the Middle Ages were also very different from those today. Edward Shorter (1975) argues that high death rates encouraged indifference and neglect, especially towards infants. For example, it was not uncommon for parents to give a newborn baby the name of a recently dead sibling, to refer to the baby as 'it', or to forget how many children they had had.

synoptic link: deviance

Many aspects of childhood regarded as normal in non-industrial cultures or in the past, such as child labour or child sexuality, might be seen as unacceptable in Britain today. This shows how ideas of deviance and normality are culturally relative: they vary between times, places and cultures.

According to Ariès, however, elements of the modern notion of childhood gradually began to emerge from the 13th century onwards:

- Schools (which previously adults had also attended) came to specialise purely in the education of the young. This reflected the influence of the church, which increasingly saw children as fragile 'creatures of God' in need of discipline and protection from worldly evils.
- There was a growing distinction between children's and adults' clothing. By the 17th century, an upper-class boy would be dressed in 'an outfit reserved for his own age group, which set him apart from adults'.
- By the 18th century, handbooks on childrearing were widely available – a sign of the growing child-centredness of family life, at least among the middle classes.

According to Ariès, these developments culminate in the modern 'cult of childhood'. He argues that we have moved from a world that did not see childhood as in any way special, to a world that is obsessed with childhood. He describes the 20th century as 'the century of the child'.

Some sociologists have criticised Ariès for arguing that childhood did not exist in the past. Linda Pollock (1983) argues that it is more correct to say that in the Middle Ages, society simply had a different notion of childhood from today's.

However, Ariès' work is valuable because it shows that childhood is socially constructed: he demonstrates how ideas about children and their social status have varied over time.

A child-centred world?

Reasons for changes in the position of children

There are many reasons for the changes in the position of children. These include the following changes during the 19th and 20th centuries:

- Laws restricting child labour and excluding children from paid work. From being economic assets who could earn a wage, children became an economic liability, financially dependent on their parents.

- The introduction of compulsory schooling in 1880 had a similar effect, especially for the children of the poor (middle- and upper-class children were already receiving education). The raising of the school-leaving age has extended this period of dependency.
- Child protection and welfare legislation, such as the 1889 Prevention of Cruelty to Children Act. Exactly a century later, the 1989 Children Act made the welfare of the child the fundamental principle underpinning the work of agencies such as social services.
- The growth of the idea of children's rights. For example, the Children Act defines parents as having 'responsibilities' rather than 'rights' in relation to children, while the United Nations Convention on the Rights of the Child (1989) lays down basic rights such as entitlement to healthcare and education, protection from abuse, and the right to participate in decisions that affect them, such as custody cases.
- Declining family size and lower infant mortality rates. These have encouraged parents to make a greater financial and emotional investment in the fewer children that they now have.
- Children's health and development became the subject of medical knowledge. Jacques Donzelot (1977) observes how theories of child development that began to appear from the 19th century stressed that children need supervision and protection.
- Laws and policies that apply specifically to children, such as minimum ages for a wide range of activities from sex to smoking, have reinforced the idea that children are different from adults and so different rules must be applied to their behaviour.

activity

Make a list of all the activities that the law prevents children engaging in. Find out the age limits for each of these. For example, what are the age restrictions governing access to alcohol?

Most sociologists agree that the process of industrialisation – the shift from agriculture to factory production as the basis of the economy – underlies many of the above changes. For example, modern industry needs an educated workforce and this requires compulsory schooling of the young. Similarly, the higher standards of living and better welfare provision that industry makes possible lead to lower infant mortality rates. Industrialisation is thus a key factor in bringing about the modern idea of childhood and the changed status of children.

Has the position of children improved?

As we have seen, childhood is socially constructed and varies between times, places and cultures. There are important differences between childhood in western societies today as compared both to present-day Third World countries and to European societies in the past. For example, in the Middle Ages, child labour was a basic fact of life for almost all children, while schooling was available only to the wealthy.

The march of progress view

These differences raise the question of whether the changes in the status of childhood that we looked at earlier represent an improvement. The 'march of progress' view argues that, over the past few centuries, the position of children in western societies has been steadily improving and today is better than it has ever been.

Writers such as Ariès and Shorter hold this view. They argue that today's children are more valued, better cared for, protected and educated, enjoy better health and have more rights than those of previous generations.

For example, children today are protected from harm and exploitation by laws against child abuse and child labour, while an array of professionals and specialists caters for their educational, psychological and medical needs. The government spends huge sums on their education – nearly £45 billion in 2003 in England.

Better healthcare and higher standards of living also mean that babies have a much better chance of survival now than a century ago. In 1900, the infant mortality rate was over 140 per 1,000 live births; a century later, it was fewer than 6 per 1,000.

Higher living standards and smaller family sizes (down from 5.7 births per woman in the 1860s to 1.64 in 2001) also mean that parents can afford to provide for children's needs properly. According to one estimate, by the time a child reaches their 17th birthday, they will have cost their parents £50,000.

March of progress sociologists argue that the family has become child-centred. Children are no longer to be 'seen and not heard', as they were in Victorian times. Instead they are now the focal point of the family, consulted on many decisions as never before. Parents invest a great deal in their children emotionally as well as financially, and often have high aspirations for them to have a better life and greater opportunities than they themselves have had.

Furthermore, it is not just the family that is now child-centred; so is society as a whole. For example, many leisure activities and much media output are designed specifically for children.

The conflict view

The march of progress view is that the position of children has improved dramatically in a relatively short period of time. However, conflict sociologists such as Marxists and feminists dispute this. They argue that society is based on a conflict between different social groups such as social classes or genders. In this conflict, some groups have more power, status or wealth than others. Conflict sociologists see the relationship between groups as one of domination and subordination, in which the dominant group act as oppressors.

Conflict sociologists argue that the march of progress view of modern childhood is based on a false and idealised image that ignores important inequalities. They criticise the march of progress view on two grounds:

- There are inequalities *among children* in terms of the opportunities and risks they face: many today remain unprotected and badly cared for.
- The inequalities *between children and adults* are greater than ever: children today experience greater control, oppression and dependency, not greater care and protection.

synoptic link: stratification

We cannot speak of 'children' in general as if they were all equal: social class, gender and ethnic differences affect their life chances.

Inequalities among children

Not all children share the same status or experiences. For example, children of different *nationalities* are likely to experience different childhoods and different life chances. 90% of the world's low birth-weight babies are born in the Third World.

There are also *gender* differences between children. For example, according to Hillman (1993), boys are more likely to be allowed to cross or cycle on roads, use buses, and go out after dark unaccompanied. Similarly, there are *ethnic* differences: Julia Brannen's (1994) study of 15–16 year olds found that Asian parents were more likely than other parents to be strict towards their daughters.

Table 2B: Children and young people on child protection registers, year ending 31 March 2000: England

Type of abuse	numbers	percentages
Neglect	10,400	39
Physical injury	5,000	19
Sexual abuse	3,200	12
Emotional abuse	4,800	18
Other	500	2
More than one type of abuse	2,900	12
Total of all types of abuse	26,800	100

Source: Government Statistical Office

question

Suggest two reasons why statistics on child abuse might not give an accurate picture of the extent of abuse.

There are also important *class* inequalities between children:

- Poor mothers are more likely to have low birth-weight babies, which in turn is linked to delayed physical and intellectual development.
- According to Caroline Woodroffe (1993), children of unskilled manual workers are over three times more likely to suffer from hyperactivity and four times more likely to experience conduct disorders than the children of professionals.
- According to Marilyn Howard (2001), children born into poor families are also more likely to die in infancy or childhood, to suffer longstanding illness, to be shorter in height, to fall behind at school, and to be placed on the child protection register.

Inequalities between children and adults

There are also major inequalities of power between children and adults. March of progress writers argue that adults use this power for the benefit and protection of children, for example by passing laws against child labour.

However, critics such as Shulamith Firestone (1979) and John Holt (1974) argue that many of the things that march of progress writers see positively as care and protection are in fact just new forms of oppression and control. For example, Firestone argues that 'protection' from paid work is not a benefit to children but a form of inequality. It is a way of forcibly segregating children, making them more dependent, powerless and subject to adult control than previously.

These critics see the need to free children from adult control, and so their view is described as 'child liberationism'. Adult control takes a number of forms.

neglect and abuse

Adult control over children can take the extreme form of physical neglect or physical, sexual or emotional abuse. In 2000, over 26,800 children were on child protection registers because they were deemed to be at risk of significant harm – most often from their own parents (see Table 2B). The charity ChildLine receives over 20,000 calls a year from children saying that they have been sexually or physically abused. Such figures indicate a 'dark side' to family life of which children are the victims.

controls over children's space

Children's movements in industrial societies such as Britain are highly regulated. For example, shops may display signs such as 'no schoolchildren'. Children are told to play in some areas and forbidden to play in others. There is increasingly tight surveillance over children in public spaces such as shopping centres, especially at times when they should be in school. Fears about road safety and 'stranger danger' have led to more and more children being driven to school rather than travelling independently, as Figure 2.1 shows.

This control and surveillance contrasts with the independence of many children in Third World countries today. For example, Cindi Katz (1993) describes how rural Sudanese children roam freely both within the village and for several kilometres outside it.

controls over children's time

Adults in modern society control children's daily routines, including the times when they get up, eat, go to school, come home, go out, play, watch

Figure 2.1: Children's unaccompanied journeys to school, 1971 and 1990

% going to school unaccompanied
100
80
60
40
20
0
7
8
9
10
11
Age
1971
1990

Source: M. Hillman (1993)

television and sleep. Adults also control the speed at which children 'grow up'. It is they who define whether a child is too old or too young for this or that activity, responsibility or behaviour. This contrasts with Holmes' finding that among Samoans, 'too young' is never given as a reason for not letting a child undertake a particular task.

Should smacking be banned?

controls over children's bodies

Adults exercise enormous control over children's bodies, including how they sit, walk and run, what they wear (sun hats, make-up, glasses), their hairstyles and whether or not they can have their ears pierced. It is taken for granted that children's bodies may be touched (in certain ways by certain adults): they are washed, fed and dressed, have their heads patted and hands held, are picked up, cuddled and kissed, and they may be disciplined by smacking. At the same time, adults restrict the ways in which children may touch their own bodies. For example, a child may be told not to pick their nose, suck their thumb or play with their genitals. This contrasts with the sexual freedoms enjoyed by children in some non-industrial cultures such as the Trobriand Islands.

control over children's access to resources

In industrial societies, children have only limited opportunities to earn money, and so they remain dependent economically on adults:

- Labour laws and compulsory schooling exclude them from all but the most marginal, low-paid, part-time employment.
- Although the state pays child benefit, this goes to the parent not the child.
- Pocket money given by parents may depend on 'good behaviour' and there may be restrictions on what it can be spent on.

All this contrasts with the economic role of children in Third World societies and in European societies in the past. For example, Katz found that Sudanese children were already engaged in productive work from the age of three or four.

activity

If you have any younger brothers or sisters, ask them for their views on childhood – what they like and don't like about being a child, and how they resist adult control (parents, teachers). Alternatively, think back to your own experiences as a child.

Age patriarchy

Diana Gittins (1998) uses the term 'age patriarchy' to describe inequalities between adults and children. Just as feminists use the concept of patriarchy to describe male domination and female dependency, Gittins argues that there is also an *age* patriarchy of adult domination and child dependency. In fact, patriarchy means literally 'rule by the father' and as Gittins points out, the term 'family' referred originally to the power of the male head over all other members of the household, including children and servants as well as women.

Today this power may still assert itself in the form of violence against both children and women. For example, according to the Women's Aid Federation of England (1999), 70% of children staying in refuges with their abused mothers had themselves been abused by their father, while most convicted child abusers are male. (See page 28 for further discussion of domestic violence.) Such findings support Gittins' view that patriarchy oppresses children as well as women.

Evidence that children may experience childhood as oppressive comes from the strategies that they use to resist the status of child and the restrictions that go with it. Jennifer Hockey and Allison James (1993) describe one strategy as 'acting up' – acting like adults by doing things that children are not supposed to do, such as swearing, smoking, drinking alcohol, joy riding and under-age sexual activity. Similarly, children may exaggerate their age ('I'm nearly 9').

'Acting down' – behaving in ways expected of younger children – is also a popular strategy for resisting adult control (e.g. by reverting to 'baby talk' or insisting on being carried). Hockey and James conclude that modern childhood is a status from which most children want to escape.

However, critics of the child liberationist view argue that some adult control over children's lives is justified on the grounds that children cannot make rational decisions and so are unable to safeguard their interests themselves.

Critics also argue that, although children remain under adult supervision, they are not as powerless as the child liberationists claim. For example, as we saw earlier, the 1989 Children Act and the United Nations Convention on the Rights of the Child establish the principle that children have legal rights to be protected and consulted.

activity

Draw up a two-column table entitled, 'Has the position of children improved?' Head the left-hand column 'Yes' and the right-hand column 'No'. In each column, list evidence and arguments in support of that view.

Then write a brief conclusion saying whether on balance you think the position of children has improved, giving your reasons.

synoptic link: deviance

Sociologists studying deviance are interested in how society controls its members to ensure they act in ways appropriate to their status. Adults exercise controls over children's behaviour and bodies to ensure that they act as children are expected to in our society.

Sociologists are also interested in how individuals – including children – resist authority and refuse to conform to society's norms.

The future of childhood

If the idea of children's rights is gaining ground, could this be a sign that children are becoming more powerful and that the distinction between childhood and adulthood is breaking down? Is childhood as we know it in western society disappearing? Sociologists and others have put forward several different answers to these questions. We examine these now.

The disappearance of childhood

Neil Postman (1994) argues that childhood is 'disappearing at a dazzling speed'. He points to the trend towards giving children the same rights as adults, the disappearance of children's traditional unsupervised games, the growing similarity of adult and children's clothing, and even to cases of children committing 'adult' crimes such as murder. In his view, the cause both of the emergence of childhood, and now of its disappearance, lies in the rise and fall of print culture and its replacement by television culture.

- During the Middle Ages, most people were illiterate, so speech was the only skill needed for participation in the adult world. Children were able to enter adult society from an early age. Childhood was not associated with innocence, nor the adult world with mystery. There was no division between the world of the adult and that of the child.
- Childhood emerged as a separate status along with mass literacy, from the 19th century on.

This is because the printed word creates an information hierarchy: a sharp division between adults, who can read, and children, who cannot. This gave adults the power to keep knowledge about sex, money, violence, illness, death and other 'adult' matters a secret from children. These things became mysteries to them, and childhood came to be associated with innocence and ignorance.

- Television blurs the distinction between childhood and adulthood by destroying the information hierarchy. Unlike the printed word, television does not require special skills to access it, and it makes information available to adults and children alike. The boundary between adult and child is broken down, adult authority diminishes and the ignorance and innocence of childhood is replaced by knowledge and cynicism. The counterpart of the disappearance of childhood is the disappearance of adulthood, where adults' and children's tastes and styles become indistinguishable.

Postman's study is valuable in showing how different types of communication technology, such as print and television, can influence the way in which childhood is constructed. However, he over-emphasises a single cause – television – at the expense of other factors that have influenced the development of childhood, such as rising living standards or changes in the law.

Street child, San Cristobal de las Casas, Mexico. Is this oppression or preparation for adult life?

question

Suggest three examples of ways in which children's activities, leisure, dress or food and those of adults have become similar in recent years.

A separate childhood culture

Unlike Postman, Iona Opie (1993) argues that childhood is not disappearing. Based on a lifetime of research into children's games, rhymes and songs, conducted with her husband Peter Opie, she argues that there is strong evidence of the continued existence of a separate children's culture over many years. Their findings contradict Postman's claim that children's own unsupervised games are dying out. Their studies show that children can and do create their own independent culture separate from that of adults.

The globalisation of western childhood

As we saw earlier, child liberationists argue that modern childhood is oppressive and that children today are subject to adult authority. In their view, childhood is not disappearing.

Another version of this view is the claim that western notions of childhood are being globalised. International humanitarian and welfare agencies have exported and imposed on the rest of the world, western norms of what childhood should be – a separate life stage, based in the nuclear family and school, in which children are innocent, dependent and vulnerable and have no economic role.

For example, campaigns against child labour, or concerns about 'street children' in Third World countries, reflect western views about how childhood 'ought' to be – whereas in fact, such activity by children may be the norm for the culture and an important preparation for adult life. In this view, 'childhood' is not disappearing, but spreading throughout the world.

Contradictory trends

It is difficult to draw firm conclusions about whether the modern notion of childhood is disappearing. It depends on which aspects we look at:

- Children have more rights, but still do not have equal rights with adults and are still subject to adult authority.
- There are growing similarities between children and adults in leisure activities, dress, diet etc.
- The extension of compulsory and post-compulsory education has made young people economically dependent 'children' for longer and longer.
- Children's freedom of movement has become more restricted with fears over road safety and 'stranger danger'.
- At the same time children now have greater access to means of communication.
- Many adults remain concerned about children's behaviour and discipline and about exposure to media sex and violence.

One way in which childhood may be 'disappearing' is in terms of falling birth and death rates. These two trends produce an ageing population in which there are more old people and fewer young ones. Jens Qvortrup (1990) argues that as the proportion of the population who are parents with dependent children falls, so there will be fewer voices calling for resources to go to children. This may also make childhood a more isolating experience, as families become smaller and there are fewer children in the neighbourhood. However, it could also be that children's relative scarcity will make them more valued and powerful.

Growing similarities between adults' and children's leisure activities?

Although it is difficult to predict how our notion of childhood will develop in the future, we have seen that there are a number of trends that may re-shape children's future position. These possibilities of change demonstrate that childhood is not a fixed, universal fact but a status that is socially constructed. Whether it will be reconstructed as something that segregates children further, or as a status that gives them greater freedom, remains to be seen.

QuickCheck Questions

1 True or false? The social construction of childhood means that it is likely to be similar in all societies.

2 Ruth Benedict identifies three ways in which childhood in non-industrial cultures often differs from childhood in the west. State two of these.

3 Edward Shorter gives examples of parental neglect or indifference towards children in the Middle Ages. State one of these.

4 True or false? In industrial society, children tend to be an economic asset to their parents.

5 Give one example of class differences between children.

6 What is age patriarchy?

7 Why does Neil Postman believe childhood is disappearing?

8 What is meant by the globalisation of western childhood?

Answers are on page 271.

Examining **Childhood**

Item A According to some sociologists, children in today's supposedly child-centred society lead lives that are segregated and controlled, but childhood was not always like this. Nor is it yet the case for many children in the Third World.

For example, Ariès describes a medieval world in which, if children were not actually the equals of adults, they nevertheless mixed freely with adults in both work and leisure. Little distinction was drawn between adults and children.

According to this view, however, industrialisation brought major changes to the position of children. The development of industrial society meant that their lives were increasingly confined, disciplined and regulated by adults. This was done on the grounds that children were innocent, vulnerable and in need of protection from the dangers of adult society. The result is that in the west today, adults exercise a control over children's time, space and bodies that would have been unimaginable to medieval society. In this view, children today are the victims of adult oppression.

Not all sociologists share this view of modern childhood, however. Some argue that the distinction between childhood and adulthood is once again becoming blurred, and some even go so far as to argue that childhood is disappearing.

Short questions

(a) Explain what is meant by the term 'child-centred society' (**Item A**, lines 1-2). (2 marks)

(b) Give **two** examples of ways in which the distinction between childhood and adulthood is 'becoming blurred' (**Item A**, line 15). (4 marks)

(c) Suggest **three** ways in which adults control 'children's time, space and bodies' (**Item A**, lines 11-12). (6 marks)

(d) Identify **two** changes linked to industrialisation and briefly explain how each one may have led to changes in the position of children (**Item A**, lines 7-8). (8 marks)

Mini-essay

Using material from **Item A** and elsewhere, assess the view that 'children today are the victims of adult oppression'(**Item A**, lines 12–13). (20 marks)

This is a type (f) question of the kind found in the exam, carrying 6 AO1 marks (knowledge and understanding) and 14 AO2 marks (identification, interpretation, analysis and evaluation).

The Examiner's advice **In the mini-essay, the emphasis is on AO2 skills such as evaluation, so don't just describe the view – make judgements and draw conclusions about it too. You could start by identifying it as a 'child liberationist' view, bring in concepts like age patriarchy and examine some of the ways that adults control children. You could evaluate (e.g. by asking whether control equals oppression, or whether it is in children's own interests). The 'march of progress' view is relevant, as are cross-cultural or historical comparisons, but consider also the view that childhood is disappearing; how might this link to oppression? Go carefully through the Item to find points you can bring in and build on. Write a separate conclusion.**

Changing patterns and family diversity

In the past 30 or 40 years there have been some major changes in family patterns. For example:

- The number of traditional nuclear family households has fallen.
- Divorce rates have increased.
- There are fewer first marriages, but more re-marriages. People are marrying later.
- More couples are cohabiting.
- Women are having fewer children and having them later.
- There are more births outside marriage.
- There are more lone-parent families.
- More people live alone.
- There are more stepfamilies, and more couples without children.

A traditional nuclear family?

In this section, we examine the changes in patterns of family life in Britain and the reasons for them. These changes include marriage, cohabitation and divorce. Such changes are contributing to greater family diversity and we examine how sociologists have interpreted them.

Divorce

We look first at divorce because divorce is a major cause of changing family patterns and greater family diversity. For example, most re-marriages involve a divorcee, and divorce creates both lone-parent families and one-person households.

Changing patterns of divorce

Since the 1960s, there has been a great increase in the number of divorces in the United Kingdom, as Figure 2.2 shows. The number of divorces doubled between 1961 and 1969, and doubled again by 1972. The upward trend continued, peaking in 1993 at 180,000. Since then, numbers have fallen somewhat, but still stood at 157,000 in 2001 – about six times higher than in 1961. This rate means that about 40% of all marriages will end in divorce.

About 7 out of every 10 petitions (applications) for divorce now come from women. The most common reason for a woman to be granted a divorce is the unreasonable behaviour of her husband.

Some couples are more likely than others to divorce. Couples whose marriages are at greatest risk include those who marry young, have a child before they marry, or cohabit before marriage, and those where one or both partners have been married before.

Figure 2.2: Marriages and divorces

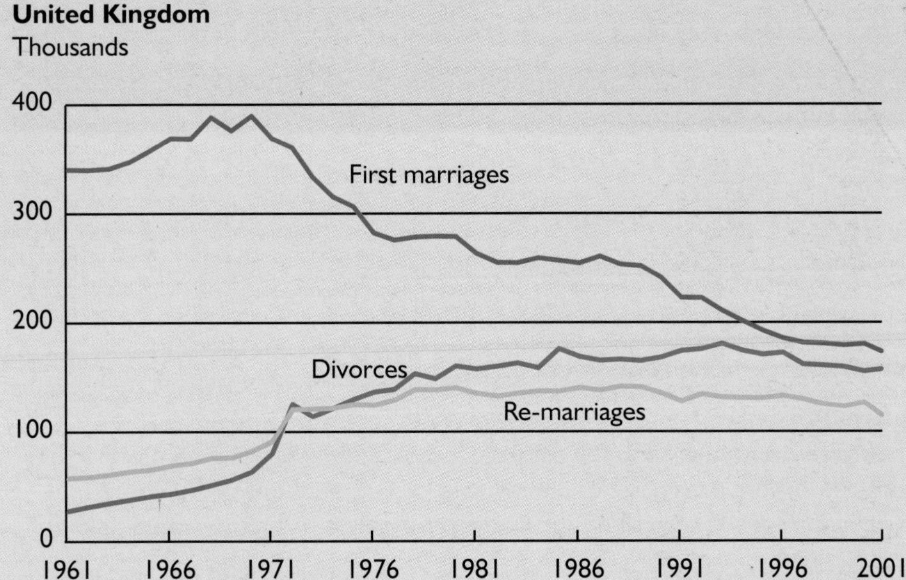

Source: Office for National Statistics

questions

1 Study Figure 2.2 and answer the following questions:

(a) Roughly how many divorces were there in 1971?

(b) Approximately what was the total number of marriages (first marriages plus re-marriages) in 2001?

(c) Describe the trends shown in the number of first marriages, re-marriages and divorces over the period shown.

2 By 1993, civil rather than church marriages made up over half the total number of marriages and three-quarters of re-marriages. Suggest reasons why:

(a) there has been such a decline in church marriages

(b) re-marriages are much less likely than first marriages to take place in church.

Explanations of the increase in divorce

Sociologists have identified the following reasons for the increase in divorce:

1 changes in the law
2 declining stigma and changing attitudes
3 secularisation
4 rising expectations of marriage
5 changes in the position of women.

1 Changes in the law

Divorce was very difficult to obtain in 19th-century Britain, especially for women. Gradually, changes in the law have made divorce easier. There have been three kinds of change in the law:

- equalising the grounds (the legal reasons) for divorce between the sexes
- widening the grounds for divorce
- making divorce cheaper.

When the grounds were equalised for men and women in 1923, this was followed by a sharp rise in the number of divorce petitions from women. Similarly, the widening of the grounds in 1971 to 'irretrievable breakdown' made divorce easier to obtain and produced a doubling of the divorce rate almost overnight. The introduction of legal aid for divorce cases in 1949 lowered the cost of divorcing. Divorce rates have risen with each change in the law.

Box 7: A brief history of divorce law

Pre-1857: Divorce virtually non-existent: only obtainable by special and costly Act of Parliament.

1857: Men could divorce unfaithful wives, but women also had to prove husbands' cruelty or another matrimonial offence in addition to adultery. Divorce still very costly.

1921: 3,000 divorces.

1923: Grounds for divorce equalised for men and women.

1937: Grounds widened to include desertion and cruelty.

1949: Legal aid available, making divorce more affordable.

1961: 27,000 divorces – nine times higher than in 1921.

1969: Divorce Law Reform Act passed (came into effect in 1971). This made 'irretrievable breakdown' of marriage the sole ground for divorce, established by proving unreasonable behaviour, adultery, desertion, or separation either with or without consent. Divorce available after two years' agreed separation, or five years if only one spouse wants divorce.

1984: The minimum period after marriage before a divorce petition could be filed was reduced from three years to one.

1996: Family Law Act encourages couples to seek mediation but allows divorce by agreement after a 'period of reflection'.

Although divorce is the legal termination of a marriage, couples can and do find other solutions to the problem of an unhappy marriage. These include:

- desertion, where one partner leaves the other but the couple remain legally married
- legal separation, where a court separates the financial and legal affairs of the couple but where they remain married and are not free to re-marry
- 'empty shell' marriage, where the couple continue to live under the same roof but remain married in name only.

However, as divorce has become more easily available, these solutions have become less popular.

Yet although changes in the law have given people the freedom to divorce more easily, this does not in itself explain why more people should choose to take advantage of this freedom. To explain the rise in divorce rates we must therefore look at other changes too. These include changes in public attitudes towards divorce.

2 Declining stigma and changing attitudes

Stigma refers to the negative label or social disapproval attached to a person, action or relationship. In the past, divorce and divorcees have been stigmatised. For example, churches tended to condemn divorce and often refused to conduct marriage services involving divorcees. Juliet Mitchell and Jack Goody (1997) note that an important change since the 1960s has been the rapid decline in the stigma attached to divorce.

As stigma declines and divorce becomes more socially acceptable, couples are more willing to resort to divorce as a means of solving their marital problems. In turn, the fact that divorce is now more common begins to 'normalise' it and reduces the stigma attached to it.

synoptic link: deviance

Until fairly recently, divorce was widely regarded as shameful – a form of deviance from the expected norm. With 40% of marriages now ending in divorce, today it is more likely to be seen simply as a misfortune. Other family patterns once regarded as deviant, such as cohabitation, lone parenthood, births outside marriage and same-sex relationships, are also increasingly seen as normal or tolerable.

3 Secularisation

Secularisation refers to the decline in the influence of religion in society. Many sociologists argue that religious institutions and ideas are losing their influence and society is becoming more secular. For example, church attendance rates continue to decline.

As a result of secularisation, the traditional opposition of the churches to divorce carries less weight in society and people are less likely to be influenced by religious teachings when making decisions about divorce. At the same time, many churches have also begun to soften their views on divorce and divorcees, perhaps because they fear losing credibility with large sections of the public and with their own members.

activity

Which churches now allow divorce and re-marriage and under what circumstances? Try to find out about a range of churches, e.g. Church of England, Catholic, Baptist, Jehovah's Witnesses, Pentecostalist. Also, find out about the attitudes of non-Christian religions.

4 Rising expectations of marriage

Functionalist sociologists such as Ronald Fletcher (1966) argue that the higher expectations that people place on marriage today are a major cause of rising divorce rates. As a result of higher expectations, couples nowadays are less willing to tolerate an unhappy marriage.

This is linked to the ideology of romantic love – an idea that has become dominant over the last couple of centuries. This is the belief that marriage should be based solely on love, and that for each individual there is a Mr or Miss Right out there. It follows that if love dies, there is no longer any justification for remaining married and every reason to divorce so as to be able to renew the search for one's true soulmate.

In the past, by contrast, individuals often had little choice in whom they married, and at a time when the family was also a unit of production, marriages were often contracted largely for economic reasons or out of duty to one's family.

Under these circumstances, individuals were unlikely to have the high expectations about marriage as a romantic union of two souls that many couples have today. Entering marriage with lower expectations, they were less likely to be dissatisfied by the absence of romance and intimacy.

Despite today's high divorce rates, functionalists take an optimistic view. They point to the continuing popularity of marriage. Most adults marry, and the high rate of re-marriage after divorce shows that although divorcees may have become dissatisfied with a particular partner, they have not rejected marriage as an institution.

However, critics argue that this is too rosy a view. Feminists argue that the oppression of women within the family is the main cause of marital conflict and divorce, but functionalists ignore this. Although functionalists offer an explanation of rising divorce rates, they fail to explain why it is mainly women rather than men who seek divorce.

5 Changes in the position of women

One reason for women's increased willingness to seek divorce is that improvements in their economic position have made them less financially dependent on their husband and therefore freer to end an unsatisfactory marriage.

- Women today are much more likely to be in paid work. The proportion of women working rose from 47% to 70% between 1959 and 2003.
- Although women generally still earn less than men, equal pay and anti-discrimination laws have helped to narrow the pay gap.
- Girls' greater success in education now helps them achieve better-paid jobs than previous generations.
- The availability of welfare benefits means that women no longer have to remain financially dependent on their husbands.

These developments mean that women are more likely to be able to support themselves in the event of divorce.

Many feminists also argue that the fact that women are now wage earners as well as homemakers has itself created a new source of conflict between husbands and wives and that this is leading to more divorces.

While there have been big improvements in women's position in the public sphere of employment, education, politics and so on, feminists argue that in the private sphere of family and personal relationships, change has been slow. They argue that marriage remains patriarchal, with men benefiting from their wives' 'triple shift' of paid work, domestic work and emotion work (see page 24).

Similarly, Arlie Hochschild (1997) argues that for many women, the home compares unfavourably with work. At work, women feel valued. At home, men's continuing resistance to doing housework is a source of frustration and makes marriage less stable. In addition, the fact that both partners now go out to work leaves less time and energy for the emotion work needed to address the problems that arise. Both these factors contribute to the rising divorce rate.

Radical feminists such as Jessie Bernard (1976) observe that many women feel a growing dissatisfaction with patriarchal marriage. She sees the rising divorce rate, and the fact that most petitions come from women, as evidence of their growing acceptance of feminist ideas: women are becoming conscious of patriarchal oppression and more confident about rejecting it.

The meaning of high divorce rates

Sociologists disagree as to what today's high divorce rate tells us about the state of marriage and the family.

- **The New Right** see a high divorce rate as undesirable because it undermines the traditional nuclear family. In their view, divorce creates an underclass of welfare-dependent female lone parents and leaves boys without the adult male role model they need.
- **Feminists** disagree. They see a high divorce rate as desirable because it shows that women are breaking free from the oppression of the patriarchal nuclear family.
- **Postmodernists** see a high divorce rate as giving individuals the freedom to choose to end a relationship when it no longer meets their needs. They see it as a cause of greater family diversity.
- **Functionalists** argue that a high divorce rate does not necessarily prove that marriage as a social institution is under threat. It is simply the result of people's higher expectations of marriage today. The high rate of re-marriage shows people's continuing commitment to the idea of marriage.
- **Interactionists** aim to understand what divorce means to the individual. David Morgan (1996) argues that we cannot generalise about the meaning of divorce because every individual's interpretation of it is different. Mitchell and Goody provide an example of this. One of their interviewees described the day her father left as the best day of her life, whereas another said she had never recovered from her father deserting the family.

Divorced fathers campaigning for rights of custody and access. Why do the courts usually give custody to mothers?

Partnerships

Marriage

There have been a number of important changes in the pattern of marriage in recent years:

- Fewer people are marrying: marriage rates are at their lowest since the 1920s. In 2001, there were under 150,000 first marriages – less than half the total for 1970.
- However, there are more re-marriages (marriages where one or both partners has been married before). In 2001, more than 4 out of every 10 marriages were re-marriages. For many people, this is leading to 'serial monogamy': a pattern of marriage – divorce – re-marriage.
- People are marrying later: the average age of first marriage rose by 6 years between 1971 and 2000, when it reached 30 for men and 28 for women.
- Couples are less likely to marry in church. In 1981, three-fifths of weddings were conducted with religious ceremonies, but by 2001 this had fallen to below two-fifths.

Reasons for changing patterns of marriage

Many of the reasons for a fall in the number of *first marriages* are similar to the reasons for the increase in divorce examined earlier. They include the following:

- Changing attitudes to marriage. There is less pressure to marry and more freedom for individuals to choose the type of relationship they want. There is now a widespread belief that the quality of a couple's relationship is more important than its legal status. The norm that everyone ought to get married has greatly weakened. This may be linked to secularisation. The churches are in favour of marriage, but as their influence declines, people feel freer to choose not to marry.
- Declining stigma attached to alternatives to marriage. Cohabitation or remaining single are now widely regarded as acceptable, as is having children outside marriage, so that pregnancy no longer automatically leads to a 'shotgun wedding'. Seventy per cent of those interviewed for the British Social Attitudes Survey in 1989 believed that couples who want children should get married; but by 2000 only 54% thought so.
- Changes in the position of women. With better educational and career prospects, many women are now less economically dependent on men. This gives them greater freedom not to marry. The growing impact of the feminist view that marriage is an oppressive patriarchal institution may also dissuade some women from marrying.
- Fear of divorce. With the rising divorce rate, some may be put off marrying as they see the increased likelihood of marriage ending in divorce.

The main reason for the increase in *re-marriages* is the rise in the number of divorces. As Figure 2.2 shows, the two have grown together, so that the rising number of divorcees provides a supply of people available to re-marry.

The *age* at which couples marry is rising because young people are postponing marriage in order to spend longer in full-time education, and perhaps to establish themselves in a career first. Another reason is that more couples are now cohabiting for a period before they marry.

Couples nowadays are less likely to marry *in church* for two main reasons:

- Secularisation: fewer people see the relevance of a religious ceremony.
- Many churches refuse to marry divorcees (who make up a growing proportion of those marrying) and divorcees may in any case have less desire to marry in church.

questions

1 What is meant by a 'pre-nuptial agreement'?

2 What does the rise of pre-nuptial agreements tell us about attitudes to marriage today?

Estimated cost of a white wedding: £14,000.

Cohabitation

Cohabitation involves an unmarried couple in a sexual relationship living together. While the number of marriages has been falling, the number of couples cohabiting continues to increase:

- There are over 1.5 million cohabiting couples in England and Wales. About a quarter of all unmarried adults under 60 are now cohabiting – double the number in 1986.
- The number of cohabiting couples is expected to double again by 2021.

Reasons for the increase in cohabitation

- Increased cohabitation rates reflect the decline in stigma attached to sex outside marriage. In 1989, only 44% of people agreed that 'premarital sex is not wrong at all', whereas by 2000, 62% took this view (British Social Attitudes, 2000). The young are more likely to accept cohabitation: a third of the over-60s thought cohabitation was always wrong, but less than a tenth of the under-30s thought so.
- Increased career opportunities for women may also mean that they have less need for the financial security of marriage and are freer to opt for cohabitation.

The relationship between cohabitation and marriage

Although cohabitation is increasing as marriage decreases, the relationship between the two is not clear-cut. For some couples, cohabitation is just a step on the way to getting married, whereas for others it is a permanent alternative to marriage.

Robert Chester (1985) argues that for most people, cohabitation is part of the process of getting married. For example, evidence from the British Household Panel Survey (1998) shows that about three-quarters of cohabiting couples expect to marry each other. Many see cohabitation as a trial marriage and intend to marry if it goes well. Most couples who cohabit decide to marry if they have children. In some cases, cohabitation is a temporary phase before marriage because one or both partners is awaiting a divorce.

On the other hand, some couples see

cohabitation as a permanent alternative to marriage. André Bejin (1985) argues that cohabitation among some young people represents a conscious attempt to create a more personally negotiated and equal relationship than conventional patriarchal marriage. For example, Shelton and John (1993) found that women who cohabit do less housework than their married counterparts.

Clearly, then, cohabitation does not mean the same thing to every couple. Eleanor Macklin (1980) argues that the term covers a diverse range of partnerships, and that the relationship between marriage and cohabitation is a complex and variable one.

activity

Group discussion: Cohabitation is becoming 'marriage by another name'.

You might like to consider issues such as whether cohabitation is just a temporary phase before marriage; same-sex couples; why some couples choose to cohabit permanently rather than marry; similarities and differences in the rights and obligations of married versus cohabiting couples; the significance of high divorce rates.

Same-sex relationships

According to a survey in the *Lancet* (2002), about 5% of the adult population now have same-sex relationships. However, it is hard to judge whether this represents an increase because in the past, stigma and illegality meant that such relationships were more likely to be hidden.

There is evidence of increased social acceptance of same-sex relationships in recent years. Male homosexual acts were decriminalised in 1967 for consenting adults over 21. More recently the age of consent has been equalised with heterosexuals. Opinion polls show more tolerance of homosexuality.

Social policy is now beginning to treat all couples more equally, whether homosexual or heterosexual, cohabiting or married. For example, since 2002, cohabiting couples have had the same right to adopt as married couples. From 2004, the proposed civil partnership scheme gave same-sex couples similar legal rights to married couples in respect of pensions, inheritance, tenancies and property.

Jeffrey Weeks (1999) argues that increased social acceptance may explain a trend in recent years towards same-sex cohabitation and stable relationships resembling those found among heterosexuals. Weeks sees gays as creating families based on the idea of 'friendship as kinship', where friendships become a type of kinship network. He describes these as 'chosen families' and argues that they offer the same security and stability as heterosexual families.

Similarly, Kath Weston (1992) describes same-sex cohabitation as 'quasi-marriage' and notes that many gay couples are now deciding to cohabit as stable partners. She contrasts this with the gay lifestyle of the 1970s, which largely rejected monogamy and family life in favour of casual relationships.

One-person households

Fewer people today are living in couples:

- There has been a big rise in the number of people living alone. In 2000, almost three in ten households (7 million people) contained only one person – nearly three times the figure for 1961.
- Just over half of all one-person households are people of pensionable age. Pensioner one-person households doubled between 1961 and 2000; those of non-pensioners tripled. Men under 65 were the group most likely to live alone.

Reasons for the changes

The increase in separation and divorce has created more one-person households, especially among men under 65. This is because, following divorce, any children are more likely to live with their mother; their father is more likely to leave the family home.

The decline in the numbers marrying, and the trend towards people marrying later, mean that more people are remaining single. The proportion of adults who are single has risen by about half since 1971. Many of these are living alone. Peter Stein (1976) argues that a growing number of people are choosing 'creative singlehood'.

However, while many of these choose to remain single and live alone, some are alone because there are too few partners available in their age group. These are mainly older widows.

Parents and children

Childbearing

- About four in every ten children are now born outside marriage: nearly five times more than in 1971. However, most of these births are jointly registered by both parents. In most cases, the parents are cohabiting.
- Women are having children later: the average age at the birth of their first child rose from 26.2 years in 1971 to 29.3 in 2002.
- Women are having fewer children. In 1961 the average was 2.77 children. By 2001, this had fallen to 1.64.
- More women are remaining childless: it is predicted that nearly a quarter of those born in 1974 will be childless when they reach the age of 45.

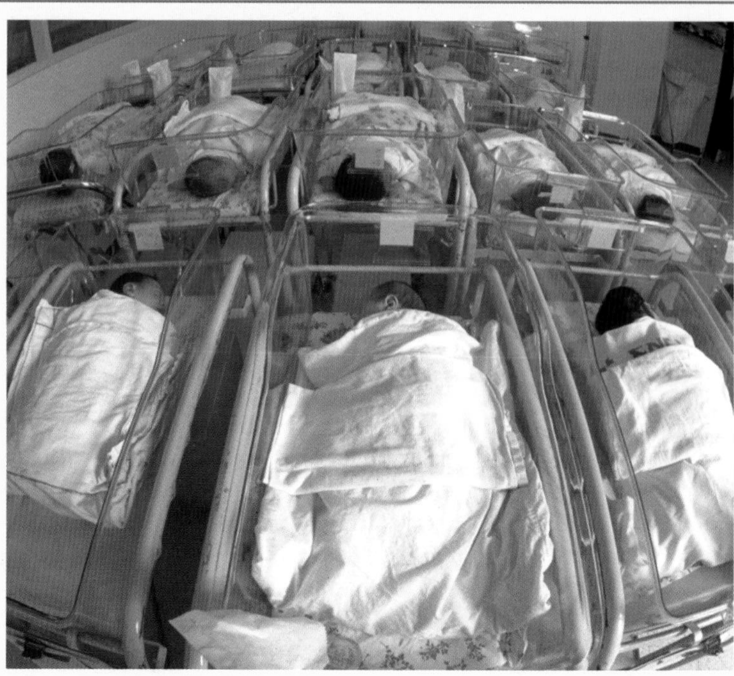

Birth rates have fallen by 40% since 1961.

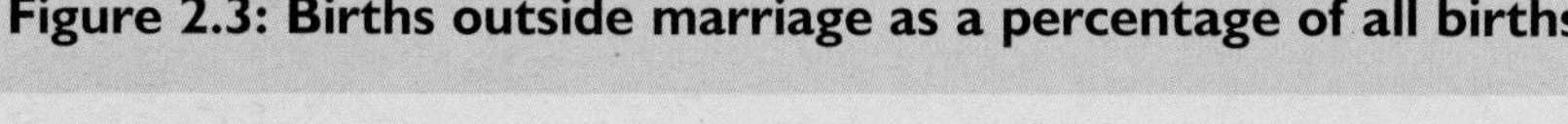

Figure 2.3: Births outside marriage as a percentage of all births

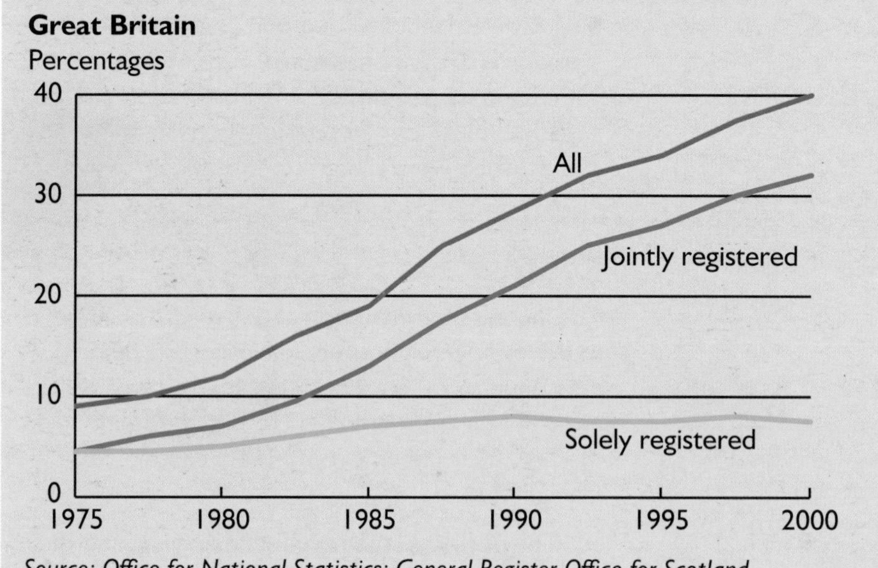

Source: Office for National Statistics; General Register Office for Scotland

questions

1. By how many percentage points did the births that were solely registered by the mother alone increase between 1975 and 2000?
2. By how many percentage points did the births that were jointly registered by both parents increase during this period?

Reasons for the changes

- Reasons for the increase in births outside marriage include a decline in stigma and increase in cohabitation. For example, only one-third of 18–24 year olds now think marriage should come before parenthood. The rise is largely the result of an increase in births to cohabiting couples rather than to women living alone.
- The later age at which women are having children, smaller family sizes and the fact that more women are remaining childless, all reflect the fact that women now have more options than just motherhood. Many are seeking to establish themselves in a career before starting a family, or instead of having children at all.

Lone-parent families

- Lone-parent families now make up 22% of all families. One child in five lives in a lone-parent family.
- Over 90% of these families are headed by lone mothers.
- Until the early 1990s, divorced women were the biggest group of lone mothers. From the early 1990s, single (never married) women became the biggest group of lone mothers.

synoptic link: stratification

Lone parenthood is a major source of inequality. A child living with a lone parent is more than twice as likely to be in poverty as a child living with two parents.

Reasons for the patterns

The *number* of lone-parent families has increased due to the increase in divorce and separation and more recently, the increase in the number of never-married women having children. This is linked to the decline in stigma attached to births outside marriage. In the past, the death of one parent was a common cause of lone-parent families, but this is no longer very significant.

Lone-parent families tend to be *female-headed* for several reasons. These include the widespread belief that women are by nature suited to an 'expressive' or nurturing role; the fact that divorce courts usually give custody of children to mothers and the fact that men may be less willing than women to give up work to care for children.

Many lone-parent families are female-headed because the mothers are single by choice. They may not wish to cohabit or marry, or they may wish to limit the father's involvement with the child. Jean Renvoize (1985) found that professional women were able to support their child without the father's involvement.

Equally, as Ellis Cashmore (1985) found, some working-class mothers with less earning power chose to live on welfare benefits without a partner, often because they had experienced abuse. Feminist ideas, and greater opportunities for women, may also have encouraged an increase in the number of never-married lone mothers.

Lone parenthood, the welfare state and poverty

The New Right thinker Charles Murray (1984) sees the growth of lone-parent families as resulting from an over-generous welfare state providing benefits for unmarried mothers and their children.

Murray argues that this has created a 'perverse incentive'; that is, it rewards irresponsible behaviour, such as having children without being able to provide for them. The welfare state creates a 'dependency culture' in which people assume that the state will support them and their children.

For Murray, the solution is to abolish welfare benefits. This would reduce the dependency culture

Many lone mothers are single by choice.

that encourages births outside marriage.

However, critics of New Right views argue that welfare benefits are far from generous and lone-parent families are much more likely to be in poverty. Reasons for this include:

- Lack of affordable childcare prevents lone parents from working: three-fifths of them are unemployed.
- Inadequate welfare benefits.
- Most lone parents are women, who generally earn less than men.
- Failure of fathers to pay maintenance, especially if they have formed another family that they have to support.

questions

1. Suggest two reasons for the increased number of lone-parent families today.
2. Suggest two reasons why so few lone-parent families are headed by fathers.
3. Why is it easier for women today to choose to have a child without marrying?

Stepfamilies

- Stepfamilies (often called reconstituted families) account for about 8% of all families with dependent children.
- In 84% of stepfamilies, at least one child is from the woman's previous relationship, while in 12% there is at least one child from the man's previous relationship. In 4% of stepfamilies there are children from both partners' previous relationships.
- Elsa Ferri and Kate Smith (1998) found that stepfamilies are very similar to first families in all major respects, and that the involvement of stepparents in childcare and childrearing is a positive one. However, they found that in general stepfamilies are at greater risk of poverty.

Reasons for the patterns

- Stepfamilies are formed when lone parents form new partnerships. Thus the factors causing an increase in the number of lone parents, such as divorce and separation, are also responsible for the creation of stepfamilies.
- More children in stepfamilies are from the woman's previous relationship than the man's because, when marriages and cohabitations break up, children are more likely to remain with their mother.
- Stepparents are at greater risk of poverty because there are often more children and because the stepfather may also have to support children from a previous relationship.

Ethnic differences in family patterns

Immigration into Britain over the last 50 years has helped to create greater ethnic diversity. In 2001, Britain had a total ethnic minority population of approximately 3.6 million. Of these, 1.8 million people were of Indian, Pakistani or Bangladeshi origin, there were 1 million black people and a further 0.8 million people belonging to other ethnic minorities. Greater ethnic diversity has contributed to changing family patterns.

Black families

Black people have a higher proportion of lone-parent households. In 2002, just over half of families with dependent children headed by a black person were lone-parent families (see Table 2C). This compared with one in 11 Indian families and just under a quarter for the population as a whole.

The high rate of female-headed, lone-parent black families has sometimes been seen as evidence of family disorganisation that can be traced back to slavery or, more recently, to high rates of unemployment among black males.

Under slavery, when couples were sold separately, children stayed with the woman. It is argued that this established a pattern of family life that persists today. It is also argued that male unemployment and poverty have meant that black men are less able to provide for their family, resulting in higher rates of desertion.

However, Heidi Safia Mirza (1997) argues that the higher rate of lone-parent families among blacks is not the result of disorganisation, but rather reflects the high value that black women place on independence. Tracey Reynolds (1997) argues that the statistics are misleading, in that many apparently 'lone' parents are in fact in stable, supportive but non-cohabiting relationships.

Asian families

Indian and Pakistani/Bangladeshi households tend to be larger than those of other ethnic groups, at 3.5 and 4.6 persons per household respectively, compared with 2.4 for the population as a whole. Such households sometimes contain three generations, with grandparents living with a married couple and their children, but most are in fact nuclear rather than extended.

Larger Asian household sizes to some extent reflect the value placed on the extended family in Asian cultures. However, practical considerations, such as the need for support and assistance when migrating to Britain, are also important, as Ballard argues (see page 38).

Larger household sizes are also partly a result of the younger age profile of British Asians, since a higher proportion are in the childbearing age groups compared to the population as a whole.

Table 2C: Families with dependent children: by ethnic group, 2002

United Kingdom		Percentages
	Couples	**Lone parents**
White	77	23
Mixed	39	61
Asian or Asian British		
Indian	91	9
Pakistani	85	15
Bangladeshi	89	11
Other Asian	90	10
All Asian groups	89	11
Black or Black British		
Black Caribbean	46	54
Black African	54	46
All Black groups	49	51
Chinese	79	21
Other ethnic group	80	20
All families	77	23

Source: Office for National Statistics

activity

Test your knowledge of the changes in family patterns. When you have finished, check the text to see how many you got right.

1 What proportion of children lives in a lone-parent family?
(a) 1 in 3
(b) 1 in 5
(c) 1 in 10

2 What proportion of households contains one person living alone?
(a) 1 in 10
(b) 2 in 10
(c) 3 in 10

3 What proportion of unmarried adults under 60 is cohabiting?
(a) a tenth
(b) a quarter
(c) a half

4 In 2002, the average age of women at the birth of their first child was:
(a) 24 (b) 26 (c) 29

5 What percentage of families with dependent children are stepfamilies?
(a) 8 (b) 12 (c) 16

6 Out of every 10 petitions for divorce, how many are filed by women?
(a) 5 (b) 6 (c) 7

7 Out of every 5 marriages, how many are religious ceremonies?
(a) 2 (b) 3 (c) 4

8 What percentage of adults have same-sex relationships?
(a) 5 (b) 10 (c) 15

9 Out of every 10 marriages, how many are likely to end in divorce?
(a) 2 (b) 4 (c) 6

Understanding family diversity

The changing family patterns we have examined are bringing about increased family diversity in Britain today. For example, there are now fewer households containing a nuclear family and more lone-parent families and one-person households than 30 years ago. More couples, both straight and gay, now cohabit, many more children are born outside marriage, and many more marriages end in divorce.

Challenging patriarchy: a women's liberation march, 1971. Are women now liberated?

We now turn our attention to the ways in which sociologists have classified the different types of family diversity and how they have tried to understand the meaning and significance of increased diversity today. For example, does it mean the decline of the family, or a new era of choice and personal fulfilment?

The New Right

The New Right have a conservative and anti-feminist perspective on the family. They are firmly opposed to family diversity.

They hold the view that there is only one correct or normal family type. This is the traditional or conventional patriarchal nuclear family consisting of a married couple and their dependent children, with a clear-cut division of labour between the breadwinner-husband and homemaker-wife.

The New Right see this family as 'natural' and based on fundamental biological differences between men and women. In their view, this family is the cornerstone of society; a place of refuge, contentment and harmony.

question

What similarity is there between the New Right view of the roles of husbands and wives and that of the functionalist Talcott Parsons?

The New Right argue that the decline of the traditional nuclear family and the growth of family diversity are the cause of many social problems, such as higher crime rates and educational failure. They oppose most of the changes in family patterns that we examined earlier:

- They see lone-parent families as both unnatural and harmful, especially to children. They argue that lone mothers cannot discipline their children properly, they are a burden on the welfare state and they leave boys without an adult male role model, resulting in higher rates of delinquency.
- They see marriage as the essential basis for creating a stable environment in which to bring up children. They regard both cohabitation and divorce as undermining family stability and making it easier for adults to avoid commitment and responsibility.

- They disapprove of women going out to work because they believe women should make caring for their family their first priority. As the Conservative politician, Patrick Jenkin, said:

  'Quite frankly, I don't think that mothers have the same right to go out to work as fathers do. If the good Lord had intended us to have equal rights to go out to work, he would not have created men and women. These are biological facts.'

The New Right oppose many of the recent trends in family life on economic and political grounds. As conservatives, they are strongly opposed to high levels of taxation and government spending. They argue that the increase in numbers of lone-parent families has led to more spending on welfare benefits. As this has to be paid for out of public funds, it places a bigger tax burden on the working population.

High levels of benefits and taxation act as perverse incentives; that is, they punish responsible behaviour and reward irresponsible behaviour. They undermine the traditional family by discouraging men from working to support their families, and they encourage a dependency culture of living off welfare benefits. The New Right therefore favour cutting or abolishing welfare benefits to reduce the dependency culture and encourage the conventional family.

synoptic link: deviance

The New Right see lone-parent families as deviant and as threatening social stability by discouraging hard work and encouraging criminality.

However, the New Right view has been criticised:

- Oakley (1997) argues that the New Right wrongly assume that husbands' and wives' roles are fixed by biology. In fact, cross-cultural studies show great variation in the roles men and women perform within the family. Oakley believes that the New Right view of the family is a negative reaction against the feminist campaign for women's equality.
- Critics argue that there is no evidence that children from lone-parent families are more likely to be delinquent than those brought up in a two-parent family of the same social class.

synoptic link: stratification

Feminists argue that the traditional patriarchal nuclear family favoured by the New Right is based on the oppression of women and is a fundamental cause of gender inequality.

For example, it prevents women from working and so keeps them financially dependent, and denies them an equal say in decision-making.

Chester: the neo-conventional family

Robert Chester (1985) recognises that there has been some increased family diversity in recent years. However, unlike the New Right, he does not regard this as very significant. Chester argues that the only important change is a move from the dominance of the traditional or conventional nuclear family, to what he describes as the neo-conventional family.

By the conventional family, Chester means the type of nuclear family described by the New Right and Parsons (see page 19), with its division of labour between a male breadwinner and a female homemaker.

By contrast, Chester defines the neo-conventional family as a dual-earner family in which both spouses go out to work. This is similar to the symmetrical family described by Young and Willmott (see page 20).

Apart from this, Chester does not see any other evidence of major change. He argues that most people are not choosing to live in alternatives to the nuclear family (such as lone-parent families) on a long-term basis and the nuclear family remains the ideal to which most people aspire.

Although many people are not part of a nuclear family at any one time, Chester argues that this is largely due to the life-cycle. Many of the people who are currently living in a one-person household, such as elderly widows, divorced men or young people who have not yet married, were either part of a nuclear family in the past or will be in the future.

Statistics on household composition are thus a misleading snapshot of where everyone is living at a single moment in time; they don't show us the fact that most people will spend a major part of their lives in a nuclear family.

As evidence of his view that little has changed, Chester identifies a number of patterns:

- Most people live in a household headed by a married couple.
- Most adults still marry and have children. Most children are reared by their two natural parents.
- Most marriages continue until death. Divorce has increased, but most divorcees remarry.
- Cohabitation has increased, but for most couples it is a temporary phase before marrying. Most couples get married if they have children.
- Although births outside marriage have increased, most are jointly registered, indicating that the parents are committed to bringing up children as a couple.

In Chester's view, then, the extent and importance of family diversity has been exaggerated. The only important change has been from a conventional to a neo-conventional nuclear family.

The Rapoports: five types of family diversity

Unlike Chester, Rhona and Robert Rapoport (1982) argue that diversity is of central importance in understanding family life today. They believe that we have moved away from the traditional nuclear family as the dominant family type, to a range of different types. Families in Britain have adapted to a pluralistic society; that is, one in which cultures and lifestyles are more diverse.

In their view, family diversity represents greater freedom of choice and the widespread acceptance of different cultures and ways of life. Unlike the New Right, the Rapoports see diversity as a response to people's different needs and wishes and not as a deviation from the assumed norm of the nuclear family.

They identify five different types of family diversity in Britain today:

activity

1. Either as a whole class or in groups of four, devise a set of questions that you will use to ask a sample of people of different generations about their attitudes to family and personal relationships. You will need to include questions about divorce, cohabitation, homosexuality, births outside marriage, lone-parent families and abortion.
2. Each of you should interview at least two people. Try to ensure that as a group you have a good spread of ages (e.g. from under 20s to over 60s).
3. When you have completed the interviews, get back together to collate and discuss your results. How far did attitudes vary according to age? How would you account for any differences?

Shopping for one: the number of pensioners living alone has doubled since the 1960s.

- **Organisational diversity:** this refers to differences in the ways family roles are organised. For example, some couples have joint conjugal roles and two wage-earners, while others have segregated conjugal roles and one wage-earner.
- **Cultural diversity:** different cultural, religious and ethnic groups have different family structures. For example, there is a higher proportion of female-headed families among Afro-Caribbeans.
- **Social class diversity:** differences in family structure are partly the result of income differences between households of different classes. Likewise, there are class differences in child-rearing practices.
- **Life-stage diversity:** family structures differ according to the stage reached in the life-cycle – for example, newlyweds, couples with children, retired couples whose children have left home, and widows and widowers who are living alone.
- **Generational diversity:** older and younger generations have different attitudes and experiences that reflect the historical periods in which they have lived. For example, they may have different views about the morality of cohabitation and divorce (see page 58).

questions

1 Suggest two reasons why there might be differences in child-rearing practices between middle-class and working-class families.

2 Suggest two ways in which cultural or religious factors may affect family structures or relationships.

Postmodernism and family diversity

While the Rapoports have identified a range of types of family diversity, postmodernists such as David Cheal (1993) go much further. They argue that we are now living in a new, chaotic postmodern stage of society in which family structures are fragmented and individuals have much more choice in their lifestyles and personal relationships (see Box 8).

As a result, family life has become more diverse. In today's postmodern society there is no longer one single type of family that is dominant (such as the nuclear family) – only families *plural*.

Some writers argue that this greater diversity and choice brings with it both advantages and disadvantages:

- It gives individuals greater freedom to choose the kind of family and personal relationships that meet their needs.
- But greater freedom of choice in relationships means greater risk of instability, since they are more likely to break up.

While not accepting everything postmodernism says about the nature of society today, a number of sociologists have been influenced by postmodernist ideas about family life. We shall now examine their views on family diversity.

Giddens: choice and equality

Anthony Giddens (1992) argues that in recent decades the family and marriage have been transformed by greater choice and a more equal relationship between men and women. This transformation has occurred because:

- contraception has allowed sex and intimacy rather than reproduction to become the main reason for the relationship's existence.
- women have gained independence as a result of feminism and because of greater opportunities in education and work.

As a result, the basis of marriage and the family has changed into one in which the couple are free to define their relationship themselves, rather than simply acting out roles that have been defined by law or tradition. For example, a couple nowadays can choose to cohabit rather than marry.

The couple's relationship now exists solely to meet each partner's needs and is likely to continue only so long as it succeeds in doing so. Couples stay together because of love, happiness or sexual attraction, rather than because of tradition, a sense of duty or for the sake of the children.

Giddens notes that with more choice, personal relationships inevitably become less stable. Relationships can be ended more or less at will by either partner.

Beck: 'risk society' and the negotiated family

Ulrich Beck (1992) puts forward a similar view. He argues that we now live in a 'risk society' where people have more choice and tradition has less influence. As a result, we are more aware of risks. This is because making choices involves calculating the risks and rewards of the different courses of action available.

Today's risk society contrasts with an earlier time when roles were more fixed and people had much less choice in how they lived their lives. For example, people were expected to marry. Once they were married, men were expected to play the role of breadwinner and disciplinarian and to make the important financial decisions, while women took responsibility for the housework and childcare.

Although this traditional patriarchal family was unequal and oppressive, it did provide a stable and predictable basis for family life by defining each member's role and responsibilities. However, the patriarchal family has been undermined by two trends:

- Greater gender equality, which has challenged male domination in all spheres of life. Women now expect equality both at work and in marriage.
- Greater individualism, where people's actions are influenced more by calculations of their own self-interest than by a sense of obligation to others.

These trends have led to a new type of family replacing the patriarchal family. Ulrich Beck and Elisabeth Beck-Gernsheim (1995) call this the 'negotiated family'. Negotiated families do not conform to the traditional family norm, but vary according to the wishes and expectations of their members, who decide what is best for themselves by negotiation. They enter the relationship on an equal basis.

However, although the negotiated family is more equal than the patriarchal family, it is less stable. This is because individuals are free to leave if their needs are not met.

Thus although in today's uncertain risk society, people turn to the family as a haven of security, the irony is that family relationships are themselves now subject to greater risk than ever.

question

Suggest three reasons why there is now greater gender equality in the family and society.

Box 8: Modernism and postmodernism

Sociological perspectives such as functionalism have been described as 'modernist'. That is, they see modern society as having a fairly fixed, clear-cut and predictable structure. They see one 'best' family type, the nuclear family, as slotting into this structure and helping to maintain it. As Parsons puts it, there is a 'functional fit' between the nuclear family and modern society. This means that we can generalise about the type of family that we will find in modern society.

However, postmodernists argue that since the late 20th century, society has entered a new 'postmodern' phase. Postmodern society has two key characteristics:

- **Diversity and fragmentation:** Society today is increasingly fragmented, with an ever greater diversity of cultures and lifestyles – more a collection of subcultures than a single culture shared by all. People can 'pick and mix', creating their identities and lifestyles from a wide range of choices. For example, different ethnic and youth subcultures, sexual preferences and social movements such as environmentalism all offer sources of identity.
- **Rapid social change**: New technology and the electronic media have dissolved old barriers of time and space, transformed our patterns of work and leisure and accelerated the pace of change. One effect of this rapid change is to make life less predictable.

Not surprisingly, family life in postmodern society is less stable, but at the same time gives individuals more choice about their personal relationships. As a result, family life is now much more diverse than previously. This means that it is no longer possible to generalise about it in the way that modernist sociologists such as Parsons have done.

Stacey: the divorce-extended family

Judith Stacey (1998) argues that greater choice has benefited women. It has enabled them to free themselves from patriarchal oppression and to shape their family arrangements to meet their needs.

Stacey used life history interviews to construct a series of case studies of postmodern families in Silicon Valley, California. She found that women rather than men have been the main agents of changes in the family. Many of the women she interviewed had rejected the traditional housewife-mother role. They had worked, returned to education as adults, improved their job prospects, divorced and re-married. These women had often created new types of family which better suited their needs.

One of these new family structures Stacey calls the 'divorce-extended family', whose members are connected by divorce rather than marriage. The key members are usually female and may include former in-laws, such as mother- and daughter-in-law, or a man's ex-wife and his new partner.

For example, Stacey describes in one of her case studies how Pam Gamma created a divorce-extended family. Pam married young in the 1950s, then divorced and cohabited for several years before re-marrying. Her second husband had also been married before. By the mid-1980s the children of Pam's first marriage were in their twenties and she had formed a divorce-extended family with Shirley, the woman cohabiting with her first husband. They helped each other financially and domestically, for example by exchanging lodgers in response to the changing needs of their households.

Such cases illustrate the idea that postmodern families are diverse and that their shape depends on the active choices people make about how to live their lives; for example, whether to get divorced, cohabit, come out as gay etc.

Thus, as David Morgan (1996) argues, it is pointless trying to make large-scale generalisations about '*the* family' as if it were a single thing, as functionalists do. Instead, sociologists ought to concentrate on studying how people create their own diverse family lives and practices.

Weeks: the growing acceptance of diversity

Jeffrey Weeks (2000) identifies a long-term shift in attitudes since the 1950s. Over this period, sexual morality has become largely a matter of personal choice. At the same time, the church and state have lost much of their power to influence individual morality.

There is growing acceptance of sexual and family diversity, especially by the under-35s. Attitudes have become more favourable towards issues such as cohabitation and homosexuality.

However, Weeks observes that despite these changing attitudes, family patterns continue to be fairly traditional. Most people still live in a family; most children are brought up by couples; most couples marry and many divorcees re-marry.

Nevertheless, Weeks argues that sexual and family diversity are now an undeniable and widely accepted fact. Although the New Right continue to oppose diversity, Weeks sees them as fighting a losing battle.

synoptic link: deviance

Attitudes to homosexuality are a good example of the relativity of deviance. That is, what counts as deviant is relative to time and culture. What is seen as deviant at one time or in one culture may be seen as acceptable, normal or even desirable in another.

activity

Fill in the gaps in the table below.

Against diversity	In favour of diversity
	Different family types are equally valid.
	Postmodernism and feminism
Gender roles in the family are fixed, based on biological differences between men and women.	
	Diversity is good because it gives people more freedom of choice of lifestyle.

Two views of family diversity

From the different contributions made by sociologists to our understanding of family diversity, we can identify two broad views – one against diversity and the other in favour of it.

Against diversity

The first view opposes greater family diversity. It is held by functionalists and the New Right. It is based on the belief that there is only one 'best' or normal type of family. This is the traditional patriarchal nuclear family, consisting of a married couple and their dependent children, with a division of labour between an 'instrumental' male breadwinner role and an 'expressive' female housewife role.

Its supporters see the nuclear family as based on natural biological differences between men and women that suit them to their different roles. As such, they see the nuclear family as best equipped to meet the needs of society and its members. By contrast, other family types are seen as unnatural and dysfunctional. For example, the New Right see lone-parent families as causing juvenile delinquency.

In favour of diversity

The second view is held by postmodernists and feminists. It rejects the New Right's view that only the nuclear family is a 'proper' family. Instead, writers such as Weeks take the view that a family is simply whatever arrangements those involved choose to *call* a family: the family is not 'natural', but rather socially constructed by its members.

A lesbian couple and their son: how far has society moved towards accepting same-sex families?

Postmodernists and feminists are in favour of greater family diversity. Writers like Stacey see diversity as desirable because it brings people the freedom to choose the personal relationships and ways of living that meet their needs. In particular, it enables women to liberate themselves from the oppression of the traditional patriarchal family.

However, while many sociologists recognise the trend to greater diversity and choice they also see the continuing importance of factors such as patriarchy and class inequality in restricting people's choices and shaping family life.

QuickCheck Questions

1. Identify three changes in family patterns where decline in stigma may be partly responsible for the changes.
2. True or false? There are now more re-marriages than first marriages.
3. What is meant by secularisation?
4. Identify two changes in patterns of childbearing in recent years.
5. Give two reasons why Asian households tend to be larger than the national average size.
6. True or false? The New Right favour greater welfare spending to meet the needs of lone-parent families.
7. True or false? In Chester's view, the only important change in the family has been a move from the dominance of the conventional nuclear family, to the neo-conventional family.
8. Complete the list of Rapoport and Rapoport's five types of family diversity: cultural, social class…
9. True or false? Functionalism is a modernist perspective.
10. Name two factors that according to Giddens have led to greater choice and more equal relationships between men and women.
11. Why do Beck and Beck-Gernsheim see the negotiated family as less stable than the patriarchal family?
12. What does Stacey mean by the divorce-extended family?

Answers are on page 271.

Examining Changing patterns and family diversity

Item A Along with the trend towards people getting married later in life, there has been an increase in the proportion of people getting divorced. The number of divorces doubled between 1961 and 1969 in the United Kingdom, and doubled again by 1971. Although there was a drop in the number of divorces in 1973, the number increased again in 1974 and peaked in 1993 at 180,000. By 1999 the annual number of divorces had declined to 159,000. Average divorce rates across the European Union have more than trebled since 1961. One effect of higher divorce rates is to contribute to greater family diversity, including a trend towards 'serial monogamy'.

Source: adapted from Social Trends, *volume 32 (2002)*

Item B New Right thinking can be described as the modern equivalent of functionalism as it sees the nuclear family both as 'normal' and the ideal towards which we should all be striving. The New Right deplore the breakdown they feel has occurred in family life, the growing diversity of family forms and the steady rise in social problems resulting from these changes. The nuclear family should therefore be defended against such threats. Children need to be socialised in a stable environment, women need to make care of their families their first priority, and the spread of cohabitation, divorce and single-parent families should be curbed. Any attempts to deviate from the nuclear family pattern are likely to lead to the collapse of society.

Charles Murray agrees. He argues that an underclass has developed, composed of single mothers, and absent fathers who leave the state to pick up the bill. Their illegitimate children are socialised into a culture of dependency and grow up lacking discipline and morality.

Source: adapted from Liz Steel and Warren Kidd (2001)

Examining Changing patterns and family diversity

Short questions

(a) Explain what is meant by 'serial monogamy' (**Item A**, line 8). (2 marks)

(b) Suggest **two** reasons for 'the trend towards people getting married later in life'(**Item A**, line 1). (4 marks)

(c) Suggest **three** ways in which higher divorce rates may 'contribute to greater family diversity' **apart from** serial monogamy (**Item A**, lines 7-8). (6 marks)

(d) Identify and briefly explain **two** reasons for the increase in the number of divorces (**Item A**). (8 marks)

Mini-essay

Using material from **Item B** and elsewhere, assess the view that family diversity is harmful both to individuals and to society. (20 marks)

This is a type (f) question of the kind found in the exam, carrying 6 AO1 marks (knowledge and understanding) and 14 AO2 marks (identification, interpretation, analysis and evaluation).

The Examiner's advice

For the mini-essay, start by identifying the view as one held by the New Right and functionalism. Explain why they believe diversity to be harmful – both to individuals and to society – and why they see the nuclear family as best. You can illustrate the view by looking at lone-parent families in relation to socialisation of children, the dependency culture, delinquency, higher taxation to pay for benefits etc. You also need to assess the view (e.g. by contrasting New Right with feminist and/or postmodernist views about the patriarchal nuclear family, divorce, lone parenthood, same-sex relationships, cohabitation). Use the Item to get a start on some of these issues. Write a separate conclusion to pull together your main points.

Families and social policy

Social policy refers to the plans and actions of government agencies, such as the health and social services, the benefits system, schools and other public bodies. Policies are usually based on laws that provide the framework within which these agencies operate.

Most social policies affect families in some way or other. Some are aimed directly at families, such as laws governing marriage and divorce, abortion and contraception, child protection, adoption and so on. Other policies, although not necessarily aimed directly at families, still have an effect on them. For example:

Chinese government poster urging couples to practise family planning as part of the one-child policy.

- The policy of compulsory education enables parents to go out to work while schools provide a free 'childminding' service.
- The policy of 'care in the community' often means that it is family members rather than hospitals or nursing homes who have to care for the sick or elderly.

Cross-cultural examples

Cross-cultural examples show some of the more extreme ways in which the state's policies can affect family life. For example, according to Adrian Wilson (1985), in China the government's population control policy discourages couples from having more than one child. The policy is supervised by workplace family planning committees; women must seek their permission to try to become pregnant, and there is often both a waiting list and a quota for each factory.

Couples who comply with the policy get extra benefits, such as free child healthcare and higher tax allowances. An only child will also get priority in education and housing later in life. Couples who break their agreement to have only one child must repay the allowances and pay a fine. Women face pressure to undergo sterilisation after their first child.

At the other extreme, the former communist government of Romania in the 1980s introduced a series of policies to try to drive up the birth rate, which had been falling as living standards declined. It restricted contraception and abortion, set up infertility treatment centres, made divorce more difficult, lowered the legal age of marriage to 15, and made unmarried adults and childless couples pay an extra 5% income tax.

In Nazi Germany in the 1930s, the state pursued a twofold policy. On the one hand, it encouraged the healthy and supposedly 'racially pure' to breed a 'master race' (e.g. by restricting abortion and contraception). Official policy sought to keep women out of the workforce and confine them to 'children, kitchen and church', the better to perform their biological role. On the other hand, the state compulsorily sterilised 375,000 disabled people deemed unfit to breed on grounds of 'physical malformation, mental retardation, epilepsy, imbecility,

…s'. Many of these people were … concentration camps.

…vith these extreme examples, some …at in democratic societies such as …ily is a private sphere of life in which …ent does not intervene, except perhaps when t… 'go wrong', for example in cases of child abuse. However, sociologists argue that in fact, even in democratic societies, the state's social policies play a very important role in shaping family life. In this section we shall encounter a range of ways in which this occurs.

question

How might laws on equal pay for men and women affect family roles?

Perspectives on families and social policy

Although sociologists agree that social policy can have an important influence on family life, they hold different views about what kinds of effects it has and whether these are desirable. We shall examine a range of different sociological views or perspectives on the impact of social policy on families.

Functionalism

Functionalists see society as built on harmony and consensus (shared values) and free from major conflicts. They see the state as acting in the interests of society as a whole and its social policies as being for the good of all. Functionalists see policies as helping families to perform their functions more effectively and make life better for their members.

For example, Ronald Fletcher (1966) argues that the introduction of health, education and housing policies in the years since the industrial revolution has gradually led to the development of a welfare state that supports the family in performing its functions more effectively. For example, the existence of the National Health Service means that with the help of doctors, nurses, hospitals and medicines, the family today is better able to take care of its members when they are sick.

The functionalist view has been criticised on two main counts:

- It assumes that all members of the family benefit from social policies, whereas feminists argue that policies often benefit men at the expense of women.
- It assumes that there is a 'march of progress', with social policies steadily making family life better and better, whereas Marxists argue that policies can also turn the clock back and reverse progress previously made, for example by cutting welfare benefits to poor families.

questions

1 Identify two functions that families perform for their members apart from healthcare.

2 Suggest ways in which welfare policies may help families to carry out each of these two functions more effectively.

The New Right

The New Right have had considerable influence on government thinking about social policy and its effects on the family. They see the traditional nuclear family, with its division of labour between a male provider and a female home-maker, as self-reliant and capable of caring for its members. In their view, social policies should therefore avoid doing anything that might undermine this 'natural', self-reliant family.

activity

Much of the New Right perspective arose as a criticism of the welfare state that had been introduced following the 1942 Beveridge Report.

Using the library or the Internet, find out about the Beveridge Report and the setting up of the welfare state.

1 Who was Beveridge?

2 What were the main parts of the welfare state set up at the end of the Second World War and what 'giant evils' were these meant to combat?

3 What is meant by the phrase 'welfare from the cradle to the grave'? What principles underlie this phrase?

The New Right criticise many existing government policies for undermining the family. In particular, they argue that governments often weaken the family's self-reliance by providing generous welfare benefits. These include providing council housing for unmarried teenage mothers and cash payments to support lone-parent families.

Charles Murray (1984) argues that these benefits offer perverse incentives; that is, they reward irresponsible or anti-social behaviour. For example:

- If fathers see that the state will maintain their children, some of them will abandon their responsibilities towards their families.
- Providing council housing for unmarried teenage mothers encourages young girls to become pregnant.
- The growth of lone-parent families encouraged by generous benefits means more boys grow up without a male role model and authority figure. This lack of paternal authority is responsible for a rising crime rate among young males.

Thus for the New Right, social policy can have a major impact on family roles and relationships. It can encourage a dependency culture, where individuals come to depend on the state to support them and their children rather than being self-reliant.

The New Right's solution to these problems is simple. They argue that the policy must be changed, with cuts in welfare spending and tighter restrictions on who is eligible for benefits.

This would have a number of advantages. For example, cutting benefits would mean that taxes could also be reduced, and both these changes would give fathers more incentive to work and provide for their families. Similarly, denying council housing to unmarried teenage mothers would remove at least one incentive to become pregnant when very young.

The New Right also advocate policies to support the traditional nuclear family, such as taxes that favour married rather than cohabiting couples, and the Child Support Agency, whose main role is to make absent fathers financially responsible for their children.

Whereas functionalists take the view that state welfare policies can benefit the family and make it better able to meet its members' needs, the New Right disagree. In their view, the less the state 'interferes' in families, the better family life will be. Greater self-reliance, and not reliance on the state, is what will enable the family to meet its members' needs most effectively (see page 65).

The New Right view has been criticised on several counts:

- Feminists argue that it is an attempt to justify a return to the traditional patriarchal family that subordinated women to men and confined them to a domestic role.
- It wrongly assumes that the patriarchal nuclear family is 'natural' rather than socially constructed.
- Cutting benefits would simply drive many poor families into even greater poverty.

activity

Divide into groups of 3 or 4. Each group is allocated the role of either supporters or critics of New Right ideas.

When you have noted down your arguments, get together with an opposing group to debate the ideas. Each group should put forward their ideas and then the other group be given a chance to criticise them. Try to be polite!

New Labour

Although the New Right's ideas are usually associated with the Conservative Party, many commentators have noted similarities between these ideas and New Labour views on the family and social policy. Both before and after being elected to government in 1997, New Labour politicians have made statements supporting the traditional family. For example, New Labour favours strengthening the institution of marriage and regards a family headed by a married couple as normally the best place in which to bring up children. New Labour has also cut benefits to some lone parents.

On the other hand, New Labour takes a more positive view of the role of social policy than the New Right and believes that certain kinds of state intervention can improve life for families. New Labour has introduced a number of policies that are at odds with a New Right view. For example:

- New Labour changed the law on adoption to give unmarried cohabiting couples, including gay couples, the right to adopt on the same basis as married couples.

- New Labour's welfare, taxation and minimum wage policies have been partly aimed at lifting children out of poverty by re-distributing income to the poor through higher benefits, whereas the New Right disapprove of income re-distribution through increased benefits.

However, in keeping with New Right thinking, many of New Labour's main anti-poverty benefits, such as Working Families Tax Credit, are means-tested (only available to those on a low income) rather than being universal benefits available to everyone, like child benefit, for example.

question

Identify two other means-tested benefits that are only available to families on a low income.

Feminism

Feminists take a conflict view (see Box 9). They see society as patriarchal (male-dominated), benefiting men at women's expense. They argue that all social institutions, including the state and its policies, help to maintain women's subordinate position and the unequal gender division of labour in the family.

In the case of social policy, the way this often works is that policies are based on assumptions about what the 'normal' family is like. In turn, the effect of the policies is often to reinforce that type of family at the expense of other types.

For example, if the state assumes that 'normal' families are based on marriage and offers benefits and tax incentives to married couples that are not available to cohabiting couples, these policies may encourage marriage and discourage cohabitation. In effect, this creates a 'self-fulfilling prophecy', making it more difficult for people to live in other family types than the one that policy-makers *assume* they live in.

Feminists such as Hilary Land (1978) argue that social policies often assume that the ideal family is the patriarchal nuclear family with a male provider and female home-maker, along with their dependent children. This is the family type that Edmund Leach (1967) calls the 'cereal packet norm' because it is the kind of family that often appears in advertisements for breakfast cereals.

This norm of what the family should be like affects the kind of policies governing family life. In turn, these policies reinforce existing patriarchal roles and relationships. For example:

- Tax and benefits policies may assume that husbands are the main wage-earners and that wives are their financial dependants. This can make it impossible for wives to claim social security benefits in their own right, since it is expected that their husbands will provide. This then reinforces women's dependence on their husbands.
- Courts may assume that women should have custody of children in divorce cases because they are seen as the 'natural' carers.

Diana Leonard (1978) argues that even where policies appear to support women, they may still reinforce the patriarchal family and act as a form of social control over women.

For example, although maternity leave policies benefit women, they also reinforce patriarchy in the family. Maternity leave entitlement is much more generous than that for paternity leave and this encourages the assumption that the care of infants is the responsibility of mothers rather than fathers.

Similarly, child benefit is normally paid to the mother and, although this gives her a source of income that does not depend on the father, it also assumes that the child's welfare is primarily her responsibility.

Box 9: Conflict theories

Conflict theories do not share the functionalist view that society is built on harmony and consensus. Conflict theories of the family and social policy have two key features:

- They see society as based on a conflict of interest between social groups with unequal power – for example, rich and poor, or men and women.
- They see the state and its policies as serving the interests of powerful groups in society. State policies shape family life and define what counts as a 'normal' family in ways that benefit the powerful.

Conflict theories of the family and social policy include feminism, Marxism and Jacques Donzelot's surveillance theory.

activity

Find out about maternity and paternity leave provision. How do the two differ? What effects might it have on family life if they were the same?

Examples like these show the importance of social policies in the social construction of family roles and relationships. By making it easier for women to take responsibility for the care of infants or by assuming that men are the main economic providers, social policies help to create and maintain the patriarchal roles and relationships that they assume to be the norm.

The feminist view of social policy has been criticised. Not all policies are directed at maintaining patriarchy. For example, equal pay and sex discrimination laws, benefits for lone parents, refuges for women escaping domestic violence and equal rights to divorce could all be said to challenge the patriarchal family.

Gender regimes

As we have seen, feminists argue that social policy reinforces the patriarchal family. By examining policy from a comparative perspective across different societies, we can see whether this is inevitable, or whether different policies can encourage more equal family relationships.

For example, a country's policies on taxation, childcare, welfare services and equal opportunities will affect whether women can work full-time, or whether they have to forego paid work to care for children or elderly relatives.

Eileen Drew (1995) uses the concept of 'gender regimes' to describe how social policies in different countries can either encourage or discourage gender equality in the family and at work. She identifies two types of gender regime following different types of family policies:

- traditional 'familistic' gender regimes
- more equal 'individualistic' gender regimes.

familistic gender regimes

These base their family policies on the assumption that the husband works to support the family while his wife stays at home and is responsible for domestic work, childrearing and the care of family members.

In Greece, for example, there is little state welfare or publicly funded childcare. Women have to rely heavily on support from their extended kin and there is a traditional division of labour.

question

Which of Young and Willmott's three stages of the development of the family do familistic gender regimes resemble?

individualistic gender regimes

These base their family policies on the belief that husbands and wives should be treated the same. Wives are not assumed to be financially dependent on their husbands. This means that each partner has a separate entitlement to state benefits.

In Sweden, for example, policies treat husbands and wives as equally responsible both for breadwinning and domestic tasks. Equal opportunities policies, state provision of childcare, parental leave and good quality welfare services mean that women are less dependent on their husbands and have more opportunities to work.

How might state provision of childcare affect women's position in the family?

Drew argues that most European Union countries are now moving away from familistic gender regimes and towards individualistic ones. This is likely to bring a move away from the traditional patriarchal family and towards greater gender equality in family roles.

However, policies such as publicly funded childcare do not come cheap, and they involve major conflicts about who should benefit from social policies and who should pay for them. It would therefore be naïve to assume that there is an inevitable 'march of progress' towards gender equality.

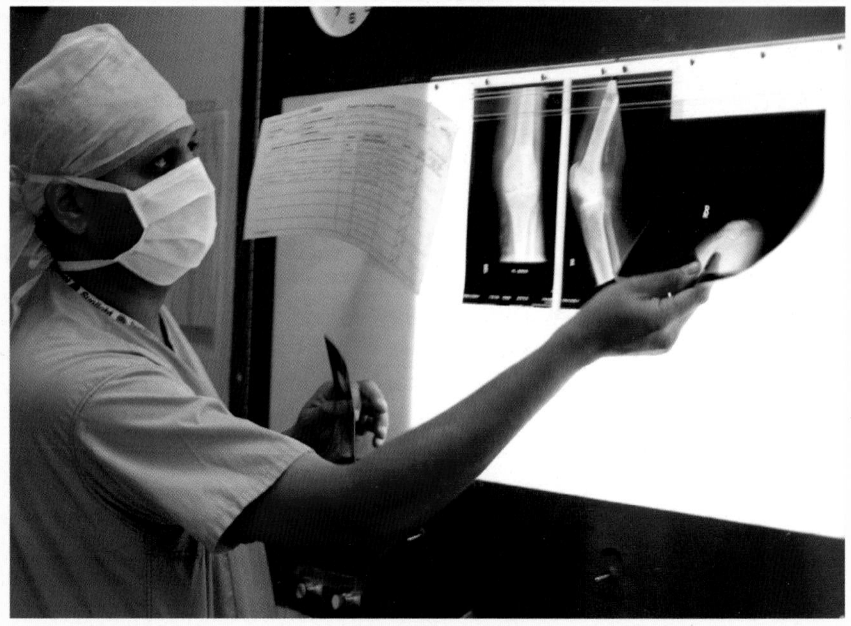

Free healthcare: a concession won through class struggle?

Nevertheless, the differences between European countries show that social policies can play an important role in promoting or preventing gender equality in the family.

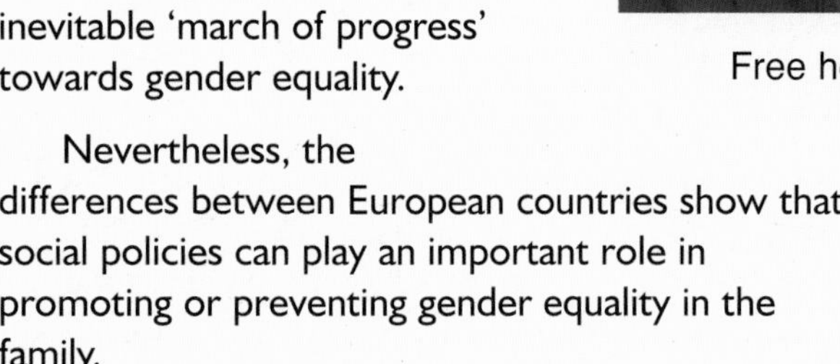

Marxism

Marxists are conflict theorists (see Box 9). They see society as based on class conflict. Capitalist society contains two classes – capitalists and workers. The dominant capitalist class owns the means of production, such as factories, machinery and raw materials, while the working class owns nothing but its labour power.

To survive, therefore, the workers must sell their labour to the capitalists in return for wages. This enables the capitalists to exploit the workers, making profits by paying them less than the value of what they produce. This produces conflict between the classes.

activity

Research any three areas of government policy for their effects on family roles and relationships. For example, you could look at policies on areas such as immigration and asylum, adoption and fostering, taxation, the social security system, child support etc.

1 What assumptions are made about 'normal' family life?
2 Have the policies been changed in any way recently?

In capitalist society, all institutions – such as education, the media and religion – help to maintain class inequality and exploitation. The family too serves the interests of capitalism, for example by reproducing the labour power of the workforce.

Unlike functionalists, Marxists do not see social policies as benefiting all members of society equally. They see the state and its policies as serving capitalism. For example, they see the low level of state pensions as evidence that once workers are too old to produce profits, they are 'maintained' at the lowest possible cost.

Similarly, Marxists do not accept that there is a steady march of progress towards ever better welfare policies producing ever happier families. They argue that improvements for working-class families, such as pensions or free healthcare, have often only been won through class struggle to extract concessions from the capitalist ruling class. Furthermore, these improvements can easily be lost again, as when Mrs Thatcher's government made major cuts to public services in the 1980s.

Marxists also argue that some policies affecting families have come about because of the needs of capitalism. For example, during the Second World War, when large numbers of male workers were conscripted into the armed forces, women were needed as a reserve army of labour to fill the jobs the men had left vacant in the factories. According to Wilson, the government quickly set up 1,450 full-time nurseries for the children of working mothers.

However, at the end of the war, when the men had returned and women were no longer needed in the labour force, the nurseries were closed down. This prevented many women from working, making them financially dependent on their husbands and weakening their bargaining power within the family. This example illustrates how social policies simultaneously serve the needs of capitalism and affect family relationships.

Donzelot: the policing of families

Like Marxists and feminists, Jacques Donzelot (1977) sees policy as a form of state power over families. He uses Michel Foucault's (1976) concept of surveillance. Foucault sees power not just as something held by the government or state, but as diffused (spread) throughout society and found within all relationships. In particular, Foucault sees professionals such as doctors and social workers as exercising power over their clients by using their expert knowledge.

Donzelot applies these ideas to the family. He is interested in how professionals carry out surveillance (observing and monitoring) of families. He argues that social workers, health visitors and doctors use their knowledge to control and change families. Donzelot calls this 'the policing of families'.

Surveillance is not targeted equally on all social classes. Poor families are more likely to be seen as 'problem' families and as the cause of crime and anti-social behaviour. These are the families that professionals target for 'improvement'. For example, parents of badly behaved or truanting children may be encouraged or forced to attend parenting classes to learn the 'correct' way to bring up their children.

Donzelot rejects the march of progress view that social policy and the professionals who carry it out have created a better, freer or more humane society. Instead he agrees with other conflict theorists that social policy is a form of state control of the family.

By focusing on the micro level of how the 'caring professions' act as agents of social control through their surveillance of families, Donzelot shows the importance of professional knowledge as a form of power and control.

However, Marxists and feminists criticise Donzelot for failing to identify clearly who benefits from such policies of surveillance. Marxists argue that social policies generally operate in the interests of the capitalist class, while feminists argue that men are the main beneficiaries.

synoptic link: deviance

Both feminists and Donzelot see policy as enforcing a norm of proper family life – in other words, policy is a form of social control of deviance.

synoptic link: stratification

Conflict theorists such as Marxists and feminists see policies towards the family as maintaining class, gender and other inequalities. Donzelot shows how poor families are more likely to be labelled as 'problem' families.

QuickCheck Questions

1 True or false? Functionalists see social policy as benefiting men at the expense of women.

2 Why do the New Right believe that welfare benefits are a 'perverse incentive'?

3 Identify one social policy that reinforces gender roles.

4 Explain the difference between familistic and individualistic gender regimes.

5 Which of the two gender regimes would feminists favour?

6 True or false? Marxism and functionalism are both consensus views of the family and social policy.

Answers are on page 271.

Examining Families and social policy

Item A In November 1998 Tony Blair's New Labour government published a paper on family life entitled *Supporting Families*, which gave a clear indication of New Labour's position on the role of the family – and of social policy. The paper was aimed at strengthening the family and marriage. 'Family' here means two opposite-sex parents. The family and marriage are seen as vital to moral stability in society, while divorce and single parenthood are viewed as potentially disruptive and damaging both to children and to society as a whole. Jack Straw, then Labour home secretary, commented that, 'it plainly makes sense for the Government to do what it can to strengthen the institution of marriage'. Like most other recent political thinking on family life, the paper mainly advocates the traditional nuclear family and pays only lip service to other forms of family and household. Many of New Labour's ideas are very similar to those of the New Right.

Roger Sapsford (1995) argues that even though families are seen as 'private spaces', they are often held responsible for social problems that occur in the 'public sphere' of wider society. Equally, although both New Labour and the New Right see families as important private spaces where we can be 'free', families are in fact massively controlled, policed and regulated by the state, for example by welfare, medical and educational professionals.

Source: adapted from Liz Steel and Warren Kidd (2001)

Short questions

(a) Explain what is meant by the idea that 'families are seen as "private spaces"' (**Item A,** line 12). (2 marks)

(b) Suggest **two** 'social problems' that the family is often held responsible for (**Item A,** line 13). (4 marks)

(c) Suggest **three** examples of ways in which professionals control, police and regulate families (**Item A,** lines 15-16). (6 marks)

(d) Identify and briefly describe **one** similarity and **one** difference between New Labour and New Right views on family policy (**Item A,** line 11). (8 marks)

Mini-essay

Examine some of the ways in which laws and social policies affect family life. (20 marks)

This is a type (e) question of the kind found in the exam, carrying 14 AO1 marks (knowledge and understanding) and 6 AO2 marks (identification, interpretation, analysis and evaluation).

The Examiner's advice **For the mini-essay, look at a range of laws and policies. These can be directly about family life (e.g. on marriage, divorce, abortion, homosexuality, child support, child protection, benefits etc) and ones about other areas that still affect family life (e.g. compulsory schooling, child labour laws, immigration restrictions). How might policies affect the rights, duties or positions of different family members – e.g. couples, parents, children, other relatives? How do different policies support or undermine different kinds of family (e.g. nuclear, lone parent, gay, extended)? Bring in different perspectives – e.g. New Right, feminism, Donzelot. You could also look at policies from different countries and times (Nazi Germany, China, Romania, gender regimes in Europe today). Write a conclusion.**

Chapter summary

Couples

Sociologists disagree as to whether couples are becoming more equal. Functionalists and the New Right argue for the necessity of **segregated conjugal roles** based on biological differences between the sexes. However, 'march of progress' sociologists argue that the family is becoming more **symmetrical**, with joint conjugal roles. Feminists disagree, arguing that men's contribution remains minimal and women now shoulder a **dual burden** of paid and unpaid work, or even a triple burden that also includes emotion work.

Couples remain unequal in terms of **decision making** and control of resources. Men earn more and are more likely to take the major decisions, even where incomes are pooled. Radical feminists argue that **domestic violence** is an extreme form of patriarchal power over women. However, though most victims are female, not all women are equally at risk.

The family and industrialisation

According to functionalists, there is a **functional fit** between family and society: the extended family fits the needs of pre-industrial society, while the nuclear family, by promoting social and geographical mobility, fits the needs of industrial society. However, critics challenge this with evidence of the existence of the pre-industrial nuclear family and of the extended family in early industrial society, where it was a valuable source of support in harsh conditions. Others argue that the extended family remains important today.

Childhood

Childhood is a **social construction** and varies between times, places and groups. Most sociologists see our idea of childhood as a fairly recent one, the result of industrialisation and other social changes.

'March of progress' sociologists believe we live in an increasingly **child-centred society**. They state that children have never had it so good. Critics argue that this ignores the continued existence of child poverty, abuse and exploitation. Child liberationists argue that children in modern western society are victims of **age patriarchy** and are subject to adult control. Some argue that we are witnessing the **disappearance of childhood** as the media erode the boundary between childhood and adulthood. Others argue that the West is imposing its ideas of childhood on the Third World.

Changing patterns and family diversity

Recent decades have seen some major **changes in family patterns**: fewer first marriages, more divorce, re-marriage, cohabitation, births outside marriage, lone parents, stepfamilies, one-person households and same-sex families. Reasons for these changes include greater individualism and changes in attitudes, the law and the position of women.

Sociologists disagree about **diversity**. The New Right and functionalists see only the conventional nuclear family as normal and other family types as deviant. Postmodernists welcome diversity as giving individuals greater freedom to shape relationships to meet their needs. Feminists see diversity as liberating women from the patriarchal family.

Families and social policy

Social policies may work to undermine or support different kinds of family. The **New Right** argue that over-generous welfare benefits to unmarried mothers encourage a dependency culture. **Feminists** disagree, arguing that government policies legitimate the heterosexual patriarchal nuclear family and make other family types seem less valid.

Countries with individualistic **gender regimes** follow policies promoting women's equality. Familistic regimes perpetuate women's patriarchal dependence. **Marxists** see policies on the family as serving the needs of capitalism. **Donzelot** argues that state professionals exercise control and surveillance, intervening to regulate family life.

Examining Families and Households

Item A Industrialisation has had a major impact on the family, although sociologists do not all agree as to exactly what its effects have been. However, most sociologists accept that the family changed from being a unit of both consumption and production, to being a unit of consumption only.

There is more disagreement about the effects of industrialisation on family structure. Parsons' view is that it brought about a change in structure from extended to nuclear, and left the nuclear family to perform just two essential functions. Others argue that industrialisation encouraged the growth of the extended family, especially among the working class, because it performed many functions for its members and for society.

On the other hand, most sociologists agree that industrialisation, and the many social and legal changes it brought, have had a major effect on children. For example, the introduction of various laws and social policies concerned with children has altered their status and helped to shape our ideas of what childhood should be like.

Item B Marriage, and the roles and relationships within it, continue to be an unequal 'partnership'. The domestic division of labour may not be as clear-cut as it once was, but it is still a highly gendered division in most marriages. Just as the employment structure continues to discriminate against women in the opportunities available for well-paid work, so too the tasks of childcare and housework remain defined predominantly as female ones. Current high levels of divorce also highlight the gap between the ideology and the reality of marriage, as does the prevalence of domestic violence.

Source: adapted from Graham Allan (1996)

Examining Families and Households

(a) Explain what is meant by the idea that the family was a unit of production (**Item A,** line 3). (2 marks)

(b) Name the **two** 'essential functions' that Parsons believes the nuclear family now performs (**Item A,** line 7). (4 marks)

(c) Suggest **three** functions that the **extended** family might perform, **apart from** the 'essential functions' to which Parsons refers (**Item A,** line 7). (6 marks)

(d) Identify **two** laws and/or social policies that have affected the status of children and briefly explain how each one has done so (**Item A,** lines 11-13). (8 marks)

(e) Examine the reasons for changes in the divorce rate in the last 40 years. (20 marks)

(f) Using material from **Item B** and elsewhere, assess the view that roles and relationships among couples are becoming more equal. (20 marks)

The Examiner's advice

For (e), you need to be familiar with the general pattern of changes: very big increases until the 1990s, then a smaller fall and levelling off. Examine a range of reasons: decline in stigma, secularisation, changes in women's position, higher expectations, changes in the law etc. Write at least a paragraph on each, explaining clearly how each factor might affect the rates. Link different perspectives (feminist, New Right, functionalist, postmodernist) to these reasons. Write a conclusion.

For (f), deal with both 'roles' and 'relationships'. 'Roles' refers to conjugal roles – both domestic labour and breadwinning. 'Relationships' involves power and control – who controls resources, makes decisions, uses violence? Use Item B: build on the references to gendered housework and childcare, paid work, domestic violence. Bring in heterosexual and same-sex cohabitation – are these more equal than married couples? Evaluate the view through a debate: e.g. march of progress or functionalists versus feminists on domestic labour; radical feminists and their critics on domestic violence. Consider whether women working makes roles and relationships more equal. Use a range of studies and explanations. Write a conclusion.

Chapter 3

Education

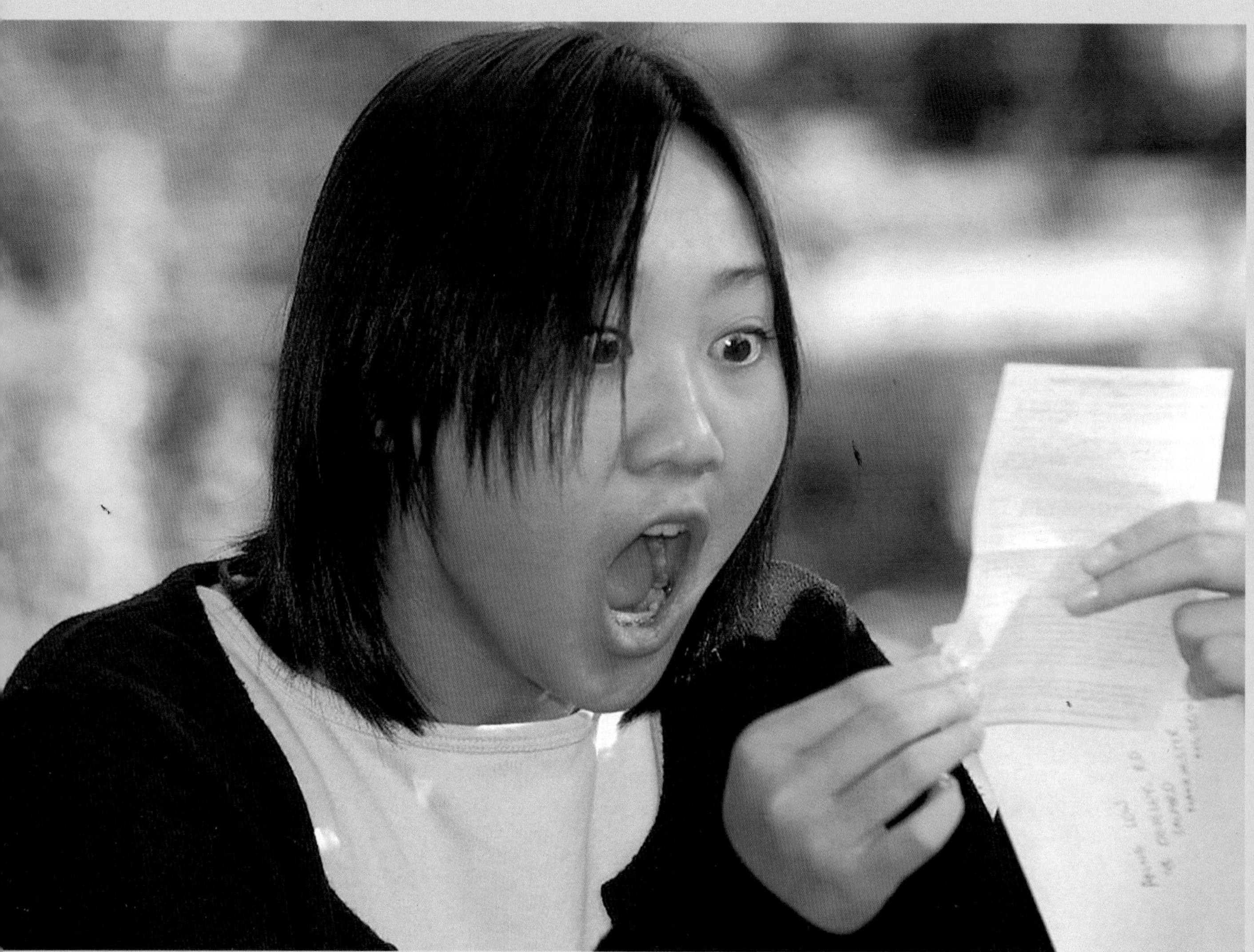

Introduction

In simpler, pre-industrial societies of the past, socialisation was largely informal: most people learnt their culture from relatives, workmates and so on. By contrast, in today's complex society, much of our socialisation is formal, carried out by specialist educational institutions and professional educators, following set curricula.

Education plays a large part in the life of society. We spend huge sums of public money on it. We see it as so important the law makes parents ensure their children receive an education. For these and other reasons, sociologists are interested in education.

Key questions about education

Sociologists are interested in four main questions about education.

Firstly, **why do some pupils achieve more than others?** On average, middle-class pupils do better than working-class pupils and girls do better than boys, and there are differences in the achievements of pupils from different ethnic groups.

To explain these differences, sociologists have studied the impact of processes within schools such as the ways teachers label pupils, as well as factors outside school such as children's home background.

Secondly, sociologists have examined **the role of education in society** and who benefits from it. For example, functionalists claim that education acts as a way of allocating people to jobs on the basis of ability, while Marxists see it as a means of providing capitalism with an obedient workforce.

Thirdly, sociologists are interested in **how pupils experience schooling**. For example, girls and boys often study different subjects, while pupils from minority groups may face racism in school. Such experiences may affect pupils' identity, achievement and self-esteem.

Fourthly, the government makes **laws and policies** that affect education. Sociologists are interested in their impact. For example, do they produce equal opportunity for all pupils? Do they produce the kind of labour force the economy needs?

A brief history of education

Before the industrial revolution in the late 18th and early 19th centuries, education was available only to a minority of the population. It was provided either by private tutors or fee-paying schools for the well-to-do, or by the churches and charities for a few of the poor. Before 1833, the state spent no public money on education.

However, industrialisation increased the need for an educated workforce, and from the late 19th century the state began to become more involved

The AQA Specification

The specification is the syllabus produced by the exam board, telling you what you have to study. The AQA specification for Education requires you to examine the following:

- Different explanations of the role of the education system
- Different explanations of the different educational achievement of social groups, by social class, gender and ethnicity
- Relationships and processes within schools, with particular reference to teacher/pupil relationships, pupil subcultures, the hidden curriculum and the organisation of teaching and learning.
- The significance of state policies for an understanding of the role, impact and experience of education.

Note on the OCR Specification

If you are studying the OCR specification, this chapter will help you if you are doing the Education option at A2. This option module covers very similar issues to the AQA specification above and comprises:

- Education, socialisation and identity
- Patterns and trends in educational achievement
- Power, control and the relationship between education and the economy.

If you are unsure which specification (AQA or OCR) you are studying, check with your teacher.

in education. Miriam David (1993) identifies three phases in the history of state education in Britain.

School class in 1958

phase 1 (1870–1944)

In this period, the type of education children received depended on their class background. Schooling did little to change pupils' ascribed status (the position they were born into). Middle-class pupils were given an academic curriculum to prepare them for careers in the professions or office work.

By contrast, working-class pupils were given a schooling to equip them with the basic numeracy and literacy skills needed for routine factory work and to instil in them an obedient attitude to their superiors. Reflecting the growing importance of education, the state made schooling compulsory from the ages of 5 to 13 in 1880 (rising to 15 by 1947).

phase 2 (1944–88)

In this period, education was shaped by the idea of meritocracy – that individuals should be able to achieve their status in life through their own efforts and abilities, rather than their status being ascribed at birth by their class background.

Thus, the 1944 Education Act brought in *the tripartite system*, in which the 11+ exam (taken at age 11) was used to identify pupils' aptitudes and abilities and to allocate them to the appropriate type of secondary school. Those with academic ability went to grammar schools, while non-academic pupils went to secondary modern schools.

In practice, however, education remained class-divided, with most middle-class pupils going to grammar schools and most working-class children to secondary moderns. The tripartite system also discriminated against girls, often requiring them to gain higher marks than boys in the 11+ to get a grammar school place.

The comprehensive system was introduced from 1965 partly to overcome this class divide. This system abolished selection at age 11, replacing grammars and secondary moderns with comprehensive schools that all pupils would attend. However, these changes had only a limited impact on class inequalities.

phase 3 (since 1988)

The 1988 Education Reform Act created an 'education market' with competition between schools and greater choice of school for parents and pupils. The aim was to cater for the needs of different pupils and to raise standards in schools. For example, specialist schools in technology, languages and sport were set up, while publication of exam league tables and Ofsted inspection reports provided parents with information about the performance of every school.

David describes this phase as a 'parentocracy' (literally, 'rule by parents'). The Conservative government introduced these policies in 1988, but the Labour government, after its election in 1997, followed similar policies, emphasising standards, diversity and choice.

Critics argue that many of these changes have served to increase inequalities between pupils because middle-class parents are better placed to take advantage of the available choices.

Social class differences in educational achievement

One of the most striking features of education in Britain is the difference in achievement between pupils from different social classes. Despite great improvements in the educational level of the nation as a whole since state education began in 1870, social class differences continue. In this section of the chapter we shall look at the evidence of these differences and at how sociologists have explained them.

Boys at Eton: fees are £21,000 per year.

Evidence of class differences

When examining social class differences in achievement, the main comparison sociologists make is between working-class and middle-class pupils. Most sociologists use parental occupation to determine a pupil's social class. Box 10 shows a classification of occupations that has been widely used to present official statistics on education and class.

Box 10: Social classes

Middle class

Class I	Professional e.g. doctor, lawyer
Class II	Intermediate e.g. teacher, sales manager
Class IIIN*	Skilled non-manual e.g. clerk, nurse

Working class

Class IIIM**	Skilled manual e.g. electrician, plumber
Class IV	Semi-skilled manual e.g. lorry driver, waitress
Class V	Unskilled manual e.g. office cleaner, labourer

* N stands for non-manual.
** M stands for manual.

Social class background has a powerful influence on a child's chances of success in the education system. Children from middle-class families on average perform better than working-class children, and the class gap in achievement grows wider as children get older. Children of the middle class do better at GCSE (see Figure 3.1), stay longer in full-time education and take the great majority of university places (see Table 3A on page 94).

activity

Why do you think some parents are willing to pay to send their child to a high-status public school? Make a list of the advantages they might hope to gain from this. Are there any disadvantages?

Figure 3.1: Pupils achieving 5 or more GCSE grades A*–C or equivalent, by parents' social class, 1989 and 2000

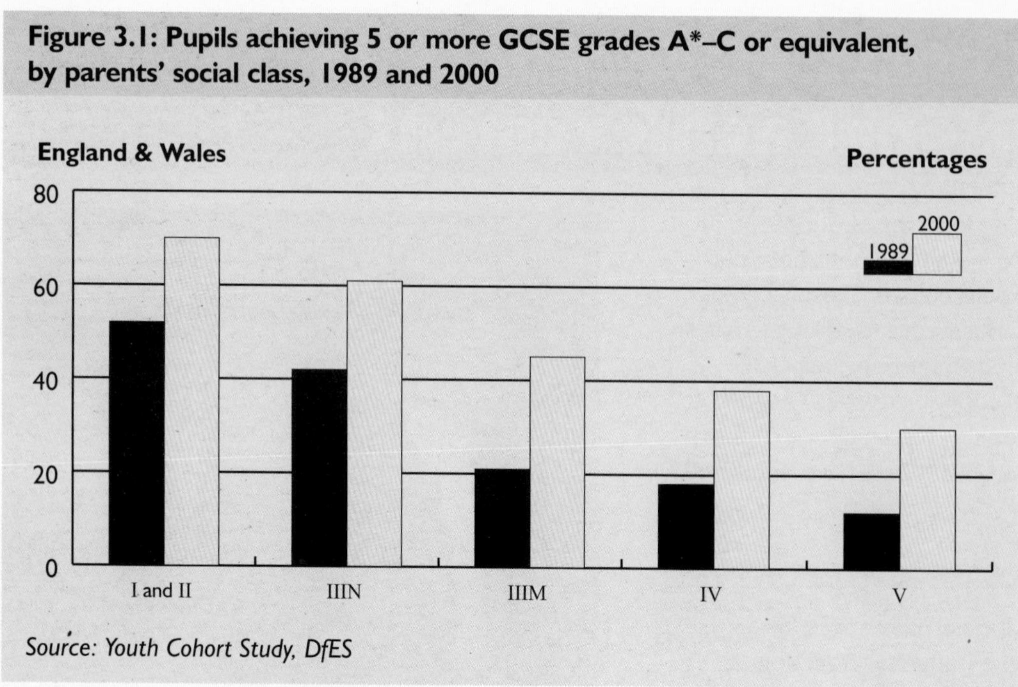

Source: Youth Cohort Study, DfES

Internal and external factors

Sociologists are interested in why these class differences in educational achievement exist and have put forward a number of explanations. We can group these into 'internal' and 'external' explanations or factors – though in reality, of course, these factors are very often linked:

- **External factors** – these are factors outside the education system, such as the influence of home and family background and wider society.
- **Internal factors** – these are factors within schools and the education system, such as interactions between pupils and teachers and inequalities between schools.

We shall focus first on the following external factors that affect pupils' educational achievement:

1. Cultural deprivation
2. Material deprivation
3. Cultural capital

One popular explanation of class differences in achievement is that better-off parents can afford to send their children to private schools, which many believe provide a higher standard of education. For example, average class sizes are less than half those in state schools. Although these schools educate less than 7% of Britain's children, nearly all these pupils (88%) go on to university and they account for nearly half of all students entering the elite universities of Oxford and Cambridge. Andrew Adonis and Stephen Pollard (1998) see private education as a major way in which class privileges are transmitted from generation to generation.

However, the existence of private education does not account for class differences within state education and most sociological research has focused on why middle-class pupils do better than working-class pupils within the state sector itself.

Cultural deprivation

Cultural deprivation theorists argue that most of us begin to acquire the basic values, attitudes and skills that are needed for educational success through primary socialisation in the family. This basic 'cultural equipment' includes things such as language, self-discipline and reasoning skills.

However, according to cultural deprivation theorists, many working-class families fail to socialise their children adequately. These children grow up 'culturally deprived'; that is, they lack the cultural equipment needed to do well at school and so they under-achieve.

There are three main aspects of cultural deprivation:

- intellectual development
- language
- attitudes and values.

Intellectual development

This refers to the development of thinking and reasoning skills, such as the ability to solve problems and use ideas and concepts.

Cultural deprivation theorists argue that many working-class homes lack the books, educational toys and activities that would stimulate a child's intellectual development. Thus children from such homes start school without having developed the intellectual skills needed to progress.

For example, J.W.B. Douglas (1964) found that working-class pupils scored lower on tests of ability than middle-class pupils. He argues that this is because working-class parents are less likely to support their children's intellectual development through reading with them or other educational activities in the home.

In what ways do middle-class parents give their children a head start?

Basil Bernstein and Douglas Young (1967) reached similar conclusions. They found that the way mothers think about and choose toys has an influence on their children's intellectual development. Middle-class mothers are more likely to choose toys that encourage thinking and reasoning skills and prepare children for school.

Language

The importance of language for educational achievement is highlighted by Carl Bereiter and Siegfried Engelmann (1966). They claim that the language used in lower-class homes is deficient. They describe lower-class families as communicating by gestures, single words or disjointed phrases.

As a result, their children fail to develop the necessary language skills. They grow up incapable of abstract thinking and unable to use language to explain, describe, enquire or compare. Because of this, they are unable to take advantage of the opportunities that school offers.

Like Bereiter and Engelmann, Basil Bernstein (1975) also identifies differences between working-class and middle-class language that influence achievement. He distinguishes between two types of speech code:

- **The restricted code** is the speech code typically used by the working class. It has a limited vocabulary and is based on the use of short, often unfinished, grammatically simple sentences. Speech is predictable and may involve only a single word, or even just a gesture instead. It is descriptive not analytic. The restricted code is context-bound: the speaker assumes that the listener shares the same set of experiences.
- **The elaborated code** is typically used by the middle class. It has a wider vocabulary and is based on longer, grammatically more complex sentences. Speech is more varied and communicates abstract ideas. The elaborated code is context-free: the speaker does not assume that the listener shares the same experiences and so uses language to spell out his or her meanings explicitly for the listener. Box 11 gives examples of the two codes.

Box 11: Restricted and elaborated codes: an illustration

The difference between speech codes is illustrated by these descriptions given by two five-year-old children, one working-class, the other middle-class, who were each shown the same set of pictures and asked to tell the story:

'They're playing football and he kicks it and it goes through there it breaks the window and they're looking at it and he comes out and shouts at them because they've broken it so they run away and then she looks out and she tells them off.'

'Three boys are playing football and one boy kicks the ball and it goes through the window the ball breaks the window and the boys are looking at it and a man comes out and shouts at them because they've broken the window so they run away and then the lady looks out of her window and she tells the boys off.'

The first child uses the restricted code, where the speech is context-bound. The second child is using the elaborated code, where the speech is context-free.

Source: adapted from Bernstein (1976)

questions

1 Explain why the first example is context-bound speech and the second is context-free.

2 In what ways might the context-free elaborated code be more useful when writing in an exam or answering questions at an interview for university?

These differences in speech code give middle-class children an advantage at school and put working-class children at a disadvantage. This is because the elaborated code is the language used by teachers, textbooks and exams. Not only is it taken as the 'correct' way to speak and write, but in Bernstein's view it is a more effective tool for analysing and reasoning and for expressing thoughts clearly and effectively – essential skills in education.

Early socialisation into the elaborated code means that middle-class children are already fluent users of the code when they start school. Thus they feel 'at home' in school and are more likely to succeed. By contrast, working-class children, lacking the code in which schooling takes place, are likely to feel excluded and to be less successful.

Critics argue that Bernstein is a cultural deprivation theorist because he describes working-class speech as inadequate. However, unlike most cultural deprivation theorists, Bernstein recognises that the school – and not just the home – influences children's achievement. He argues that working-class pupils fail not because they are culturally deprived, but because schools fail to teach them how to use the elaborated code.

Attitudes and values

Cultural deprivation theorists argue that parents' attitudes and values are a key factor affecting educational achievement. For example, Douglas found that working-class parents placed less value on education, were less ambitious for their children, gave them less encouragement and took less interest in their education. They visited schools less often and were less likely to discuss their children's progress with teachers. As a result, their children had lower levels of achievement motivation.

Similarly, Leon Feinstein (1998) found that working-class parents' lack of interest was the main reason for their children's under-achievement and was even more important than financial hardship or factors within school. Feinstein argues that middle-class children are more successful because their parents provide them with the necessary motivation, discipline and support.

Cultural deprivation theorists argue that lack of parental interest in their children's education reflects the subcultural values of the working class. A subculture is a group whose attitudes and values differ from those of the mainstream culture. According to cultural deprivation theorists, large sections of the working class have different goals, beliefs, attitudes and values from the rest of society and this is why their children fail at school.

Herbert Hyman (1967) takes this view. He argues that the values and beliefs of lower-class subculture are a 'self-imposed barrier' to educational and career success. The lower class believe that they have less opportunity for individual advancement and place little value on achieving high-status jobs, so they see no point in education. They are less willing to make the sacrifices involved in staying on at school and leave early to take manual work. Their subcultural beliefs and values ensure that they neither want, nor know how to get, educational success.

Similarly, Barry Sugarman (1970) argues that working-class subculture has four key features that act as a barrier to educational achievement:

- **Fatalism:** a belief in fate – that 'whatever will be, will be' and there is nothing you can do to change your status. This contrasts with middle-class values, which emphasise that you can change your position through your own efforts.
- **Collectivism:** valuing being part of a group more than succeeding as an individual. This contrasts with the middle-class view that an individual should not be held back by group loyalties.
- **Immediate gratification:** seeking pleasure now rather than making sacrifices in order to get rewards in the future. By contrast, middle-class values emphasise deferred gratification, making sacrifices now for greater rewards later.
- **Present-time orientation:** seeing the present as more important than the future and so not having long-term goals or plans. By contrast, middle-class culture has a future-time orientation that sees planning for the future as important.

Working-class children internalise the beliefs and values of their subculture through the socialisation process and this results in them under-achieving at school.

Why do these differences in values exist? Sugarman argues that they stem from the fact that middle-class jobs are secure *careers* offering more prospects for continuous individual advancement. This encourages ambition, long-term planning and a willingness to invest time and effort in gaining qualifications. By contrast, working-class jobs are less secure and have no career structure through which individuals can advance. There are few promotion opportunities and earnings peak at an early age.

Cultural deprivation theorists argue that parents pass on the values of their class to their children through primary socialisation. Middle-class values equip children for success, whereas working-class values fail to do so.

questions

Explain why:

1 working-class job insecurity may lead to an attitude of fatalism

2 lack of a clear career ladder for manual workers may encourage a present-time orientation

3 an attitude of fatalism and present-time orientation may lead to educational failure.

Compensatory education

Compensatory education is a policy designed to tackle the problem of cultural deprivation by providing extra resources to schools and communities in deprived areas. Compensatory education programmes attempt to intervene early in the socialisation process to compensate children for the deprivation they experience at home.

The best known example of such programmes is Operation Head Start in the United States, a multi-billion dollar scheme of pre-school education in poorer areas introduced in the 1960s. Its aim was 'planned enrichment' of the deprived child's environment to develop learning skills and instil achievement motivation. It included improving parenting skills, setting up nursery classes, home visits by health visitors and educational psychologists and the creation of intensive learning programmes for deprived children.

The well known television programme *Sesame Street* was initially conceived as part of Head Start, providing a means of reaching young children and transmitting – in this case literally – values and attitudes needed for educational success. These included the importance of punctuality, numeracy, literacy and general knowledge.

In Britain, there have been several compensatory education programmes. Educational

Priority Areas were created in the 1960s. More recently, Education Action Zones were introduced in the late 1990s, while Sure Start, a nationwide programme aimed at pre-school children and their parents was launched in 2000. Although it also has non-educational goals such as improving children's health, Sure Start has similarities to earlier compensatory education programmes (see Box 12).

The myth of cultural deprivation?

Although it draws our attention to the role of the child's social background, cultural deprivation theory has been widely criticised as an explanation of class differences in achievement.

Nell Keddie (1973) describes cultural deprivation as a 'myth' and sees it as a victim-blaming explanation. She dismisses the idea that failure at school can be blamed on a culturally deprived home background. She points out that a child cannot be deprived of its own culture and argues that working-class children are culturally different, not culturally deprived. They fail because they are put at a disadvantage by an education system that is dominated by middle-class values.

Keddie argues that rather than seeing working-class culture as deficient, schools should recognise and build on its strengths and should challenge teachers' anti-working class prejudices.

Likewise, Barry Troyna and Jenny Williams (1986) argue that the problem is not the child's language but the school's attitude towards it. Teachers have a 'speech hierarchy': they label middle-class speech highest, followed by working-class and finally black speech.

Other critics reject the view that working-class parents are not interested in their children's education. They attend fewer parents' evenings, not because of a lack of interest, but because they work longer hours or are put off by the school's middle-class atmosphere. They may want to help their child progress but they lack the knowledge and education to do so.

Finally, some critics argue that compensatory education schemes act as a smokescreen concealing the real cause of under-achievement, namely social inequality and poverty. They argue that the real problem is not cultural deprivation, but poverty and material deprivation.

questions

Explain briefly Keddie's arguments that:

1 'a child cannot be deprived of its own culture'

2 cultural deprivation theory 'blames the victims'

3 it is the education system that is at fault.

Box 12: Sure Start

Sure Start is a major element in the British government's policies to tackle poverty and social exclusion. By 2004, there were around 500 local Sure Start programmes. The government has invested over £1 billion in these.

The aim of Sure Start is to work with parents to promote the physical, intellectual and social development of babies and young children, particularly those who are disadvantaged, so that they can flourish at home and when they go to school, and thereby break the cycle of disadvantage.

One objective of Sure Start is to improve children's ability to learn, by encouraging high quality environments that promote early learning, provide stimulating and enjoyable play, improve language skills and ensure early identification and support of children with special needs.

Source: adapted from DfES (2001)

question

What similarities can you see between Sure Start and Operation Head Start?

Material deprivation

Unlike cultural deprivation theorists, who blame educational failure on the inadequacy of working-class subculture, many other sociologists see material deprivation as the main cause of under-achievement. The term 'material deprivation' refers to poverty and a lack of material necessities such as adequate housing and income.

Material factors such as inadequate housing can have a powerful effect on children's achievement.

Poverty is closely linked to educational under-achievement. For example, according to Marilyn Howard (2001), children entitled to free school meals (a widely used measure of child poverty) are less likely than others to obtain five or more GCSE grades A* to C. Truants and those excluded from school are also more likely to be from poorer families. A third of all persistent truants leave school with no qualifications.

There is a close link between poverty and social class. Working-class families are much more likely to have low incomes or inadequate housing. Factors such as these can affect their children's education in several ways.

> **synoptic link: deviance**
>
> There is a strong link between truancy and crime. The Home Office has found that truants were over three times more likely to offend than non-truants. Almost half of school-age offenders have been excluded from school.

Housing

Poor housing can affect pupils' achievement both directly and indirectly. For example, overcrowding can have a direct effect by making it harder for the child to study. Overcrowding means less room for educational activities, nowhere to do homework, disturbed sleep from sharing beds or bedrooms and so on. For young children especially, development can be impaired through lack of space for safe play and exploration. Families living in temporary (bed and breakfast) accommodation may find themselves having to move frequently, resulting in constant changes of school and disrupted education.

Poor housing can also have indirect effects, notably on the child's health and welfare. For example, children in crowded homes run a greater risk of accidents. Cold or damp housing can also cause ill health, especially respiratory illnesses. Families in temporary accommodation suffer more psychological distress, infections and accidents. Such health problems mean more absences from school.

Diet and health

Howard notes that young people from poorer homes have lower intakes of energy, vitamins and minerals. Poor nutrition affects health, for example by weakening the immune system and lowering children's energy levels. This may result in more absences from school due to illness and difficulties concentrating in class.

Children from poorer homes are also more likely to have emotional or behavioural problems.

According to Richard Wilkinson (1996), among ten year olds, the lower the social class, the higher the rate of hyperactivity, anxiety and conduct disorders, all of which are likely to have a negative effect on the child's education.

synoptic link: stratification

Material deprivation is strongly class-related and powerfully affects the life-chances (i.e. opportunities) of working-class children in education, health and future employment.

Financial support and the costs of education

Lack of financial support means that children from poor families have to do without equipment and miss out on experiences that would enhance their educational achievement. David Bull (1980) refers to this as 'the costs of free schooling'. Items such as transport, uniform, books, computers, calculators, and sports, music and art equipment are a heavy burden on poor families. A pupil who has to make do with hand-me-downs and cheaper but unfashionable equipment may also be stigmatised or bullied by peers.

synoptic link: deviance

Stigmatisation – the negative labelling of 'outsiders' – is an important concept in the study of deviance. Stigmatisation leads to exclusion from mainstream life and may push individuals into a 'deviant career'.

Lack of funds also means that children from low-income families often need to work part-time to support their studies. Dan Finn (1984) found 75% of teenagers doing paid work, often over 10 hours per week.

These financial restrictions help to explain why many working-class pupils leave school at 16 and why relatively few go on to university, as Table 3A shows. There is evidence that fear of debt is deterring poor students from applying. Students from poorer families starting university can expect to leave with substantial debts as a result of the introduction of fees for higher education.

Drop-out rates are also higher for universities with a large proportion of poor students: up to 40% at some universities with a large working-class intake, but only 1% at Oxford and Cambridge. The National Audit Office (2002) found that working-class students spent twice as much time in paid work to reduce their debts as middle-class students.

Table 3A: Percentage of young people (under 21) participating in higher education, by social class

Social class	2003
I Professional	79
II Intermediate	50
IIIN Skilled non-manual	33
IIIM Skilled manual	21
IV Semi-skilled manual	18
V Unskilled manual	15
All social classes	35

Source: DfES

question

Roughly how many times greater was the participation rate in higher education for young people from the professional class than for those from the unskilled manual class?

Cultural or material factors?

While material factors clearly play a part in achievement, the fact that some children from poor families do succeed suggests that material deprivation is only part of the explanation.

For example, the cultural, religious or political values of the family may play a part in creating and sustaining the child's motivation, despite poverty. Similarly, the quality of the school may play an important part in enabling some poor children to achieve.

Nevertheless, Peter Mortimore and Geoff Whitty (1997) argue that material inequalities have a greater effect on achievement than school factors. For this reason, Peter Robinson (1997) argues that tackling child poverty would be the most effective way to boost achievement.

Cultural capital

Bourdieu: three types of capital

Pierre Bourdieu (1984) argues that both cultural and material factors contribute to educational achievement and are not separate but interrelated. He uses the concept of 'capital' to explain why the middle class are more successful in education.

The term capital usually refers to wealth but in addition to this economic capital, Bourdieu identifies two further types of capital. These are 'educational capital' or qualifications, and 'cultural capital'. He argues that the middle class generally possess more of all three types of capital.

cultural capital

Bourdieu uses the term cultural capital to refer to the knowledge, attitudes, values, language, tastes and abilities of the middle class. He sees middle-class culture as a type of capital because, like wealth, it gives an advantage to those who possess it. Like Bernstein, he argues that middle-class children acquire through their socialisation the ability to grasp, analyse and express abstract ideas. They are more likely to develop intellectual interests and an understanding of what the education system requires for success.

This gives middle-class children an advantage in school, where such abilities and interests are highly valued and rewarded with qualifications. This is because the education system is not neutral, but favours and transmits the dominant middle-class culture.

By contrast, working-class children find that school devalues and rejects their culture as 'rough' and inferior. Their lack of cultural capital leads to exam failure. Many working-class pupils also 'get the message' that education is not meant for people like them and respond by truanting, early leaving or just not trying.

educational and economic capital

Bourdieu argues that educational, economic and cultural capital can be converted into one another.

For example, middle-class children with cultural capital are better equipped to meet the demands of the school curriculum and gain qualifications. Similarly, wealthier parents can convert their economic capital into educational capital by sending their children to private schools, moving into the catchment area of 'good' state schools or paying for extra tuition.

Gewirtz: marketisation and parental choice

Another example of how cultural and economic capital can lead to differences in educational achievement is via the impact of marketisation and parental choice. Since the creation of an education market by the 1988 Education Reform Act (see Box 13 on page 97), sociologists have been interested in the effect of increased parental choice that the Act introduced. Has greater parental choice of school benefited one social class more than the other?

This question is examined by Sharon Gewirtz (1995) in a study of class differences in parental choice of secondary school. Her study is based on interviews with teachers and parents and secondary data from 14 London schools. She uses Bourdieu's ideas to explain her findings.

Gewirtz found that differences in economic and cultural capital lead to class differences in how far parents can exercise choice of secondary school. She identifies three main types of parents, whom she calls privileged-skilled choosers, disconnected-local choosers and semi-skilled choosers.

privileged-skilled choosers

These were mainly professional middle-class parents who used their economic and cultural capital to gain educational capital for their children. Being prosperous, confident and well educated, they were able to take full advantage of the choices open to them.

Their cultural capital meant that these parents knew how school admissions systems work, 'how to approach schools, present and mount a case, maintain pressure, make an impact and be remembered'. They understood the importance of putting a particular school as first choice, meeting deadlines, and using appeals procedures and waiting lists to get what they wanted. They saw choosing a school as part of the process of planning their child's future and had time to visit schools and the skills to research the options available.

Their economic capital also meant they could afford to move their children around the education system to get the best deal out of it, for example by paying extra travel costs so that their children could attend 'better' schools out of their area.

Cultural capital includes developing a taste for fine art, classical music and other 'high culture'.

disconnected-local choosers

These were working-class parents whose choices were restricted by their lack of economic and cultural capital.

They found it difficult to understand school admissions procedures. They were less confident in their dealings with schools, less aware of the choices open to them and less able to manipulate the system to their own advantage. Many of them attached more importance to safety and the quality of school facilities than to league tables or long-term ambitions.

Distance and cost of travel were major limitations on their choice of school. Their funds were limited and a place at a local comprehensive was often the only realistic option for their children.

semi-skilled choosers

These parents were also mainly working-class, but unlike the disconnected-local choosers, they were ambitious for their children. However, they too lacked cultural capital and found it difficult to make sense of the education market, often having to rely on other people's opinions about schools. They were often frustrated at their inability to get their children into the schools they wanted.

Gewirtz concludes that middle-class families with cultural and economic capital are better placed to take advantage of the available opportunities for a good education. Although in theory the education market gives everyone greater choice, in practice those who possess cultural and economic capital have more choice than others.

As Geoff Whitty (1998) notes, the marketisation of education since 1988 has not led to more opportunities for working-class children. Instead, it has allowed the middle class to use their wealth and knowledge even more effectively than before.

activity

Cultural capital includes aspects such as taste (e.g. in music, art and literature); language and communication skills; experiences; knowledge and manners.

Choose three of these and suggest how each of them might give a middle-class child an advantage in school.

synoptic link: stratification

Bourdieu and Gewirtz both show how economic and social inequalities of wealth and culture translate into educational inequalities and vice versa.

Box 13: Marketisation

The education market

Marketisation is the process where market forces of supply and demand are introduced into areas that were previously run by the state, such as education and the NHS. The New Right argue that state control leads to low standards, inefficiency and lack of choice for parents and pupils.

Marketisation means that schools are run more like businesses that have to attract customers (pupils and parents) by competing with each other in an 'education market'. Schools that provide customers with what they want – such as success in exams – will thrive, and those that don't will 'go out of business'.

Private schools have always operated within a market: they charge fees and compete with each other for customers. Within the state sector, however, the creation of a market began with the 1988 Education Reform Act.

The claimed advantages of marketisation

Supporters claim that marketisation of education brings several benefits to parents and pupils:

- It makes education more responsive to the needs of parents by making them into consumers with choice of the school they send their children to.
- This encourages diversity among schools as they seek to meet the different needs of different parents and communities.
- It improves standards – by opening up schools to competition, the best will survive and the 'failing' schools must improve their performance or close down.
- It ensures greater efficiency – competition forces schools to make better use of their resources.

Policies to introduce the market into education

The 1988 Education Reform Act and the 1993 Parents' Charter introduced these measures to create an education market:

- Open enrolment: allowing successful schools to recruit more pupils.
- Head teachers given more responsibility for school budgets and how their school is run.
- The opportunity to 'opt out' of local education authority control and become grant maintained (GM) schools.
- Business sponsorship of schools – e.g. City Technology Colleges.
- Publication of exam league tables and school inspection reports so parents can see how schools are performing and make informed choices about where to send their child.

Labelling

While external factors may play an important part in creating class differences in achievement, we also need to examine the part played by factors *within* schools and the education system in causing these differences. These internal factors include:

1. Labelling
2. The self-fulfilling prophecy
3. Pupil subcultures
4. Marketisation and selection

To label someone is to attach a meaning or definition to them. For example, teachers may label a pupil as bright or thick, trouble maker or hardworking.

Studies show that teachers often attach such labels regardless of the pupil's actual ability or attitude. Instead, they label pupils on the basis of stereotyped assumptions about their class background, labelling working-class pupils negatively and middle-class positively.

A number of studies of labelling have been carried out by interactionist sociologists. Interactionists study small-scale, face-to-face interactions between individuals. They are interested in how people attach labels to one another, and the effects this has on those who are labelled.

Labelling in secondary schools

Howard Becker (1971) carried out an important interactionist study of labelling. Based on interviews with 60 Chicago high school teachers, he found that they judged pupils according to how closely they fitted an image of the 'ideal pupil'.

Pupils' work, conduct and appearance were key factors influencing teachers' judgements. The teachers saw children from middle-class backgrounds as the closest to the ideal, and lower working-class children as furthest away from it because they saw the latter as badly behaved.

Aaron Cicourel and John Kitsuse's (1963) study of educational counsellors in an American high school shows how such labelling can disadvantage working-class students. Counsellors play an important role in deciding which students will get on to courses that prepare them for higher education.

Cicourel and Kitsuse found inconsistencies in the way the counsellors assessed students' suitability for courses. Although they claimed to judge students according to their ability, in practice they judged them largely on the basis of their social class and/or race. Where students had similar grades, counsellors were more likely to label middle-class students as having college potential and to place them on higher-level courses.

Labelling in primary schools

Labelling occurs from the outset of a child's educational career, as Ray Rist's (1970) study of an American kindergarten shows. He found that the teacher used information about children's home background and appearance to place them in separate groups, seating each group at a different table. Those she decided were fast learners, whom she labelled the 'tigers', tended to be middle-class and of neat and clean appearance. She seated these at the table nearest to her and showed them greatest encouragement.

The other two groups – whom she labelled the 'cardinals' and the 'clowns' – were seated further away. These groups were more likely to be working-class. They were given lower-level books to read and fewer opportunities to demonstrate their abilities. For example, they had to read as a group, not as individuals.

activity

Working in pairs and drawing on your own experiences:

1 List the characteristics you think teachers see as making up the 'ideal pupil'.

2 Teachers gradually build up a picture of the 'type' of child they are dealing with. Make a list of all the facts, influences etc that might determine how a particular child is labelled by a teacher.

British studies show similar patterns. Rachel Sharp and Tony Green (1975) studied Mapledene, a primary school that operated along 'child-centred' lines, where children were allowed to choose activities for themselves and develop at their own pace. The teachers felt that when a child was ready to learn they would seek help, for example with reading.

On the other hand, the teachers believed that children who were not yet ready to learn should be allowed to engage in 'compensatory play' in the

Do teachers label some children as 'ready to learn' and give them more attention?

Wendy House until they too were ready. In practice, however, this meant that middle-class children, who started reading earlier, gained the help they needed, while working-class children were ignored.

Sharp and Green's findings support the interactionist view that children of different class backgrounds are labelled differently. However, their explanation goes beyond the level of small-scale, face-to-face interactions. They argue that the negative labelling of working-class children is also the result of inequalities between the social classes in wider society, not just classroom interactions.

High- and low-status knowledge

These studies show how the labelling of working-class pupils puts them at a disadvantage. Other studies show that labelling can be applied not just to pupils, but also to the knowledge they are taught. As Nell Keddie (1971) found, both pupils and knowledge can be labelled high- or low-status.

The comprehensive school classes she observed were streamed by ability, but all streams followed the same humanities course and covered the same course content. However, Keddie found that although teachers believed they were teaching all pupils in the same way, in practice when they taught the A stream, they gave them abstract, theoretical, high-status knowledge. The 'less able' C stream pupils, on the other hand, were given descriptive, commonsense, low-status knowledge, related more to everyday experience. As lower streams generally contain more working-class pupils (see Box 14 on page 102), this withholding of high-status knowledge from the C stream is likely to increase class differences in achievement.

The self-fulfilling prophecy

A self-fulfilling prophecy is a prediction that comes true simply by virtue of it having been made. Interactionists argue that labelling can affect pupils' achievement as a result of the self-fulfilling prophecy, as the following example illustrates:

Step 1: The teacher labels a pupil (e.g. as being very intelligent) and on the basis of this label, makes predictions about him (e.g. he will make outstanding academic progress).

Step 2: The teacher treats the pupil accordingly, acting as if the prediction is already true (e.g. by giving him more attention and expecting a high standard of work from him).

Step 3: The pupil internalises the teacher's expectation, which becomes part of his self-concept or self-image, so that he now actually becomes the kind of pupil the teacher believed him to be in the first place. He gains confidence, tries harder and is successful. The prediction is fulfilled.

Teachers' expectations

In their study of Oak community school, a California primary school, Robert Rosenthal and Leonora Jacobson (1968) show the self-fulfilling prophecy at work. They told the school that they had a new test specially designed to identify those pupils who would 'spurt' ahead. This was untrue because the test was in fact a standard IQ test. Importantly, however, the teachers believed what they had been told.

The researchers tested all the pupils, but then picked 20% of them purely at random and told the school, again falsely, that the test had identified these children as 'spurters'. On returning to the school a year later, they found that almost half (47%) of those identified as spurters had indeed made significant progress. The effect was greater on younger children.

question

Why do you think the effect was greater on younger children?

Rosenthal and Jacobson suggest that the teachers' beliefs about the pupils had been influenced by the supposed test results. The teachers had then conveyed these beliefs to the pupils through the way they interacted with them – through their body language and the amount of attention and encouragement they gave them.

This demonstrates the self-fulfilling prophecy: simply by accepting the prediction that some children would spurt ahead, the teachers brought it about. The fact that the children were selected at random strongly suggests that if teachers believe a pupil to be of a certain type, they can make him or her into that type. The study's findings illustrate an important interactionist principle: that what people believe to be true will have real effects – even if the belief was not true originally.

The self-fulfilling prophecy can also produce under-achievement. If teachers have low expectations of certain children and communicate these expectations in their interaction, these children may develop a negative self-concept. They may come to see themselves as failures and give up trying, thereby fulfilling the original prophecy.

activity

Rosenthal and Jacobson's study is entitled *Pygmalion in the Classroom* – from George Bernard Shaw's play *Pygmalion* (later made into the film *My Fair Lady*). Find out the plot of the play or film and see why Rosenthal and Jacobson borrowed from it.

Streaming and the self-fulfilling prophecy

Streaming involves separating children into different ability groups or classes called 'streams'. Each ability group is then taught separately from the others for all subjects. Studies show that the self-fulfilling prophecy is particularly likely to occur when children are streamed.

As Becker shows, teachers do not usually see working-class children as ideal pupils. They tend to see them as lacking ability and have low expectations of them. As a result, working-class children are more likely to find themselves put in a lower stream.

Once streamed, it is usually difficult to move up to a higher stream; children are more or less locked into their teachers' low expectations of them. Children in the lower streams 'get the message' that their teachers have written them off as no-hopers.

This creates a self-fulfilling prophecy in which the pupils live up to their teachers' low expectations by under-achieving. For example, Douglas found that children placed in a lower stream at age 8 had suffered a decline in their IQ score by age 11.

By contrast, middle-class pupils tend to benefit from streaming. They are likely to be placed in higher streams, reflecting teachers' view of them as ideal pupils. As a result, they develop a more positive self-concept, gain confidence, work harder and improve their grades. For example, Douglas found that children placed in a higher stream at age 8 had improved their IQ score by age 11.

Pupil subcultures

A pupil subculture is a group of pupils who share similar values and behaviour patterns. Pupil subcultures often emerge as a response to the way pupils have been labelled, and in particular as a reaction to streaming.

A number of studies have shown how pupil subcultures may play a part in creating class differences in achievement. We can use Colin Lacey's (1970) concepts of differentiation and polarisation to explain how pupil subcultures develop:

- **Differentiation** is the process of teachers categorising pupils according to how they perceive their ability, attitude and/or behaviour. Streaming is a form of differentiation, since it categorises pupils into separate classes. Those that the school deems 'able' are given high status by being placed in a high stream, whereas those deemed 'less able' and placed in low streams are given an inferior status.
- **Polarisation**, on the other hand, is the process in which pupils respond to streaming by moving towards one of two opposite 'poles' or extremes.

In his study of Hightown boys' grammar school, Lacey found that streaming polarised boys into a pro-school and an anti-school subculture.

the pro-school subculture

Pupils placed in high streams (who are largely middle-class) tend to remain committed to the values of the school. They gain their status in the approved manner, through academic success. Their values are those of the school: they tend to form a pro-school subculture.

the anti-school subculture

Those placed in low streams (who tend to be working-class) suffer a loss of self-esteem: the school has undermined their self-worth by placing them in a position of inferior status.

This label of failure pushes them to search for alternative ways of gaining status. Usually this involves inverting (turning upside down) the values that the school holds dear, such as hard work, obedience and punctuality. As Lacey says, 'a boy who does badly academically is predisposed to criticise, reject or even sabotage the system where he can, since it places him in an inferior position'.

Such pupils form an anti-school subculture as a means of gaining status among their peers, for example by cheeking a teacher, truanting, not doing homework, smoking, drinking or stealing.

Unfortunately, however, although joining an anti-school subculture may solve the problem of lack of status, it creates further problems for the pupils who become involved in it. As Lacey says,

> *'the boy who takes refuge in such a group because his work is poor finds that the group commits him to a behaviour pattern which means that his work will stay poor – and in fact often gets progressively worse'.*

In other words, joining an anti-school subculture is likely to become a self-fulfilling prophecy of educational failure.

Lacey's study is a striking example of the power of labelling and streaming to actually *create* failure. The boys had all been successful at primary school and were among an elite of about 15% of the town's pupils who had passed the 11+ exam to get into grammar school.

Once there, however, the competitive atmosphere and streaming meant that many boys were soon labelled as failures, and many showed extreme physical reactions such as bed-wetting and insomnia. By their second year, many boys had become distinctly anti-school as they adjusted to their status as failures.

David Hargreaves (1967) found a similar response to labelling and streaming in a secondary modern school. From the point of view of the education system, boys in the lower streams were triple failures: they had failed their 11+ exam; they had been placed in low streams; and they had been labelled as 'worthless louts'.

One solution to this status problem was for pupils to seek each other out and form a group within which high status went to those who flouted the school's rules. In this way, they formed a delinquent subculture that helped to guarantee their educational failure.

synoptic link: deviance

Interactionists use labelling, the self-fulfilling prophecy and subculture to explain deviance as well as educational failure. In fact, one of their main interests in education is 'deviance in classrooms' – how labelling pupils as 'trouble' may lead to a self-fulfilling prophecy and the creation of an anti-school subculture in which the pupils act out their deviant label as a way of gaining status, thus embarking on a 'deviant career'.

abolishing streaming

Stephen Ball (1981) takes the analysis a step further in his study of Beachside, a comprehensive that was in the process of abolishing banding (a form of streaming) in favour of teaching mixed-ability groups. As Box 14 shows, banding had produced the kind of polarisation described by Lacey.

Ball found that when the school abolished banding, the basis for pupils to polarise into subcultures was largely removed and the influence of the anti-school subculture declined.

Nevertheless, although pupil polarisation all but disappeared, differentiation continued. Teachers continued to categorise pupils differently and were more likely to label middle-class pupils as cooperative and able. This positive labelling was reflected in their better exam results, suggesting that a self-fulfilling prophecy had occurred. Ball's study shows that class inequalities can continue as a result of teachers' labelling, even without the effect of subcultures or streaming.

Pro- and anti-school subcultures are two possible responses to labelling and streaming. However, as Peter Woods (1979) argues, other responses are also possible. These include ingratiation: being the 'teacher's pet'; ritualism: going through the motions and staying out of trouble; retreatism: daydreaming and mucking about; and rebellion: outright rejection of everything the school stands for.

Moreover, as John Furlong (1984) observes, pupils are not committed permanently to any one response, but may move between different types of response, acting differently in lessons with different teachers.

The theme of pupil subcultures is an important one in several areas of education, and elsewhere in this chapter there are further examples in relation to ethnicity and gender as well as class, including studies by Fuller, Sewell, Willis and Mac an Ghaill (see pages 113, 114, 141 and 146).

The limitations of labelling theory

The approaches we have examined start from the idea that under-achievement is the result of pupils being negatively labelled. This results in a self-fulfilling prophecy, with pupils often joining anti-school subcultures that help to guarantee their failure.

These studies are useful in showing how the interactions within schools actively create class inequalities. Schools are not neutral institutions, as cultural deprivation theorists assume. However, labelling theory has been accused of determinism. That is, it assumes that pupils who are labelled have no choice but to fulfil the prophecy and will inevitably fail. However, studies such as Fuller's show that this is not always true.

Marxists criticise labelling theory for ignoring the wider structures of power within which labelling takes place. Labelling theory tends to blame teachers for labelling pupils but fails to explain *why* they do so. Marxists argue that labels are not merely the result of teachers' individual prejudices, but stem from the fact that teachers work in a system that reproduces class divisions.

Box 14: Banding and polarisation

Comparison of top band and middle band year 8 pupils at Beachside Comprehensive

	Top band	Middle band
Teachers' stereotypes of each band	Academic potential Neat workers Bright, alert and enthusiastic Wanting to get on Rewarding	Not up to much Rowdy and lazy Cannot take part in discussions Not interested Unrewarding
Proportion of pupils from working-class homes	36%	78%
Proportion of teachers' time in class devoted to maintaining order	1.5%	12.5%
Average number of detentions, per pupil per year	0.4	3.8
Average number of absences per pupil in term 1	8.1	12.6
Average number of minutes spent on homework per pupil	47	16
Proportion of end-of-year subject tests graded at 50% or higher	58%	11%
Number of extra-curricular activities or club memberships, per class	43	10
Proportion of pupils who dislike school	13%	48%
Views held about each band by pupils in the other band	Brainy Unfriendly Stuck-up Arrogant	Thick Rough Boring Simple

Source: adapted from Bilton (1987) table 8.4 (compiled from Ball, 1981)

activity

Working alone or in pairs, use the concepts of labelling, the self-fulfilling prophecy and pupil subcultures to write an explanation of as many of the above differences between the two bands as you can.

Marketisation and selection

Another way in which factors within the education system may cause class differences in achievement is through the impact of the policy of marketisation (see Box 13). Marketisation brought in:

- **a funding formula** that gives a school the same amount of funds for each pupil
- **exam league tables** that rank each school according to its exam performance and make no allowance for the level of ability of its pupils
- **competition** between schools to attract pupils.

These changes explain why schools are under pressure to select more able, largely middle-class pupils who will gain the school a higher ranking in the league tables. Those schools with a good league table position will then be better placed to attract other able/middle-class pupils. This will further improve the school's results and make it more popular still, thus increasing its funding. Increased popularity will enable it to select from a larger number of applicants and recruit the most able, thereby improving its results once again, and so on.

However, while popular schools can afford to screen out less able or more 'difficult' pupils from disadvantaged backgrounds, unpopular schools are obliged to take them, get worse results, become less popular still and see their funding further reduced.

These pressures have resulted in increased social class segregation between schools. Will Bartlett (1993) argues that marketisation has led to popular schools:

- **cream-skimming:** selecting able pupils, who gain the best results and cost less to teach
- **silt-shifting:** off-loading pupils with learning difficulties, who are expensive to teach and get poor results.

One example of how this can disadvantage working-class children is through the use of home/school contracts. Selective schools often require parents to sign demanding home/school contracts before being offered a place. Gewirtz describes one school where the contract required parents to:

Why might marketisation discourage schools from taking pupils with special educational needs?

> *'ensure attendance and punctuality, encourage and support their daughter with her work, supervise her homework, attend parents' evenings and school functions in which their daughter is involved, keep her in the correct uniform, provide her with a well-stocked pencil-case, a calculator, dictionary and recorder, pay for the replacement of damaged or lost books, and support the policies of the school.'*

She quotes a school governor as saying that having the contracts 'will really be influential in bringing the right sort of parents into this school'.

questions

1 In what ways might working-class parents find it more difficult to meet the requirements of such a contract?

2 Explain in your own words what advantages attracting 'the right sort of parents' might have for a school.

There is evidence, then, that marketisation and selection processes have created a polarised education system, with popular, successful, well-resourced schools with a more able, largely middle-class intake at one extreme and unpopular, 'failing', under-resourced schools with mainly low-achieving working-class pupils at the other. Gewirtz describes this as a 'blurred hierarchy' of schools.

Sheila Macrae (1997) sees a similar pattern in post-16 education. At the top are highly selective sixth form colleges attracting middle-class students and providing academic courses leading to university and professional careers. Then come general further education colleges catering for mainly working-class students and providing largely vocational courses. At the bottom are government-funded training organisations providing low-level courses leading to low-paid jobs.

An image to attract middle-class parents

Some schools have responded to marketisation by creating a 'traditional' image to attract middle-class parents and this has reinforced class divisions. Studies of Grant Maintained (GM) schools and City Technology Colleges (CTCs) show how this has occurred.

Geoffrey Walford's (1991) research on CTCs found that although they were intended to provide vocational education in partnership with employers and to recruit pupils from all social backgrounds, in practice they have come to be just another route to elite education. They became attractive to middle-class parents not because of a hi-tech image, but because they were seen as the next best thing to a traditional grammar school.

Similarly, John Fitz's (1997) study of GM schools, which were allowed to opt out of local education authority control, found them 're-inventing tradition'. One school had spent £10,000 on a new pipe organ for assemblies and had re-named its canteen the 'dining hall'. The organ was in fact newer than the school's computer suite. Fitz concludes that the reason most schools adopted a traditional image was to attract middle-class parents.

City Technology Colleges – just grammar schools by another name?

QuickCheck Questions

1 Explain the difference between:
   (a) deferred and immediate gratification
   (b) the elaborated and restricted codes
   (c) cultural and economic capital.

2 Suggest three ways in which poverty may affect achievement.

3 Explain briefly what is meant by marketisation.

4 Name one policy that has helped to create an education market.

5 Explain the difference between labelling and the self-fulfilling prophecy.

6 Give one criticism of labelling theory.

7 True or false? Streaming is an example of polarisation.

8 Identify one reason why anti-school subcultures develop.

Answers are on page 272.

Examining Class and education

Item A Government plans are that the great majority of secondary schools will soon either be specialist or boast a distinctive ethos as a 'beacon' school or one based on a single religious faith. As Labour prepares to put the expansion of these specialist schools at the heart of its drive to raise standards, some worry that it signals the end of the 'bog standard' comprehensive and will create a two-tier education system. Specialist schools will flourish at the expense of poorer rivals, which will gradually become unpopular sink schools.

Why has Labour embraced a scheme originally launched by Margaret Thatcher in the shape of her city technology colleges (CTCs)? Evidence of high achievement in specialist schools has helped to sway the government. CTCs' results are better and improving faster than other schools'.

Specialist schools already enjoy extra funding. They have to raise £50,000 in private sponsorship, for which they get an extra £600,000 from government. By 2006, the government aims to have 1,500 specialist schools – eight times the number when they took office in 1997. There will be six specialisms: arts and media, technology, languages, sport, business and engineering. There are plans for more single-faith schools, which deliver good results, and even for 'advanced specialist schools', which might be used to train teachers.

With this daunting array of labels, the impression is of more choice. But will this really be the case? Parents may find themselves having no choice except the specialist school on their doorstep. The thorny issue of selection also raises its head. Specialist schools are allowed to select up to 10% of pupils by aptitude.

Head teachers fear that the government's plans will lead to one set of schools being treated as high-status and high-funded and the rest – low-status and low-funded.

Source: adapted from Rebecca Smithers (2001)

Item B J.W.B. Douglas' 1964 study, *The Home and the School*, explained working-class failure as being the result of a lack of parental interest and stimulation in the home. Two of the measures of parental interest were the number of times parents visited their child's school, and what teachers said about parents. Douglas proposed an improvement in primary school teaching and an increase in nursery schools to give working-class children the stimulus lacking in their homes. This picture of the culturally deprived child was given further weight by the publication of several official reports into child development.

These reports and studies like Douglas' led to the setting up of Educational Priority Areas (EPAs) in a number of inner-city areas. An area acquired its EPA status, which brought extra funds, by virtue of its measurable indices of poverty, such as the proportion of its children receiving free school dinners. Educational factors included pupils' average reading ages and truancy rates. A major aim of the EPAs was to increase the involvement of parents in their children's education.

Source: adapted from Karen Chapman (1986)

Examining Class and education

Short questions

(a) Explain briefly what is meant by the 'ethos' of a school (**Item A**, line 2). (2 marks)

(b) Suggest **two** criticisms of the measures of parental interest in their child's education referred to in **Item B**, lines 3-4. (4 marks)

(c) Suggest **three** reasons why governments may want to introduce more specialist schools (**Item A**). (6 marks)

(d) Identify and briefly explain **two** reasons why increasing the number of specialist schools might not lead to more choice for all parents (**Item A**, lines 18-19). (8 marks)

Mini-essay

Using material from **Item B** and elsewhere, assess the view that working-class children under-achieve because they are culturally deprived.

(20 marks)

This is a type (f) question of the kind found in the exam, carrying 6 AO1 marks (knowledge and understanding) and 14 AO2 marks (identification, interpretation, analysis and evaluation).

The Examiner's advice For the mini-essay, explain how cultural deprivation may affect achievement. Use evidence from studies and Item B to do so. Make reference to policies to overcome cultural deprivation (Head Start, EPAs, Sure Start). You need to evaluate the view: a good focus is that cultural deprivation (CD) theory lets both social inequality (poverty) and teachers/the education system off the hook, by 'blaming the victim' for failure. Use Keddie's claim that CD is a myth, as well as criticisms from other explanations – e.g. material deprivation, Bourdieu, Gewirtz, internal factors (labelling, pupil subcultures, selection processes). Write a separate conclusion.

Ethnic differences in educational achievement

In the previous section we saw that social class plays an important part in educational achievement. Just as we can think of everyone as 'belonging to' a class, so too we can see individuals as being part of an ethnic group – whether a minority or a majority group.

Why are students from some ethnic groups more successful than others?

Tony Lawson and Joan Garrod (2000) define ethnic groups as 'people who share common history, customs and identity, as well as, in most cases, language and religion, and who see themselves as a distinct unit'. When we use terms such as customs, language and religion, we are talking about culture – that is, about all those things that are learned, shared and valued by a social group.

One difficulty in studying ethnicity and education is the problem of deciding whom to include in an ethnic group. For example, should all 'Asians' be classified together – when this would include people of many different nationalities, religions and languages?

It is a mistake to think of ethnic groups as always being defined by physical features such as skin colour. Although many ethnic minority groups in Britain are non-white, this is not true of all groups. However, it happens that the largest minority groups in Britain are non-white: mainly of African, Caribbean or South Asian origin. There are, however, many other minority groups. According to David Crystal (1997), well over 100 languages are in routine use in the UK. Today, children from ethnic minority backgrounds make up over 11% of the pupils in English schools.

questions

1. What ethnic group do you see yourself as belonging to?
2. What makes it a group (e.g. what cultural features make it distinct from other groups)?
3. Do you feel you belong to more than one group (e.g. English, British, European)?
4. What problems might this pose for recording people's educational achievements in terms of their ethnicity?

Evidence of ethnic differences in achievement

We can see from Figure 3.2 that there are inequalities in the educational achievement of different ethnic groups. For example, whites and Asians on average do better than blacks. However, as Figure 3.2 also shows, there are significant variations among Asians. For example, Indians do better than Pakistanis and Bangladeshis.

Figure 3.2: Percentage of 16 year olds attaining 5 or more GCSE grades A* – C by ethnic origin, England and Wales, 2002

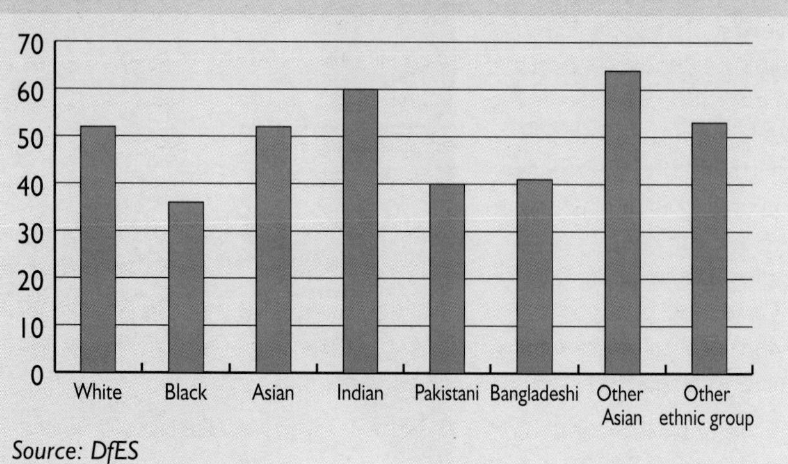

Source: DfES

Similarly, there are class and gender differences within and between ethnic groups. For example, among black and white working-class pupils, girls do better than boys, whereas among Asians the reverse is true. Comparing females of different ethnic groups, working-class blacks do better than working-class whites.

Other differences remain important. For example, children of middle-class East African Asian families do better than children of working-class Bangladeshi families.

Sociologists are interested in the reasons for these differences in achievement and have put forward a number of explanations of them. Some of these are similar to the explanations of social class differences we examined in the previous section. As with class differences in achievement, we can separate them into internal and external factors, though in reality, these two factors are very often linked.

- **External factors** – factors outside the education system, such as the influence of home and family background and wider society.
- **Internal factors** – factors within schools and the education system, such as interactions between pupils and teachers and inequalities between schools.

External factors and ethnic differences in achievement

Many sociologists argue that ethnic differences in achievement can best be explained by looking at factors outside the school – in the home, family and culture of the child and the impact of wider society. The main explanations of this kind are:

1 Cultural deprivation
2 Material deprivation and class
3 Racism in wider society

1 Cultural deprivation

As with explanations of class differences in achievement (see page 88), cultural deprivation theory sees the under-achievement of some ethnic groups as the result of inadequate socialisation in the home. The explanation has three main aspects:

- intellectual and linguistic skills
- attitudes and values
- family structure.

Intellectual and linguistic skills

Cultural deprivation theorists see the lack of intellectual and linguistic skills as a major cause of under-achievement for many minority children. They argue that many children from low-income black families lack intellectual stimulation and enriching experiences. This leaves them ill-equipped for school because they have not been able to develop reasoning and problem-solving skills.

Similarly, Bereiter and Engelmann (see page 89) consider the language spoken by low-income black American families as inadequate for educational success. They see it as ungrammatical, disjointed and incapable of expressing abstract ideas. Likewise, Gordon Bowker (1968) identifies their lack of standard English as a major barrier to progress in education and integration into wider society.

synoptic links: stratification and deviance

The New Right argue that such families form part of an underclass – a class below the working class with a separate, deviant subculture and lifestyle, and high rates of lone-parent families, male unemployment and criminality. Educational failure results from, and helps to perpetuate, this subculture.

Attitudes and values

Cultural deprivation theorists see lack of motivation as a major cause of the failure of many black children. Most other children are socialised into mainstream culture, which instils ambition, competitiveness and willingness to make the sacrifices necessary to achieve long-term goals. This equips them for success in education. By contrast, cultural deprivation theorists argue, some black children are socialised into a subculture that instils a fatalistic, 'live for today' attitude that does not value education and leaves them ill-equipped for success.

question

What term might sociologists use to describe a 'live for today' attitude?

Family structure

Cultural deprivation theorists argue that this failure to socialise children adequately is the result of a dysfunctional family structure. For example, Daniel Moynihan (1965) argues that the fact that many black families are headed by a lone mother means that children are deprived of adequate care because she has to struggle financially in the absence of a male breadwinner. His absence also means that boys lack an adequate role model of male achievement. Moynihan sees cultural deprivation as a cycle where inadequately socialised children from unstable families go on to fail at school and become inadequate parents themselves.

The New Right put forward similar explanations. For example, Charles Murray (1984) argues that a high rate of lone parenthood and a lack of positive male role models leads to the under-achievement of some minorities. Similarly, Anthony Flew (1984) believes that ethnic differences in achievement stem from cultural differences outside the education system, not discrimination within it. Roger Scruton (1986) sees the low achievement levels of some ethnic minorities as resulting from a failure to embrace mainstream British culture.

Ken Pryce (1979) also sees family structure as contributing to the under-achievement of black Caribbean pupils in Britain. From a comparison of black and Asian pupils, he claims that Asians are higher achievers because their culture is more resistant to racism and gives them a greater sense of self-worth. By contrast, he argues, black Caribbean culture is less cohesive and less resistant to racism. As a result, many black pupils have low self-esteem and under-achieve.

Is motivation the key to success in school?

Pryce argues that the difference is the result of the differing impact of colonialism on the two groups. He argues that Asian family structures, languages and religions were not destroyed by colonial rule, whereas the experience of slavery was culturally devastating for blacks. Being transported and sold into slavery meant that they lost their language, religion and entire family system.

Some sociologists have also criticised the Asian family as an obstacle to success, despite the high levels of achievement of some Asian minorities. For example, Verity Khan (1979) describes Asian families as 'stress ridden', bound by tradition and controlling in their attitude towards children, especially girls. This may explain why Asian girls do less well than Asian boys.

compensatory education

The main policy that has been adopted to tackle cultural deprivation is compensatory education. For example, the aim of Operation Head Start (see page 91) was to compensate children for the cultural deficit they are said to suffer because of deprived backgrounds.

Criticisms of cultural deprivation

Geoffrey Driver (1977) criticises cultural deprivation theory for ignoring the positive effects of ethnicity on achievement. He shows that the black Caribbean family, far from being dysfunctional, provides girls with positive role models of strong independent women. Driver argues that this is why black girls tend to be more successful in education than black boys.

Errol Lawrence (1982) challenges Pryce's view that black pupils fail because their culture is weak and they lack self-esteem. He argues that black pupils under-achieve not because of low self-esteem, but because of racism.

Keddie sees cultural deprivation as a victim-blaming explanation (see page 92). She argues that ethnic minority children are culturally different, not culturally deprived. They under-achieve because schools are ethnocentric: biased in favour of white culture and against minorities.

Critics oppose compensatory education because they see it as an attempt to impose the dominant culture on children who already have a coherent culture of their own. They propose two main alternatives:

- multicultural education: a policy that recognises and values minority cultures and includes them in the curriculum
- anti-racist education: a policy that challenges the prejudice and discrimination that exists in schools and wider society.

Some sociologists argue that material deprivation rather than cultural deprivation is the main cause of under-achievement. We examine their view next.

2 Material deprivation and class

Material deprivation means a lack of those physical necessities that are seen as essential or normal for life in today's society. In general, working-class people are more likely to face poverty and material deprivation.

Material deprivation explanations see educational failure as resulting from factors such as substandard housing and low income. Ethnic minorities are more likely to face these problems. For example, according to Howard (2001):

- Pakistanis and Bangladeshis are three times more likely than whites to be in the poorest fifth of the population.
- Male unemployment is three times higher for ethnic minorities than for whites.
- 15% of ethnic minority households live in overcrowded conditions, compared with only 2% of white households.

Similarly, according to David Mason (1995):

- 19% of white men, but 70% of Bangladeshi men, were in unskilled or semi-skilled jobs.
- Minority employees earn 10–30% less than whites, and are more likely to work shifts and to be engaged in low-paid homeworking.

question

How might (a) parents working shifts and (b) parents engaged in low-paid homeworking affect their children's education?

These inequalities parallel those seen in educational achievement. For example, on average Indians, Chinese and whites have a higher social class position than Bangladeshis and Pakistanis, who often face high levels of poverty. The material deprivation explanation argues that such class differences explain why Bangladeshi and Pakistani pupils tend to do worse than Indian, Chinese and white pupils.

Evidence for this view comes from the Swann Report (1985), which estimated that social class accounts for at least 50% of the difference in achievement between ethnic groups. If we fail to take the different class positions of ethnic groups into account when we compare their educational achievements, there is a danger that we may over-estimate the effect of *cultural* deprivation and under-estimate the effect of poverty and *material* deprivation.

3 Racism in wider society

While material deprivation has an impact on the educational achievement of some ethnic minority children, some sociologists argue that deprivation is itself the product of another factor – namely, racism. As Mason puts it, 'discrimination is a continuing and persistent feature of the experience of Britain's citizens of minority ethnic origin'.

John Rex (1986) shows how racial discrimination leads to social exclusion and how this worsens the material deprivation faced by ethnic minorities. In housing, for instance, discrimination means that minorities are more likely to be forced into substandard accommodation than white people of the same class.

In employment, too, there is evidence of direct and deliberate discrimination. For example, Mike Noon (1993) sent matched letters of enquiry about future employment opportunities to the top 100 UK companies, signed by fictitious applicants called 'Evans' and 'Patel' with the same qualifications and experience. In terms of both the number and helpfulness of replies, the companies were more encouraging to the 'white' candidate.

This helps to explain why members of ethnic minorities are more likely to face unemployment and low pay, and this in turn has a negative effect on their children's educational prospects.

Internal factors and ethnic differences in achievement

While external factors may play an important part in creating differences in achievement between ethnic groups, factors internal to the education system itself are also important. These internal factors include:

1 Labelling and teacher racism
2 Pupil responses and subcultures
3 The ethnocentric curriculum
4 Institutional racism
5 Selection and segregation

1 Labelling and teacher racism

To label someone is to attach a meaning or definition to them. For example, teachers may label a pupil as a trouble maker or cooperative, bright or thick. Interactionist sociologists study the face-to-face interactions in which such labelling occurs.

When looking at ethnic differences in achievement, interactionists focus on the different labels teachers give to children from different ethnic backgrounds. Their studies show that teachers often see black and Asian pupils as being far from the 'ideal pupil' (see page 98). For example, black pupils are often seen as disruptive and Asians as passive. Negative labels may lead teachers to treat ethnic minority pupils differently. This disadvantages them and may result in their failure.

Black pupils

A good illustration of the impact of labelling on black pupils is David Gillborn's (1990) study. He found that teachers were quick to discipline black students because they saw them as a threat to their authority and safety. Teachers often misinterpreted their behaviour as threatening when no threat was intended. When teachers acted on this misperception, the pupils responded negatively and further conflict resulted.

Gillborn concludes that much of the conflict between white teachers and black pupils stems from the racial stereotypes teachers hold rather than the pupils' actual behaviour. Teachers were less likely to see pupils from other ethnic backgrounds as a threat or to punish them, even if they behaved in the same way as the black pupils.

This may explain the higher level of exclusions from school of black boys (see Figure 3.3). As Jenny Bourne (1994) found, schools tend to see black boys as a threat and to label them negatively, leading eventually to exclusion.

Do teachers treat pupils from different backgrounds unequally?

Similarly, Peter Foster (1990) found that teachers' stereotypes of black pupils as badly behaved could result in them being placed in lower sets than other pupils of similar ability. Both exclusions and allocation to lower sets are likely to lead to lower levels of achievement.

Figure 3.3: Permanent exclusion rates among 5–15 year-olds in England, 2001/2, by ethnic group (% of group)

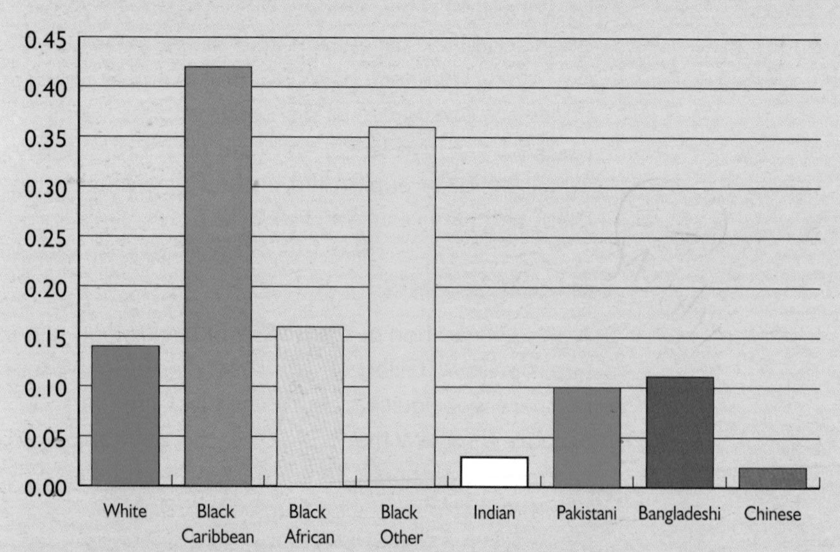

Source: DfES

question

Roughly how many times more likely were black Caribbean pupils to be excluded than (a) white and (b) Chinese pupils?

Asian pupils

Cecile Wright's (1992) study of a multi-ethnic primary school shows that Asian pupils can also be the victims of teachers' labelling. She found that despite the school's apparent commitment to equal opportunities, teachers held ethnocentric views: that is, they took for granted that British culture and standard English were superior. This affected how they related to Asian pupils. For example, teachers assumed they would have a poor grasp of English and left them out of class discussions or used simplistic, childish language when speaking to them.

Asian pupils also felt isolated when teachers expressed disapproval of their customs or failed to pronounce their names properly. In general, teachers saw them not as a threat (unlike black pupils), but as a problem they could ignore. The effect was that Asian pupils, especially the girls, were marginalised – pushed to the edges and prevented from participating fully.

2 Pupil responses and subcultures

As we have seen, there is evidence of teacher racism. However, research shows that pupils can respond in a variety of ways. For example, they may respond to negative labelling by becoming disruptive or withdrawn. Alternatively, pupils may refuse to accept the label and even decide to prove it wrong by working extra hard. Negative labels do not automatically turn into self-fulfilling prophecies.

Fuller: rejecting negative labels

A good example of pupils responding by rejecting negative labels is Mary Fuller's (1984) study of a group of black girls in year 11 of a London comprehensive school. The girls were untypical because they were high achievers in a school where most black girls were placed in low streams.

Fuller describes how instead of accepting negative stereotypes of themselves, the girls channelled their anger about being labelled into the pursuit of educational success. However, unlike other successful pupils they did not seek the approval of teachers, many of whom they regarded as racist. Nor did they limit their choice of friends to other academic achievers. Instead, they were friends with other black girls from lower streams.

Also unlike other successful pupils, they conformed only as far as the schoolwork itself was concerned. They worked conscientiously, but gave the appearance of not doing so, and they showed a deliberate lack of concern about school routines. They had a positive attitude to academic success but rather than seeking the approval of teachers, they preferred to rely on their own efforts and the impartiality of external exams.

Fuller sees the girls' behaviour as a way of dealing with the contradictory demands of succeeding at school while remaining friends with black girls in lower streams and avoiding the ridicule of black boys, many of whom were anti-school. They were able to maintain a positive self-image by relying on their own efforts rather than accepting the teachers' negative stereotype of them.

A positive attitude to academic success.

The study highlights two important points. Firstly, pupils may still succeed even when they refuse to conform. Secondly, negative labelling does not always lead to failure. These girls were able to reject the labels placed on them and they remained determined to succeed. There was no self-fulfilling prophecy.

Mirza: failed strategies for avoiding racism

Like Fuller, Heidi Safia Mirza (1992) studied ambitious black girls who faced teacher racism. However, the girls in Mirza's study failed to achieve their ambitions because the strategies they used to cope restricted their opportunities and resulted in under-achievement.

Mirza found that racist teachers discouraged black pupils from being ambitious through the kind of advice they gave them about careers and option choices. For example, teachers discouraged them from aspiring to professional careers.

A large majority of teachers in the study held racist attitudes. Mirza identifies three main types of teacher racism:

- **The colour-blind:** teachers who believe all pupils are equal but in practice allow racism to go unchallenged.
- **The liberal chauvinists:** teachers who believe black pupils are culturally deprived and who have low expectations of them.
- **The overt racists:** teachers who believe blacks are inferior and actively discriminate against them.

Much of the girls' time at school was spent trying to avoid the effects of teachers' negative attitudes. The strategies they employed to do this included being selective about which staff to ask for help; getting on with their own work in lessons without taking part and not taking certain option choices to avoid teachers with racist attitudes.

Although the girls had high self-esteem, however, these strategies put them at a disadvantage by restricting their opportunities. Unlike the girls in Fuller's study, their strategies were unsuccessful.

Sewell: the variety of boys' responses

Like Mirza, Tony Sewell (1998) examines the responses and strategies black pupils adopt to cope with racism. In his study of a boys' secondary school, he found that many teachers have a stereotype of 'black machismo', which sees all black boys as rebellious, anti-authority and anti-school. One effect of this stereotyping is that black boys are more likely to be excluded from school.

Using Robert Merton's (1949) classification of conformity and deviance, Sewell identifies four ways in which the boys respond to racist stereotyping.

the rebels

The rebels were the most visible and influential group but were only a small minority of black pupils. The rebels were often excluded from school. They rejected both the goals and the rules of the school and expressed their opposition through peer group membership, conforming to the stereotype of the 'black macho lad'. They believed in their own superiority based on the idea that black masculinity equates with sexual experience and virility. They were contemptuous of white boys, who they saw as effeminate, and dismissive of conformist black boys.

the conformists

The conformists were the largest group. These boys were keen to succeed, accepted the school's goals and had friends from different ethnic groups. They were not part of a subculture and were anxious to avoid being stereotyped either by teachers or their peers.

the retreatists

The retreatists were a tiny minority of isolated individuals who were disconnected from both school and black subcultures, and were despised by the rebels.

the innovators

The innovators were the second largest group. Like Fuller's girls, they were pro-education but anti-school. They valued success, but did not seek the approval of teachers and conformed only as far as schoolwork itself was concerned. This distanced them from the conformists and allowed them to maintain credibility with the rebels while remaining positive about academic achievement.

Sewell shows that only a small minority fit the stereotype of the 'black macho lad'. Nevertheless, teachers tend to see them all in this way and this contributes to the under-achievement of many boys, whatever their attitude to school. Furthermore, many of the boys' negative attitudes are themselves a response to this racism.

In addition to teacher stereotyping, however, Sewell recognises that other factors also contribute to the under-achievement of black boys. These include low aspirations and the absence of fathers as role models in some black families. He also blames a media inspired role model of anti-school black masculinity whose ideal Chris Arnot (2004) describes as 'the ultra-tough ghetto superstar, an image constantly reinforced through rap lyrics and MTV videos'.

synoptic link: deviance

Merton defines conformity as acceptance both of society's goals (e.g. a high income) and its legitimate means of achieving them (e.g. hard work).

He identifies four types of deviance: innovation, ritualism, retreatism and rebellion. He distinguishes between the four in terms of whether they reject society's goals and/or the legitimate means of achieving them.

Evaluation of labelling and pupil responses

Rather than blaming the child's home background, as cultural deprivation theory does, labelling theory shows how teachers' stereotypes can be a cause of failure. However, there is a danger of seeing these as simply the product of individual teachers' prejudices, rather than of racism in wider society. Factors outside school, such as the influence of role models in the family and media, also play a part.

There is also a danger of assuming that once labelled, pupils automatically fall victim to the self-fulfilling prophecy and fail. Nevertheless, as Mirza shows, although pupils may devise strategies to try to avoid teachers' racism, these too can limit their opportunities.

3 The ethnocentric curriculum

The term 'ethnocentric' describes an attitude or policy that gives priority to the culture and viewpoint of one particular ethnic group while disregarding others.

Troyna and Williams describe the curriculum in British schools as ethnocentric because it gives priority to white culture and the English language. Similarly, Miriam David (1993) describes the National Curriculum as a 'specifically British' curriculum that teaches the culture of the 'host community', while largely ignoring non-European languages, literature and music.

Equally, Stephen Ball (1994) criticises the National Curriculum for ignoring cultural and ethnic diversity and for promoting an attitude of 'little Englandism'. For example, the history curriculum tries to recreate a 'mythical age of empire and past glories', while ignoring the history of black and Asian people.

Bernard Coard (1971) explains how the ethnocentric curriculum may produce under-achievement. For example, in history the British are presented as bringing civilisation to the 'primitive' peoples they colonised. This image of black people as inferior undermines black children's self-esteem and leads to their failure.

However, it is not clear what impact the ethnocentric curriculum has. For example, while it may ignore Asian culture, Indian and Chinese pupils' achievement is above the national average. Similarly, Maureen Stone (1981) argues that black children do not in fact suffer from low self-esteem.

activity

In small groups, discuss the following questions.

1 How ethnocentric was the curriculum you followed in school? How much non-European history, geography, literature, music etc did you study? Did you study any non-European languages or non-Christian religions?

2 How far do your experiences support Troyna and Williams' view?

4 Institutional racism

Troyna and Williams argue that explanations of ethnic differences in achievement need to go beyond an understanding of the effects of individual teacher racism and look at how schools and colleges routinely discriminate against ethnic minorities. They therefore make a distinction between:

- individual racism that results from the prejudiced views of individuals
- institutional racism – discrimination that is built into the way schools and colleges operate.

From this point of view, the ethnocentric curriculum is a prime example of institutional racism. Troyna and Williams see the meagre provision for teaching Asian languages as institutional racism because it is an example of racial bias being built into schools and colleges.

Studies of school governing bodies provide further examples of institutional racism. Richard Hatcher (1996) found that they gave low priority to race issues and failed to deal with pupils' racist behaviour. In the schools he studied, there were no formal channels of communication between school governors and ethnic minority parents. This meant, for example, that nothing was done about parents' concerns over lack of language support.

These examples show that institutional racism may create an environment in which ethnic minority pupils are routinely disadvantaged by a system that disregards their needs.

synoptic link: stratification

The concept of institutional racism is used to explain the way in which systematic discrimination against minorities across a wide range of social institutions (education, employment, housing, health care, policing etc) serves to create and maintain an ethnically stratified society.

5 Selection and segregation

David Gillborn (1997) argues that marketisation has given schools greater scope to select pupils (see Box 13 on page 97) and this has put some ethnic minority pupils at a disadvantage because selection gives more scope for negative stereotypes to influence decisions about school admissions.

Gillborn's view is supported by Donald Moore and Susan Davenport's (1990) American research, which focuses on how selection procedures lead to ethnic segregation, with minority pupils failing to get into better schools. They found that these schools discriminated against 'problem students'. For example, they used primary school reports to screen out pupils with language or learning difficulties, while the application process was difficult for less educated or non-English speaking parents to understand.

These procedures favoured white, middle-class pupils and put those from low-income and ethnic minority backgrounds at a disadvantage. Moore and Davenport thus conclude that selection leads to an ethnically stratified education system.

The Commission for Racial Equality (1993) has identified similar biases in British education. Their report notes that racism in school admissions procedures means that ethnic minority children are more likely to end up in unpopular schools. The report identifies the following reasons:

- reports from primary schools that stereotype minority pupils
- racist bias in interviews for school places
- lack of information and application forms in minority languages
- ethnic minority parents are often unaware of how the waiting list system works and the importance of deadlines.

However, schools' selection policies are not the only cause of segregation. It can also be the result of an active choice by parents, as Gewirtz's study of 'Gorse' and 'Flightpath' schools shows. Gorse attracted a mainly Asian intake. Many white parents refused to consider it because of this, opting instead for Flightpath. By contrast, Asian parents saw Gorse as 'safe' and having an academic orientation and firm discipline. They viewed Flightpath as 'a bit rough', with a reputation for racism.

activity

Some minorities have set up their own schools. For example, black communities have set up Saturday or supplementary schools for their children, while Muslims and Seventh Day Adventists have set up their own faith schools. Alone or in small groups:

1 Research the different reasons for setting up such schools.

2 List the arguments for and against having schools for a single ethnic or religious group.

QuickCheck Questions

1 List the following groups in order of achievement at GCSE, highest first: whites, blacks, Bangladeshis.

2 True or false? Among both white and black working-class pupils, girls do better than boys.

3 State one criticism of cultural deprivation theory as an explanation of ethnic differences in achievement.

4 Name one sociologist who has studied the labelling of black pupils.

5 List three ways in which pupils may respond to negative labels.

6 What is meant by the ethnocentric curriculum?

Answers are on page 272.

Examining Ethnicity and education

Item A

According to a report produced by the Cabinet Office in summer 2002, 'Bangladeshi, black and Pakistani pupils achieve less well than other pupils at all stages of education. Black Caribbean children have equal, if not higher, ability than white children on entrance to school, but Black Caribbean boys make the least progress through school.' Black Caribbean boys are also more likely than other groups to be excluded from school.

There are also considerable differences in the achievements of different ethnic groups. For example, in 2000, 62% of Indians achieved five or more A*–C grades at GCSE, but only 37% of blacks and 30% of Pakistanis and Bangladeshis did so. Indian children's results improved almost twice as fast as Pakistani and Bangladeshi children's between 1992 and 2000.

There are also important gender differences between ethnic groups. On average, boys and girls have similar staying-on rates, but among blacks and Chinese the rate is higher for females, while among Indians, Bangladeshis and Pakistanis males have the higher rate.

In higher education, a bigger proportion of ethnic minority students (like white working-class students) attend the new universities rather than the old established universities. Even when factors such as parents' social class and level of qualifications are taken into account, minority students are less likely than whites to get into the traditional universities.

The report concludes that the education system encourages competition and separation. White parents, and middle-class black and Asian parents, tend to try to select schools with few students from ethnic minority groups.

Short questions

(a) Explain what is meant by an ethnic group (**Item A**, line 6). (2 marks)

(b) Identify and briefly explain **one** problem in trying to categorise pupils by their ethnicity. (4 marks)

(c) Suggest **three** ways in which the education system may encourage separation between children of different ethnic backgrounds (**Item A**, line 17). (6 marks)

(d) Identify and briefly describe **two** ways in which factors in children's home background may lead to differences in achievement levels between or within ethnic groups (**Item A**, lines 6-12). (8 marks)

Mini-essay

Examine the ways in which racism and discrimination may affect the achievement of pupils from ethnic minority backgrounds. (20 marks)

This is a type (e) question of the kind found in the exam, carrying 14 AO1 marks (knowledge and understanding) and 6 AO2 marks (identification, interpretation, analysis and evaluation).

The Examiner's advice

For the mini-essay, probably most of your answer will be about racism and discrimination inside school, but the question is broader than this so you should say something about outside school too. Inside school, look at studies of teacher racism/stereotyping of pupils and at the different ways pupils respond to this (e.g. Wright, Gillborn, Sewell, Mirza, Fuller). Does teacher racism inevitably affect achievement, and are all minorities (and both genders/classes within each minority) equally affected? Do all pupils react to it in the same way? How does racism affect pupil subcultures and thus achievement? You could also look at the role of the ethnocentric curriculum. Lastly, what role does racism outside school (e.g. in housing and employment) play?

Gender differences in education

Along with class and ethnicity, gender has a major impact on people's experience of education. In recent years, there have been some important changes in this area. For example, while both sexes have raised their level of attainment, girls have now overtaken boys.

On the other hand, an area where gender patterns have been slower to change is in subject choice, with boys and girls often preferring to study traditional 'sex-typed' subjects and courses. Similarly, there is evidence that schooling continues to reinforce differences in gender identity between boys and girls.

A growing gender gap in educational achievement.

The main questions that interest sociologists in this area are:

- Why do girls now generally achieve better results than boys?
- Why do girls and boys opt to study different subjects?
- How does schooling help to reinforce gender identities?

This section of the chapter examines some of the answers sociologists have given to these questions.

The growing gender gap

Official statistics provide evidence of differences in the achievements of girls and boys at several important stages of their education:

- **On starting school**, children are given baseline assessments, where the teacher assesses what each child knows, understands and can do. A national survey of 6,953 children by the government's Qualifications and Curriculum Authority (1999) found that girls scored higher in all tests. While 62% of girls could concentrate without supervision for 10 minutes, only 49% of boys could do this. Similarly, 56% of girls could write their own name and spell it correctly, but only 42% of boys could do so.
- **At Key Stages 1 to 3**, girls do consistently better than boys in both teacher assessments and tests, especially in English, where the gender gap steadily widens with age. In science and maths the gap is much narrower, but girls still do better.
- **At GCSE**, as Figure 3.4 shows, the gender gap has widened to over 10 percentage points.
- **At AS and A level**, girls are more likely than boys to pass their exams, and to get higher grades. In 2002, for all AS subjects, 88.5% of girls passed, as against 84% of boys. For all A level subjects, the figures were 95.4% and 93% respectively. At both AS and A level, girls were more likely to gain A, B and C grades, even in so-called 'boys'' subjects such as maths, physics and chemistry.

- **On vocational courses**, such as Advanced level VCE, results show a similar pattern. In 2000, 19.5% of girls achieved a distinction, but only 11.1% of boys. In fact, a larger proportion of girls achieved distinctions in every subject, including those such as engineering and construction where girls are a tiny minority of the students.

Although results for both sexes have improved at all levels over the years, the girls' rate of improvement has been more rapid and a significant gap has opened up, particularly at GCSE.

Figure 3.4: Percentage of pupils achieving five or more grades A*–C or equivalent at GCSE, 1976/7 to 2001/2, by gender

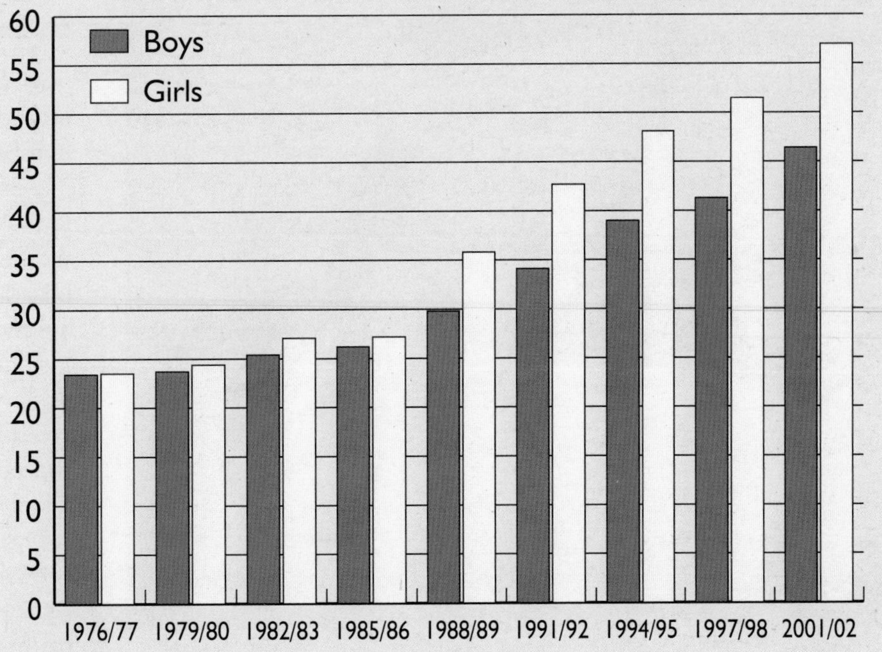

Boys
Girls

0 5 10 15 20 25 30 35 40 45 50 55 60

1976/77 1979/80 1982/83 1985/86 1988/89 1991/92 1994/95 1997/98 2001/02

Source: DfES

Explaining changes in boys' and girls' achievement

There are a number of reasons for gender differences in achievement. As with explanations of class and ethnic differences in achievement, we can divide them into external and internal factors:

- **External factors** – factors outside the education system, such as home and family background and wider society.
- **Internal factors** – factors within schools and the education system, such as the effect of schools' equal opportunities policies.

External factors and gender differences in achievement

Many sociologists argue that gender differences in achievement, and especially the more rapid improvement in girls' results, can best be explained by changes that have occurred in factors outside the school, such as the following:

1 The impact of feminism

2 Changes in the family

3 Changes in women's employment

4 Girls' changing perceptions and ambitions

1 The impact of feminism

Feminism is a social movement that strives for equal rights for women in all areas of life. Since the 1960s, the feminist movement has challenged the traditional stereotype of a woman's role as solely that of mother and housewife, subordinate to her breadwinner husband in a patriarchal nuclear family and inferior to men outside the home, in work, education and the law.

Although feminists argue that we have not yet achieved full equality between the sexes, the feminist movement has had considerable success in improving women's rights and opportunities through changes in the law. More broadly, feminism has raised women's expectations and self-esteem.

These changes are partly reflected in media images and messages. A good illustration of this comes from Angela McRobbie's (1994) comparison

Do magazines influence girls' attitudes and expectations?

of girls' magazines in the 1970s and the 1990s. In the 1970s, girls' magazines like *Jackie* emphasised the importance of getting married and not being 'left on the shelf', whereas nowadays, they contain images of assertive, independent women. Similarly, current affairs programmes and soap operas now highlight the importance of self-esteem and personal choice for young women.

As we shall see, the changes encouraged by feminism may affect girls' self-image and ambitions with regard to the family and careers. In turn, this may explain improvements in their educational achievement.

activity

Carry out an analysis of girls' magazines. Get a range of magazines and analyse them to find any evidence (a) supporting and (b) contradicting McRobbie's views. Are there any differences between the magazines?

2 Changes in the family

There have been major changes in the family since the 1970s. These include:

- an increase in the divorce rate
- an increase in cohabitation and a decrease in the number of first marriages
- an increase in the number of lone-parent families (mainly female-headed)
- smaller families.

These changes are affecting girls' attitudes towards education in a number of ways. For example, increased numbers of female-headed lone-parent families may mean more women need to take on a breadwinner role. This in turn creates a new adult role model for girls – the financially independent woman. To achieve this independence, of course, women need well-paid jobs and therefore good qualifications. Likewise, increases in the divorce rate may suggest to girls that it is unwise to rely on a husband to be their provider. Again, this may encourage girls to look to themselves and their own qualifications to make a living.

3 Changes in women's employment

There have been a number of important changes in women's employment in recent decades. These include the following:

- The 1970 Equal Pay Act makes it illegal to pay women less than men for work of equal value, and the 1975 Sex Discrimination Act outlaws sex discrimination in employment.
- The proportion of women in employment has risen from 47% in 1959 to 70% in 2003. The growth of service sector and flexible part-time work has offered opportunities for women, while traditional 'men's' jobs have declined.
- Since 1975, the pay gap between men and women has fallen from 30% to 18%.
- Some women are now breaking through the 'glass ceiling' – the invisible barrier that keeps them out of high-level professional and managerial jobs.

These changes are likely to encourage girls to see their future in terms of paid work rather than as full-time housewives. Greater career opportunities for women, and the role models that successful career women offer, provide an incentive for girls to gain qualifications.

4 Girls' changing perceptions and ambitions

What policies might encourage more girls to pursue a career in construction?

The view that changes in the family and employment are producing changes in girls' ambitions is supported by evidence from sociological research. For example, Sue Sharpe (1994) compared the results of interviews she conducted with girls in the 1970s and 1990s. Her findings show a major shift in the way girls see themselves and their future.

In 1974, the girls Sharpe interviewed had low aspirations; they felt educational success was unfeminine and believed that if they appeared to be ambitious and intelligent they would be considered unattractive. They gave their priorities as 'love, marriage, husbands, children, jobs and careers, more or less in that order'.

By the 1990s, girls' ambitions had changed and they had a different order of priorities – jobs, careers and being able to support themselves. Girls are now more likely to see their future as an independent woman with a career rather than as dependent on their husband and his income. Clearly, this ambition requires educational qualifications, whereas those of the 1970s girls did not.

Internal factors and gender differences in achievement

While factors outside school may play an important part in explaining gender differences in educational achievement, factors within the education system itself are also important. These include:

1. Equal opportunities policies
2. Positive role models in schools
3. GCSE and coursework
4. Challenging stereotypes in the curriculum
5. Teacher attention and classroom interaction
6. Selection and league tables

1 Equal opportunities policies

Many sociologists argue that feminist ideas have had a major impact on the education system. Those who run the system are now much more aware of gender issues and teachers are more sensitive to the need to avoid gender stereotyping. The belief that boys and girls are equally capable and entitled to the same opportunities is now part of mainstream thinking in education and it influences educational policies.

For example, policies such as GIST (Girls into Science and Technology) and WISE (Women into Science and Engineering) aim to encourage girls to pursue careers in these non-traditional areas. Female scientists have visited schools, acting as role models; efforts have been made to raise science teachers' awareness of gender issues; non-sexist careers information and advice has been provided and learning materials in science have been developed that reflect girls' interests.

Similarly, the introduction of the National Curriculum in 1988 removed one source of gender inequality by making girls and boys study mostly the same things, which was often not the case before its introduction. Alison Kelly (1987) argues that making science part of the compulsory core curriculum for all pupils helps to equalise opportunities.

Jo Boaler (1998) sees the impact of equal

opportunities policies as a key reason for the changes in girls' achievement. Many of the barriers have been removed and schooling has become more meritocratic (based on equal opportunities) – so that girls, who generally work harder than boys, achieve more.

2 Positive role models in schools

As Table 3B shows, in recent years there has been an increase in the proportion of female heads, deputy heads and classroom teachers. Similarly, the proportion of new recruits to secondary teaching who are female rose from 57% to 64% between 1997 and 2002. These women in positions of authority and seniority may act as role models for girls, showing them women can achieve positions of importance and giving them non-traditional goals to aim for.

Women teachers are likely to be particularly important role models as far as girls' educational achievement is concerned, since to become a teacher, the individual must undertake a lengthy and successful education herself. It could be argued that primary schools in particular have become 'feminised', with a virtually all-female staff. This may have an impact on how far each gender sees schooling as part of their 'gender domain' or territory (see page 126).

Table 3B: Teachers in maintained schools who are women, by grade

England & Wales	Nursery/primary		Secondary	Percentages
	1990	1999	1990	1999
Heads	49	58	20	28
Deputy heads	65	73	34	36
Classroom teachers	88	88	49	55
All teachers	81	83	48	53

Source: DfES

questions

1 Approximately how many times more male than female secondary head teachers were there in 1999?

2 Suggest reasons why there is a bigger proportion of (a) female classroom teachers and (b) female heads and deputy heads in primary schools than in secondary schools.

3 GCSE and coursework

The introduction of GCSE in 1988 brought with it coursework as a new form of assessment. Patricia Murphy and Jannette Elwood (1998) argue that this change has benefited girls more than boys because coursework rewards girls' aptitude for organisation and sustained application.

Eirene Mitsos and Ken Browne (1998) support this view. They conclude that girls are more successful in coursework because they are more conscientious and better organised than boys. Girls:

- spend more time on their work
- take more care with the way it is presented
- are better at meeting deadlines
- bring the right equipment and materials to lessons.

Mitsos and Browne argue that these factors have helped girls to benefit from the introduction of coursework in GCSE, AS/A level and VCE. They also note that girls gain from maturing earlier than boys and from their ability to concentrate for longer.

Along with GCSE has come the greater use of oral exams. This is also said to benefit girls because of their generally better developed language skills.

Sociologists argue that these characteristics and skills are the result of early gender role socialisation in the family. For example, girls are more likely than boys to be encouraged to be neat, tidy and patient. These qualities become an advantage in today's assessment system, helping girls achieve greater success than boys. The New Right thinker, Madsen Pirie, makes a similar point (see page 130, Item B).

activity

As a group, design and carry out a survey on gender differences in how conscientious and organised students are, and differences in their attitudes to coursework. Ask about time spent on homework, meeting deadlines, how much revision they did for GCSE, whether they prefer coursework or exams etc. Do your results support Mitsos and Browne's views?

4 Challenging stereotypes in the curriculum

Some sociologists argue that the removal of gender stereotypes from textbooks, reading schemes and other learning materials in recent years has removed a barrier to girls' achievement. Research in the 1980s found that reading schemes portrayed women mainly as housewives and mothers, that physics books showed them as frightened or amazed by science, and that maths books depicted boys as more inventive than girls.

Gaby Weiner (1995) argues that since the 1980s, teachers have challenged such stereotypes. Also, in general, sexist images have been removed from learning materials. This may have helped to raise girls' achievement by presenting them with more positive images of what women can do.

5 Teacher attention and classroom interaction

The way teachers interact with boys and girls differs. Dale Spender (1983) found that teachers spend more time interacting with boys than with girls. However, when Jane and Peter French (1993) analysed classroom interaction, they found that the amount of attention teachers paid to boys and girls for academic reasons was similar. Boys only received more attention because they attracted more reprimands.

Similarly, Joan Swann and David Graddol (1994) found that boys are generally more boisterous and attract the teacher's gaze more often than girls, and so get more opportunity to speak. However, they found that the way teachers interacted with girls was more positive because it focused on schoolwork rather than behaviour.

Swann (1998) also found gender differences in communication styles. Boys dominate in whole-class discussion, whereas girls prefer pair-work and group-work and are better at listening and cooperating. When working in groups, girls' speech involves turn-taking, and not the hostile interruptions that often characterise boys' speech.

This may explain why teachers respond more positively to girls, whom they see as cooperative, than to boys, whom they see as potentially disruptive. This may lead to a self-fulfilling prophecy in which successful interactions with teachers promote girls' self-esteem and raise their achievement levels.

6 Selection and league tables

Marketisation (see Box 13, page 97) has created a more competitive climate in which schools see girls as desirable recruits because they achieve better exam results.

David Jackson (1998) notes that the introduction of exam league tables, which place a high value on academic achievement, has improved opportunities for girls: high-achieving girls are attractive to schools whereas low-achieving boys are not. This tends to create a self-fulfilling prophecy: because girls are more likely to be recruited by schools with a good academic record, they are more likely to get good results.

Roger Slee (1998) argues that boys are less attractive to schools because they are more likely to suffer from behavioural difficulties and are four times more likely to be excluded. As a result, they may be seen as 'liability students' – obstacles to the school improving its league table scores. They give the school a 'rough, tough' image that deters high-achieving girls from applying.

activity

Investigate what steps your school or college has taken to encourage girls or boys to take non-traditional subjects and courses. What further steps could be taken?

Two views of girls' achievement

While there have clearly been changes in gender and educational achievement, sociologists differ in their interpretation of the importance of these changes.

liberal feminists

Liberal feminists celebrate the progress made so far in improving achievement. They believe that further progress will be made by the continuing development of equal opportunities policies, encouraging positive role models and overcoming sexist attitudes and stereotypes. This is similar to the functionalist view that education is a meritocracy where all individuals, regardless of gender, ethnicity or class, are given an equal opportunity to achieve (see page 133).

radical feminists

Radical feminists take a more critical view. While they recognise that girls are achieving more, they emphasise that the system remains patriarchal (male-dominated) and conveys the clear message that it is still a man's world. For example:

- Sexual harassment of girls continues at school.
- Education still limits their subject choices and career options (see page 125).
- Although there are now more female head teachers, male teachers are still more likely to become heads.
- Women are under-represented in many areas of the curriculum. For example, their contribution to history is largely ignored. Weiner (1993) describes the secondary school history curriculum as a woman-free zone.

Boys and achievement

We have focused so far on the thing that appears to have changed most – girls' performance. Recently, the gender gap in achievement has given rise to concern about boys falling behind and several possible reasons for this have been suggested:

- 'Laddish' subcultures – boys gain peer group status from being anti-school.
- Parents spend less time with sons on reading; mothers do most of the reading to young children, who come to see it as a feminine activity.
- Some boys see education as feminine.
- Boys have more behavioural problems, are more likely to be disruptive in class and more likely to be excluded.
- Boys' over-confidence in their abilities means they prepare less thoroughly for exams.
- The decline of traditional 'men's' jobs leads some boys to believe they have limited prospects and so they give up trying to get qualifications.

question

Suggest two reasons why boys are more likely to be seen as disruptive in school.

Some of these explanations are illustrated in Debbie Epstein's (1998) study of how masculinity is constructed within school. She found that working-class boys are likely to be harassed, labelled as sissies and subjected to homophobic (anti-gay) verbal abuse if they appear to be 'swots'.

This is because in working-class culture, masculinity is equated with being tough and doing manual work. Non-manual work, and by extension schoolwork, is seen as effeminate and inferior. As a result, working-class boys tend to reject schoolwork to avoid being called 'gay'. As Epstein observes, 'real boys don't work' – and if they do they get bullied. She notes that:

> *'The main demand on boys within their peer group, but also sometimes from teachers, is to appear to do little or no work, to be heavily competitive at sports and hetero-sex, to be rough, tough and dangerous to know.'*

Epstein's findings on working-class masculinity and schooling parallel those of Willis and Mac an Ghaill (see pages 141 and 146).

However, it would be wrong to conclude that boys are a 'lost cause'. In fact, as Figure 3.4 (page 119) shows, the performance of both sexes has actually improved in recent years. As Tracey McVeigh (2001) notes, the similarities in girls' and boys' achievement are far greater than the differences.

On the other hand, there are important class and ethnic differences *within* each gender. This is because pupils define their gender differently according to their class and ethnicity. For example, as Fuller shows, many black girls are successful at school because they define their femininity in terms of educational achievement and independence. Conversely, Sewell shows that some black boys fail at school because they define their masculinity in opposition to education, which they see as effeminate.

This shows that we need to take the interplay of class, gender and ethnicity into account in order to understand differences in educational achievement.

synoptic links: deviance and stratification

As males are generally seen as more criminally inclined than females, a moral panic about male under-achievement has been fuelled by the fear that unqualified, unskilled, unemployable working-class and/or black males are a breeding ground for crime and disorder.

The New Right sees this male under-achievement as perpetuating the existence of a welfare-dependent underclass.

Subject choice and gender identity

In the previous section we looked at how sociologists have explained the growing gender gap in achievement. In this section we examine two closely related issues.

Firstly, despite the improvement in girls' achievement relative to boys', there continues to be a fairly traditional pattern of 'boys' subjects' and 'girls' subjects'. Boys still tend to opt for subjects such as maths and physics, while girls are more likely to choose modern languages, for example.

Ninety-four per cent of all hairdressing apprentices are girls.

Secondly, schooling reinforces gender identity in various ways, both through the curriculum and in the interactions between teachers and pupils and among pupils themselves.

Subject choice

The introduction of the National Curriculum reduced pupils' freedom to choose or drop subjects by making most subjects compulsory until 16. However, where choice is possible, both in the National Curriculum and much more so after 16, boys and girls tend to follow different gender routes through the education system and there are some clear gender differences in subject choices. This is shown in National Curriculum options, AS and A levels, and vocational courses.

National Curriculum options

Andrew Stables and Felicity Wikeley (1996) found that where there is a choice in the National Curriculum, girls and boys choose differently. For example, although design and technology is a compulsory subject, girls tend to choose the food technology option whereas boys choose graphics and resistant materials.

AS and A levels

Gendered subject choices become more noticeable after the National Curriculum, when students have greater freedom of choice. For example, there are big gender differences in entries for different A level subjects (see table 3C), with boys opting for maths and physics and girls choosing literature, languages and social studies (about three quarters of AS and A level sociology students are female). These differences are also mirrored in subject choice at university level.

vocational courses

Vocational courses prepare students for particular careers. Evidence shows a similar but more exaggerated pattern to that for A levels. As Table 3D shows, gender segregation is a very noticeable feature of vocational training. For example, almost 19 out of 20 hairdressing apprentices are female, while only one in 100 construction apprentices is a girl.

Table 3C: GCE A level entries by gender, UK, 2002

	Percentages	
	Males	Females
Home economics	5	95
Modern languages	31	69
Art and design	31	69
Biological sciences	37	63
History	47	53
Mathematics	60	40
Physical education	62	38
Economics	69	31
Computer studies	74	26
Physics	76	24
All entries	46	54

Source: DfES; NAfW; SE; NIDfE

Table 3D: Advanced Modern Apprenticeships by gender, England, 2001

	Percentages	
	Males	Females
Hairdressing	6	94
Health and social care	10	90
Business administration	20	80
Retailing	38	62
Hospitality	50	50
Information technology	79	21
Engineering manufacturing	97	3
Motor industry	98	2
Electrical engineering	99	1
Construction	99	1
All	62	38

Source: DfES

Explanations of gender differences in subject choice

Why do boys and girls tend to choose different subjects? Sociologists have put forward a number of explanations:

1 Early socialisation and gender domains
2 Gendered subject images
3 Peer pressure
4 Gendered career opportunities

1 Early socialisation and gender domains

According to Ann Oakley (1973), sex refers to inborn physical differences between males and females, whereas gender refers to the learned cultural differences between them. Gender role socialisation is the process of learning the behaviour expected of males and females in society.

Early socialisation shapes children's gender identity. As Fiona Norman (1988) notes, from an early age, boys and girls are dressed differently, given different toys and encouraged to take part in different activities. Parents tend to reward boys for being active and girls for being passive.

Schools also play an important part. Eileen Byrne (1979) shows that teachers encourage boys to be tough and show initiative and not be weak or behave like sissies. Girls on the other hand are expected to be quiet, helpful, clean and tidy, not rough or noisy.

As a result of differences in socialisation, boys and girls develop different tastes in reading. Murphy and Elwood (1998) show how these lead to different subject choices. Boys read hobby books and information texts, while girls are more likely to read stories about people. This helps to explain why boys prefer science subjects and why girls prefer subjects such as English.

Naima Browne and Carol Ross (1991) argue that children's beliefs about 'gender domains' are shaped by their early experiences and the expectations of adults. By gender domains, they mean the tasks and activities that boys and girls see as male or female 'territory' and therefore as relevant to themselves. For example, mending a car is seen as falling within the male gender domain but looking after a sick child is not.

question

Suggest two reasons why so few females choose construction courses.

Children are more confident when engaging in tasks that they see as part of their own gender domain. For example, when they are set the same mathematical task, girls are more confident in tackling it when it is presented as being about food and nutrition, whereas boys are more confident if it is about cars.

Sex-typing of jobs influences boys' and girls' choice of vocational courses.

Boys and girls also interpret tasks differently. Patricia Murphy (1991) set primary and lower secondary pupils open-ended tasks where they were asked to design boats and vehicles and to write estate agents' adverts for a house.

- Boys designed powerboats and battleships with elaborate weaponry and little living accommodation, whereas girls designed cruise ships, paying attention to social and domestic details.
- Boys designed sports cars and army vehicles, whereas girls designed family cars.
- When writing an estate agent's advert, boys focused on 'masculine' spheres such as garage space, whereas girls focused on 'feminine' ones such as décor and kitchen design.

This study shows that boys and girls pay attention to different details even when tackling the same task. In general, girls focus more on how people feel, whereas boys focus on how things are made and work. This in turn helps to explain why girls choose humanities and arts subjects, while boys choose science.

question

Suggest six interests or activities that are seen as part of the masculine gender domain and six that are seen as part of the feminine gender domain.

2 Gendered subject images

The gender image that a subject 'gives off' affects who will want to choose it. Sociologists have tried to explain why some subjects are seen as boys' or girls' subjects in the first place. For example, Kelly argues that science is seen as a boys' subject for several reasons:

- Science teachers are more likely to be men.
- The examples that teachers use, and those found in textbooks, have often drawn on boys' rather than girls' interests and experiences.
- In science lessons, boys monopolise the apparatus and dominate the laboratory, acting as if it is 'theirs'.

Similarly, Anne Colley (1998) notes that computer studies is seen as a masculine subject for two reasons:

- It involves working with machines – part of the male gender domain.
- The way it is taught is off-putting to females. Tasks tend to be abstract and teaching styles formal, with few opportunities for group work which, as we saw earlier, girls tend to favour.

3 Peer pressure

Subject choice can be influenced by peer pressure. Other boys and girls may apply pressure to an individual if they disapprove of his or her choice. For example, boys tend to opt out of music and dance because such activities fall outside their gender domain and so are likely to attract a negative response from peers.

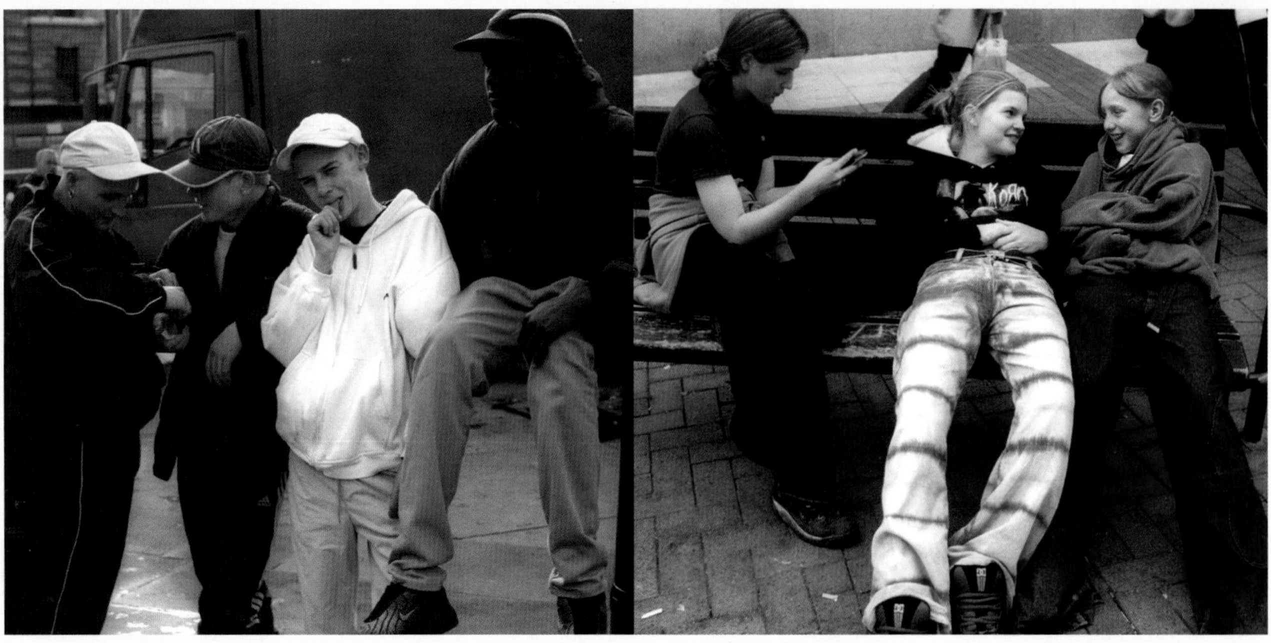

How do peer groups reinforce gender identity?

Carrie Paetcher (1998) found that as sport is seen as mainly within the male gender domain, girls who are 'sporty' have to cope with an image that contradicts the conventional female stereotype. This explains why girls are more likely than boys to opt out of sport.

Similarly, a study of American college students by Alison Dewar (1990) found that male students would call girls 'lesbian' or 'butch' if they appeared to be more interested in sport than in boys.

By contrast, an absence of peer pressure from the opposite sex may explain why girls in single-sex schools are more likely to choose traditional 'boys'' subjects. The absence of boys may mean there is less pressure on the girls to conform to restrictive stereotypes of what subjects they can or cannot study.

4 Gendered career opportunities

An important reason for differences in subject choice is the fact that work is highly gendered: jobs tend to be sex-typed as 'men's' or 'women's'. Women's jobs often involve work similar to that performed by housewives, such as childcare and nursing. Women are concentrated in a narrow range of occupations. Over half of all women's employment falls within four categories: clerical, secretarial, personal services and 'other elementary' occupations, such as cleaning. By contrast, only a sixth of male workers work in these jobs.

This sex-typing of occupations affects boys' and girls' ideas about what kinds of job are possible or acceptable. Thus for example, if boys get the message that nursery nurses are women, they will be less likely to opt for a career in childcare. In turn, this affects what subjects and courses they will choose.

This also helps to explain why vocational courses are much more gender-specific than academic courses, since vocational studies are by definition more closely linked to students' career plans.

Gender identity

We have seen how early socialisation into a gender identity strongly influences children's subject preferences. Here we examine how pupils' experiences in school reinforce their gender and sexual identities. These experiences include:

1 verbal abuse

2 the male gaze

3 teachers and discipline

4 double standards

1 Verbal abuse

Verbal abuse is one of the ways in which dominant gender and sexual identities are reinforced. For example, boys use name-calling to put girls down if they behave or dress in certain ways. Sue Lees

(1986) found that boys called girls 'slags' if they appeared to be sexually available – and 'drags' when they didn't.

Similarly, Paetcher sees name-calling as helping to shape gender identity and maintain male power. The use of negative labels such as 'gay', 'queer' and 'lezzie' are ways in which pupils 'police' each other's sexual identities. For example, Andrew Parker (1996) found that boys were labelled 'gay' simply for being friendly with girls or female teachers. Both Lees and Paetcher note that these labels often bear no relation to pupils' actual sexual behaviour. Their function is simply to reinforce gender norms.

Similarly, male peer groups use verbal abuse to reinforce their definitions of masculinity. For example, as studies by Epstein, Willis and Mac an Ghaill show, boys in anti-school subcultures often accuse boys who want to do well of being gay or effeminate (see pages 124, 141 and 146).

2 The male gaze

There is also a visual aspect to the way pupils control each other's identities. Mac an Ghaill refers to this as the 'male gaze': the way male pupils and teachers look girls up and down, seeing them as sexual objects and making judgements about their appearance.

Mac an Ghaill sees this as a form of surveillance through which dominant heterosexual masculinity is reinforced and femininity devalued. It is one of the ways boys prove their masculinity to their friends and is often combined with constant telling and retelling of stories about sexual conquests. Boys who do not display their heterosexuality in this way run the risk of being labelled gay.

3 Teachers and discipline

Research shows that teachers also play a part in reinforcing dominant definitions of gender identity. Chris Haywood and Mairtin Mac an Ghaill (1996) found that male teachers told boys off for 'behaving like girls' and teased them when they gained lower marks in tests than girls. Teachers tended to ignore boys' verbal abuse of girls and even blamed girls for attracting it.

Sue Askew and Carol Ross (1988) show how male teachers' behaviour can subtly reinforce messages about gender. For example, male teachers often have a protective attitude towards female colleagues, coming into their classes to 'rescue' them by threatening pupils who are being disruptive. However, this reinforces the idea that women cannot cope alone.

4 Double standards

A double standard exists when we apply one set of moral standards to one group but a different set to another group. In the case of gender identity, Sue Lees (1993) identifies a double standard of sexual morality in which boys boast about their own sexual exploits but call a girl a 'slag' if she doesn't have a steady boyfriend or if she dresses and speaks in a certain way. Sexual conquest is approved of and given status by male peers and ignored by male teachers, but 'promiscuity' among girls attracts negative labels. Feminists see double standards as an example of a patriarchal ideology that justifies male power and devalues women.

synoptic links: deviance and stratification

Verbal abuse, the male gaze, school discipline and double standards can all be seen as forms of social control to prevent individuals deviating from their allotted roles.

They also act to reinforce gender stratification by keeping females in subordinate positions to males.

activity

Working alone or in pairs, review the section on Gender differences in education (pages 118 – 29) and decide:

1 Which of the factors you have read about contribute to the continuation of patriarchy (male dominance) in society?

2 Which factors are leading to greater gender equality in society?

QuickCheck Questions

1 True or false? At GCSE, AS and A level, girls do better overall, but boys do better in maths.

2 Identify two changes in wider society that may have contributed to girls' improved achievement.

3 Suggest two possible reasons for boys' lower achievement levels.

4 True or false? Gender differences in subject choices are more noticeable on vocational courses than on academic courses.

5 Suggest two reasons why science is seen as a 'boys'' subject.

6 Suggest one way in which male teachers may reinforce pupils' gender identities.

Answers are on page 272.

Examining Gender and education

Item A The lack of men choosing childcare as a career is the subject of a study by the Daycare Trust, the national childcare charity. Despite widespread recognition that good male role models are important in a child's early years, the report says that fewer than one in 100 nursery assistants are men, while only 3% of nursery teachers and classroom assistants and 1.5% of playgroup leaders are men.

The report says that many men are wary of being seen to undertake work with young children and this is reflected in the fact that very few males are to be found training for this area. In many further education colleges, for example, it is rare to find even one male student studying traditional 'sex-typed' subjects like childcare. The related 'caring' field of health and social care is almost as bad, with males outnumbered by over 15 to 1 among students gaining an Advanced certificate in this subject. These patterns may reflect the different gender domains into which boys and girls are socialised and the ways in which different features of school life help to shape their gender identities.

Item B According to Madsen Pirie of the New Right Adam Smith Institute, the modular courses and continuous assessment found in education today favour the systematic approach of girls as against the risk-taking approach of boys. He argues that the old O level (replaced by GCSE in 1988), 'with its high risk, swot it all up for the final throw… was a boys' exam'. By contrast, GCSE, AS and A levels – which emphasise preparation and modules that can be worked on over time – favour what Pirie calls the 'more systematic, consistent, attention-to-detail qualities' of girls. In his view, it is the examination system, not laddish anti-school subcultures, that explain why girls have now overtaken boys.

Examining Gender and education

Short questions

(a) Explain what is meant by 'gender domains' (**Item A,** line 12). (2 marks)

(b) Identify **two** policies that may have helped reduce the likelihood of boys and girls only 'studying traditional "sex-typed" subjects' (**Item A,** line 9). (4 marks)

(c) Suggest **three** ways in which features of school life may help to shape pupils' gender identities (**Item A,** line 13). (6 marks)

(d) Identify and briefly explain **two** reasons why so few males study for a qualification in childcare (**Item A**). (8 marks)

Mini-essay

Using material from **Item B** and elsewhere, assess the view that gender differences in achievement are largely the result of changes in the types of courses and assessment found in the education system. (20 marks)

This is a type (f) question of the kind found in the exam, carrying 6 AO1 marks (knowledge and understanding) and 14 AO2 marks (identification, interpretation, analysis and evaluation).

The Examiner's advice

For the mini-essay, briefly describe achievement differences and use the Items to identify the 'types of courses and assessment'. You need to evaluate – that is, weigh up how true the view in the question actually is. You will need to consider arguments and evidence for (e.g. Mitsos and Browne on coursework) and against (e.g. changes in the family, employment, girls' aspirations, equal opportunities policies etc). You could also consider the following: trends in girls' achievement before GCSEs were brought in in 1988 (do they support Pirie's claim?); the role of 'laddish subcultures' mentioned in the Item; why are boys doing better at GCSE than they did at the old O level?

The role of education in society

When studying the role of education in society, sociologists are interested in questions such as:

- How far does education provide all individuals with equal opportunities for achievement?
- How far does education recreate existing social inequalities?
- In what ways does education serve the needs of the economy?
- What kinds of knowledge, skills, attitudes and values does education transmit?

Does education recreate existing social inequalities?

As we shall see, sociologists hold different and conflicting views on these questions. Often, this is because they have different sociological perspectives or viewpoints that see society differently. In this section of the chapter, we shall examine the following perspectives on the role of education in society:

- **Functionalism** – a consensus approach
- **The New Right** – a conservative approach
- **Marxism** – a class conflict approach
- **Postmodernism** – a diversity approach
- **Critical modernism** – a diversity-with-conflict approach.

The functionalist perspective on the role of education

Functionalism is based on the view that society is a system of interdependent parts held together by a shared culture or value consensus – an agreement among society's members about what values are important. Each part of society, such as the family, economy or education system, performs functions that help to maintain society as a whole. This is rather like the way each of our different organs has specific tasks to perform to maintain the body as a whole. When studying education, functionalists seek to discover what functions it performs – that is, what does it do to help meet society's needs?

Durkheim: solidarity and skills

The French sociologist Emile Durkheim (1903), the founder of functionalist sociology, identified two main functions of education:

- creating social solidarity
- teaching specialist skills.

Social solidarity

Durkheim argues that society needs a sense of solidarity; that is, its individual members must feel themselves to be part of a single 'body' or community. He argues that without social solidarity, social life and cooperation would be impossible because each individual would pursue their own selfish desires.

The education system helps to create social solidarity by transmitting society's culture – its shared beliefs and values – from one generation to the next. For example, Durkheim argues that the teaching of a country's history instils in children a sense of a shared heritage and a commitment to the wider social group.

School also acts as a 'society in miniature', preparing us for life in wider society. For example, both in school and at work we have to cooperate with people who are neither family nor friends – teachers and pupils at school, colleagues and customers at work. Similarly, both in school and at work we have to interact with others according to a set of impersonal rules that apply to everyone.

synoptic link: deviance

Functionalists see education as helping to reduce deviance and promote conformity by instilling into each individual the same shared norms and values and a sense of belonging to wider society.

Specialist skills

Modern industrial economies have a complex division of labour, where the production of even a single item usually involves the cooperation of many different specialists. This cooperation promotes social solidarity but for it to be successful, each person must have the necessary specialist knowledge and skills to perform their role.

Durkheim argues that education teaches individuals the specialist knowledge and skills that they need to play their part in the social division of labour.

Parsons: meritocracy

The American functionalist Talcott Parsons (1961) draws on many of Durkheim's ideas. Parsons sees the school as the 'focal socialising agency' in modern society, acting as a bridge between the family and wider society. This bridge is needed because family and society operate on different principles, so children need to learn a new way of living if they are to cope with the wider world.

Within the family, the child is judged by *particularistic* standards; that is, rules that apply only to that particular child. Similarly, in the family, the child's status is *ascribed*; that is, fixed by birth. For example, an elder son and a younger daughter may be given different rights or duties because of differences of age and sex.

By contrast, both school and wider society judge us all by the same *universalistic* and impersonal standards. For example, in society, the same laws apply to everyone. Similarly, in school each pupil is judged against the same standards (e.g. they all sit the same exam and the pass mark is the same for everyone).

Likewise, in both school and wider society, a person's status is largely *achieved*, not ascribed. For example, at work we gain promotion or get the sack on the strength of how good we are at our job, while at school we pass or fail through our own individual efforts.

Parsons sees school as preparing us to move from the family to wider society because school and society are both based on meritocratic principles. In a meritocracy, everyone is given an equal opportunity, and individuals achieve rewards through their own effort and ability.

activity

The education system has some meritocratic features, such as equal opportunities policies for gender, and comprehensive schooling. However, critics argue that education is not meritocratic. From your knowledge of educational achievement and class, gender and ethnicity, list some of the evidence in support of the critics' view.

Davis and Moore: role allocation

Do high achievers get there purely on merit?

Parsons argues that schools also perform a second function: that of selecting and allocating pupils to their future work roles. By assessing individuals' aptitudes and abilities, schools help to match them to the job they are best suited to.

Like Parsons, Kingsley Davis and Wilbert Moore (1945) also see education as a device for selection and role allocation, but they focus on the relationship between education and social inequality.

They argue that inequality is necessary to ensure that the most important roles in society are filled by the most talented people. For example, it would be inefficient and dangerous to have less able people performing roles such as surgeon or airline pilot. Not everyone is equally talented, so society has to offer higher rewards for these jobs. This will encourage everyone to compete for them and society can then select the most talented individuals to fill these positions.

synoptic link: stratification

Functionalists see a meritocratic education system as vital to a meritocratic or 'open' stratification system, since it ensures that people's social status and rewards are based on their own achievements (as measured by their qualifications), and not on ascribed characteristics such as their class, gender or ethnic background.

Education plays a key part in this process, since it acts as a proving ground for ability. Put simply, education is where individuals show what they can do. It 'sifts and sorts' us according to our ability. The most able gain the highest qualifications, which then give them entry to the most important and highly rewarded positions.

Similarly, Peter Blau and Otis Duncan (1978) argue that a modern economy depends for its prosperity on using its 'human capital' – its workers' skills. They argue that a meritocratic education system does this best, since it enables each person to be allocated to the job best suited to their abilities. This will make most effective use of their talents and maximise their productivity.

questions

1. Name three functions that functionalists see education as performing.
2. In what ways can school be seen as a 'society in miniature'?
3. In your own words, explain why a meritocratic education system might enable society to make best use of people's talents.

Evaluation of the functionalist perspective

- As we have seen, there is evidence that equal opportunity in education does not exist. For example, achievement is greatly influenced by characteristics such as class background.

- Melvin Tumin (1953) criticises Davis and Moore for putting forward a circular argument, as follows: How do we know that a job is important? Answer: because it's highly rewarded. Why are some jobs more highly rewarded than others? Answer: because they are more important!
- Functionalists see education as a process that instils the shared values of society as a whole, but Marxists argue that education in capitalist society only transmits the ideology of a minority – the ruling class.
- The interactionist Dennis Wrong (1961) argues that functionalists have an 'over-socialised view' of people as mere puppets of society. Functionalists wrongly imply that pupils passively accept all they are taught and never reject the school's values.
- Unlike Davis and Moore, the New Right argue that the state education system fails to prepare young people adequately for work. This is because state control of education discourages efficiency, competition and choice.

activity

Complete the following criticisms of the functionalist perspective. If you get stuck, choose the right word from the missing words list.

1. Other perspectives, such as Marxism, believe that education only passes on the ideology of the ______.
2. Interactionists criticise functionalists for their __________ view of pupils that sees them as passively accepting all they are taught.
3. We do not have a meritocracy as functionalists suggest. For example, _____ and ____ are not the only factors that determine achievement.
4. Some sociologists argue that the ______ and ______ taught in school are not particularly useful for life at work.

Missing words

knowledge	skills	ruling class
ability	effort	over-socialised

The New Right perspective on the role of education

The New Right is a conservative political perspective. However, its ideas have influenced the policies of Labour as well as Conservative governments (see Boxes 15 and 17). A central principle of New Right thinking is the belief that the state cannot meet people's needs and that people are best left to meet their own needs through the free market. For this reason, the New Right favour the marketisation of education (see Box 13 on page 97).

The New Right are similar in many ways to functionalists:

- They believe that some people are naturally more talented than others.
- They broadly accept the desirability of an education system run on meritocratic principles of open competition and serving the needs of the economy by preparing young people for their future work roles.
- They believe that education should socialise pupils into shared values, such as competition, and instil a sense of national identity.

However, a key difference with functionalism is that the New Right do not believe that the current education system is achieving these goals. The reason for its failure, in their view, is that it is run by the state.

The New Right argue that in all state education systems, politicians and educational bureaucrats use the power of the state to impose their view of what kind of schools we should have. The state tends to take a 'one size fits all' approach, imposing uniformity and disregarding local needs. The local consumers who use the schools – pupils, parents and employers – have no say. State education systems are therefore unresponsive and breed inefficiency. Schools that waste money or get poor results are not answerable to their consumers. This means lower standards of achievement for pupils, a less qualified workforce and a less prosperous economy.

Box 15: Conservative education policy: widening choice

Speaking at the 2002 Conservative Party Conference, Damian Green MP, Shadow Secretary of State for Education, said:

'My vision is that excellent schools and colleges will flourish if, and only if, we trust them to take their own decisions. Heads and teachers know more than any Minister about what the children in their school really need. Parents deserve more of a say about where their child goes to school. Those are our principles. And here are some policies to make those principles real, and to create a better society. We would:

- Give head teachers more power over discipline in the classroom.
- Allow head teachers to make parents sign a contract guaranteeing their child's good behaviour.
- Allow head teachers to decide how to spend their money.
- Make it easier for good schools to expand, and make it possible for new schools to start up.
- Introduce state scholarships, starting in our most deprived areas, which will allow parents and other groups to set up new schools, funded by the state, but run by independent bodies.

'This will be a revolution in our school system. The sort of choice in schools now enjoyed only by the well-off will be spread to many more families. We want to give people the chance to choose the school they really want for their children. That's the way to give every child a fair start in life: give power to the parents, not the politicians.'

question

Critics argue that in fact those in deprived areas are unlikely to benefit from such policies. Suggest reasons why the well-off might benefit more from the policy of 'making it easier for good schools to expand'.

The New Right's solution to these problems is the marketisation of education. They believe that competition and the laws of supply and demand will empower the consumers, bringing greater diversity, choice and efficiency to schools and increasing their ability to meet the needs of pupils, parents and employers.

Chubb and Moe: consumer choice

A good example of the New Right perspective on education comes from the work of the Americans, John Chubb and Terry Moe (1990). They argue that American state education has failed and they make the case for opening it up to market forces of supply and demand. They make a number of claims:

- Disadvantaged groups – the lower classes, ethnic and religious minorities and rural communities – have been badly served by state education. State education has failed to create equal opportunity.
- State education is inefficient because it fails to produce pupils with the skills needed by the economy.
- Private schools deliver higher quality education because unlike state schools, they are answerable to paying consumers – the parents.

Chubb and Moe base their arguments on a comparison of the achievements of 60,000 pupils from low-income families in 1,015 state and private high schools, together with the findings of a parent survey and case studies of 'failing' schools apparently being 'turned around'. Their evidence shows that pupils from low-income families consistently do about 5% better in private schools.

Based on these findings, Chubb and Moe call for the introduction of a market system in state education that would put control in the hands of the consumers (parents and local communities). They argue that this would allow consumers to shape schools to meet their own needs and would improve quality and efficiency.

Most improved schools

	School	LEA
1	Sir John Cass Foundation	Tower Hamlets
2	All Saints Cath & Tech Col	Barking & Dagenham
3	Guru Nanak Sikh VA Sec	Hillingdon
4	Jaamiatul Imaam Muhammad Zakaria	Bradford
5	Turves Green Boys	Birmingham
6	Brownhills High	Stoke on Trent
7	Waverley	Birmingham
8	Archbishop Holgate	York
9	Croxteth Comm Comp	Liverpool
10	Kingsmeadow Comm Comp	Gateshead
11	Halifax High	Calderdale
12	Shipston High	Warwickshire
13	Bishop Challoner Cath	Birmingham
14	Central Foundation Boys	Islington
15	Christ's CoE Comp Sec	Richmond
16	Walker Tech Col	Newcastle
17	Oxclose Community	Sunderland
18	Ernest Bevin Col	Wandsworth
19	Bnos Yisroel Schs	Salford
20	Kingsdale Sec	Southwark

League table of the top 20 most improved schools: does marketisation bring rising standards?

To achieve this, Chubb and Moe propose an end to the system where schools automatically receive guaranteed funding from the state, regardless of how good or bad they are. Instead they propose a system in which each family would be given a voucher to spend on buying education from a school of their choice. This would force schools to become more responsive to parents' wishes, since the vouchers would be the school's main source of income. Like private businesses, schools would have to compete to attract 'customers' by improving their 'product'.

These principles are already at work in the private education sector. In Chubb and Moe's view, educational standards would be greatly improved by introducing the same market forces into the state sector.

Two roles for the state

However, while the New Right stress the importance of market forces in education, this does not mean they see no role at all for the state. In the New Right view there remain two important roles for the state.

Firstly, the state imposes a framework on schools within which they have to compete. For example, by publishing inspection reports and league tables of schools' exam results, the state gives parents information with which to make a more informed choice between schools.

Secondly, the state ensures that schools transmit a shared culture. By imposing a single National Curriculum, it seeks to guarantee that schools socialise pupils into a single cultural heritage.

The New Right believe that education should affirm the national identity. For example, the curriculum should emphasise Britain's positive role in world history and teach specifically British literature, and there should be a Christian act of worship in school each day because Christianity is Britain's main religion. The aim is to integrate pupils into a single set of traditions and cultural values. For this reason, the New Right also oppose multi-cultural education that reflects the cultures of the different ethnic minority groups in British society.

questions

1. How would the introduction of a voucher system in the state sector make the state and private sectors more similar?
2. What arguments could be made against introducing a voucher system?

Evaluation of the New Right perspective

- Gewirtz and Ball both argue that competition between schools benefits the middle class, who can use their cultural and economic capital to gain access to more desirable schools.
- Critics argue that the real cause of low educational standards is not state control but social inequality and inadequate funding of state schools.
- There is a contradiction between the New Right's support for parental choice on the one hand and the state imposing a compulsory national curriculum on all its schools on the other.
- Marxists argue that education does not impose a shared national culture, as the New Right argue, but imposes the culture of a dominant minority ruling class. It devalues the culture of the working class and ethnic minorities.

The Marxist perspective on the role of education

Where functionalists see society and education as based on value consensus, Marxists see it as based on class division and capitalist exploitation. Karl Marx (1818–83) described capitalism as a two-class system.

In capitalism, the minority class, the bourgeoisie or capitalist employers who own the means of production (land, factories, machinery etc), make their profits by exploiting the labour of the majority, the proletariat or working class. As a result, work under capitalism is alienating, unsatisfying, poorly paid and something over which workers have no real control.

This creates the potential for class conflict. For example, if workers realise that they are being exploited, they may demand higher wages, better working conditions or even the abolition of capitalism itself. Marx believed that ultimately the proletariat would unite to overthrow the capitalist system.

Althusser: ideological state apparatuses

However, capitalism is able to continue because the bourgeoisie also control the state. Marxists see the state as the means by which the capitalist ruling class maintain their dominant position. According to Louis Althusser (1971), the state consists of two elements or 'apparatuses', both of which serve to keep the bourgeoisie in power:

- The repressive state apparatuses (RSAs), which maintain the rule of the bourgeoisie by force or the threat of it. RSAs include the police, courts and army. When necessary, they use physical coercion to repress the working class.
- The ideological state apparatuses (ISAs), which maintain the rule of the bourgeoisie by controlling people's ideas, values and beliefs. ISAs include religion, the mass media and the education system.

In Althusser's view, the education system is an important ISA. He argues that it performs two functions:

- Education reproduces class inequality by transmitting it from generation to generation, by failing each successive generation of working-class pupils in turn.
- Education legitimates (justifies) class inequality by producing ideologies (sets of ideas and beliefs) that disguise its true cause. The function of ideology is to persuade workers to accept that inequality is inevitable and that they deserve their subordinate position in society. If they accept these ideas, they are less likely to challenge or threaten capitalism.

activity

In pairs, explain in your own words the following Marxist terms:

capitalism	ideology
means of production	exploitation
reproduction of class inequality	ideological state apparatus
proletariat	bourgeoisie
legitimation of class inequality	

Bowles and Gintis: schooling in capitalist America

The American Marxists Samuel Bowles and Herbert Gintis (1976) develop these ideas further. They argue that capitalism requires a workforce with the kind of attitudes, behaviour and personality-type suited to their role as alienated and exploited workers willing to accept hard work, low pay and orders from above. In the view of Bowles and Gintis, this is the role of the education system in capitalist society – to reproduce an obedient workforce that will accept inequality as inevitable.

From their own study of 237 New York high school students and the findings of other studies, Bowles and Gintis conclude that schools reward precisely the kind of personality traits that make for a submissive, compliant worker. For instance, they found that students who showed independence and creativity tended to gain low grades, while those who showed characteristics linked to obedience and discipline (such as punctuality) tended to gain high grades.

Bowles and Gintis conclude from this evidence that schooling helps to produce the obedient workers that capitalism needs. They do not believe that education fosters personal development. Rather, it stunts and distorts students' development.

The correspondence principle and the hidden curriculum

Bowles and Gintis argue that there are close parallels between schooling and work in capitalist society. Both schools and workplaces are hierarchies, with head teachers or bosses at the top making decisions and giving orders, and workers or pupils at the bottom obeying. Box 16 shows some other ways in which school mirrors the workplace. As Bowles and Gintis put it, schooling takes place in 'the long shadow of work'.

Bowles and Gintis refer to these parallels between school and workplace as examples of the 'correspondence principle'. The relationships and structures found in education mirror or correspond to those of work.

Bowles and Gintis argue that the correspondence principle operates through the hidden curriculum – that is, all the 'lessons' that are learnt in school without being directly taught. For example, simply through the everyday workings of the school, pupils become accustomed to accepting hierarchy and competition, working for extrinsic rewards and so on. In this way, schooling prepares working-class pupils for their role as the exploited workers of the future, reproducing the workforce capitalism needs and perpetuating class inequality from generation to generation.

synoptic link: stratification

Marxists see education as helping to reproduce existing class inequality. It does this by ensuring that children achieve according to their class origins rather than their ability, and by mirroring the inequality found in the workplace to prepare them for their ascribed role in capitalist society.

The correspondence principle: schooling takes place in 'the long shadow of work'.

Box 16: The correspondence principle

School in capitalist society	reflects	work in capitalist society
Hierarchy of authority among teachers (e.g. head – deputy – classroom teacher) and between teachers and students	reflects	hierarchy of authority in the workplace (e.g. managers – supervisors – workers).
Alienation through students' lack of control over education (e.g. over what to study, timetabling)	reflects	alienation through workers' lack of control over production (e.g. managers decide what, how, when and where to produce).
Extrinsic satisfaction (rewards external to the work itself) e.g. from grades, rather than from interest in the subjects studied	reflects	satisfaction from extrinsic rewards, e.g. pay, rather than from doing the job itself.
Fragmentation and compartmentalisation of knowledge (e.g. into unconnected subjects)	reflect	fragmentation of work through the division of labour into small, meaningless tasks.
Competition and divisions among students (e.g. to come top of class; to be in a higher stream)	reflect	competition and divisions among the workforce through differences in status and pay.
Levels of education (streams, year groups) ■ lower levels: few choices; close supervision ■ higher levels: trusted to get on with work; self-directed learning	reflect	levels of the occupational structure ■ lower levels: workers closely supervised; given orders ■ higher levels: workers internalise company's goals; self-supervision.

question

Suggest ways in which lower ability and younger pupils are given fewer choices and supervised more closely.

The myth of meritocracy: schooling and the legitimation of class inequality

Because capitalist society is based on inequality, there is always a danger that the poor will feel that this inequality is undeserved and unfair, and that they will rebel against the system responsible for it. In Bowles and Gintis' view, the education system helps to prevent this from happening, by legitimating class inequalities. It does this by producing ideologies that explain why inequality is fair, natural and inevitable.

Bowles and Gintis describe the education system as 'a giant myth-making machine'. A key myth that education promotes is the 'myth of meritocracy'. Meritocracy means that everyone has an equal opportunity to achieve, that rewards are based on ability and effort, and that those who gain the highest rewards deserve them because they are the most able and hardworking.

Bowles and Gintis argue that meritocracy does not in fact exist. Evidence shows that the main factor determining whether or not a person has a high income is their family and class background, not their ability or their educational achievement.

By disguising this fact, the myth of meritocracy serves to justify the privileges of the higher classes, making it seem that they gained them through open and fair competition at school. This helps persuade the working class to accept inequality as legitimate, and makes it less likely that they will seek to overthrow capitalism.

The education system also justifies poverty, through what Bowles and Gintis describe as the 'poor-are-dumb' theory of failure. It does so by blaming poverty on the individual ('I'm poor because I wasn't clever enough/didn't work hard enough at school'), rather than on capitalism. It therefore plays an important part in reconciling workers to their exploited position, making them less likely to rebel against the system.

activity

Complete the following table to show the differences between functionalist and Marxist views of the role of education.

Functionalist view	Marxist view
Education …	Education …
serves the needs of the whole society.	serves the needs of …
serves as a selection mechanism to ensure that the jobs people get match their talents.	
transmits society's values and norms.	
allows the talented to rise to the top by giving everyone an equal opportunity to succeed.	

Willis: learning to labour

All Marxists agree that capitalism cannot function without a workforce that is willing to accept exploitation. Likewise, all Marxists see education as reproducing and legitimating class inequality. That is, it ensures that working-class pupils are slotted into and learn to accept jobs that are poorly paid and alienating.

However, whereas Bowles and Gintis see education as a relatively straightforward process of indoctrination into the myth of meritocracy, Paul Willis' (1977) study shows that working-class pupils can resist such attempts to indoctrinate them.

As a Marxist, Willis is interested in the way schooling serves capitalism. However, he combines this with an interactionist approach that focuses on the meanings pupils give to their situation and how these enable them to resist indoctrination.

Using qualitative methods including participant observation and unstructured interviews, Willis studied the counter-school culture of 'the lads' – a group of 12 working-class boys – as they make the transition from school to work.

The lads form a distinct counter-culture opposed to the school. They are scornful of the conformist boys they call the 'ear'oles' (so-called because unlike the lads, they listen to what the teachers tell them). The lads have their own brand of intimidatory humour, 'taking the piss' out of the ear'oles and girls. The lads find school boring and meaningless and they flout its rules and values, for example by smoking and drinking, being disruptive in class and playing truant. For the lads, such acts of defiance are ways of resisting the school. They reject as a 'con' the school's meritocratic ideology that working-class pupils can achieve middle-class jobs through hard work.

Willis notes the similarity between this anti-school counter-culture and the shopfloor culture of male manual workers. Both cultures see manual work as superior and intellectual work as inferior and effeminate. The lads identify strongly with male manual work and this explains why they see themselves as superior both to girls and to the 'effeminate' ear'oles who aspire to non-manual jobs.

However, it also explains why the lads' counter-culture of resistance to school helps them to slot into the very jobs – inferior in terms of skill, pay and conditions – that capitalism needs someone to perform. For example:

- Having been accustomed to boredom and to finding ways of amusing themselves in school, they don't expect satisfaction from work and are good at finding diversions to cope with the tedium of unskilled labour.
- Their acts of rebellion guarantee that they will end up in unskilled jobs, by ensuring their failure to gain worthwhile qualifications.

For Willis, the irony is that by helping them resist the school's ideology, the lads' counter-culture ensures that they are destined for the unskilled work that capitalism needs someone to perform.

activity

Write a short paragraph explaining in your own words:

1 how the counter-school culture enables the lads to resist the school's ideology

2 how the counter-school culture helps to reproduce class inequality.

Evaluation of Marxist approaches

Marxist approaches are useful in exposing the 'myth of meritocracy'. They show the role that education plays as an ideological state apparatus, serving the interests of capitalism by reproducing and legitimating class inequalities.

However, critical modernists such as Morrow and Torres (see page 146) criticise Marxists for taking a 'class first' approach that neglects other forms of inequality. For example, feminists such as Madeleine MacDonald (1980) point out that Bowles and Gintis ignore the fact that schools reproduce patriarchy, not just capitalism.

Similarly, as Angela McRobbie (1978) points out, females are largely absent from Willis' study. However, Willis' work has stimulated a great deal of research into how education reproduces and legitimates other inequalities, including gender, ethnicity and sexuality.

Marxists also disagree as to how reproduction and legitimation take place. Bowles and Gintis take a deterministic view. That is, they assume that pupils have no free will and passively accept indoctrination. This approach fails to explain why pupils ever reject the school's values.

By contrast, Willis rejects the view that school simply 'brainwashes' pupils into passively accepting their fate. By combining Marxist and interactionist approaches, he shows how pupils may resist the school and yet how this still leads them into working-class jobs.

However, critics argue that Willis' account of the lads romanticises them, portraying them as working-class heroes despite their anti-social behaviour and sexist attitudes. His small-scale study of only 12 boys in one school is also unlikely to be representative of other pupils' experience and it would be risky to generalise his findings.

synoptic link: deviance

Marxists see two kinds of relationship between education and deviance:

- Bowles and Gintis see education promoting conformity through the myth of meritocracy.
- Willis sees working-class youth as rebelling against the school's values.

Examining Functionalism, the New Right and education

Item A The New Right believe in reducing the role of the state and increasing the role of market forces to make the education system more effective. They aim to introduce into the state sector as many features of the private sector as possible, especially the idea of consumers (parents) exercising choice in the types of state school they can send their children to.

During the 1980s, the governments of Britain and the United States, influenced by New Right theorists, pursued policies of open enrolment and parental choice in an attempt to empower all 'parent-consumers' and make the education system more responsive to parental needs.

Evidence suggests that these changes do lead to changes in the recruitment patterns of schools, but to the disadvantage of working-class children. For example, Moore and Davenport show that in the United States the more popular schools have been taken over by better-off parents, while children from less well-off families have become concentrated in other schools. This strongly suggests that poorer parents are less able to make the kinds of choices that will benefit their children's education.

However, although the New Right wish to see a reduction in state control, they do generally see the state as continuing to have a role in education.

Examining Functionalism, the New Right and education

Item B Functionalists take a very positive view of education. They see it as a form of secondary socialisation essential to the maintenance of society. It performs vital social functions, including transmitting shared norms and values and equipping pupils with the knowledge, skills and habits needed for work. It acts as a bridge between the family and the world of work, reflecting in its own organisation the values of equal opportunity and individual achievement found in wider society. It gives everyone an equal chance of discovering and developing their talents. Education also sifts and sorts individuals, allocating them their future occupational roles on the basis of their ability and effort and enabling the talented to become upwardly mobile.

Short questions

(a) Explain what is meant by 'open enrolment' (**Item A**, line 6). (2 marks)

(b) Identify **one** similarity and **one** difference between New Right and functionalist views of education. (4 marks)

(c) Suggest **three** reasons why 'poorer parents are less able to make the kinds of choices that will benefit their children's education'(**Item A**, line 12). (6 marks)

(d) Identify and briefly explain **two** ways in which the New Right 'see the state as continuing to have a role in education' (**Item A**, lines 13-14). (8 marks)

Mini-essay

Using material from **Item B** and elsewhere, assess the contribution of functionalism to our understanding of the role of education. (20 marks)

This is a type (f) question of the kind found in the exam, carrying 6 AO1 marks (knowledge and understanding) and 14 AO2 marks (identification, interpretation, analysis and evaluation).

The Examiner's advice

For the mini-essay, you need to show what functionalists have said about education, so look at a range of functions. Use Item B for clues about the different functions you could write about. 'Assess' means you need to evaluate, e.g. by using criticisms from Tumin, Wrong, and especially Marxism (e.g. Althusser on ISAs, Bowles and Gintis on the myth of meritocracy). Mentioning studies that show inequality of opportunity/under-achievement (e.g. from the section on class and achievement earlier in the chapter) is relevant if linked to meritocracy, but don't write long descriptions of these studies, as this will take you away from the question. Write a separate conclusion.

Postmodernism, post-Fordism and education

Postmodernism is the view that society has entered a new, postmodern, phase and is now fundamentally different from the kind of modern society that functionalists and Marxists have written about. For example, rather than the well-integrated society built on value consensus that functionalists describe, postmodernists such as Jean-Francois Lyotard (1984) argue that society today is increasingly fragmented, with an ever-greater variety of cultures and communities rather than a single shared way of life.

Similarly, where Marxists see a two-class society based on exploitation, postmodernists believe that class divisions are now of little importance. Instead, new social divisions based on gender, ethnicity, sexuality and so on have become more important.

In today's more diverse, fragmented society, people can now 'pick and mix' their identities from a wide range of sources. For example, an individual may see herself as gay or straight, white, black or Asian, and able-bodied or disabled, rather than simply middle-class or working-class.

Post-Fordism

Postmodernists argue that society is now changing more rapidly that in the past, particularly under the impact of new technology and the electronic media. One effect of this is to change the way we work. We have largely shifted away from the old forms of mass production for mass markets typified by the rigid assembly-line methods found in car plants worldwide. This system of production is often called 'Fordism', because it was first introduced by the Ford Motor Company.

Instead, production is now based upon 'flexible specialisation' – where production is customised for smaller, 'niche' (specialist) markets, using advanced technology. This system is known as 'post-Fordism'.

Mass production and flexible specialisation require different kinds of workforce and different kinds of education system:

- Mass production calls for large numbers of workers with the same low level of skill, each doing much the same routine, repetitive work on assembly lines. This is the kind of work that Bowles and Gintis see the mass education systems of capitalist countries like the USA and Britain as preparing pupils for.
- By contrast, flexible specialisation requires a skilled, adaptable workforce able to use advanced technology and who can transfer their skills rapidly from one specialised task to another.
- A different kind of education system is required for this kind of work. Instead of a system that prepares pupils to be obedient workers motivated by extrinsic rewards, education needs to encourage self-motivation, self-supervision and creativity. It also needs to be able to develop transferable skills and offer re-training, because the pace of technological change nowadays rapidly makes existing skills outdated.
- Postmodernists argue that these changes in work mean that education is moving away from a mass, standardised system in which all schools are similar, to one in which education is customised to the needs of the individual.

Postmodernists welcome these changes as freeing individuals and groups from the oppressive uniformity of a mass education system where 'one size fits all' (see Box 17). They see opportunities for different communities to create the kinds of schools that suit their particular needs.

Usher and Thompson: postmodern education

One example of a postmodernist approach to education is that of Robin Usher (1997). He contrasts modern and postmodern education as follows:

- In modern society, education is controlled centrally by the state, whereas postmodern education is controlled by communities.
- In modern society, there is a 'one size fits all' approach to education, whereas postmodern education is diverse and customised to the needs of the individual learner.
- In modern society, education is fixed in time and place (e.g. it takes place on the school's

premises following a fixed timetable), whereas postmodern education is flexible. For instance, we may study through distance learning (e.g. the Open University and the Internet).

Mass production at the Ford plant in Detroit, Michigan, 1940.

- In modern society, education only takes place during a fixed period of the individual's life, whereas postmodern education is a process of lifelong learning through which individuals constantly update their skills in response to the changing needs of the economy.
- In modern society, education is teacher-led, where the learner passively absorbs knowledge from the teacher, whereas in postmodern education, the learner is active and learns through his or her own experience.

Similarly, Kenneth Thompson (1992) argues that schools in postmodern society are able to break free from the 'oppressive uniformity' of the old centralised mass education system, where all schools were expected to be the same. Thompson argues that the growing diversity and fragmentation of society mean that education is changing to meet the differing needs of diverse communities.

This is illustrated by the growth of 'faith schools' for different religious groups, and by the growing demand for specialist schools in technology, languages, media and so on. In this way, Thompson argues, postmodern education empowers minority groups.

Postmodernists such as Usher and Thompson reject Bowles and Gintis' Marxist view that class inequality is fundamental to today's society and that education still reproduces inequality. Rather than inequality, postmodernists see diversity.

Similarly, instead of an oppressive, uniform system designed to churn out factory fodder for the capitalist economy, postmodernists see a diverse education system responsive to the needs of different individuals and groups. In their view, education no longer performs the oppressive functions of reproducing and legitimating class inequality: in their view, the correspondence principle described by Bowles and Gintis no longer operates.

Evaluation of the postmodernist perspective

- Postmodernists have identified important trends towards diversity in both society and education.
- However, critics claim that postmodernists exaggerate the extent of diversity. For example, the National Curriculum is a 'one size fits all', state-controlled curriculum that gives little scope for expressing minority cultures (see page 115). Similarly, although there has been an increase in the number of specialist schools, most remain standard comprehensives.
- Critical modernists argue that postmodernists also ignore the continuing importance of inequality in education.

Box 17: New Labour and post-comprehensive education

Speaking about education and healthcare at the 2002 Labour Party Conference, the Prime Minister Tony Blair said:

> 'In education, we need to move to the post-comprehensive era, where schools keep the comprehensive principle of equality of opportunity but where we open up the system to new and different ways of education, built around the needs of the individual child. Both education and the NHS need an end to the "one size fits all" mass production public service. The purpose of the 20th-century welfare state was to treat citizens as equals. The purpose of our 21st-century reforms must be to treat them as individuals as well. And we can't make that change by more bureaucracy from the centre – by just flogging the system harder. We need to change the system. It means putting power in the hands of the patient or parent.'

question

Are there any similarities between the New Labour view of education and that of the New Right (see page 135)?

Critical modernism and education

In this section and the next, we examine two further explanations of the role of education. Both explanations recognise the importance of the social changes that postmodernists identify, but both argue that postmodernists fail to see the continuing importance of social inequality.

- The first explanation, put forward by Raymond Morrow and Carlos Torres (1998) and others is known as 'critical modernism'. This approach examines how education reproduces both class and non-class inequalities, all of which they see as equally important.
- The second explanation, put forward by Stephen Ball (1994) and Geoff Whitty (1998), focuses specifically on the role that educational policies play in reproducing and legitimating inequality.

Morrow and Torres: reproducing different inequalities

Morrow and Torres reject the view that education no longer reproduces inequality. They agree that there is now greater diversity, but they argue that inequality remains of key importance.

However, unlike the Marxists Bowles and Gintis, they argue that class inequality is not the only significant form of inequality. They criticise Bowles and Gintis for taking a 'class first' view – a view that sees class as the key inequality and ignores all other kinds. Instead, Morrow and Torres see inequalities such as gender, ethnicity and sexuality as equally important.

Morrow and Torres therefore argue that we need to be able to explain how education reproduces and legitimates *all* forms of inequality, not just class, and how the different forms of inequality are inter-related.

Here we shall explore some of these inter-relationships, through Mac an Ghaill's study of masculinity and class, Beverley Skeggs' investigation of femininity and class, and Paul Connolly's research on ethnicity and gender.

Mac an Ghaill: masculinity and class

Mairtin Mac an Ghaill's (1994) study of Parnell School examines how peer groups within the school reproduce a range of different class-based masculine identities. He identifies four male peer groups:

- **The Academic Achievers** – hard-working, mainly white and Asian boys from skilled working-class backgrounds who aspired to middle-class careers.

- **The Macho Lads** – working-class boys from a variety of ethnic backgrounds. They equated academic work with effeminacy. They described the Academic Achievers as 'dickhead achievers'. Like Willis' lads and those described by Epstein (see pages 124 and 141), they rejected non-manual work and schoolwork as unmasculine. Their definition of masculinity as 'toughness' prepared them for a life of manual work.
- **The Real Englishmen** – a group of mostly white middle-class boys who projected an image of 'effortless achievement', giving an appearance of succeeding without really trying (though in some cases actually working hard 'on the quiet'). They saw themselves as intellectually superior and regarded the hard-working Academic Achievers as 'sloggers'.
- **The New Enterprisers** – mostly working-class boys who aspired to middle-class careers. They were interested in technology and computers. However, they didn't attract the same abuse from the Macho Lads as the Academic Achievers, probably because of their interest in computers, which were seen as masculine.

Interestingly, Peter Redman and Mairtin Mac an Ghaill (1997) found that the dominant definition of masculinity in school changes from that of the Macho Lads in the lower school to that of the Real Englishmen by the sixth form. This represents a shift away from a working-class definition of masculinity based on toughness to a middle-class one based on intellectual ability. This in turn reflects the mainly middle-class composition and atmosphere of the sixth form.

These studies show how schooling prepares working-class boys for working-class jobs and middle-class boys for middle-class jobs by reproducing two different class-based masculine identities.

Skeggs: femininity and class

Beverley Skeggs (1997) argues that education reproduces and legitimates class and gender inequalities together. Her study is based on nine years of observation of working-class women on low-level 'caring' courses in further education. Skeggs describes two main ways in which the courses reproduce and legitimate both gender and class inequalities:

- The courses encourage stereotypical feminine qualities such as domesticity and putting others first. These are qualities the women value and see in themselves.
- The courses emphasise how difficult it is to care properly. They encourage the women to regard their own caring skills as inadequate and to see the expertise of middle-class professionals such as teachers and health visitors as superior to their own.

As a result, the women come to see themselves both as suited to 'feminine' caring work and as incapable of middle-class jobs. This prepares them both for low-paid work such as care assistants and for unpaid 'women's work' in the home.

Caring: work for working-class women?

Connolly: ethnicity and gender

Sociologists have also studied the ways in which ethnicity and gender intersect in schooling to reproduce an ethnic and gender hierarchy. For example, in a study of five and six year olds in a multi-ethnic, inner-city primary school, Paul Connolly (1998) shows how masculinity is constructed differently by pupils and teachers according to a child's ethnicity.

On the one hand, Connolly found that teachers saw black boys as disruptive under-achievers and controlled them by punishing them more and by channelling their energies into sport. The boys, in turn, responded by seeking status in non-academic ways, such as playing kiss-chase and football.

Though black girls were considered to be more passive, they too were seen as good at sport, music and dance, and were treated in a similar manner to the boys.

On the other hand, teachers saw Asian pupils as passive and conformist. They regarded the boys as keen and academic and when they misbehaved, they were seen as being silly or immature rather than threatening. Other boys would pick on them to assert their own masculinity, and would exclude them from playing football. Both teachers and pupils saw them as more 'feminine', vulnerable and in need of protection from bullying.

Thus we can see how schools reproduce different masculinities in boys according to their ethnic backgrounds and how black boys are seen as more 'masculine' than Asian boys. This parallels the findings of Willis and Mac an Ghaill that schools reproduce different masculinities according to boys' social class backgrounds.

However, Connolly notes that the boys' masculinity is not just a product of what happens in school. It is also influenced by the expectations of masculine behaviour that they bring into school from the outside world.

activity

Look back at the accounts of Epstein, Willis, Mac an Ghaill and Connolly. Make a list of the different groups or types of boys referred to in these studies. What similarities can you see? Try to categorise them into two main sorts and make a list of the characteristics of each category.

synoptic links: stratification and deviance

Mac an Ghaill, Skeggs and Connolly show how education maintains stratification by reproducing overlapping divisions of class, gender, ethnicity and sexuality.

Connolly shows how teachers stereotype black boys as deviant and use different forms of control over them. He also shows how black and white boys use deviant behaviour (bullying) to subordinate Asian boys.

Educational policy, reproduction and legitimation

'Educational policy' refers to the plans and strategies for education introduced by government, for example through Acts of Parliament, together with instructions and recommendations to schools and local education authorities.

Many sociologists see educational policy as playing an important part in reproducing and legitimating inequality. We can see this occurring through the policies of:

- the tripartite system
- the comprehensive system
- marketisation.

the tripartite system

The tripartite system introduced in 1944 reproduced class inequality by having two types of school broadly corresponding to the two social classes: secondary moderns for the working class and grammar schools for the middle class.

Selection took place at the age of 11, with the 11+ exam. Most working-class children failed the exam and ended up in secondary modern schools. These schools offered a non-academic curriculum for pupils destined for manual work. Most middle-class children passed the 11+ and went to grammar schools that provided an academic curriculum and access to non-manual jobs and higher education.

The tripartite system legitimated inequality through the ideology that ability is inborn rather than the product of the child's upbringing and environment, and thus can be identified early on in life (e.g. through the 11+ exam). In reality, however, children's class background greatly affects their ability to succeed at school.

Not all parents can afford to move into the catchment area of popular schools.

the comprehensive system

The comprehensive system introduced from 1965 was designed to overcome the unfairness of the tripartite system by abolishing the 11+ exam and sending all pupils to the same type of secondary school.

Nevertheless, the system continued to reproduce class inequality. For example, many comprehensives were streamed into ability groups, where middle-class pupils tended to be put into higher streams and working-class pupils into lower streams.

Even where streaming was not present, as Ball shows, teachers continued to label working-class pupils negatively and to restrict their opportunities. Comprehensives also legitimated inequality through the 'myth of meritocracy', making it appear that all pupils have an equal opportunity regardless of class background, when in reality this is not the case.

question

How might the following policies reproduce inequality?

(a) the abolition of student grants and their replacement with student loans

(b) the introduction of educational vouchers.

marketisation

More recently, both Stephen Ball and Geoff Whitty have examined how the policy of marketisation (see Box 13) also reproduces and legitimates inequality. Marketisation is largely the result of the 1988 Education Reform Act, which reduced direct state control and introduced market forces into education so as to create competition between schools and increase parental choice.

Marketisation and the reproduction of inequality

Ball and Whitty argue that marketisation reproduces inequality through:

- exam league tables
- the funding formula.

Exam league tables

The policy of publishing each school's exam results in a league table ensures that schools that achieve good results are more in demand, because parents are more likely to be attracted to schools with good league table rankings. This allows these schools to be more selective and to recruit high-achieving, mainly middle-class pupils. As a result, middle-class pupils get the best education.

For schools with poor league table positions, the opposite applies: they cannot afford to be selective and have to take less able, mainly working-class pupils. The overall effect of league tables is to produce schools that are unequal and that reproduce social class inequalities.

The funding formula

Schools are allocated funds by a funding formula based upon how many pupils they attract. As a result, popular schools get more funds and can afford better qualified teachers and better facilities. Again, their popularity allows them to be more selective and attracts more able or ambitious, generally middle-class applicants.

On the other hand, unpopular schools lose income and find it difficult to match the teacher skills and facilities of their more successful rivals. Thus, popular schools with good results and able middle-class pupils thrive; unpopular schools fail to attract pupils and their funding is reduced.

Marketisation and the myth of parentocracy

Not only does marketisation reproduce inequality; it also legitimates it. Legitimation refers to ideas that conceal the true causes of inequality and justify its existence.

Ball believes that marketisation gives the appearance of creating a 'parentocracy' (literally, 'rule by parents'). That is, the education system seems as if it is based on parents having a free choice of school. However, Ball argues that parentocracy is a myth, not a reality. It makes it appear that all parents have the same freedom to choose which school to send their children to.

In reality, however, as Gewirtz shows, middle-class parents have more economic and cultural capital and so are better able to take advantage of the choices available (see page 95). For example, they can afford to move into the catchment areas of more desirable schools.

By disguising the fact that schooling continues to reproduce class inequality in this way, the 'myth of parentocracy' makes inequality in education appear to be fair and inevitable.

synoptic link: stratification

Educational policies may reproduce class inequalities by enabling children of one class to gain better educational opportunities.

Marketisation gives middle-class children a better chance of admission to successful schools, while concealing this inequality through 'the myth of parentocracy'.

questions

1 Explain the difference between the 'myth of parentocracy' and Bowles and Gintis' 'myth of meritocracy'.

2 What similarity is there between these two 'myths'?

QuickCheck Questions

1 Explain the difference between ascribed status and achieved status.

2 Which type of status is found in meritocratic education systems?

3 True or false? The New Right believe that the state should be more involved in running the education system.

4 Give one example each of repressive and ideological state apparatuses.

5 Explain the difference between the reproduction of class inequality and the legitimation of class inequality.

6 Explain what Marxists mean by the correspondence principle, and give one example of it.

7 What is post-Fordism?

8 How does the critical modernist view of education differ from

(a) postmodernism

(b) Marxism?

9 Explain how the publication of exam league tables may help to reproduce inequality.

Answers are on page 273.

Examining Postmodernism, critical modernism and education

Item A According to some sociologists, the emergence of a globalised economy and the increased use of modern information and communication technology in production have created a need for a new kind of labour force. In the past, Fordist methods of mass production required a large mass of semi-skilled workers performing simple, repetitive tasks, such as the fitting of one particular component to a product on an assembly line. By contrast, today's economy requires more flexible post-Fordist production techniques and workers.

Many postmodernists believe that these changes in work and the economy are helping to bring about a change in the role of education. They argue that it no longer exists simply to reproduce class inequality. However, other sociologists claim that schooling not only continues to reproduce class inequality, but that it also reproduces gender, ethnic and other inequalities at the same time.

Short questions

(a) Suggest **one** criticism of the postmodernist view of the role of education (**Item A,** lines 8-10). (2 marks)

(b) Identify and briefly explain **one** difference between Fordist and post-Fordist views of the role of education (**Item A,** lines 3-7). (4 marks)

(c) Identify **three** features of postmodern society. (6 marks)

(d) Identify and briefly describe **two** ways in which schooling reproduces social class or ethnic differences in pupils' gender identities. (8 marks)

Mini-essay

Examine the ways in which educational policies may help to reproduce and legitimate social inequalities. (20 marks)

This is a type (e) question of the kind found in the exam, carrying 14 AO1 marks (knowledge and understanding) and 6 AO2 marks (identification, interpretation, analysis and evaluation).

The Examiner's advice **For the mini-essay, you need to deal with both reproduction and legitimation – so it will help if you briefly explain what these two terms mean. You should examine a range of policies (e.g. tripartite system, comprehensives, marketisation, student loans). There are many relevant concepts and issues you can refer to, including selection, streaming, innate ability, ideology, the myth of meritocracy, the funding formula, league tables, parentocracy, student loans, educational vouchers, GM schools etc. You may find it useful to refresh your memory by re-reading Box 13 on marketisation (page 97) and the section on the New Right (page 135).**

Chapter summary

Social class differences in educational achievement

Middle-class pupils tend to achieve more than working-class pupils. Explanations of these patterns include **factors outside school**, such as cultural deprivation (working-class pupils are unable to defer gratification or use the elaborated speech code); material deprivation (e.g. poverty leads to poor health and absence from school) and cultural capital.

Others see **factors inside the education system** as more important. Interactionists argue that schools actively create inequality through labelling and the self-fulfilling prophecy, streaming and polarisation into pro- and anti-school subcultures. Marketisation means that better schools recruit more middle-class pupils, widening class inequalities.

Ethnic differences in educational achievement

There are achievement differences **between** ethnic groups. For example, Indian pupils tend to do better than average, while Bangladeshi, Pakistani and black pupils do worse. There are gender differences **within** groups: e.g. black females do better than black males.

Some explanations focus on **factors outside school**, such as cultural deprivation due to unstable family structures or inadequate socialisation. Others argue that the lower class position of many minorities, along with racism in wider society, leads to material deprivation and lower achievement.

Other explanations focus on **racism within school**. Teachers' labelling may create a self-fulfilling prophecy. However, not all pupils respond by accepting negative labels. The ethnocentric curriculum may undermine achievement, while institutional racism routinely discriminates against minorities. Increased selection in schools is producing racial segregation.

Gender and education

Statistics show a widening **gender gap in achievement**, with girls doing better than boys at all stages. Some sociologists explain this in terms of **changes outside the education system** – in the family, more employment opportunities for women, the impact of feminist ideas and changes in girls' ambitions. Others focus on **changes within education**, such as the influence of feminist ideas via equal opportunities policies and challenges to stereotyping in the curriculum, more female teachers, coursework and exam league tables.

There are gender differences in **subject choice**. Choices are influenced by early socialisation into gender identities, the image subjects have, peer pressure and career opportunities.

Education reinforces **gender identities** and hierarchies e.g. through verbal abuse, the male gaze, school discipline and double standards of sexual morality.

The role of education in society

Different perspectives see the role of education differently. **Functionalists** take a consensus approach. They see education as performing important functions – socialisation into the shared culture, equipping individuals with work skills and selecting them meritocratically for work roles.

The **New Right** take a conservative view, arguing that education can only perform its role effectively if it is organised on market principles rather than run by the state. Marketisation will increase competition, ensure choice and raise standards.

Marxists take a class conflict approach. They see education as serving the needs of capitalism by reproducing and legitimating class inequality – ensuring that working-class children end up in working-class jobs, and that this labour force will accept its exploited role.

Postmodernists take a diversity approach. They argue that society has become more diverse and fragmented and the economy has become post-Fordist. Education reflects these changes and is becoming more diverse and flexible.

Critical modernists take a diversity-with-conflict approach. They accept that society is more diverse, but argue that inequalities of class, ethnicity, gender and sexuality remain important and that education reproduces them. Some focus on how policies such as marketisation reproduce inequality and legitimate it through the 'myth of parentocracy'.

Examining **Education**

Item A A child's home background and early socialisation can have profound effects on their educational achievement and the pathway that they follow through the education system. For example, many sociologists argue that material deprivation in the home can place the child at a profound educational disadvantage, while others claim that the cultural deprivation experienced in some families leaves the child with a 'deficit' or deficiency that results in under-achievement. Such ideas have been applied to the study of both class and ethnic differences in achievement, but the early socialisation of children prior to school can also affect boys' and girls' preferences for different school subjects and activities.

Item B Bowles and Gintis put forward a Marxist explanation of the role of education. They argue that its primary purpose is to reproduce a labour force for capitalism. It does this largely by virtue of the 'correspondence principle' – the principle that there is a close correspondence between the school and the workplace. For example, in schools there is a hierarchy of authority with the head teacher at the top and the youngest pupils at the bottom. In work there is a similar hierarchy of bosses, managers and supervisors down through the different grades of workers. School accustoms pupils to the kinds of authority relationships, rewards and so on that they will have to accept in work. This is achieved largely through the hidden curriculum rather than the official curriculum.

As Bowles and Gintis recognise, though, education can perform not only a reproduction role. It can also legitimate the class inequality that it helps to reproduce. However, critics argue that Bowles and Gintis neglect the role of education in reproducing other, non-class inequalities.

(a) Explain what is meant by the 'hidden curriculum' (**Item B,** line 9). (2 marks)

(b) Suggest **two** ways in which the early socialisation of young children may 'affect boys' and girls' preferences for or confidence in different school subjects and activities' (**Item A,** lines 7–8). (4 marks)

(c) Identify **three** material factors that may explain differences in educational achievement (**Item A,** line 3). (6 marks)

(d) Identify and briefly explain **two** criticisms of the view that the under-achievement of some ethnic groups is due to cultural deprivation (**Item A,** lines 4–7). (8 marks)

(e) Examine the ways in which processes within schools may lead to differences in achievement between social groups. (20 marks)

(f) Using material from **Item B** and elsewhere, assess the view that the role of education is to reproduce a labour force for capitalism. (20 marks)

The Examiner's advice For (e), there are two important aspects to deal with here: 'processes' and 'social groups'. Bring in a range of processes: labelling, streaming, self-fulfilling prophecy, anti-school subcultures, hidden curriculum. Show how these can lead to differences in achievement. Deal with at least two of the following: class, ethnicity and gender. You could apply processes such as labelling and pupil subculture formation to all three. Evaluation is not the main focus, but it is worth saying that home factors can play a part in producing differences in achievement. The view in (f) is a Marxist one. Summarise it, making sure that you use Item B. You must also evaluate: again, Item B is useful in pointing out that education may also legitimate, not just reproduce, inequalities. Develop evaluation by contrasting Bowles and Gintis with Willis, and by using non-Marxists to criticise. You could use Bowles and Gintis' correspondence principle to organise your answer, by contrasting what others (e.g. postmodernists, critical modernists) say about it. You could also contrast functionalist and Marxist views on education and the economy.

Chapter 4

Sociological Methods

Introduction

In the previous two chapters we looked at what sociologists have discovered in studying families and households, and education. But how exactly *do* sociologists go about studying the topics they are interested in? In this chapter, we examine how sociologists go about investigating society.

The purpose of sociology is to answer questions about social life and the social world. For example, why do middle-class children generally achieve better exam results than working-class children? What causes divorce? How far do the mass media influence people's behaviour?

To answer questions like these, sociologists develop **theories**. A theory is a general explanation of how or why social life follows the patterns it does.

A good theory is one that explains these patterns. That is, it explains all the available **evidence** that can be found about the topic being investigated. If a theory does not explain the evidence that we or others have gathered about the topic, we need to replace it with one that does.

Sociologists therefore try to ensure that their theories are based on sound evidence. To do otherwise would risk their work being discredited by other sociologists.

We thus need good, sound evidence to test our theories. But what methods can we use to obtain it? This chapter is concerned with the different methods sociologists use for collecting information about society, and with the issues we need to think about when deciding which methods to use.

The AQA Specification

The specification is the syllabus produced by the exam board, telling you what you have to study. The AQA specification for Sociological Methods requires you to examine the following:

- the different quantitative and qualitative methods and sources of data, including questionnaires, interviews, observation techniques and experiments, and documents and official statistics
- the distinctions between primary and secondary data, and between quantitative and qualitative data
- the relationship between positivism, interpretivism and methods
- the theoretical, practical and ethical considerations influencing the choice of topic, choice of method(s) and the conduct of research
- the nature of social facts and the strengths and limitations of different sources of data and methods of research.

Note on the OCR Specification

If you are studying the OCR specification, this chapter will help you if you are doing the Sociological Research Skills module at AS. This module covers very similar issues to the AQA specification above and comprises:

- Basic concepts in research design
- Aspects of data collection
- Interpreting and evaluating data.

If you are unsure which specification (AQA or OCR) you are studying, check with your teacher.

Types of data

Sociologists use a wide variety of different methods and sources to obtain data (information or evidence) about society. To make sense of this variety we can classify them into:

- Primary and secondary sources of data.
- Quantitative and qualitative data.

Primary and secondary sources of data

Primary data is information collected by sociologists themselves for their own purposes. These purposes may be to obtain a first-hand 'picture' of a group or society, or to test a hypothesis (an untested theory).

Methods for gathering primary data include:

- **Social surveys**: these involve asking people questions in a written questionnaire or an interview.
- **Participant observation**: the sociologist joins in with the activities of the group he or she is studying.
- **Experiments**: sociologists rarely use laboratory experiments, but they sometimes use field experiments and the comparative method.

A big advantage of using primary data is that sociologists may be able to gather precisely the information they need to test their hypotheses. However, doing so can often be costly and time consuming.

Secondary data is information that has been collected or created by someone else for their own purposes, but which the sociologist can then use.

Sources of secondary data include:

- **Official statistics** produced by government on a wide range of issues, such as crime, divorce, health and unemployment, as well as other statistics produced by charities, businesses, churches and other organisations.
- **Documents** such as novels, diaries, photographs, official reports, letters, newspapers and television broadcasts.

Using secondary data can be a quick and cheap way of doing research since someone else has already produced the information. However, those who produce it may not be interested in the same questions as sociologists, and so secondary sources may not provide exactly the information that sociologists need.

Quantitative and qualitative data

Quantitative data refers to information in a numerical form. Examples of quantitative data include official statistics on how many girls passed five or more GCSEs or on the percentage of marriages ending in divorce. Similarly, information collected by opinion polls and market research surveys often comes in the form of quantitative data – for example, on the proportion of the electorate intending to vote for a particular party or how many people take holidays abroad.

Qualitative data, by contrast, give a 'feel' for what something is like – for example, what it feels like to get good GCSE results, or for one's marriage to end in divorce. Evidence gathered by using participant observation aims to give us a sense of what it feels like to be a member of a particular group. Similarly, in-depth interviews that probe deeply into a person's views can give us an insight into what it is like to be in that person's 'shoes'. These methods can provide rich descriptions of people's feelings and experiences.

synoptic links: deviance & stratification

Both deviance and stratification can be studied using either quantitative or qualitative data. For example, official crime statistics or figures on the distribution of income and wealth can provide us with quantitative data. Qualitative data can be obtained through participant observation of a delinquent gang or through unstructured interviews with the unemployed to understand their experience of poverty.

Box 18: Types of data

	Primary sources	Secondary sources
Quantitative data	Questionnaires Structured interviews	Official statistics
Qualitative data	Participant observation Unstructured interviews	Letters Diaries

question

Which of the four categories above does each of the following belong in?

(a) experiments
(b) novels
(c) unofficial statistics
(d) newspaper articles
(e) historical documents

Factors influencing choice of methods

Given the wide range of methods available, how do we select the right one for our research? Different methods and sources of data have different strengths and weaknesses and we need to be able to evaluate these when selecting which to use.

We can look at these strengths and weaknesses in terms of a number of practical, ethical (moral) and theoretical issues.

Practical issues

Different methods present different practical problems. These include:

time and money

Different methods require different amounts of time and money and this may influence the sociologist's choice. Large-scale surveys may employ dozens of interviewers and data-inputting staff and cost a great deal of money. By contrast, a small-scale project involving a lone researcher using participant observation may be cheaper to carry out, but it can take several years to complete.

The researcher's access to resources can be a major factor in determining which methods they employ. A well-known professor will probably have access to more research funds than a young student, for example.

requirements of funding bodies

Research institutes, businesses and other organisations that provide the funding for research may require the results to be in a particular form. For example, a government department funding research into educational achievement may have targets for pass rates and so require quantitative data to see whether these targets are being achieved. This means the sociologist will have to use a method capable of producing such data, such as questionnaires or structured interviews.

personal skills and characteristics

Each sociologist possesses different personal skills, and this may affect their ability to use different methods. For example, participant observation usually requires the ability to mix easily with others as well as good powers of observation and recall, while depth interviews call for an ability to establish a rapport (relationship of empathy and trust) with the interviewee. Not all sociologists have these qualities and so some may have difficulty using these methods.

subject matter

It may be much harder to study a particular group or subject by one method than by another. For example, it might prove difficult for a male sociologist to study an all-female group by means of participant observation, while written questionnaires may be useless for studying those who cannot read.

What personal skills and characteristics might be useful for a researcher studying this group?

Ethical issues

Ethics refers to moral issues of right and wrong. Methods that sociologists use to study people may raise a range of ethical questions. For example:

1 Is covert (secret) observation, which is done without the knowledge or consent of those being observed, a morally acceptable way to study people?

2 Is it right to deceive people so that we can study them more easily?

3 Is it acceptable for the sociologist to become involved in committing criminal acts so as to study criminals?

4 Is it ever right to conduct research that might cause harm to the participants?

5 Is it acceptable to publish findings about a group without their consent?

activity

In small groups, consider each of the five ethical questions above. Under what circumstances, if any, do you feel it would be acceptable for sociologists to do any of these things? Give reasons for your answer in each case.

Theoretical issues

This refers to questions about what we think society is like and whether we can obtain an accurate, truthful picture of it. Our views on these issues will affect the kinds of methods we favour using.

validity

A valid method is one that produces a true or genuine picture of what something is really like. It allows the researcher to get closer to the truth.

Many sociologists argue that qualitative methods such as participant observation give us a more valid or truthful account of what it is like to be a member of a group than quantitative methods such as questionnaires can. This is because participant observation can give us a deeper insight through first hand experience.

reliability

Another word for reliability is replicability. A replica is an exact copy of something, so a reliable method is one which, when repeated (e.g. by another researcher), gives the same results.

For example, in physics or chemistry, different researchers can repeat the same experiment and obtain the same results every time. In sociology, quantitative methods such as written questionnaires tend to produce more reliable results than qualitative methods such as unstructured interviews.

question

Which of the two statements below is an example of validity and which of reliability? Give reasons for your answers.

1 A friend of mine was attacked recently. He told me in detail all about his feelings at the time and afterwards. Now I really understand what it must be like.

2 We were all given an intelligence test every day this week. Our results were very consistent. Each of us gained the same score every time we took the test.

representativeness

Representativeness refers to whether or not the people we study are a typical cross-section of the group we are interested in. Imagine for example that we want to know about the effects of divorce on children. It would take a great deal of time and money to study every child of divorced parents, and we might only be able to afford to study a sample of, say, 100 such children.

However, if we ensure that our sample is representative or typical of the wider population, we can then use our findings to make generalisations about *all* children of divorced parents, without actually having to study all of them.

Large-scale quantitative surveys that use sophisticated sampling techniques to select their sample (see pages 167–8) are more likely to produce representative data.

sociological perspective

Sociologists' choice of method is also influenced by their sociological perspective – their view of what society is like. Some perspectives tend to prefer quantitative data, whereas others favour qualitative data:

Functionalists and Marxists see society as a large-scale (macro-level) structure that shapes the individual's behaviour. They tend to take the *positivist* view that sees sociology as a science.

Thus, they favour methods that allow them to discover scientific laws explaining how society causes us to behave. These methods are ones such as questionnaires and official statistics that provide quantitative data to measure the effect that society has on us. Functionalists and Marxists therefore tend to favour methods that are reliable and produce objective facts.

Interactionists take a micro-level view of society, focusing on small-scale, face-to-face interactions such as those between teacher and pupil or police officer and suspect. Rather than trying to discover scientific laws, interactionists take an *interpretivist* approach – they try to interpret the meanings that social actors (individuals) give to actions and situations.

To achieve this, they use qualitative methods, such as participant observation, unstructured interviews and personal documents. These methods allow the researcher to gain access to the actor's way of seeing the world. They favour methods that are valid and give a true insight into the actor's world.

However, it would be wrong to assume that the only thing determining which method a sociologist chooses is their theoretical perspective. Practical and ethical issues also play a part, and even sheer chance may determine the methods used. For example, David Tuckett (2001) describes how one postgraduate sociology student found himself taken ill with tuberculosis and confined to a hospital ward, so he used this as an opportunity to conduct a participant observation study.

activity

Using the information on perspectives above, complete the following table.

	Positivism	Interpretivism
Perspective	Functionalism and ...	
Quantitative or qualitative methods and sources?		
Examples of preferred methods and sources	1 2	1 2
Emphasis on reliability or validity?		
Aim	To discover scientific laws of cause and effect	
Micro- or macro-level?		

QuickCheck Questions

1 Explain the difference between:
   (a) quantitative and qualitative data
   (b) primary and secondary sources of data.

2 Give one example of:
   (a) a primary method that produces quantitative data
   (b) a secondary source that gives qualitative data.

3 Identify two ethical issues that sociologists may face in studying people.

4 True or false? If a method is reliable then if another researcher uses it they should get the same results.

5 What does 'validity' mean?

6 Name two practical issues that might affect a researcher's choice of method.

7 True or false? Positivists
   (a) see sociology as a science.
   (b) prefer qualitative data.

Answers are on page 273.

20 mins ☐

Experiments

In the natural sciences such as chemistry and biology, scientists set out to discover scientific laws of cause-and-effect. For example, physicists have discovered that an increase in the temperature of a gas will cause it to expand.

Scientists use laboratory experiments to discover causes. But how useful is this method for sociologists?

The method favoured by natural scientists for discovering these laws is the laboratory experiment. The laboratory is an artificial environment in which the scientist is able to control all the different variables (factors that can vary, such as temperature) to see what effect they have.

An example will help to illustrate the basic principle of the experimental method. Suppose we want to discover what causes plants to grow. One way would be to take a set of identical plants and randomly divide them into two groups – an experimental group and a control group. We then treat them differently, as follows:

- The experimental group: with this group, we might vary the amount of nutrients that they received, carefully measuring and recording any changes in the plants' size that we observe.
- The control group: with this group, we would keep the amount of nutrients constant, also measuring and recording any changes in the size of the plants.

On comparing the results from the two groups, we notice that the plants in the experimental group have grown more rapidly than the plants in the control group after receiving extra nutrients. In other words, we may have discovered a cause-and-effect relationship: nutrients cause growth.

In scientific terms, the nutrient is the independent variable (the causal factor) and the resulting growth is the effect or dependent variable (since it depends on the first variable, nutrition).

The logic of the experimental method is that the scientist manipulates (alters) the variables in which he or she is interested, in order to discover what effect they have. By following this method, the scientist can establish a cause-and-effect relationship. In turn, this will allow the scientist to predict accurately what will happen in the future under specified conditions. In our example, the scientist will be able to predict what will happen when a certain amount of nutrient is given to the plants.

Reliability

Once an experiment has been conducted, other scientists can then replicate it. That is, they can repeat it exactly in every detail. The laboratory experiment is therefore highly reliable, producing the same results each time, for two reasons:

- The original experimenter can specify precisely what steps were followed in the original experiment, so other researchers can repeat these in future.
- It is a very detached method: the researcher merely manipulates the variables and records the results. The scientist's personal feelings and opinions have no effect on the conduct or outcome of the experiment.

The laboratory experiment therefore has major advantages as the method used to identify cause-and-effect relationships in the natural sciences. Despite this, however, there are several reasons why laboratory experiments are rarely used in sociology.

Practical problems

Society is a very complex phenomenon. In practice, it would be impossible to identify, let alone control, all the variables that might exert an influence on, say, a child's educational achievement or a worker's attitude to work.

Another practical problem is that the laboratory experiment cannot be used to study the past, since by definition it is impossible to control variables that were acting in the past rather than the present.

Ethical problems

There are ethical (moral) objections to conducting experiments on human beings, at least under certain circumstances. As a general principle, the researcher needs the informed consent of the subjects (the people being experimented on). It could therefore be considered wrong to mislead people as to the nature of the experiment, as Stanley Milgram (1974) did in his famous studies of obedience.

Milgram lied to his subjects about the purpose of the research, telling them that they were assisting in an experiment on learning, in which they were told by the researcher to administer electric shocks when the learner failed to answer questions correctly. In reality, however, the purpose was to test people's willingness to obey orders to inflict pain. Unbeknown to them, no electric shocks were actually used.

It could also be difficult to obtain informed consent from groups such as children or people with learning difficulties who may be unable to understand what is being proposed. The experiment may also cause harm to the subjects.

The Hawthorne Effect

A laboratory is not a normal or natural environment (except for scientists, maybe!). As a result, it is likely that any behaviour that occurs in these conditions is also unnatural or artificial. If people do not behave in true-to-life ways, the experiment will not produce valid results.

If people know they are being studied, they may behave differently; for example, by trying to second-guess what the researcher wants them to do and acting accordingly. This will ruin the experiment, which depends on the subjects responding to the variables that the experimenter introduces into the situation, not to the fact that they are being observed.

This problem has become known as the 'Hawthorne Effect' or 'experimental effect'. In 1927, Elton Mayo began conducting research into factors affecting workers' productivity at the Western Electric Company's Hawthorne plant in Chicago. Working with five female volunteer workers who knew he was conducting an experiment, Mayo altered different variables such as lighting, heating, rest breaks and so on to see what effect they had on the volunteers' output.

Surprisingly, not only did output go up when he improved their working conditions, but it continued to rise even when conditions were worsened. Mayo concluded that the workers were not responding to the changes he was making in the experimental variables (such as the lighting), but simply to the fact that they were being studied and wished to please the experimenter who was showing an interest in them.

Free will

Interpretivist sociologists, such as interactionists, argue that human beings are fundamentally different from plants, rocks and other natural phenomena studied by natural scientists. Unlike these objects, we have free will, consciousness and choice. This means our behaviour cannot be explained in terms of cause and effect. Instead, it can only be understood in terms of the choices we freely make. In this view, the experimental method, with its search for causes, is therefore not an appropriate method for studying human beings.

activity

Some sociologists and psychologists have used experiments to try to discover the effects of media violence on children. Write a short account of the difficulties they might face in doing this. Use the following ideas: the complexity of social life; long- and short-term effects; artificial environment; ethical problems; children's previous socialisation.

Two alternatives to the laboratory experiment

Given these problems, sociologists have developed two alternatives that follow the same logic as laboratory experiments, but which overcome some of the difficulties identified above. These are:

- Field experiments
- The comparative method or 'thought experiment'.

Field experiments

A field experiment has two features that distinguish it from a laboratory experiment:

- It takes place in the subject's natural surroundings, such as school or workplace, rather than in an artificial laboratory environment.
- Those involved are not aware that they are the subjects of an experiment, so there is no Hawthorne Effect.

The researcher manipulates one or more of the variables in the situation to see what effect it has on the unwitting subjects of the experiment. For example, Rosenthal and Jacobson manipulated teachers' expectations about children's abilities in order to discover what effects labelling has on achievement.

Similarly, in David Rosenhan's (1973) 'pseudopatient' experiment, a team of eight 'normal' researchers presented themselves at 12 California mental hospitals, complaining that they had been hearing voices. Each was admitted and diagnosed as schizophrenic solely on the basis of this claim, which obviously no-one else could prove. Once in hospital, they ceased to complain of hearing voices and acted normally throughout. Nevertheless, hospital staff treated them all as if they were mentally ill. None was found out (although some fellow patients were suspicious).

This suggests that it was not the patients' behaviour that led to them being treated as sick (since they didn't behave abnormally), but the label 'schizophrenic' itself that led staff to treat them in this way. For example, the pseudopatients kept notes of their experiences, but hospital staff interpreted this as a symptom of mental illness. On one pseudopatient's nursing notes was written 'patient exhibits writing behaviour' – writing apparently being a sign of illness!

Rosenhan's study shows the value of field experiments. They are more 'natural' and realistic, and they avoid the artificiality of laboratory experiments.

However, the more realistic we make the situation, the less control we have over the variables that might be operating. If so, we cannot be certain that the causes we have identified are the correct ones. For example, while it might have been the label 'schizophrenic' that led doctors and nurses to treat the pseudopatients as mentally ill (as Rosenhan claims), it may in fact have been some other factor that the researchers had not controlled that led the hospital staff to behave in this way.

Some critics also argue that field experiments are unethical, since they involve carrying out an experiment on their subjects (in this case, the hospital staff) without their knowledge or consent.

synoptic links: deviance & stratification

Rosenhan's work is a good example of the study of deviance using field experiments. In stratification, Sissons (1970) used an actor, first dressed as a businessman, then as a labourer, to ask passers-by for directions to see whether a person's class affects how others respond to them.

The comparative method

Unlike both the field experiment and laboratory experiment, the comparative method is carried out only in the mind. It is a 'thought experiment' and it does not involve the researcher actually experimenting on real people at all. However, it too is designed to discover cause-and-effect relationships. It works as follows:

- Identify two groups of people that are alike in all major respects except for the one variable we are interested in.
- Then compare the two groups to see if this one difference between them has any effect.

An example of the comparative method is Emile Durkheim's (1897) classic study of suicide. Durkheim's hypothesis was that low levels of integration of individuals into social groups caused high rates of suicide. He argued that different religions produced different levels of integration, with Catholicism producing higher levels than Protestantism. From this, he therefore predicted that Protestants would have a higher suicide rate than Catholics.

Durkheim then tested his prediction by comparing the suicide rates of Catholics and Protestants who were similar in all other important respects (for example, in terms of where they lived, whether they were married or single etc). His prediction was supported by the official statistics on suicide, which showed Catholics to have lower suicide rates than Protestants. Durkheim claimed from this that his hypothesis was correct.

In seeking to discover cause-and-effect relationships, the comparative method has three advantages over laboratory experiments:

- It avoids artificiality.
- It can be used to study past events.
- It poses no ethical problems, such as harming or deceiving subjects.

However, the comparative method gives the researcher even less control over variables than do field experiments, so we can be even less certain whether a thought experiment really has discovered the cause of something.

question

What are the similarities and differences between a laboratory experiment and the comparative method?

QuickCheck Questions

1 Fill in the missing words. The laboratory experiment is an artificial ...... in which the scientist is able to ...... all the different ...... to see what effect they have.

2 State
(a) one practical problem and
(b) one ethical problem of conducting laboratory experiments in sociology.

3 What is the Hawthorne Effect?

4 True or false? Field experiments enable the researcher to control all the variables in the situation.

5 Suggest two advantages of using the comparative method.

Answers are on page 273.

Social surveys

The most obvious way of gathering data about people is simply to ask them questions. Social surveys involve gathering information by asking people questions about their lives, attitudes, opinions or behaviour. Most of us are familiar with market research surveys of consumers' preferences and opinion polls on people's voting intentions, but sociologists also use surveys to collect data and test hypotheses on subjects as varied as income, family patterns, crime, social mobility, sexual behaviour, attitudes to work, religious beliefs, and housework.

Surveys take two basic forms. Questions can be put to people via:

- **written questionnaires**, which respondents are asked to complete and return
- **interviews**, either face-to-face or by telephone.

Social surveys are a good way of studying large numbers of people.

Types of question

Whether we use questionnaires or interviews to carry out our survey, the questions we ask can be of two types:

- **Closed-ended questions:** the respondent (the person answering the questions) must choose their answer from a limited range of possible answers that the researcher has decided upon in advance, such as 'Yes', 'No' or 'Don't know', or like multiple-choice questions in an exam.

  Closed-ended questions are often pre-coded for ease of analysis later. Each possible answer to the question is given a code, and the interviewer or respondent rings the number corresponding to the answer chosen. The information can then be fed into a computer for processing, enabling the researchers to quantify (count) the number of respondents choosing each of the available answers.

- **Open-ended questions:** the person answering is free to give whatever answer they wish, in their own words, and without any pre-selected choices being offered by the researcher (see Box 19).

activity

Working in pairs:

1 Choose a topic with which you are familiar (e.g. family diversity, or gender and education) and design:

(a) three open-ended questions

(b) three closed-ended questions: one with yes/no answers and two others.

2 Decide which of the following are advantages of closed-ended questions, and which are advantages of open-ended questions:

(a) can find out what the respondent really thinks

(b) can collect information quickly

(c) can ask more complex questions

(d) easier to quantify and classify results

(e) less chance of bias from the researcher

(f) allows the respondent to compose their own answer

(g) produces reliable data.

Box 19: Open-ended and closed-ended questions

The following example of a closed-ended question comes from John Goldthorpe and David Lockwood's (1969) study of 'affluent workers':

> Here are some things often thought important about a job: which one would you look for first in a job?
>
> Interest and variety
>
> Pleasant working conditions
>
> A strong and active union
>
> Good pay and the chance of plenty of overtime
>
> Good workmates
>
> A supervisor who doesn't breathe down your neck

By contrast, Gordon Marshall (1988) used the following open-ended question in his study of social class:

> When you hear someone described as 'working class', what sort of person do you think of?

Preparing to conduct a survey

Survey research begins with the choice of a topic to investigate and with formulating an aim or hypothesis. Then, before the actual survey, a pilot study needs to be conducted and a sample selected for study. We examine each of these stages below.

Choosing a topic

The first stage is choosing a topic for investigation. Sociologists use surveys to study a wide variety of issues, but survey methods are not suitable for all subjects. For example, historical topics cannot be investigated, unless there are survivors we can question.

Once we have chosen a suitable topic for research, there are a number of stages we need to go through before we can start gathering data. The first of these is to formulate an aim or hypothesis for the research.

Formulating an aim or hypothesis

Most surveys either have a general aim or seek to test a specific hypothesis. An **aim** is a statement that identifies what a sociologist intends to study and hopes to achieve by carrying out the research. Often the aim will simply be to collect data on a particular topic, for example, people's leisure patterns, religious beliefs or attitudes to cohabitation. The Census of the entire population conducted by the government every ten years is designed to collect large quantities of data about many different aspects of British society.

Other surveys seek to test one or more hypotheses. A **hypothesis** is more specific than an aim. It is a possible explanation that can be tested by collecting evidence to prove it true or false.

For example, we may be interested in the topic of educational achievement. We may have a hunch or suspicion that achievement is affected by family size. If so, we can formulate a specific hypothesis in the form of a statement, such as: 'differences in educational achievement are the result of differences in family size'. We can then collect evidence to see whether or not this is true.

The advantage of a hypothesis is that it gives direction to our research. It will give a focus to the questions that we ask in our questionnaires or interviews, since their purpose is to gather information that will either confirm (prove) or refute (disprove) our hypothesis.

question

Explain the difference between an aim and a hypothesis.

Creating a hypothesis is a work of imagination, because we have to think up a possible explanation first. Often, sociologists develop a hypothesis by studying previous work on the subject, but it could come to them from anywhere. The important thing is whether the evidence gathered in our survey supports it. If the hypothesis turns out to be false, we must discard it.

Apart from family size, what other variables might influence children's achievement?

see what social class each pupil belongs to. We can then correlate this with information we collect about their qualifications to find out whether our hypothesis is true or false.

Before we can do research, then, we need to define our sociological ideas in such a way that they can be measured. This process of converting a concept (e.g. social class) into something that can be measured is called 'operationalisation'.

Operationalising a concept may seem straightforward, but a problem can arise when different sociologists operationalise the same concept differently. For example, we might agree that occupation is a useful operational definition of class, but disagree about whether a routine office worker is working-class or middle-class. Disagreements like these can make it hard to compare the findings of different pieces of research.

Discarding a hypothesis might seem like a bad thing, but in fact it means we have made some progress. In our example of educational achievement, if the survey reveals no link with family size, we have learned something new and we can now direct our attention to another possible cause instead. Perhaps the cause is parental attitudes, or income; we simply formulate a new hypothesis and set out to test it.

Operationalising concepts

Suppose we have the hypothesis that working-class pupils achieve lower qualifications than middle-class pupils because of lower parental income. Before we can test it, we need a working definition of our key ideas or concepts – in this case, the concept of social class. The reason is simple: without a working definition, we won't be able to count the numbers of working-class pupils who have or don't have qualifications.

Now, 'social class' is a fairly abstract idea, so we need a way of measuring or indicating what class each pupil belongs to. Most sociologists would probably use parental occupation as an indicator of a pupil's social class, both because it is easily identifiable and because it seems to be the best single indicator of all those other aspects of our lives that make up our 'class' (such as income, housing etc).

Once we have a working or 'operational' definition of our concept, we can set about writing questions that measure it. In our example, we might ask the parent, 'what is your job?' This will allow us to

activity

In small groups, discuss how you might operationalise the following concepts so you could use them in researching education: poverty; homelessness; disability; achievement. What problems might you encounter in operationalising them?

The pilot study

Once we have a hypothesis we want to test, the next stage is to produce a draft version of the questionnaire or interview schedule (the list of interview questions) that we intend to use, and to give this a trial run. This is known as a pilot study.

The basic aim of the pilot study is to iron out any problems, refine or clarify questions and their wording and give interviewers practice, so that the actual survey goes as smoothly as possible. For example, Young and Willmott (1962) carried out just over 100 pilot interviews to help them decide on the design of their study, the questions to ask and how to word them.

A pilot study may reveal that some questions are badly worded and hard to understand, or that the answers are difficult to analyse. After carrying out the pilot study, it should be possible to finalise the questionnaire or interview schedule.

Sampling

Sociologists aim to produce generalisations that apply to all cases of the topic they are interested in. For example, if we were interested in educational achievement, we would ideally want our theory to explain the achievement levels of *all* pupils, not just the ones who were in our study.

Obviously, however, we do not have the time or money to include every pupil in Britain in our survey, so we have to choose a sample of pupils to include. This process is called sampling.

The basic purpose of sampling is usually to ensure that those people we have chosen to include in the study (such as pupils) are representative or typical of the whole group that we are interested in, including all the people we have *not* been able to include in the study. This will enable us to generalise our findings to the group as a whole.

Sampling frame

To choose a sample, we first need a sampling frame. This is a list of all the members of the population we are interested in studying. For example, Young and Willmott used the electoral register (the list of people entitled to vote) as their sampling frame. It is important that the list we use as a sampling frame is as complete and accurate as possible – otherwise the sample chosen from it may not be truly representative of the population.

Once we have obtained our sampling frame, we can choose our sample from it, for example by selecting every tenth name. In selecting the sample, we need to ensure it is representative of the wider population we are interested in.

Box 20: The biggest blunder in survey history?

The biggest blunder in survey history was probably the 1936 poll on voting intentions carried out by an American magazine, the *Literary Digest*, using a postal questionnaire. The poll asked respondents how they would vote in the forthcoming election: for Landon, the Republican Party candidate, or for Roosevelt, the Democratic Party candidate. Two million people responded to the poll. The great majority surveyed said they would vote for Landon and the magazine predicted a Republican victory. Yet when the election came, Roosevelt won by a landslide. How could the magazine have got it so wrong?

Roosevelt (left) celebrating his election victory.

The answer lies in the sampling frame used for the questionnaire. The magazine had used the telephone directory, wrongly assuming it would be a reasonably good list of all those who were entitled to vote. However, in 1936, telephones were still something of a luxury; many poorer voters were not telephone subscribers and did not appear in the directory. Since in America, poorer voters have tended to be Democrats and richer voters Republicans, using the directory to draw the sample was bound to over-represent the intentions of rich Republican voters and under-represent those of poor Democrats.

activity

A good sampling frame should be: complete (covering all the population concerned); without duplications; accurate; up to date and all in one place. Working in pairs, consider the following examples and decide how far each one meets these criteria. Give reasons for your answers.

(a) The annual register of electors as a sampling frame for all people entitled to vote.

(b) A telephone directory as a sampling frame for all the people in the area it covers.

(c) Members of a football team's supporters' club as a sampling frame for all fans of that team.

Sampling techniques

Sociologists use various sampling techniques to achieve a representative sample:

- **Random sampling** is the simplest technique, where the sample is selected purely at random. For example, names may be drawn out of a hat.
- **Quasi-random sampling** is similar, for instance every tenth or hundredth name on a list is selected. Young and Willmott used every thirty-sixth name on the electoral register for their general sample.

However, with both techniques, there is always the chance that the sample obtained is not truly representative. Imagine we have a city of a million people, where half the population is male and half female. Suppose we take a 1% sample (one person in every hundred). This will give us a sample of 10,000 people. Yet it could happen, by chance, that our sample contains, say, 6,000 females and only 4,000 males, rather than 5,000 of each sex.

Other more sophisticated techniques of sampling can reduce the chance of getting an unrepresentative sample like the one above. These include the following:

- **Stratified random sampling**: by first dividing ('stratifying') the population into males and females, and then taking a 1% sample of each, we can ensure that we end up with equal numbers of each sex, and that the sample is thus representative of the population as a whole. This process can be repeated for any other important variable such as people's age, income etc.
- **Quota sampling** is similar to stratified random sampling, but instead of choosing the samples for each category (e.g. male and female) randomly, the researchers go out looking for the right number (the quota) of each sort of person required in each category. In our example, the researchers would have a quota of 5,000 males and 5,000 females to find.

Whatever sampling technique is actually used, researchers will often compile a reserve sample, so that if anyone in the original sample cannot be contacted, their counterpart from the reserve list can be used as a substitute.

However, not all studies use representative sampling techniques. In **snowball sampling**, the sample is collected by contacting a number of key individuals, who are asked to suggest others who might be interviewed, and so on, adding to the sample 'snowball' fashion, until enough data has been collected. Although not representative, this can be a useful way to contact a sample of people who might otherwise be difficult to find or persuade to take part, such as criminals.

Once we have finalised the questionnaire or interview schedule and selected the sample, we can begin to collect data about the topic. To do so, we can use either questionnaires or interviews.

synoptic links: deviance & stratification

There can be difficulties finding a satisfactory sampling frame for both these topics:

- Not all criminals are convicted, so there is no complete list available from which to select a sample.
- In studying stratification, there is no comprehensive list of poor people. For instance, not all those in poverty claim the benefits they are entitled to, so a list of claimants would not provide an adequate sampling frame.

QuickCheck Questions

1. True or false? Surveys can be conducted by written questionnaires or by telephone interviews.
2. Explain the difference between an open-ended and a closed-ended question.
3. True or false? A hypothesis is a possible explanation that we have not yet tested.
4. State one advantage of having a hypothesis before starting research.
5. What does operationalisation of concepts mean?
6. What is a pilot study?
7. True or false? In a random sample, each member of the population has an equal chance of being selected.

Answers are given on page 274.

Questionnaires

Written questionnaires (sometimes called self-completed questionnaires) are the most commonly used form of social survey. The biggest survey in the UK, the ten-yearly Census of the whole population, is a written questionnaire. They can be distributed to people at home and returned by post or in person, e-mailed or completed and collected on the spot, for example in a classroom or office. Questionnaires ask respondents (the people who complete them) to provide answers to pre-set questions. Questions tend to be closed-ended, often with pre-coded answers, but open-ended questions can also be used. Written questionnaires are a relatively cheap and quick way to collect information from a large sample.

Completing a Census form.

Advantages of questionnaires

The popularity of questionnaires is undoubtedly due to the considerable range of advantages they offer to researchers.

1 Practical advantages

Questionnaires offer several major practical advantages:

- They are a quick and cheap means of gathering large quantities of data from large numbers of people, widely spread geographically, especially if a postal questionnaire is used. For example, Helen Connor and Sara Dewson (2001) posted nearly 4,000 questionnaires to students at 14 higher education institutions around the country in their study of the factors influencing the decisions of working-class students to go to university.
- There is no need to recruit and train interviewers or observers to collect the data, because respondents complete and return the questionnaires themselves.
- The data are usually easy to quantify, particularly where pre-coded, closed-ended questions are used, and can be processed quickly by computer to reveal the relationships between different variables.

synoptic links: deviance & stratification

Questionnaires are often used in large-scale, government-funded research.

- The 2002 British Crime Survey surveyed 33,000 households to ask them what crimes they had been victims of during the previous 12 months and whether they had reported these crimes to the police.
- In the study of stratification, the ten-yearly Census gathers data on many aspects of class, gender, ethnic and age differences and inequalities in the UK population.

2 Reliability

Questionnaires are seen as a reliable method of collecting data. That is, if repeated by another researcher, a questionnaire should give similar results to those gained by the first researcher. There are two reasons for this:

- When the research is repeated, a questionnaire identical to the original one is used, so new respondents are asked exactly the same questions, in the same order, with the same choice of answers, as the original respondents.
- With postal questionnaires, there is no researcher present to influence the respondent's answers (different researchers might influence respondents to give different answers) – unlike interviews, where interaction with the interviewer may affect the answer given.

In other words, the questionnaire is a fixed yardstick that can be used by any researcher to obtain the same results (provided that later researchers use a similar sample). This means one researcher's study can easily be repeated and checked by another.

The reliability of questionnaires also means that if we do find differences in the answers that respondents give, we can assume that these are the result of real differences between the respondents and not simply the result of different questions.

A related advantage of questionnaires is that they allow comparisons to be made, both over time and between different societies. By asking the same questions, we can compare the results obtained in two different societies or at two different times.

3 Hypothesis testing

Questionnaires are particularly useful for testing hypotheses about cause-and-effect relationships between different variables. For instance, using our earlier example of educational achievement, analysis of respondents' answers could show whether there is a correlation between children's achievement levels and family size. We might find, for example, that most low achievers come from large families.

From this analysis, we can make statements about the possible causes of low achievement and predictions about which children are most likely to under-achieve.

Because questionnaires enable us to identify possible causes, they are very attractive to positivist sociologists. As we saw earlier, positivists take a scientific approach and seek to discover laws of cause and effect.

4 Detachment and objectivity

Positivists also favour questionnaires because they are a detached and objective (unbiased) form of research, where the sociologist's personal involvement with their respondents is kept to a minimum. Questionnaires are often completed at a distance and involve little or no personal contact between researchers and respondents, and so they are seen as a good way of maintaining detachment and objectivity.

5 Representativeness

Because questionnaires can collect information from a large number of people, the results stand a better chance of being truly representative of the wider population than with other methods that study only very small numbers of people, such as participant observation.

In addition, researchers who use questionnaires tend to pay more attention to the need to obtain a representative sample. For these reasons, the findings of questionnaires are more likely to allow us to make accurate generalisations about the wider population from which the sample was drawn.

Disadvantages of questionnaires

Despite their advantages, questionnaires have been subject to some sharp criticisms, especially in relation to the validity of the data they produce.

1 Practical problems

The data from questionnaires tend to be limited and superficial. One practical reason for this is that they need to be fairly brief, since most respondents are unlikely to complete and return a long, time-consuming questionnaire. This limits the amount of information that can be gathered from each respondent.

Similarly, although questionnaires are a relatively cheap means of gathering data, it may sometimes be necessary to offer incentives – such as entry into a prize draw – to persuade respondents to complete the form. This will obviously add to the cost.

2 Response rate

Although questionnaires have the potential to collect data from large, representative samples, very low response rates can be a major problem, especially with postal questionnaires. This is because few of those who receive a questionnaire bother to complete and return it. For example, Shere Hite's (1991) study of 'love, passion and emotional violence' in America sent out 100,000 questionnaires, but only 4.5% of them were returned.

A higher response rate can be obtained if follow-up questionnaires are sent and if questionnaires are collected by hand. However, this adds to the cost and time.

The problem of non-response is sometimes caused by faulty questionnaire design. For example, a questionnaire that uses complex language may only be completed by the well educated.

The great danger with a low response rate is that those who return their questionnaires may be different from those who don't. For example, busy people in full-time employment or with young children may fail to respond, whereas the unemployed or socially isolated with time on their hands may be more likely to fill in their questionnaires. Similarly, those with strong views on a subject are more likely to respond than those who have little knowledge or interest in it. If the respondents are different from the non-respondents, this will produce distorted and unrepresentative results, from which no accurate generalisations can be made.

questions

1 We are often asked to return questionnaires by magazines, or to telephone a radio or television programme to give our views. Suggest two reasons why those who respond to such requests are unlikely to be representative of the population as a whole.

2 Explain in your own words why non-response is a problem for sociologists.

3 Inflexibility

Questionnaires are a very inflexible method. Once the questionnaire has been finalised, the researcher is stuck with the questions they have decided to ask and cannot explore any new areas of interest should they come up during the course of the research. This contrasts with more flexible methods of research such as unstructured interviews, where the researcher can change the direction of the interview to ask new questions if they seem relevant.

4 Questionnaires as snapshots

Questionnaires are snapshots. They give a picture of social reality at only one moment in time: the moment when the respondent answers the questions. Questionnaires therefore fail to produce a fully valid picture because they do not capture the way people's attitudes and behaviour *change*. This snapshot contrasts with the moving image of social life that methods like participant observation can provide.

5 Detachment

Interpretivist sociologists such as Aaron Cicourel (1968) argue that data from questionnaires lack validity and do not give a true picture of what has been studied. They argue that we can only gain a valid picture by using methods that allow us to get close to the subjects of the study and share their meanings. Ideally, the method should enable us to put ourselves in the subject's place and see the world through their eyes.

Questionnaires fail to do this because they are the most detached of all primary methods. For example, postal questionnaires involve no direct contact between researcher and respondent. This lack of contact means there is no opportunity to clarify what the questions mean to the respondent or to deal with misunderstandings. There is no way of knowing whether the respondent and researcher both interpret the questions, or the answers, in the same way. This can be a serious problem where there are cultural or language differences between researcher and respondent.

6 Lying, forgetting and 'right answerism'

All methods that gather data by asking questions depend ultimately on their respondents' willingness and ability to provide full and accurate answers. Problems of validity are created when respondents give answers that are not full or frank. For example, respondents may lie, forget, not know, not understand (and not wish to admit that they don't understand), or try to please or second-guess the researcher. Some may give 'respectable' answers they feel they ought to give, rather than tell the truth.

These problems put questionnaires at a disadvantage when compared with observational methods, since the observer can see for himself or herself what the subjects actually do, rather than what they say they do.

7 Imposing the researcher's meanings

A valid method is one that gives a truthful picture of people's meanings and experiences. Yet interpretivists argue that questionnaires are more likely to impose the researcher's own meanings than to reveal those of the respondent.

- By choosing which questions to ask, the researcher, not the respondent, has already decided what is important and what is not.
- If we use closed-ended questions, respondents then have to try to fit their views into the ones on offer. If they feel some other answer to be important, they have no opportunity of giving it, thus producing a distorted and invalid picture of their reality.
- On the other hand, if we use open-ended questions, respondents are free to answer as they please, but when the researcher comes to code them to produce quantitative data, similar but non-identical answers may get lumped together into the same category.

As Marten Shipman (1997) says, when the researcher's categories are not the respondent's categories, 'pruning and bending' of the data is inevitable. The questionnaire imposes a straitjacket that distorts the respondents' meanings and undermines the validity of the data.

question

In Michael Schofield's (1965) research on the sexual behaviour of teenagers, a young girl was asked in a questionnaire, 'Are you a virgin?' she answered, 'No, not yet'.

Identify the problems of questionnaire research that this suggests.

QuickCheck Questions

1 What is the Census?

2 What is a respondent?

3 Suggest one reason why data from questionnaires often tend to be limited and superficial.

4 Why might a low response rate result in the findings of a study being unrepresentative?

5 Suggest one reason why questionnaires are seen as an inflexible method.

6 Suggest two reasons why the data from questionnaires may lack validity.

Answers are given on page 274.

Examining Surveys and questionnaires

Item A Social surveys in the form of questionnaires or structured interviews are probably the most commonly used method by which sociologists test their hypotheses. To be successful, surveys require extensive planning and preparation. Once questions have been devised to gather information that will test the hypothesis, it is advisable to conduct a pilot study before carrying out the main survey.

In most cases, it will not be possible to study the whole population in which we are interested (such as criminals, housewives, Christians, manual workers or whatever). It is therefore important that the sociologist obtains a representative sample of the population to be studied, and there are a variety of sampling techniques that sociologists use to do this. However, it is not always easy to achieve a representative sample. For example, it might be difficult to obtain a representative sample of the criminals in a given town.

Short questions

(a) Explain what is meant by a 'hypothesis' (**Item A**, line 4). (2 marks)

(b) Suggest **two** reasons why 'it is advisable to conduct a pilot study before carrying out the main survey' (**Item A**, lines 4-5). (4 marks)

(c) Identify **three** types of sampling technique that a sociologist might use in conducting a survey (**Item A**, line 9). (6 marks)

(d) Identify and briefly explain **two** reasons why 'it might be difficult to obtain a representative sample of the criminals in a given town' (**Item A**, lines 10-11). (8 marks)

Mini-essay

Examine some of the reasons why sociologists use questionnaires in their research. (20 marks)

This is a type (e) question of the kind found in the exam, carrying 14 AO1 marks (knowledge and understanding) and 6 AO2 marks (identification, interpretation, analysis and evaluation).

The Examiner's advice **For the mini-essay, look at a range of different reasons. Focus on the advantages: don't waste time on the disadvantages. Reasons can be both practical and theoretical. Practical reasons include the fact that we can study large numbers of people quickly and cheaply and don't need to train interviewers. Theoretical reasons include the fact that positivists favour questionnaires because they offer a detached, objective, scientific approach and produce reliable, quantitative data for making comparisons, establishing correlations and testing hypotheses. Use different studies to illustrate some of these points. Link theoretical and practical issues where possible. For example, link their large scale (a practical advantage) to the fact that they produce representative data from which generalisations can be made (a theoretical advantage).**

30 mins

Interviews

While social surveys can be conducted by means of postal questionnaires, an alternative widely used by sociologists is to conduct face-to-face or telephone interviews instead.

Although both questionnaires and interviews gather data by asking people questions, the obvious difference between the two methods is that interviews involve a social interaction between the interviewer and respondent, whereas with postal questionnaires the respondent usually answers the questions without the involvement of the researcher.

A face-to-face interview

Types of interview

Sociologists use different types of interview in their research. These range from completely structured to completely unstructured interviews. The difference between them lies in how free the interviewer is to vary the questions and the way they are asked:

- **Structured or formal interviews** are very similar to a questionnaire: the interviewer is given strict instructions on how to ask the questions. The interview is conducted in the same standardised way each time, asking each respondent precisely the same questions, word for word, in the same order, tone of voice and so on.
- **Unstructured or informal interviews** (also called discovery interviews) are like a guided conversation. The interviewer has complete freedom to vary the questions, their wording, order and so on from one interview to the next, pursuing whatever line of questioning seems appropriate at the time, asking follow-up questions or probing more deeply.

In between these two extremes lie semi-structured interviews. Each interview has the same set of questions in common, but the interviewer can also probe for more information. For example, Aaron Cicourel and John Kitsuse (1963) always followed up their questions with 'How do you mean?' as a way of gaining more information. Additional questions can be asked where the interviewer thinks it relevant.

Most interviews are one-to-one, but some are group interviews, with up to a dozen people being interviewed together. Paul Willis (1977) used group interviews as part of his research into the 'lads' and schooling. Focus groups are a form of group interview in which the researcher asks the group to discuss certain topics (such as how well the government is performing) and records their views.

questions

1. Why might the data obtained from two semi-structured interviews on the same topic not be strictly comparable?
2. Suggest one advantage and one disadvantage of using group interviews rather than one-to-one interviews.

Structured interviews

Structured interviews are like questionnaires: both involve asking people a set of prepared questions. In both cases, the questions are usually closed-ended with pre-coded answers. The main difference is that in the interview, the questions are read out and the answers filled in by a trained interviewer rather than by the respondent.

This basic similarity between structured interviews and questionnaires means that they share many of the same advantages and disadvantages. Where there are differences, these often come from the fact that structured interviews involve interaction between researcher and respondent.

1 Practical issues

- Training interviewers is relatively straightforward and inexpensive, since all they are really required to do is follow a set of instructions. However, this is more costly than simply posting questionnaires to people.
- Surveys that use structured interviews can cover quite large numbers of people with relatively limited resources because they are quick and fairly cheap to administer (see Box 21). However, they still cannot match the potentially huge numbers reached by postal questionnaires.
- They are suitable for gathering straightforward factual information such as a person's age or job (see Box 21).
- The results are easily quantified because they use closed-ended questions with coded answers. This makes them suitable for hypothesis-testing.

2 Response rate

The large numbers who can be surveyed using structured interviews increase the chances of obtaining a representative sample of the population. Although the numbers that can be studied are lower than for questionnaires, structured interviews generally have a higher response rate. For example, of the 987 people Young and Willmott approached for their main sample, only 54 refused to be interviewed. This may be because people find it harder to turn down a face-to-face request, and some may welcome the opportunity to talk.

Response rates can be increased if the interviewer can make several callbacks to pursue those who fail to respond initially. However, this increases the cost of the survey. High response rates help to produce a more representative result and therefore a better basis for making generalisations.

On the other hand, as with questionnaires, those with the time or willingness to be interviewed may be untypical (for example, they may be lonely or have time on their hands). If so, this will make for unrepresentative data and undermine the validity of any generalisations made from the findings.

Box 21: Using structured interviews

Young and Willmott (1962) used structured interviews in their research into the extended family in east London:

'The general sample being much larger – 933 people – we could not do the interviewing ourselves; these interviews were carried out by other interviewers we employed for the purpose. The interviews were formal and standardised, the questions precise and factual, with a limited range of alternative answers, on straightforward topics like people's age, job, religion, birthplace and on the whereabouts and last contact with parents, parents-in-law, brothers and sisters, and married children. The interviewers' task was to ring the appropriate code-number opposite the answer they received or, at a few points in the interview, to write in a fairly short and simple reply. Each interview took between about ten minutes and half an hour, depending on the number of relatives possessed by a particular informant.'

activity

Using information from the above passage, explain three advantages of using structured interviews to collect data. Write at least one sentence for each advantage.

3 Reliability

If a method is reliable, another sociologist could repeat the research and get the same results. Structured interviews are seen as reliable because it is easy for the researcher to standardise and control them. They can ensure that each interview is conducted in precisely the same way, with the same questions, in the same order, with the same wording and tone of voice.

If each interviewer conducts every interview in exactly the same way, then any other researcher following the same interview procedures should get very similar results. The structured interview provides a 'recipe' for repeating the research: as in cookery, anyone who follows the recipe ought to get the same result. The fact that all respondents are asked exactly the same questions also means that we can compare their answers easily to identify similarities and differences.

4 Validity

A valid method is one that provides a true, authentic picture of the topic being researched. Critics of structured interviews argue that, like questionnaires, they often produce a false picture of the subjects they are trying to study.

- Structured interviews usually use closed-ended questions that restrict respondents to choosing from a limited number of pre-set answers. If none of these answers fits what the respondent really wishes to say, the data obtained will be invalid.
- Structured interviews give interviewers very little freedom to explain questions or clarify misunderstandings. For example, they may be given one alternative form of words to use if the respondent doesn't understand the question, but if this fails to do the trick the interviewer usually has to move on to the next question.
- People may lie or exaggerate. These responses will produce false data.

The interview is a social interaction and so there is always a risk that the interaction between interviewer and respondent will influence the answers given. For example, gender and ethnic differences can affect the answers, as can the respondent's desire to be seen in a favourable light (see page 180).

5 Inflexibility

Like self-completed questionnaires, structured interviews suffer from the inflexibility that comes from having to draw up the questions in advance. The researcher has already decided what is important – yet this may not coincide with what the respondent thinks is important.

As a result, the findings may lack validity because they do not reflect the respondent's concerns and priorities. In particular, establishing the questions beforehand and then sticking to them rigidly will make it impossible to pursue any interesting leads that emerge in the course of the interviews, thereby losing valuable insights.

Also like questionnaires, structured interviews are merely snapshots taken at one moment in time, so they fail to capture the flowing, dynamic nature of social life.

6 Feminist criticisms

Hilary Graham (1983) argues that survey methods such as questionnaires and structured interviews are patriarchal and give a distorted, invalid picture of women's experience. She argues that:

- The researcher is in control of the interview and decides the line of questioning to be followed. This mirrors women's subordination in wider society.
- Survey methods treat women as isolated individuals rather than seeing them in the context of the power relationships that oppress them.
- Surveys impose the researcher's categories on women, making it difficult for them to express their experiences and concealing the unequal power relationships between the sexes.

These feminist criticisms are similar to those put forward by interpretivist sociologists. Graham argues that sociologists need to use methods that allow the researcher to understand women's behaviour, attitudes and meanings. She therefore advocates the use of direct observation instead.

Feminists also ague that gender inequality is an important factor limiting the reliability of interviews (see Box 22).

Unstructured interviews

Whereas a structured interview follows a standardised format, in an unstructured interview the interviewer has complete freedom to vary the interview. Supporters argue that this brings a number of important advantages.

Advantages of unstructured interviews

While structured interviews are criticised for their lack of validity, unstructured interviews are widely seen as a way of gathering valid data, enabling researchers to get a deeper understanding of the respondent's world. There are several reasons for this, which we examine below.

1 Rapport and sensitivity

The informality of unstructured interviews allows the interviewer to develop a rapport (relationship of trust and understanding) with the respondent. This is more likely to put the respondent at their ease and encourage them to open up than a formal structured interview.

A good example of this is the work of William Labov (1973). When using a more formal interview technique to study the language of black American children, they appeared to be tongue-tied and 'linguistically deprived'. However, adopting a more relaxed, informal style – the interviewer sitting on the floor, the child allowed to have a friend present – brought a completely different response. The children opened up, spoke freely and showed themselves to be competent speakers.

Unstructured interviews are particularly useful when researching sensitive topics. The empathy and encouragement of the interviewer will help the respondent to feel comfortable discussing difficult or personal subjects such as abuse.

2 The respondent's view

Because there are no set questions, unstructured interviews allow the respondent more opportunity to speak about those things they think are important. This contrasts with the structured interview, where the researcher decides in advance what questions are worth asking and limits respondents to a fixed range of possible answers. By allowing them greater freedom to express their views, an unstructured interview is more likely to produce fresh insights and valid data. Similarly, the interviewer's probing can help formulate and develop respondents' thoughts more clearly.

In their study of claimants' experiences of unemployment, Hartley Dean and Peter Taylor-Gooby (1992) used unstructured tape-recorded interviews, lasting up to 90 minutes, with 85 claimants. In their words:

> *'Questions were not put in any set order; the wording of questions was adapted to fit the circumstances of the respondent and/or the interview situation; questions which were evidently inappropriate were omitted altogether; additional questions or prompts were used at the interviewer's discretion to clarify or develop themes as they emerged.'*

This approach gives respondents the freedom to talk in their own terms about the issues that concern them.

questions

1. Explain the advantages of allowing respondents 'the freedom to talk in their own terms'.
2. What do you see as the disadvantages of tape-recorded interviews?

3 Checking understanding

A great danger in structured interviews is that the respondent misunderstands the question, or the interviewer misunderstands the answer.

A major advantage of unstructured interviews is that they make it much easier for interviewer and respondent to check each other's meanings. If the respondent doesn't understand a question, it can be explained. Similarly, if the interviewer is unsure what the respondent's answer means, follow-up questions can be put to clarify matters.

4 Flexibility

Unstructured interviews are highly flexible. The interviewer is not restricted to a fixed set of questions in advance, but can explore whatever seems interesting or relevant. The researcher can formulate new ideas and hypotheses and then put them to the test as they arise during the course of the interview. There is no need to go away and draw up a new interview schedule, as there would be if using structured interviews.

5 Exploring unfamiliar topics

With structured interviews, researchers need to have some knowledge of the subject and preferably also a clear hypothesis before they start interviewing; otherwise, they would have little idea of what questions to ask.

However, where the subject is one that we don't yet know much about, unstructured interviews may be more useful, precisely because they are open-ended and exploratory. As with an ordinary conversation, we can start out knowing nothing and, by asking questions, learn as we go along. Some sociologists use unstructured interviews as a starting point to develop their initial ideas about a topic before going on to use more structured methods of investigation.

Disadvantages of unstructured interviews

Despite their strengths, using unstructured interviews as a method of collecting data has a number of disadvantages.

1 Practical problems

Being in-depth explorations, unstructured interviews take a long time to conduct – often several hours each. This limits the number that can be carried out and means that the researcher will have a relatively small sample compared with the larger numbers who can be studied using structured interviews or questionnaires.

Training also needs to be more thorough than for someone conducting structured interviews. The interviewer needs to have a background in sociology so they can recognise when the respondent has made a sociologically important point and can probe further with an appropriate line of questioning. All this adds to the cost of conducting unstructured interviews.

Interviewers also need good interpersonal skills so they can establish the rapport that is essential if respondents are to answer fully and honestly.

2 Representativeness

The smaller numbers involved mean a greater likelihood that the sample interviewed will not be representative. This means that it will be harder to make valid generalisations based on the findings of the interviews.

3 Reliability

Unstructured interviews are not reliable because they are not standardised. Each interview is unique: interviewers are free to ask different questions in each case if they feel it is relevant to do so. This makes it virtually impossible for another researcher to replicate the interviews and check the findings or compare them with their own.

4 Quantification

Because unstructured interviews use mainly open-ended questions, answers cannot be pre-coded. This makes it very difficult to count up and quantify the numbers of respondents giving this or that answer. In turn, the lack of quantitative data makes unstructured interviews less useful for establishing cause-and-effect relationships and hypothesis testing that positivists prefer.

5 Validity

Unstructured interviews are generally seen as producing valid data. However, critics argue that the fact that they involve an interaction between researcher and respondent inevitably distorts the information obtained. As we have seen, structured interviews are also susceptible to the same problem, even if not to the same extent. We examine the problems of interviews as interactions next.

What effect might age, gender or ethnic differences between the interviewer and respondent have on the response rate and on the validity of the answers given?

The interview as a social interaction

All interviews, whether structured or unstructured, involve a social interaction between interviewer and respondent. The danger is that the respondent may be responding not to the questions themselves but the social situation in which they are asked.

Social interactions can threaten the validity of interviews in several ways.

1 Interviewer bias

The interviewer may ask 'leading' questions, where the wording 'tells' the respondent how to answer. For example, the question, 'Wouldn't you agree that women should not go out to work when they have young children?' clearly implies that the interviewer expects the answer, 'Yes'. This is a greater danger in unstructured than in structured interviews, where the interview schedule restricts the interviewer to a particular set of questions and fixed wording.

Interviewers may also consciously or unconsciously influence the answer by their facial expression, body language or tone of voice.

Another source of interviewer bias is where the interviewer identifies too closely with the respondents. For example, Ann Oakley (1982) admits that, as a mother herself, she found it difficult to remain detached and neutral when interviewing other women about maternity and childbirth.

2 Artificiality

Even the most relaxed of unstructured interviews is still an interview and not a normal conversation: both parties know it is an interview, in which one 'side' takes the initiative and asks the questions. Under these artificial conditions, it is doubtful whether truthful answers can be obtained.

Box 22: Interviewing in patriarchal society

In a patriarchal society, female sociologists interviewing men may find that the power difference between them undermines the conventional notion of the interviewer as the 'dominant' actor in the interview, as Lorna McKee and Margaret O'Brien (1983) discovered in their study of fathers.

The men frequently tried to manipulate the interview for their own ends: for example, lone fathers often used it to express grievances against their ex-wives. Sometimes the interview came to resemble a 'wooing process', with one lone father even going so far as to prepare a meal of cheese soufflé and wine.

Although the authors experienced no physical abuse, there were instances of being pestered for further contact, and McKee and O'Brien took conscious decisions about make-up and clothes, and about maintaining a professional manner during the interviews. For example, they used 'props' such as tape-recorder, clipboard and interview schedule to define themselves as detached and scientific researchers rather than as potential sexual partners.

It seems unlikely that male sociologists conducting similar research would have had to take such precautions, which suggests that gender is an important factor limiting the reliability of interviews: if gender affects interactions and responses in the interview, then sociologists of a different gender are likely to obtain different answers to the same questions.

The researchers also found that their interviews with fathers were generally shorter and more formal than those they conducted with mothers, reflecting what they call the 'legitimacy of the topic'. British culture prescribes a 'sturdy oak' role for men – 'the strong, silent male' – and this restricts their ability to talk about personal feelings.

As McKee and O'Brien show, gender inequalities can have an important bearing on the data produced by cross-gender interviewing. The wider patriarchal structure of gender relationships in society influences the way interviews are conducted and the kinds of responses they produce.

question

Identify two ways in which gender differences might affect the relationship between interviewers and respondents.

3 Status and power inequalities

Inequalities between interviewer and respondent may affect the respondent's honesty or willingness to answer. In general, the bigger the status difference, the less valid the data. For example, Josephine Rich (1968) shows that when adults interview children, the child's need to please the interviewer will affect their answers.

Similarly, gender differences in power and status can shape the interview, as Box 22 shows, while ethnic inequalities between interviewer and respondent may make interviewing very difficult. This led John Howard Griffin (1962) to abandon interviewing in favour of participant observation (see Box 23 page 185).

synoptic link: stratification

Inequalities between interviewer and respondent may make it difficult to obtain full and valid data. If the respondent has less power, they may lie to please the interviewer. If they have more power, they may challenge the interviewer's aims or hijack the interview for their own ends, as McKee and O'Brien show.

4 Cultural differences

These may also undermine validity. There may be misunderstandings as a result of different meanings being given to the same words.

The cultural gap may also mean that interviewers cannot tell when they are being lied to. For example, Margaret Mead's (1943) research on adolescents in Samoa in the western Pacific has been criticised on the grounds that Mead, who couldn't speak the language, was unable to spot that the girls she interviewed had deliberately misled her.

5 The social desirability effect

In social interaction, people often seek to win approval. This may be even truer in an interview, where respondents may be on their best behaviour and give answers that present themselves in a favourable light.

They may also wish not to appear ignorant or uninteresting and so, instead of saying that they don't know or don't understand the question, they offer any answer at all rather than none.

While all interviews risk distorting the data as a result of these factors, structured interviews may be less susceptible. This is because in a structured interview there are more controls over the nature of the interaction. For example, the interviewer has to follow a standard list of pre-set questions.

synoptic link: deviance

Where the interview is about apparently deviant behaviour or attitudes, respondents may be tempted to lie and give 'respectable' answers, for instance by stating the formal rules of behaviour (what people are *supposed* to do) rather than saying what they *actually* do or think. This produces invalid data.

Improving the validity of interviews

Some researchers use techniques to improve the chances of obtaining valid data. For example, to reduce the chance of respondents making up answers or telling lies, Alfred Kinsey's (1953) interviews on sexual behaviour asked questions rapidly, giving respondents little time to think, and used some questions to check the answers given to others. Follow-up interviews 18 months later were also used as a way of checking earlier answers.

Howard Becker (1971) developed another approach in his interviews with 60 Chicago schoolteachers. He used aggression, disbelief and 'playing dumb' as ways of extracting sensitive information from them that they might not otherwise have revealed, about how they classified pupils in terms of their social class and ethnic background. It should be stressed, however, that the success of such tactics requires the researcher to have special skills. For the same reason, this approach might also prove difficult to replicate.

Other researchers have overcome the problem of cultural differences by ensuring that interviewers and respondents are ethnically- and language-matched. For example, the interviews for James Nazroo's (1997) survey of the health of Britain's ethnic minorities were carried out in the language of the respondent's choice. Questions and other materials were translated and tested in pilot studies before being used in the main study.

All these techniques can help to improve the validity of answers.

QuickCheck Questions

1 Which of the following do you associate with structured interviews and which with unstructured?
   - (a) rapport
   - (b) similar to a questionnaire
   - (c) informal
   - (d) pre-coded questions
   - (e) standardised
   - (f) probing
   - (g) freedom to vary the questions
   - (h) quantitative data
   - (i) findings easily analysed.

2 What is a focus group?

3 Identify (a) one similarity and (b) one difference between structured interviews and postal questionnaires.

4 True or false? Structured interviews produce valid data, whereas unstructured interviews produce reliable data.

5 Give two examples of ways that an interviewer might influence a respondent's answer.

6 What is the social desirability effect?

Answers are on page 274.

Examining Interviews

Item A Structured interviews are based on an interview schedule administered by a trained interviewer. In many respects, they are similar to postal or other self-completed questionnaires, and are sometimes known as 'questionnaire interviews'. In both cases, the number of people who can be studied is quite large, but the depth of understanding gained is likely to be superficial. Both methods tend to use closed-ended questions with pre-coded answers. This makes data quantifiable and easier to analyse. Despite these similarities, however, there are important differences between the two methods, and structured interviews offer both advantages and disadvantages as compared to postal questionnaires.

Item B Tony Parker carried out unstructured tape-recorded interviews with prisoners, conducting them in prison visiting rooms, ex-prisoners' homes or on days out with prisoners on day release. The interviews took the form of a conversation, and did not include a predetermined set of questions. Rather, Parker encouraged prisoners to tell their own story with as little prompting and questioning as possible. Parker offers excellent guidance on carrying out unstructured interviews:

- Before I begin, I explain that it will take between 45 minutes and an hour.
- At the end, I ask if there is any part of our conversation they want me not to use. If there is, I give them an undertaking not to use it.
- Always remember the interview is about the other person. Don't be afraid of remaining silent, giving them time and space to think. Don't rush in with another question until you're sure they've said all they want to say.
- Never assume you understand what they are telling you. Ignorance can be invaluable. If someone says, 'do you know what I mean?' say, 'I'm not sure, could you explain it a bit more?'
- Avoid asking a question that can be answered with a straight 'yes' or 'no'.
- Write down beforehand exactly what you want to know and memorise the list.

Source: adapted from Jonathan Blundell and Janis Griffiths (2003)

Examining **Interviews**

Short questions

(a) Explain what is meant by an 'interview schedule' (**Item A,** line 1). (2 marks)

(b) Name **two** other types of interview **apart from** those referred to in **Items A and B.** (4 marks)

(c) Suggest **three disadvantages** of structured interviews compared to postal questionnaires (**Item A,** lines 7-8). (6 marks)

(d) Identify and briefly explain **two advantages** of structured interviews compared to postal questionnaires (**Item A,** lines 7-8). (8 marks)

Mini-essay

Using material from **Items A and B** and elsewhere, assess the usefulness of unstructured interviews in sociological research. (20 marks)

This is a type (f) question of the kind found in the exam, carrying 6 AO1 marks (knowledge and understanding) and 14 AO2 marks (identification, interpretation, analysis and evaluation).

The Examiner's advice

For the mini-essay you must show the skill of Evaluation by weighing up the advantages and disadvantages of unstructured interviews. Describe their main features (e.g. rapport, open-ended questions). Advantages centre on validity, so explain and apply this to unstructured interviews, e.g. in researching sensitive or unfamiliar topics, producing new insights, flexibility, allowing respondents to express themselves. Disadvantages include time; cost of trained interviewers; unrepresentative samples; unreliability and unquantifiable data. Look at the criticism that unstructured interviews may not even produce valid data, e.g. because of interviewer bias, status differences, or social desirability effect. Use the Items, examples from studies and brief contrasts with structured interviews. Develop evaluation further by linking points to interpretivist (in favour of unstructured interviews) and positivist perspectives (against). Write a separate conclusion.

Participant observation

As we have seen, one problem of using survey methods to study people is that what they *say* they do and what they *actually* do may not be the same thing. One way of overcoming this problem might be to see for ourselves what people do by observing them in their normal everyday environment rather than questioning them in an artificial interview situation.

What problems might a sociologist face in using participant observation to study this group?

Types of observation

There are several different types of observation. Firstly, we can distinguish between:

- **Non-participant observation:** the researcher simply observes the group or event without taking part in it.
- **Participant observation:** the researcher actually takes part in the event or the everyday life of the group while observing it.

Secondly, we can distinguish between:

- **Overt observation:** the researcher makes their true identity and purpose known to those being studied. The sociologist is open about what they are doing.
- **Covert observation:** the study is carried out 'under cover'. The researcher's real identity and purpose are kept concealed from the group being studied. The researcher takes on a false identity and role, usually posing as a genuine member of the group.

However, actual research does not always fit neatly into one or other of these categories. For example, William Whyte's (1955) study of 'Street Corner Society' was semi-overt (partly open). He revealed his real purpose to a key member of the group, Doc, but not to others.

question

What advantages might there be for the researcher in revealing their real purpose to a key member of the group?

activity

Look at the three examples of observational studies below and decide which one is most likely to be done using
(a) covert participant observation,
(b) overt non-participant observation and
(c) covert non-participant observation.

1 Observing the interactions of mothers and children using a hidden camera
2 Joining a criminal gang
3 Sitting in to observe a school class

In sociology, most observation is participant observation. However, sociologists do occasionally use non-participant observation. For example, they may use a two-way mirror to observe children playing. In such cases, sociologists sometimes use a structured observational schedule to record what happens.

The schedule is a list of the types of behaviour or situations the sociologist is interested in. Each time an instance of such behaviour occurs, the sociologist records it on the schedule, for example, how often boys and girls in a nursery play with particular toys. This allows the researcher to produce quantitative data from the observation.

Conducting a participant observation study

Sociologists face two main issues when conducting a participant observation study:

- getting in, staying in and getting out of the group being studied
- whether to use overt or covert observation.

We examine these two issues below.

Getting in

To do the study, we must first gain entry to the group. Some groups are easier to enter than others. For example, joining a football crowd is likely to be easier than joining a criminal gang.

making contact

Making the initial contact with the group may depend on personal skills, having the right connections, or even pure chance. Ned Polsky (1971), who was a good pool player himself, found his skill useful in gaining entry to the world of the poolroom hustler. James Patrick (1973) – not his real name – was able to join a Glasgow gang because he looked quite young and knew one of its members from having taught him in approved school. Eileen Fairhurst (1977) found herself hospitalised by back trouble and used the opportunity to conduct a study on being a patient.

acceptance

To gain entry to a group, the researcher will have to win their trust and acceptance. It may help to make friends with a key individual, as Sarah Thornton (1995) did with Kate in her study of the clubbing and rave scene. Sometimes, though, the researcher's age, gender, class or ethnicity may prove an obstacle. Thornton found her age and nationality a barrier:

> *'I began my research when I was 23 and slowly aged out of the peer group I was studying. Also, as a Canadian investigating British clubs and raves, I was quite literally a stranger in a strange land.'*

Thornton was met with suspicion at first. As Kate's brother put it, 'How do you know she won't sell this to the *Daily Mirror*?' However, such barriers can sometimes be overcome. Elliot Liebow (1967), a white man, succeeded in gaining acceptance by a black street-corner gang in Washington DC. Some researchers have gone to remarkable lengths to gain acceptance and pass as one of the group, but probably none more so than John Howard Griffin (1962) (see Box 23).

synoptic link: stratification

Griffin's research is a good example of the use of participant observation to study social inequality. By taking on the role and identity of a black man, he was able to gain some insight into the experience of racism. However, critics argue that, as a white person, Griffin could never really experience what it means to be black.

observer's role

'Getting in' poses the question of what role the researcher should adopt. Ideally, it should:

- be one that does not disrupt the group's normal patterns
- offer a good vantage point from which to make observations.

Whyte succeeded in achieving both these aims by refusing all leadership roles, with the one exception of secretary of the community club, a position that allowed him to take ample notes under the guise of taking the minutes of meetings.

However, it is not always possible to take a role that is both unobtrusive and a good vantage point. Some roles may also involve taking sides in conflicts, with the result that the researcher may become estranged from one faction or the other, making observation more difficult.

questions

1. Suggest two reasons why characteristics such as a researcher's age, gender, social class, ethnicity or personal appearance may prove an obstacle to 'getting in' to a group.
2. Why might it be a good idea to avoid taking leadership roles when doing participant observation?

Box 23: John Howard Griffin: 'Black Like Me'

Some researchers have gone to great lengths to pass as one of the group. An extraordinary example is John Howard Griffin, a white man who in 1959 used medication and sun lamp treatments to change his skin colour and pass as black. He then travelled around the Deep South of the USA experiencing first hand the impact of white racism.

Griffin with his key informant, Stirling Williams, in New Orleans. Though he told him he was really white, Williams was unconvinced.

Griffin working at a shoeshine stand, New Orleans

Griffin rejected the use of interviews because 'Though we lived side by side, communication between the two races had simply ceased to exist. The Southern Negro [the term used at the time to describe black people] will not tell the white man the truth. He long ago learned that if he speaks a truth unpleasing to the white, the white will make life miserable for him.'

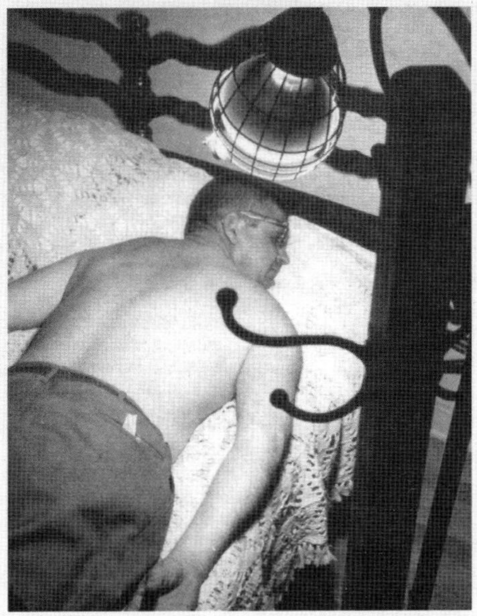

Griffin under the sun lamp

Griffin in a 'Negro diner'. In the Deep South, public amenities such as schools, cafés, hotels, transport and toilets were all racially segregated.

And so, 'the only way I could see to bridge the gap between us was to become a Negro. I decided I would do this. With my decision to become a Negro I realised that I, a specialist in race issues, really knew nothing of the Negro's problems.'

Staying in

Once accepted, the researcher needs to be able to stay in the group and complete the study. Here we can see a key problem for the participant observer: having to be both *involved* in the group so as to understand it fully, and yet at the same time *detached* from the group so as to remain objective and unbiased.

going native

One danger of staying in the group is that of becoming over-involved or 'going native'. By over-identifying with the group, the researcher becomes biased. When this happens, they have stopped being an objective observer and have simply become a member of the group.

For example, in his study of the Amsterdam police, Maurice Punch (1979) found that in striving to be accepted by the tightly-knit patrol group he was studying, he over-identified with them, even acting as a 'policeman' himself – chasing and holding suspects, searching houses, cars and people, and shouting at people who abused his police 'colleagues'.

At the other extreme, the researcher may preserve their detachment so as to avoid bias, but by remaining detached they risk not understanding the events they observe. Striking a balance between these two extremes is immensely difficult. As David Downes and Paul Rock (1989) put it:

> *'Participant-observers try to perform a most intricate feat. They are required to reach the probably unattainable state of one who is both insider and outsider, a person who sees a social world from within it in the manner of a member yet who also stands apart and analyses it in the manner of a stranger.'*

A further problem of staying in is that the longer the researcher spends with the group, the less strange its ways come to appear. After a while, the researcher may cease to notice things that would have struck them as unusual or noteworthy at an earlier stage of the research: the observer becomes less observant. As Whyte put it, 'I started as a non-participating observer and ended as a non-observing participator.'

Getting out

In practical terms, getting out of the group at the end of the study generally presents fewer problems than getting in or staying in. If the worst comes to the worst, the researcher can simply call a halt and leave. This was Patrick's experience of studying a Glasgow gang when, sickened by the violence, he abandoned the study abruptly. Others can leave more gracefully, particularly if their observation has been overt. Nevertheless, leaving a group with whom one has become close can be difficult.

Re-entering one's normal world can also be difficult. Whyte found that when he returned to Harvard University after his research, he was tongue-tied and unable to communicate with fellow academics. These problems can be made worse if the research is conducted on and off over a period of time, with multiple 'crossings' between the two worlds.

The researcher may also find that loyalty prevents them from fully disclosing everything they have learnt, for fear that this might harm members of the group. For example, in the case of criminal groups, exposure of their activities might lead to prosecution, or reprisals against the author. Clearly, such concealment of data will reduce the validity of the study.

questions

1. Explain what is meant by 'going native'.
2. How might going native lead to invalid data?

Overt observation

Sociologists face the decision whether to use overt or covert observation. Many sociologists favour the use of overt observation, where the researcher reveals his or her true identity and purpose to the group and asks their permission to observe. This has several advantages:

- It avoids the ethical (moral) problem of obtaining information by deceit and, when studying deviant groups, that of being expected to join in their activities.
- It allows the observer to ask the kind of naïve but important questions that only an outsider could ask. For example, the researcher could ask a gang member, 'Why do you rob and steal?'
- The observer can take notes openly.
- It allows the researcher to use interview methods to check insights derived from observations.

However, overt observation has two major disadvantages:

- A group may refuse the researcher permission to observe them, or may prevent them from seeing everything. As two of the Amsterdam police officers with whom Punch had done his research later told him, 'When you were with us, we only let you see what we wanted you to see'.
- It risks creating the Hawthorne Effect (see page 161), where those who know they are being observed begin to behave differently as a result. This undermines the validity of the data.

Covert observation

Because of these disadvantages, some sociologists choose to carry out covert observation. However, the use of covert observation raises several practical and ethical issues.

Practical issues

The main practical advantage of covert observation is that it reduces the risk of altering people's behaviour, and sometimes it is the only way to obtain valid information. This is particularly true where people are engaged in activities that they would rather keep secret. As Laud Humphreys (1970), who studied gay men's sexual encounters in public toilets, notes: 'There is only one way to watch highly discreditable behaviour and that is to pretend to be in the same boat with those engaging in it.'

If they knew they were being observed, they would change or conceal their behaviour and so the main advantage of observation – that it preserves the naturalness of people's behaviour – would be lost.

On the other hand, covert participant observation can pose practical problems:

- It requires the researcher to keep up an act, and may call for detailed knowledge of the group's way of life even before joining it. There is always a risk of one's cover being 'blown' by even a trivial mistake. Patrick was almost found out when he bought his suit with cash instead of credit and when he fastened the middle button of his jacket rather than the top one – things the gang would never have done. This is likely to bring the research to an abrupt end and may, in the case of some criminal groups, lead to physical harm. As Polsky advises, therefore:

  'You damned well better not pretend to be "one of them" because they will test this claim out and you will either find yourself involved in illegal activities, or your cover will be blown.'

  This was something Patrick also discovered when the gang handed him an axe to use in an expected fight.
- The sociologist cannot usually take notes openly and must rely on memory and the opportunity to write them in secret. Both Leon Festinger (1956), studying a religious sect that had predicted the imminent end of the world, and Jason Ditton (1977), studying 'fiddling' among bread deliverymen, had to use toilets as a place for recording their observations. In Ditton's case, this eventually aroused suspicion.
- The researcher cannot ask naïve but important questions, or combine observation with other methods, such as interviews.
- Although pretending to be an insider rather than an outsider reduces the risk of the Hawthorne Effect, the addition of a new member (the researcher) can still change the group's behaviour, thus reducing validity.

synoptic link: deviance

The use of covert participant observation to study deviance raises particularly difficult practical problems.

- Getting into a deviant group may be especially difficult, since such groups may well be suspicious of outsiders.
- Joining a deviant group may demand a detailed knowledge of a way of life that is alien to the researcher.
- With certain deviant groups, the sociologist may also risk physical injury if his or her cover is blown.

Ethical issues

Covert participant observation raises serious ethical (moral) issues for researchers. These often conflict with the practical advantage it brings of observing natural behaviour.

- It is immoral to deceive people, obtaining information by pretending to be their friend or 'in the same boat'. Researchers should obtain the informed consent of their subjects, and reveal the purpose of the study and the use to which its findings will be put. With covert observation, this cannot normally be done.

- Covert observers may have to lie about their reasons for leaving the group at the end of their research. Others, such as Patrick, simply abandon the group without explanation. Critics argue that this is unethical.
- They may have to participate in immoral or illegal activities as part of their 'cover' role.
- Similarly, as witnesses to such activities, they may have a moral or legal duty to intervene or to report them to the police.

Advantages of participant observation

According to its supporters, participant observation offers a range of advantages.

1 Validity

What people say they do when filling in a questionnaire, and what they actually do in real life, are not always the same thing. By contrast, by actually observing them we can obtain a rich source of qualitative data that provides a picture of how they really live. Supporters of participant observation argue that this is the method's main strength, and most of its other advantages are linked to this.

2 Insight

The best way to truly understand what something is like is to experience it for ourselves. Sociologists call this personal or subjective understanding *'verstehen'*, a German word meaning 'empathy', or understanding that comes from putting yourself in another person's place.

Participant observation allows the researcher to gain empathy through personal experience. By actually living as a member of a group, we can gain insight into their way of life, their meanings and viewpoints, their values and problems. We can come to understand their 'life-world' as they themselves understand it. This closeness to people's lived reality means that participant observation can give uniquely valid, authentic data.

synoptic link: deviance

Participant observation has been widely used to study crime and deviance. By joining in with the deviants, the respectable middle-class sociologist can gain a first hand understanding of the world of the hustler, pimp, vandal or petty thief that might normally be alien to him or her.

3 Flexibility

Survey methods involve beginning the research with a specific hypothesis and pre-set questions. Even before starting to collect the data, therefore, the researcher has already decided what questions are important. The obvious problem with this is that the questions the researcher thinks are important may not be the same as the ones the subjects think are important.

By contrast, participant observation is a much more flexible method. Rather than starting with a fixed hypothesis, it allows the sociologist to enter the situation with a relatively open mind about what they will find. As new situations are encountered, new explanations can be formulated and the sociologist can change direction to follow them up there and then. In this way, any theories that the researcher produces are 'grounded' in real life.

This open-mindedness allows the researcher to discover things that other methods may miss. As Whyte noted, simply by observing, 'I learned answers to questions that I would not have had the sense to ask if I had been using interviews.' Similarly, Polsky offers some sound, if blunt, advice: 'initially, keep your eyes and ears open but keep your mouth shut'.

4 Practical advantages

Sometimes participant observation may be the only method for studying certain groups, particularly those engaged in activities that wider society sees as deviant or disreputable. Such groups are likely to be suspicious of outsiders who come asking questions. As Lewis Yablonsky (1973) points out, a teenage gang is likely to see researchers who come armed with questionnaires as the unwelcome representatives of authority.

By contrast, because participant observation enables the sociologist to build a rapport with the group and gain its trust, it has proved a successful method of studying delinquent gangs, football hooligans, thieves, drug users, religious sects and other 'outsider' groups.

Participant observation can also be used in other situations where questioning would be ineffective. This is shown in Aaron Cicourel's (1968) study of how police and probation officers categorise juveniles by making unconscious assumptions about whether they are criminal 'types'. Precisely because they are unaware of their assumptions, it would be pointless for the sociologist to ask them questions about them. For Cicourel, therefore, the only way to get at these assumptions is to observe the police directly in their work.

Disadvantages of participant observation

Despite the advantages offered by participant observation, it also suffers from a number of disadvantages.

1 Practical disadvantages

There are several practical disadvantages in using participant observation:

- It is very time-consuming. Whyte's study took him four years to complete.
- The researcher needs to be trained so as to be able to recognise aspects of a situation that are sociologically significant and worth further attention.
- It can be personally stressful and demanding, especially if covert.
- It requires observational and interpersonal skills that not everyone possesses.
- Personal characteristics such as age, gender or ethnicity may restrict what kinds of groups can be studied. As Downes and Rock put it, 'not everyone would pass uneventfully into the world of punk rockers or Hell's Angels'.
- Many groups may not wish to be studied in this way, and some have the power to make access difficult. This is one reason why participant observation often focuses on relatively powerless groups who are less able to resist being studied, such as petty criminals.

2 Ethical problems

As we have seen, covert participant observation in particular raises serious ethical difficulties, including deceiving people in order to obtain information about them and participating in illegal or immoral activities in the course of their research.

3 Representativeness

Sociologists who use quantitative survey methods usually study large, carefully selected representative samples that provide a sound basis for making generalisations. By contrast, in participant observation studies, the group studied is usually very small and the 'sample' is often selected haphazardly, for example by a chance encounter with someone who turns out to be a key informant.

This does not provide a sound basis for making generalisations. As Downes and Rock note, although participant observation may provide valid insights into the particular group being studied, it is doubtful how far these 'internally valid' insights are 'externally valid', that is, generalisable to the wider population.

4 Reliability

Reliability means that if another researcher repeats the method, they will obtain the same results. To achieve reliability, research procedures must be standardised so that other researchers can reproduce them. For example, in structured interviews all interviewers ask the same standard questions in the same way.

By contrast, in participant observation so much depends on the personal skills and characteristics of a lone researcher that it is unlikely any other investigator would be able to replicate the original study. For example, as Whyte recognised, his method was to some extent unique to him alone.

Also, because participant observation usually produces qualitative data, this can make comparisons with other studies difficult. As a result, it is unlikely to produce reliable data. Positivists, who see sociology as scientific, thus reject participant observation as an unsystematic method that cannot be replicated by other researchers.

5 Bias and lack of objectivity

Critics argue that participant observation studies lack objectivity.

- As the term 'going native' indicates, it can be difficult to remain objective and the sociologist may end up presenting a one-sided or biased view of the group.
- Sometimes, loyalty to the group or fear of reprisals leads the sociologist to conceal 'sensitive' information. This denies those who read the published study a full and objective account of the research.
- Participant observation often attracts sociologists whose sympathies lie with the underdog. Since it is seen as an effective method for 'telling it like it is' from the actor's point of view, some of those who use it may be biased in favour of their subjects' viewpoint.

6 Validity

According to its supporters, the great strength of participant observation lies in its validity. As a form of *verstehen*, allowing the sociologist to become an insider, it gives an authentic account of the actor's world.

Positivists reject this claim. They argue that the findings from such studies are merely the subjective and biased impressions of the observer. Rather than truly 'telling it like it is', participant observation simply tells it as the observer sees it.

Supporters of participant observation claim that it does not impose the sociologist's own categories and ideas on the facts, but positivists argue that in reality the researcher selects what facts they think are worth recording, and that these are likely to fit in with the researcher's pre-existing views and prejudices.

A further threat to validity comes from the Hawthorne Effect: the very presence of the observer may make the subjects act differently. This defeats the main aim of participant observation, to produce a 'naturalistic' account of human behaviour.

7 Lack of a concept of structure

Interactionists favour the use of participant observation. They see society as constructed through the small-scale, face-to-face interactions of its members and the meanings that individual actors give to their situation. In their view, participant observation is a useful tool for examining these micro-level interactions and meanings at first hand.

However, structural sociologists such as Marxists and functionalists see this as inadequate. They argue that because it focuses on the 'micro' level of actors' meanings, participant observation research tends to ignore the wider structural forces that shape our behaviour, such as class inequality or the norms and values into which we are socialised.

In the structuralist view, therefore, seeing things only through the actors' eyes will never give us the complete picture. For example, if the actors are unaware of the structural forces shaping their behaviour, then their own account of their lives, revealed through participant observation, will give us only a partial view.

QuickCheck Questions

1. What do sociologists mean by '*verstehen*'?
2. Why can participant observation be described as a flexible method?
3. What problems might the observer have in leaving the group they have been observing?
4. State two advantages of using overt participant observation.
5. Why might participant observation not produce:
   (a) representative data
   (b) reliable data?
6. Suggest two reasons why participant observation may produce valid data.

Answers are on page 274.

Examining Participant observation

Item A Researchers may choose to use either overt or covert participant observation. In covert observation, the researcher conceals his or her true identity and purpose from the group being studied. For example, Laud Humphreys passed himself off as a 'watch queen' or lookout in his study of gay men's sexual encounters in public toilets, enabling him to study their behaviour without arousing suspicion.

However, whether using covert or overt methods, there may be many practical problems getting into a group in order to observe it. In addition, those using covert participant observation also face ethical problems in conducting their research.

According to its supporters, the great advantage of participant observation is that by allowing the researcher to participate in the lives of the subjects and study them 'from the inside', it provides a wealth of uniquely valid data. However, critics argue that this is not necessarily the case.

Short questions

(a) Explain what is meant by 'overt' participant observation (**Item A**, line 1). (2 marks)

(b) Suggest **two** practical problems a researcher might face in 'getting into a group in order to observe it' (**Item A**, lines 6-7). (4 marks)

(c) Identify **three** ethical problems of using covert participant observation (**Item A**, lines 7-8). (6 marks)

(d) Identify and briefly explain **two** reasons why participant observation might not necessarily produce valid data (**Item A**, line 11). (8 marks)

Mini-essay

Examine the reasons why sociologists sometimes use observational methods in their research. (20 marks)

This is a type (e) question of the kind found in the exam, carrying 14 AO1 marks (knowledge and understanding) and 6 AO2 marks (identification, interpretation, analysis and evaluation).

The Examiner's advice The mini-essay doesn't ask for problems of these methods and you won't gain marks for giving them. Note that 'methods' is plural: look at two or more (e.g. covert, overt, participant, non-participant). Examine a range of practical and theoretical reasons. Practical reasons could include that it may be the only feasible method (e.g. studying deviants) and that it can be done by a lone researcher on a small scale. Theoretical advantages centre on validity: apply this via ideas about rapport and *verstehen* (insight through direct experience). Flexibility in developing hypotheses during the research is also important. Give the specific advantages of covert and/or overt methods (e.g. covert may give more naturalistic behaviour; overt may save researchers from involvement in undesirable activities). Use examples from studies, and write a separate conclusion summing up.

Secondary sources

Sociologists not only use data they have gathered themselves by primary methods such as observation or surveys. They also make use of information that other people have already created or gathered. For example, governments collect data on the number of births, marriages and deaths, and private individuals often keep diaries as a record of their experiences. Sociologists often make use of information from such sources.

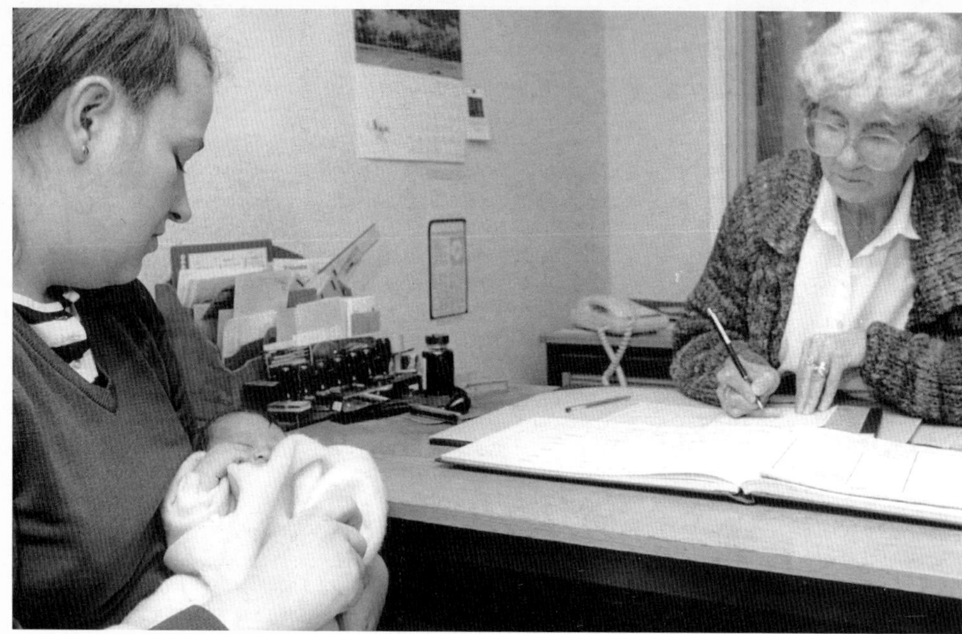

Compulsory registration of births, marriages and deaths is a major source of statistics.

These are known as secondary sources, and the information from them is called secondary data. Secondary data are therefore data gathered or produced by other people for their own particular purposes, but which sociologists make use of in their research. For example, we could use birth rate statistics to develop or test hypotheses about the family, or use diaries to obtain a feeling for what life was like for people in the past.

There are two main sources of secondary data:

- official statistics
- documents.

Official statistics

Official statistics are quantitative data gathered by the government or other official bodies. Examples include statistics on births, deaths, marriages and divorces, crime, suicide, exam results, school exclusions, unemployment and health. The Census is a major source of official statistics. Examples of many other official statistics can be found in the annual publication, *Social Trends*.

The government collects official statistics to use in policy-making. For example, statistics on births help the government to plan the number of school places for the future.

There are two ways of collecting official statistics:

- registration – for example, the law requires parents to register births
- official surveys, such as the Census or the General Household Survey.

In addition to official statistics produced by government, organisations and groups such as trade unions, businesses, churches and pressure groups also produce various kinds of statistics.

Both the advantages and the disadvantages of official statistics stem largely from the fact that they are secondary data. That is, they are not collected by sociologists but by official agencies for their own particular purposes – which may not always be the same as those of the sociologist.

question

Despite the legal requirement for every household to complete the Census form, in inner city areas there are often lower rates of completion than elsewhere. Suggest two reasons for this.

1 Practical advantages and disadvantages

Official statistics offer several practical advantages.

- They are a free source of huge amounts of quantitative data. Only the state can afford to conduct large-scale surveys costing millions of pounds, such as the ten-yearly Census covering every household in the UK. Likewise, only the government has the power to compel citizens to provide it with information, for example by requiring parents to register births. Sociologists can make use of this data, saving them both time and money.
- Statistics allow comparisons between groups. For example, we can compare statistics on educational achievement, crime rates or life expectancy between classes, genders or ethnic groups.
- Because official statistics are collected at regular intervals, they show trends and patterns over time. This means sociologists can use them for 'before and after' studies to show cause-and-effect relationships. For example, we can compare divorce statistics before and after a change in the divorce law to measure what effect the new legislation has had.

However, official statistics can have practical disadvantages.

- The government collects statistics for its own purposes, and not for the benefit of sociologists, so there may be none available on the topic we are interested in. For example, Durkheim in his study of suicide found that there were no statistics specifically on the religion of suicide victims, presumably because the state had no use for the information. However, this was crucial to Durkheim's hypothesis about integration and suicide.
- The definitions that the state uses in collecting the data may be different from those that sociologists would use. For example, they may define 'poverty' or 'homelessness' differently. In turn, this may lead to different views of how large the problem is.
- If definitions change over time, it may make comparisons difficult. For example, the official definition of unemployment changed over 30 times during the 1980s and early 1990s – so the unemployment statistics are not comparing like with like.

2 Representativeness

Because official statistics often cover very large numbers (even the entire population), and because care is taken with sampling procedures, they often provide a more representative sample than surveys conducted with the limited resources available to the sociologist. They may thus provide a sounder basis for making generalisations and testing hypotheses.

However, some statistics may be less representative than others. For example, statistics gathered by compulsory registration, such as birth and death statistics, are likely to cover virtually all cases and therefore be 'representative', while statistics produced from official surveys, such as the British Crime Survey or the General Household Survey, may be less representative because they are only based on a sample of the relevant population. Nonetheless, such official surveys are usually much bigger than most sociologists could carry out themselves. For example, the British Crime Survey in 2002 used a sample of 33,000 adults.

3 Reliability

Official statistics are generally seen as a reliable source of data. They are compiled in a standardised way by trained staff, following set procedures. For example, government statisticians compile death rates for different social classes following a standard procedure which uses the occupation recorded on each person's death certificate to identify their class. Official statistics are therefore reliable because, in principle, any person properly trained will allocate a given case to the same category.

However, official statistics are not always wholly reliable. For example, census coders may make errors or omit information when recording data from census forms, or members of the public may fill in the form incorrectly.

4 Validity: the 'dark figure'

A major problem with using official statistics is that of validity. Do they actually measure the thing that they claim to measure?

Some official statistics do succeed in doing this. For example, statistics on the number of births, deaths, marriages and divorces generally give a very accurate picture (although a small number of births and deaths do go unrecorded). However, other statistics give a much less valid picture. For example, police statistics do not record all crimes.

Attempts have been made to compensate for the shortcomings of police statistics by using self-report or victim studies to give a more accurate picture of the amount of crime. For example, the British Crime Survey (BCS) asks people what crimes they have been victims of.

By comparing the BCS results with the police statistics, we can see that the latter underestimate the 'real rate' of crime and from this we can make a more accurate estimate of the extent of crime. For example, the 2002 BCS found that only 42% of crimes were reported to the police and of these, the police only recorded three-fifths.

Not all crimes get reported or recorded.

synoptic link: deviance

Official crime statistics produced by the police are widely regarded as an invalid measure. Many crimes go unnoticed or unreported. Even where crimes are reported, the police may not record them. As a result, police statistics give a distorted picture of the extent of crime. They miss the 'dark figure' of unrecorded crimes.

questions

1 Suggest three types of crime that may not be reported to the police.

2 For each example, suggest why this may be so.

3 Suggest three reasons why the police do not record all the crimes reported to them.

5 Perspectives on official statistics

Whether we see official statistics as useful or not also depends in part on which theoretical perspective we adopt.

positivism

Positivists such as Emile Durkheim (1897) see statistics as a valuable resource for sociologists. They take for granted that official statistics are 'social facts'; that is, true and objective measures of the real rate of crime, suicide etc. They see sociology as a science and they develop hypotheses to discover the causes of the patterns of behaviour that the statistics reveal.

Positivists often use official statistics to test their hypotheses. For example, Durkheim put forward the hypothesis that suicide is caused by a lack of social integration. He argued that Protestant and Catholic religions differ in how well they integrate individuals into society. Using official suicide statistics, he was able to show that Protestants had a higher suicide rate than Catholics, and so was able to argue that this statistical evidence proved his hypothesis correct.

interpretivism

By contrast, interpretivists such as Maxwell Atkinson (1971) regard official statistics as lacking validity. They argue that statistics are not real things or 'social facts' that exist out there in the world. Instead, statistics merely represent the labels some people give to the behaviour of others.

In this view, suicide statistics do not represent the 'real rate' of suicides that have actually taken place, but merely the total number of *decisions* made by coroners to label some deaths as suicides. The statistics therefore tell us more about the way coroners label deaths than about the actual causes of deaths.

Rather than taking statistics at face value, therefore, interpretivists argue that we should investigate how they are socially constructed. For example, Atkinson uses qualitative methods such as observing the proceedings of coroners' courts to discover how coroners reach their decisions to label some deaths as suicides, others as accidents and so on.

Two rough sleepers in Edinburgh: what problems might there be in defining homelessness and collecting accurate statistics on it?

Marxism

Marxists such as John Irvine (1987) take a different view. Unlike interpretivists, they do not regard official statistics as merely the outcome of the labels applied by officials such as coroners, but instead see official statistics as serving the interests of capitalism.

Marxists see capitalist society as made up of two social classes in conflict with each other, the capitalist ruling class and the working class. In this conflict, the state is not neutral, but serves the interests of the capitalist class. The statistics it produces are part of ruling class ideology – part of the ideas and values that help to maintain the capitalist class in power.

synoptic link: deviance

While positivists use official statistics to study suicide, interpretivists use qualitative methods and sources such as interviews, the analysis of suicide notes and observation of coroners' courts.

However, these still pose problems of interpretation. For example, how can we be sure that we have correctly interpreted what the writer of a suicide note really meant by it?

synoptic link: stratification

Unemployment statistics are a good example of the Marxist view that statistics serve the interests of the ruling class. The state has regularly changed the definition of unemployment over the years, almost always with the result that the numbers officially defined as unemployed have been reduced.

Marxists see this as an attempt to disguise the harsh reality of life under capitalism and so protect ruling-class interests.

Documents

The term 'document' refers to any written text, such as personal diaries, government reports, medical records, novels, newspapers, letters, parish registers, train timetables, shopping lists, bank statements – the list is almost endless. In fact, we can also take the term to include 'texts' such as paintings, drawings, photographs, maps and so on. We can also include sounds and images from film, television, radio and the Internet and other media output.

Public and personal documents

We can distinguish between public and personal documents:

public documents

Public documents are produced by organisations such as government departments, schools, welfare agencies, businesses and charities. Some of this output may be available for researchers to use. It includes documents such as minutes of council meetings, published company accounts and records of parliamentary debates.

Public documents also include the official reports of public enquiries such as the Black Report (1980) into inequalities in health, which has become a major source of information for sociologists.

personal documents

Personal documents include items such as letters, diaries, photo albums and autobiographies. These are first-person accounts of social events and personal experiences, and they generally also include the writer's feelings and attitudes.

An early example of a study using personal documents is William Thomas and Florian Znaniecki's (1919) *The Polish Peasant in Europe and America*, a study of migration and social change. As interactionists, they were particularly interested in people's experiences of these events.

They used personal documents to reveal the meanings and interpretations that individuals gave to their experience of migration. The documents included 764 letters bought after an advertisement in a Polish newspaper in Chicago, as well as several autobiographies.

Thomas and Znaniecki also used public documents, such as newspaper articles and court and social work records. With these documents, they were able to explore the experiences of social change of some of the thousands of people who migrated from rural Poland to the United States of America in the early 20th century.

Historical documents

A historical document is simply a personal or public document created in the past. If we want to study the past, historical documents are usually the only source of information (although in the case of the recent past, there may still be people alive who can be interviewed).

We can use the study of families and households to illustrate some of the types of historical documents that have been used:

- Peter Laslett used parish records in his study of family structure in pre-industrial England.
- Michael Anderson used parliamentary reports on child labour, as well as statistical material from the 1851 Census, to study changes in family structure in 19th century Preston.
- Tamara Hareven's study of kinship networks among French Canadian migrants in the textile industry in New Hampshire, USA, from 1880 to 1930, used local government and insurance records and company employee files.
- Philippe Ariès used child-rearing manuals and paintings of children in his study of the rise of the modern notion of childhood.

Assessing documents

As John Scott (1990) argues, when it comes to assessing documentary sources, the general principles are the same as those for any other type of sociological evidence. He puts forward four criteria for evaluating documents: authenticity, credibility, representativeness and meaning.

authenticity

Is the document what it claims to be? Are there any missing pages, and if it is a copy, is it free from errors? Who actually wrote the document? For example, the so-called 'Hitler Diaries' were later proven to be fakes.

credibility

Is the document believable? Was the author sincere? Politicians may write diaries intended for publication that inflate their own importance. Thomas and Znaniecki's Polish immigrants may have lied in their letters home about how good life in the USA was, to justify their decision to emigrate.

Is the document accurate? For example, was the account of a riot written soon after the event, or years later?

representativeness

Is the evidence in the document typical? If we cannot answer this question, we cannot know whether it is safe to generalise from it:

- Not all documents survive: are the surviving documents typical of the ones that get destroyed or lost?
- Not all surviving documents are available for researchers to use. The 30-year rule prevents

access to official documents for 30 years and, if classified as official secrets, they may not be available at all. Private documents such as diaries may never become available.

- Certain groups may be unrepresented: the illiterate, and those with little leisure time, are unlikely to keep diaries.

meaning

The researcher may need special skills to understand a document. It may have to be translated from a foreign language; words may change their meaning over time.

We also have to interpret what the document actually means to the writer and the intended audience. Different sociologists may interpret the same document differently. Thomas later admitted that the interpretations he and Znaniecki had offered in the book were not founded on the data.

activity

Working in pairs, and using Scott's four criteria, assess the value of each of the following documents as a source of evidence:

(a) crime reports in newspapers

(b) letters from soldiers at war

(c) photographs of a riot

(d) *The Diary of Anne Frank* (www.annefrank.com is a useful source of information).

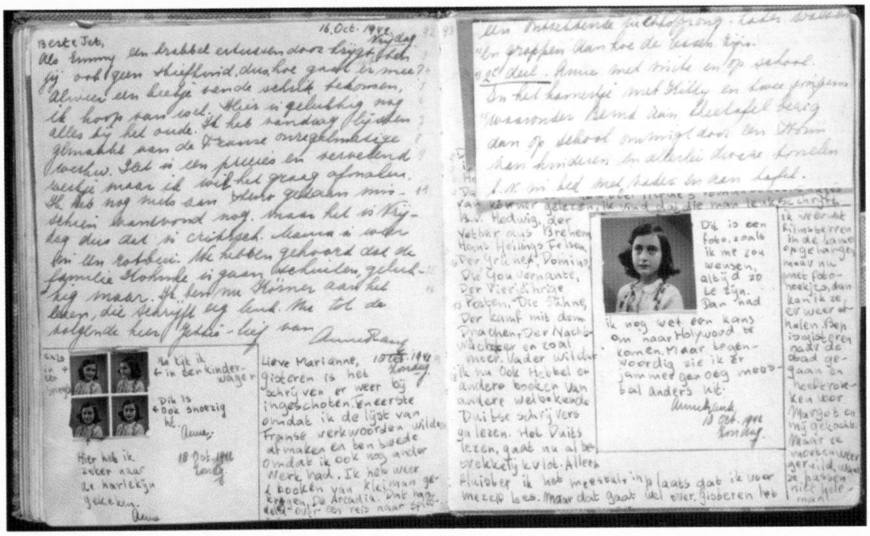

The Diary of Anne Frank, a Jewish schoolgirl in Amsterdam during World War Two. She kept a diary while hiding from the Nazis but was discovered shortly before the end of the war and died in a concentration camp.

Advantages of documents

Although documents need to be assessed carefully by the sociologist before they are used as sources of evidence, nevertheless they have several important advantages:

- Personal documents such as diaries and letters enable the researcher to get close to the social actor's reality, giving insight through their richly detailed qualitative data. Interactionists favour them for this reason.
- Sometimes documents are the only source of information, for example in studying the past.
- By providing another source of data, documents offer an extra check on the results obtained by primary methods.
- They are a cheap source of data, because someone else has already gathered the information.
- For the same reason, using existing documents saves the sociologist time.

Content analysis

Content analysis is a method for dealing systematically with the contents of documents. It is best known for its use in analysing documents produced by the mass media, such as television news bulletins or advertisements.

Although such documents are usually qualitative, content analysis enables the sociologist to produce quantitative data from these sources.

Ros Gill (1988) describes how content analysis works as follows. Imagine we want to measure particular aspects of a media message; for example, how many female characters are portrayed as being in paid employment.

- First we decide what categories we are going to use, such as employee, full-time housewife etc.
- Next, we study the source (television broadcast, magazine article etc) and place the characters in it into the categories we have decided upon.

- We can then count up the number in each category, for example to compare how often women are portrayed as full-time housewives rather than employees.

We might then go on to compare the results of our content analysis with the official statistics for female employment to see if the media were presenting a false or stereotypical picture of women's roles.

Glenys Lobban (1974) uses content analysis to analyse gender roles in children's reading schemes, and Gaye Tuchman (1978) uses it to analyse television's portrayal of women. Both studies found that females were portrayed in a range of roles that was both limited and stereotyped. For example, Lobban found that female characters were generally portrayed playing domestic roles.

Content analysis has several advantages:

- It is cheap.
- It is usually easy to find sources of material in the form of newspapers, television broadcasts and so on.
- Positivists see it as a useful source of objective, quantitative, scientific data.

However, interpretivist sociologists argue that simply counting up the number of times something appears in a document tells us nothing about its meaning.

activity

Working in small groups, carry out a content analysis of one of the following to find out how men and women are portrayed.

1 One episode of a soap
2 The adverts from one or two commercial breaks on television
3 Stories in women's magazines.

You will need to devise some appropriate categories in advance, such as different roles played by males and females, where they play them etc.

Carry out your analysis following the steps outlined by Gill above.

Did everyone in your group agree on which categories to use and on where to put different characters?

synoptic link: stratification

Content analysis can be used to study social inequalities and differences such as gender, class, ethnicity, disability, age and sexuality. It can show us how the media under-represent certain groups and portray them in stereotypical ways. For example, Guy Cumberbatch and Ralph Negrine (1992) found that people with disabilities are under-represented in television programmes.

QuickCheck Questions

1 What does the term 'secondary data' mean?
2 What are the two main ways that official statistics are collected?
3 Give three examples of official statistics.
4 Apart from government, name three other types of organisation that produce statistics.
5 State three advantages of official statistics to sociologists.
6 A major problem with using official statistics is that of validity. Explain
 (a) what validity means
 (b) why official statistics may lack validity.
7 State three other disadvantages of official statistics apart from lack of validity.
8 Give two examples of personal documents.
9 Give two examples of sociological studies that have used historical documents.

Answers are on page 275.

Examining Secondary sources

Item A Documents are an important source of data for sociologists. The types of document used range from public ones produced by government and others, to personal documents such as diaries and letters written by individuals and not intended for publication. Documents may be historical or present day.

The mass media are another important source of documents. However, while documents such as diaries generally claim to be factual accounts of real events, media output includes not only supposedly factual content such as news broadcasts, but also fictional material such as TV soaps. Sociologists study both types of output using content analysis.

However, there are many problems in using documents in sociological research.

Item B The government's Rough Sleepers Unit (RSU) said its headcount showed that by 2002 there were 500 people sleeping on the streets, compared with 1,850 in 1998, indicating that it had met its target.

But campaigners accuse the RSU of fixing the figures by moving rough sleepers off the street for one night and threatening some with arrest if they didn't go to hostels. One reporter doing his own count in Nottingham found ten rough sleepers. The official figure was three.

According to Val Chinn, chief executive of the Big Issue in the North, it is notoriously difficult to count rough sleepers, so it is probably unwise to rely too much on the official figures. She argues that rough sleepers do not sleep rough for months on end. Big Issue's research shows that, while only 14% of its vendors had slept rough the night before they were questioned, 75% had done so at some point during the year. Often, individuals who are moved into temporary accommodation are back on the streets a few months later. Homeless people often regard hostels as no better than sleeping rough. According to the housing charity Crisis, there is a 'hidden homeless' population of 400,000, including those living in squats and bed and breakfasts or sleeping on friends' sofas.

Short questions

(a) Explain what is meant by 'content analysis' (**Item A**, line 8). (2 marks)

(b) Give **two** examples of public documents (**Item A**, lines 1-2). (4 marks)

(c) Suggest **three** reasons why sociologists use documents in research (**Item A**). (6 marks)

(d) Identify and briefly explain **two** 'problems in using documents in sociological research' (**Item A**, line 9). (8 marks)

Mini-essay

Using material from **Item B** and elsewhere, assess the usefulness of official statistics in sociological research. (20 marks)

This is a type (f) question of the kind found in the exam, carrying 6 AO1 marks (knowledge and understanding) and 14 AO2 marks (identification, interpretation, analysis and evaluation).

The Examiner's advice For the mini-essay, you must show the skill of Evaluation by weighing up the advantages and disadvantages. A good approach is to link these to different perspectives, examining why positivists see statistics as valuable and why interpretivists don't. Theoretical issues about quantitative data, reliability, validity, representativeness, and hypothesis-testing are important here, so explain what these mean and how they relate to statistics. Link these issues to disagreements between positivists and interpretivists about whether statistics represent social facts or just social constructs (try using suicide or crime as your example). You can also bring in Marxist criticisms. Look too at practical issues (time, cost, availability, usefulness in identifying patterns etc). Item B provides lots of clues to their disadvantages, so make full use of it. Write a separate conclusion.

Other types of research

So far in this chapter, we have looked at a range of specific primary and secondary methods and sources. In this final section, we look at three other types of research: case studies, longitudinal studies and life histories.

In each of these types of research, one or more different methods or sources may be used to carry out the study.

Case studies have been used to investigate events such as strikes.

Case studies

A case study involves the detailed examination of a single case or example, such as a school, family or workplace. It may even be the study of one individual. For example, Elizabeth Burn (2001) carried out a case study of Jenny, an inner-city primary school teacher from a working-class background. Tony Lane and Ken Roberts (1971) studied a single strike at Pilkington's glass factory in Warrington.

Because case studies examine only one or at most a few cases, they cannot claim to be representative or typical. Their main limitation is that we cannot generalise from our findings: whatever we may have discovered to be true of that one case, we cannot guarantee it will be true of other cases. Nevertheless, case studies have many different uses:

- To provide a detailed insight into a particular group. Studies that use qualitative methods such as participant observation studies are usually case studies.
- To study exceptional cases. An example is Max Weber's (1905) famous study of the role of the Calvinist religion in the rise of capitalism in Western Europe, which he saw as unique.
- In a large-scale quantitative study, case studies can be used to illustrate general points in more detail and give the study a qualitative dimension. Peter Townsend's (1979) national survey of poverty also includes cases of individual families to show what living in poverty means for those affected by it.
- To test a theory. The Kendal Project (2004) is an ongoing case study of religious belief and practice focused on one town, which is being used to test a range of different theories about religion.
- To suggest hypotheses in the early stages of a research project. Looking closely at one case may give us ideas that can be tested on a larger group. Questions asked later are more likely to be relevant if they emerge from an initial case study.

Longitudinal studies

A longitudinal study is one that follows the same sample or group over an extended period of time. We can use the study of education and families and households to see how longitudinal studies have been used:

- J.W.B. Douglas' (1964) study followed a sample of 5,632 children who were all born in the first week of March 1946 through their schooling.
- The National Child Development Study (NCDS) has been running since 1958. It is a birth cohort

study tracing the lives of all those born in Great Britain in the same week in 1958. It has collected extensive information on them at regular intervals from birth, through childhood into adulthood. This has provided the basis for other studies. For example, Ferri and Smith's (1998) study of step-parenting used a sample of almost 6,000 adults, drawn from the NCDS.

- Most participant observation studies are longitudinal. For example, Colin Lacey spent four years studying pupils at Hightown grammar school.

An example of a longitudinal study from a different area is David Gauntlett and Annette Hill's (1999) study of television viewing. This ran for five years and used an original sample of 509 respondents, who were each asked to complete three questionnaire diaries per year on their viewing habits.

By the end of the study, 427 of the sample were still involved. One reason for this was that the researchers maintained regular contact by sending Christmas and birthday cards and even writing personally when diaries indicated events such as illness or bereavement. The research produced over 3.5 million words of material for analysis.

Longitudinal studies have both advantages and disadvantages:

- Their major advantage is that they trace developments over a period of time, rather than just offering a 'snapshot' of one moment in time. This also allows a more detailed picture to be built up.
- By making comparisons between groups over time, we can identify causes. For example, Douglas followed children of different class backgrounds but similar ability to discover why middle-class children did better at school.
- There can be problems keeping track of the sample. The NCDS lost a third of its sample of 17,400 between 1958 and 1999. This is called sample attrition. However, using methods like Gauntlett and Hill's to keep in touch can reduce sample attrition.
- A further problem is that those who drop out may not be typical of those who stay in, making the remaining sample less representative.
- The large amount of data produced can be difficult to analyse and, by definition, results cannot be obtained quickly.
- They can be costly. Howard Parker's (1998) five-year study of illegal drug use among 1,125 adolescents in Greater Manchester and Merseyside cost £380,000.
- The Hawthorne Effect may occur: those in the sample may act differently as a result of the prolonged attention they receive through being in the study.

activity

Working in groups of two or three, imagine you are conducting a large-scale longitudinal study of members of Alcoholics Anonymous groups from different social backgrounds who have given up alcohol. Your aim is to find out why some people are more successful than others at giving up alcohol.

1. What would be the advantages of re-interviewing your sample every year for five years?
2. What problems might you face in carrying out this longitudinal study?

Life histories

Life histories are often used in case studies of individuals. They are a qualitative method used mainly by interpretivist sociologists to understand how individuals construct and interpret their 'life worlds'. They involve collecting and recording individuals' experiences. This can be done either:

- by the individual writing down their own life story (an autobiography), or
- by a semi-structured or unstructured interview, often tape recorded, which the researcher then writes up as a life story (a biography).

Life histories are a rich source of insight into both a person's individual experiences, presented from their own point of view, and into the wider social forces that affect their lives. For example, they can give us insight into how mass unemployment or war affects those who live through these events.

According to Graham Hitchcock (1995), the life history adds a historical dimension to our understanding of individuals and social structures. It 'enables the researcher to build up a mosaic-like picture of the individual and the events and people surrounding them, so that relations, influences and patterns may be observed'. For example,

Chamberlain and Goulbourne (cited in Silva, 1999) carried out life story interviews with three generations of 60 families who had originated in the Caribbean and migrated to Britain in the 1950s and 1960s.

However, life histories conducted through interviews require the ability to empathise with the subject, and good listening skills. They are also very time-consuming and labour-intensive.

synoptic link: deviance

Interpretivists use life histories to study deviance because it allows deviants to speak for themselves and so enables us to see things from their viewpoint. For example, Clifford Shaw's (1930) study, 'The Jackroller', used this method to explore the world of a mugger.

Using a combination of methods

In practice, many sociological studies use more than one method. For example, a study may begin with a limited number of in-depth, unstructured interviews to gain insights; these can then be used to develop questions for a questionnaire administered to a larger sample.

The term 'triangulation' is sometimes used to describe this process. Fiona Devine and Sue Heath (1999) define triangulation as a technique that aims to obtain a more rounded picture by studying the same thing from more than one viewpoint, using a number of different sources or methods.

The idea is that different methods can complement each other – the weaknesses of one can be countered by the strengths of the other. For example, Howard Newby's (1977) study of Suffolk farm workers uses a variety of methods and sources including participant observation and a survey. He argues that these two methods complement each other:

> *'Insights gained from participant observation could be checked against survey data, while on the other hand, much of this data only became meaningful through the experiences gained from living with a farm worker and his family in their cottage for six months.'*

By combining different methods in this way, we can get the best of both worlds: both reliable quantitative data covering large numbers of cases, and valid qualitative data looking at a smaller number of cases in depth.

QuickCheck Questions

1. True or false? A case study follows the same group over an extended period of time.
2. Give two examples of research that has been carried out by means of case studies.
3. True or false? Case studies can be used to suggest hypotheses that can then be tested on a larger sample.
4. True or false? A longitudinal study involves the detailed examination of a single example.
5. Give two examples of longitudinal studies.
6. What is 'sample attrition' in a longitudinal study?
7. Identify one advantage of longitudinal studies.
8. Explain what it means to say that two methods 'complement' one another.

Answers are on page 275.

Chapter summary

Sociologists test their theories using **quantitative** or **qualitative** data. Sociologists obtain **primary** data themselves, using methods including questionnaires, interviews and observation. **Secondary** data are produced by others but used by sociologists.

In choosing a method, sociologists take several issues into account. **Practical** issues include time and funding. **Ethical** issues include whether the researcher deceives the subjects. **Theoretical** issues include **validity** (does the method give a truthful picture?), **reliability** (can it be replicated?) and **representativeness** (does it study a typical cross-section?). Sociological **perspective** also affects choice of method. Positivists prefer quantitative data; interpretivists favour qualitative data.

Experiments

In laboratory experiments, scientists manipulate variables to discover **laws** of cause and effect. Although they produce reliable data, experiments are rare in sociology. They suffer from **practical problems** (e.g. they cannot be used to study the past), **ethical problems** of experimenting on humans, and are prone to the **Hawthorne Effect**. Field experiments and the comparative method are used as alternatives to laboratory experiments.

Surveys, questionnaires and interviews

Surveys gather data by asking questions, using interviews or questionnaires. Before conducting the survey, the researcher needs a **hypothesis** (a testable statement) or aim, and concepts need to be **operationalised** (defined so that they are measurable). A **pilot study** may be used to iron out problems. A **representative sample** is essential so findings can be generalised.

Questionnaires are lists of written questions, usually **closed-ended** and often posted. They can gather data on **large numbers** cheaply and quickly. Positivists favour them because they are **reliable** and objective. However, **low response** rates can make findings unrepresentative. Interpretivists claim they **lack validity**: they are inflexible, superficial snapshots and don't give a true account of respondents' meanings.

Structured interviews use closed-ended questions. They are quicker and cheaper than unstructured interviews, cover larger numbers and produce **reliable** data, but lack validity and flexibility.

Unstructured interviews use open-ended questions, producing **valid** data by allowing respondents to express themselves fully. However, they are less representative, and quantification is difficult. Interviews are **social interactions** and face problems of interviewer bias, status or cultural differences between interviewer and respondent.

Participant observation

Participant observation (PO) involves joining in with a group to gain **insight**, and can be overt or covert. Research goes through three phases: getting in, staying in and getting out. **Covert** PO may produce more **valid** data, but is **ethically** questionable and faces **practical** problems of maintaining one's cover. **Interpretivists** claim that PO produces valid data, but **positivists** argue that it is unreliable, unrepresentative and lacks objectivity.

Secondary data

These include **official statistics** and **documents** such as government reports, diaries and letters. Some sociologists apply **content analysis** to documents. Secondary sources save time and money and provide useful data, but they may not always be available. Statistics may lack validity, measuring officials' decisions rather than real events, while documents may not be authentic or representative.

Other types of research include case studies, longitudinal studies and life histories. Sociologists often use **triangulation**, where two or more methods complement one another.

Examining **Sociological Methods**

Item A Sociologists researching a topic can use a variety of methods and sources of data. For example, they may analyse secondary data such as official statistics or documents. Alternatively, they may carry out primary research, collecting their own data through social surveys, observation or even laboratory experiments. However, there are many problems involved in using laboratory experiments to study human behaviour and sociologists rarely use this method of data collection.

Longitudinal studies are another way of studying society, although these tend to be an expensive method of research. Often, sociologists use several different methods and sources, sometimes to conduct an intensive case study of a single example.

Item B Covert participant observation involves a large element of deception, as Festinger's study of a religious cult shows. He and his colleagues traced a Mrs Keech, who had prophesied that a flood would cover the earth's surface from the Artic Circle to the Gulf of Mexico. Only the true believers would be saved, by a flying saucer at midnight on the day of the flood.

Four researchers were equipped with fake stories of psychic experiences to help them gain entry to the cult. Posing as believers, they were able to observe what happened when midnight came and went without Mrs Keech's prophecy being fulfilled.

Throughout the research, they had to maintain their deception while playing a full part in the group, and at the same time also trying to avoid influencing the group. This proved difficult on occasions when one or other of them was asked to take on responsibility or initiate action, such as becoming the group's 'medium' or 'messenger'. In fact, the researchers acknowledge that their presence lent support to the beliefs and activities of the existing members.

(a) Explain what is meant by a 'longitudinal' study (**Item A,** line 7). (2 marks)

(b) Explain the difference between primary and secondary data (**Item A,** lines 2-4). (4 marks)

(c) Suggest **three** 'problems involved in using laboratory experiments to study human behaviour' (**Item A,** line 5). (6 marks)

(d) Identify and briefly explain **two** reasons why sociologists might choose 'to conduct an intensive case study of a single example' (**Item A,** line 9). (8 marks)

(e) Examine the reasons for using secondary sources of data in sociological research. (20 marks)

(f) Using material from **Item B** and elsewhere, assess the usefulness of covert participant observation in sociological research. (20 marks)

Examining Sociological Methods

The Examiner's advice

For question (e), you should begin with a definition of secondary sources and give some examples of them. You need to consider a range of different types of secondary sources and so you should examine official statistics and the different types of documents (e.g. public and personal; historical). You should distinguish between sources that provide quantitative data (e.g. statistics) and those that provide qualitative data (e.g. diaries and letters). Refer also to content analysis as a way of producing quantitative data from media or other sources. Focus on the advantages that different secondary sources offer to sociologists, such as time and cost, availability, theoretical perspective (e.g. positivists' use of statistics, interpretivists' use of qualitative documents such as diaries), and issues of reliability, validity and representativeness. Write a separate conclusion.

For question (f), you need to focus on *covert* PO. Start by briefly defining it. 'Assess' means evaluate the usefulness of the method, so you need to put forward arguments and evidence for and against. You could organise your answer in terms of practical, ethical and theoretical issues. 'Practical' includes time and cost; getting in and out; having the right knowledge or appearance to 'pass' successfully; maintaining cover and the possible consequences of being 'uncovered'. 'Ethical' includes deception, informed consent, 'spying', and the possibility of being involved in illegal activities. 'Theoretical' includes reliability, validity, representativeness, lack of objectivity (e.g. 'going native'), lack of a concept of structure. Link these to how positivists and interpretivists rate the method. Make use of Item B (e.g. ethical issues of deception; theoretical issues of the observer's presence affecting the group). Use relevant studies (e.g. Festinger, Patrick, Griffin, Ditton). Write an evaluative conclusion on the main strengths and weaknesses.

Chapter 5

The Coursework Guide

Completing your coursework successfully

In this chapter, we look at how to succeed in the coursework task.

The chapter is divided into two sections:

- The first section provides a step-by-step guide on how to complete your coursework successfully.
- The second section looks at an example of a student's coursework and gives the examiner's marks, comments and advice on how to improve it.

The coursework task

For AS level coursework, you need to write a research proposal on an issue of your choice, setting out the steps you would follow in carrying out a sociological study of it.

Your proposal does not have to be a study you could actually carry out yourself. You might have an idea for a study that, in practice, you wouldn't have the time or funds to carry out.

For example, you could propose a large-scale survey to be carried out by a team of trained interviewers. Alternatively, you may prefer to propose a small-scale study that you would be able to carry out alone over a short period of time.

Your research proposal must be no more than 1,200 words long. Therefore, it is important that what you write is concise and relevant.

You can of course discuss your ideas with others and work as a group on the activities in this chapter. However, your coursework must be your own work. Your teacher will give you a deadline by which you will need to complete and hand it in.

You must set out your proposal in four sections, as shown.

We shall look at each of these sections more closely later on. First, you need to consider what issue to choose for your coursework proposal.

Coursework sections

Section	Maximum words	Marks
Hypothesis or aim	100	8
Context and concepts	400	20
Main research method and reasons	400	20
Potential problems	300	12
Total	1,200	60

Choice of issue

You must choose one sociological issue for your research proposal. For example, you could choose an issue from family diversity, childhood, or ethnicity and education.

You can choose any issue from the AS sociology Specification for your coursework. However, we strongly recommend that you choose one that you have already studied on your AS level course. This has the advantage that you will already be aware of the questions sociologists are interested in.

The issue you choose needs to be one you find interesting and want to investigate further. Your interest may have come purely from studying it in sociology, or it may have been sparked off by a press report, something you saw on television, or events in your own life or community. Once you have chosen the issue, you can begin to read around it and discuss it with classmates, your teacher and others who are interested.

You need to consider whether you want to link your AS level coursework to the coursework you may do next year for A2. The Specification states that if you intend to take the A2 coursework option, you can use your AS coursework as a starting point. However, you are not required to do so. You therefore have two alternatives:

1 Do your AS and A2 coursework on completely different issues. The advantage of this is that you don't need to restrict your AS research proposal to a study that you could actually carry out as an A2 student. (At A2 you have to carry out the research yourself, not just make a proposal for research.) Deciding on this option means you can put forward a proposal for a study that you may not have the resources to carry out yourself.

2 Use your AS coursework as preparation for your A2 coursework by choosing the same issue for both. This has the advantage that you can build on the work you do at AS. However, for your AS proposal you will need to design a study that you can actually carry out single-handed as an A2 student. Remember that if you choose this option, you can always change your mind later and do your A2 coursework on a different issue.

activity

1. Choose any one issue from Chapters 2 and 3, e.g. gender and education.
2. Identify which aspect of this issue you find most interesting, e.g. gender differences in achievement.
3. Suggest one or two questions you could ask about this issue, e.g. has girls' performance at school improved because they now have positive role models?

Hypothesis or aim

This section of the coursework carries 8 marks and has a maximum length of 100 words.

In this section, you need to:

- choose one issue and develop a single hypothesis or aim from it that could provide the basis for research
- state your reasons for choosing this particular aspect to research.

This first section is quite brief, but what you write here will strongly influence the rest of your research proposal. By formulating a clear hypothesis or aim, you will point your whole proposal in the right direction.

What is a hypothesis? What is an aim?

An **aim** is a fairly open-ended statement about what you propose to study and hope to achieve. It almost always begins with the phrase, 'My aim is to…'. For example:

- My aim is to find out about gender differences in educational achievement.
- In this research, my aim is to discover the extent of equality between husbands and wives today.

You might achieve the first aim by gathering information on how well boys and girls do in school and on the reasons for differences between them. You might achieve the second aim by investigating how far husbands and wives share housework and decision-making.

A **hypothesis** is more precise than an aim. It is a statement that can be tested by using factual evidence to prove it true or false. A hypothesis is therefore a statement with which you can agree, disagree or partly agree, depending on the evidence for or against it. For example:

- Boys are achieving less than girls at school because of the influence of peer groups.
- Husbands and wives are still unequal because men remain the main breadwinners.

Both these hypotheses could be tested by collecting evidence to see if they are true or false. For example, you might test the first hypothesis by undertaking research to see whether there are differences between male and female peer groups in terms of their attitudes to education. You could test the second hypothesis by conducting research on couples where men are the main breadwinners and couples where they are not, to see whether the former are more unequal than the latter.

When devising your hypothesis, it is essential for you to state it in such a way that it can be tested against the evidence. This would then allow you to say whether your hypothesis is true, false, or partly true.

Remember, though, that you will not be collecting this evidence yourself. Your task is simply to say how the research *could* be carried out.

questions

1 Explain what is meant by (a) an aim (b) a hypothesis.

2 Which of the following statements is an aim and which are hypotheses?

(a) The decline in the number of first marriages in recent years is due to the fact that people are less religious nowadays.

(b) Working-class boys are less likely than other groups of pupils to feel school is worthwhile.

(c) I would like to know why working-class boys are more likely to play truant.

Hypothesis or aim?

For your coursework, you can choose to have either a hypothesis or an aim. However, we would strongly recommend that you choose a hypothesis rather than an aim.

The main advantage of opting for a hypothesis is that a clear, precise hypothesis is more likely to keep you focused as you work through the remaining sections of your coursework – and well focused coursework will score higher marks. The danger with an aim is that it can tend to be too broad and unfocused, and this can mean that the later sections of your coursework start to go adrift.

However, because an aim is a more open-ended statement than a hypothesis, it can be more appropriate when you don't know anything about an issue or are very unsure as to what your research will find.

Thinking of a general aim may also be useful at an early stage of planning your research proposal, as a first step towards devising a precise hypothesis to test. For example, you might start with an aim such as, 'I aim to investigate social class differences in extended family relationships today'. Then as you find out more about the issue, you may be able to devise a more precise and testable hypothesis, in the form of a statement such as, 'Working-class families are more likely than middle-class families to maintain contact with extended kin'.

Formulating your hypothesis

If you find it hard to put forward a clear and precise hypothesis straight away, these steps may help you:

1 Select a broad issue that interests you and that you have already studied as part of your course, such as labelling and educational achievement.

2 Read around the issue, review your existing notes, discuss it with classmates, your teacher and anybody else who is interested, and generally immerse yourself in it.

3 Try to think of two or three questions you could ask about the issue. Try to make sure your questions don't overlap too much. For example, you could ask, 'How do teachers label pupils?' 'Why are working-class pupils more often labelled negatively?' 'What effect does this have on their achievement?'

4 From these questions, you need to come up with the one question that you think is the most important or interesting. This might involve combining two or more of your original questions, or choosing one of them. For example, you might focus on how teachers label pupils rather than on the effects of labelling.

5 Finally, re-phrase your question as a statement that can be tested. For example, 'Teachers label working-class pupils negatively even when they have high ability'. This is your hypothesis.

Box 24: Presentation points to remember

- Write in full sentences, not notes or bullet points.
- Don't exceed the word limits. Provide a word count after each section and a total count at the end.
- Ideally, you should wordprocess your work. Make a back-up copy.
- Secure the final copy with treasury tags. Don't put it in a plastic wallet or folder.
- When you refer to a source, give the author and date. You don't need to give a bibliography at the end of your proposal.
- Hand in the 1,200 words you have written, but not the articles, handouts or other source material you have used.

Reasons for your choice

What hypothesis would you suggest?

As well as stating your aim or hypothesis, you also need to give your reasons for choosing it. It is not enough simply to say, 'I am interested in this issue'. You need to spell out exactly *what* interests you about it and why you want to find out more.

It is best to limit your reasons to two. At least one of these should be a sociological reason. The other could be either a second sociological reason or a more personal reason.

For example, let's assume your hypothesis is that 'Boys are achieving less than girls at school because of the influence of peer groups'. Your sociological reason for choosing this hypothesis could be that studies have found male peer groups are often anti-school, and you want to test this. You may also have a personal reason for choosing this hypothesis. For example, you may have experienced or witnessed peer-group pressure on boys not to take school seriously and noticed that those boys who were most influenced by their peers did less well.

Keeping your hypothesis in view

The whole of your proposal is built upon your hypothesis or aim, so it's important that you don't lose sight of it in later sections. Therefore, when completing the remaining three sections, you should keep checking back to ensure that what you write in these is clearly relevant to your hypothesis or aim.

You should also treat your hypothesis or aim as a working or provisional one. You should be prepared to change it if necessary as you write the other sections.

You will need to write several drafts of your coursework until all the sections fit together properly.

activity

Working alone or in pairs:

1 Turn the following aims into hypotheses:

(a) My aim is to investigate boys' and girls' attitudes towards higher education.

(b) My aim is to investigate the relationship between social class and GCSE results.

(c) My aim is to investigate the impact of childbirth on women's domestic roles.

(d) My aim is to investigate the different attitudes of boys and girls towards school sport.

2 Write one hypothesis on each of the following issues:

(a) childhood

(b) cohabitation

(c) lone-parent families

(d) gender and subject choice

(e) material deprivation and educational achievement

(f) social class and selective schools.

Context and concepts

This section of your coursework carries 20 marks and has a maximum length of 400 words.

In this section you must:

- summarise two relevant pieces of material to provide a context for your research proposal
- choose two or three major sociological concepts that are relevant to your research proposal. You must define these concepts and give your reasons for including them.

We shall look at each of these two aspects in turn.

Context

Context refers to the background to your chosen issue. It consists of the studies and theories that have already been produced by sociologists on the issue, as well as the views, ideas and evidence put forward by other people.

You must choose two pieces of material to give a suitable context to your proposal. These two pieces will set the scene for your research by linking it to relevant arguments and/or evidence.

Your context material can come from either sociological or non-sociological sources, or both. For example, it could come from sociological studies, historical documents, official statistics, newspaper or magazine articles etc.

However, we strongly recommend that you take at least one of your two pieces of context material from a sociological source. You can of course take both pieces from sociological sources if you wish.

For example, if you were testing the hypothesis that 'boys are achieving less than girls at school because of the influence of peer groups', you might choose a sociological source such as Mac an Ghaill's study of masculine identities among boys in secondary school, or Willis' study of lads' counter-school culture. Non-sociological sources could include media reports of 'failing boys' or official statistics on gender and achievement.

Don't copy out chunks of material from this or other textbooks. Be selective and stick to the point in showing how the material you have chosen can provide a context for your research proposal.

Concepts

A concept is an idea or mental picture of something that is summed up in a word or phrase – such as 'meritocracy', 'cultural deprivation' or 'the social construction of childhood'. You must choose two or three major concepts relevant to your proposal.

- **The concepts you choose must be sociological.** You should take them from this coursebook or other sociological sources.
- **Define each concept clearly.** One sentence for each concept should be enough. For examples of such definitions, see Key Concepts (page 250).
- **Explain your reasons** for including each of your concepts. The best way to do this is to show how they link to your context material. For example, if you had chosen Mac an Ghaill's study as context for researching the hypothesis on boys' achievement, it would make sense to choose the concept of 'masculine identities'. This is because he shows how different peer groups create different identities for boys, some of which lead to anti-school attitudes.
- **Ensure your concepts are relevant** to your hypothesis or aim. For example, in the hypothesis above, the concept of masculine identities is relevant because it helps us to understand how peer groups shape boys' attitudes to school.

Remember also to check back to your hypothesis or aim while you are working on this section to make sure you are still focusing on it and to see if it needs adjusting in the light of what you have done.

activity

1. Working in small groups, consider the following hypothesis: 'Teachers label working-class and middle-class pupils differently.'
2. Using material from Chapter 3, choose:
   (a) two sociological studies or theories that could be used as context for research to test this hypothesis
   (b) two relevant sociological concepts.
3. Write a 250-word summary of the pieces that shows their relevance to the hypothesis.
4. Write a brief definition of each concept.

Main research method and reasons

This section carries 20 marks and has a maximum length of 400 words. In this section you need to:

- identify **one** main method you will use in your proposed research
- give reasons why you have chosen it as your method of testing your hypothesis or achieving your aim.

Identifying your main method

You must identify and briefly describe your chosen method and how you would study your topic. Depending on the method you choose, you should give details of features such as:

- **Interviews and questionnaires**: the sampling frame, type and size of sample, pilot study, type of question (e.g. open or closed), main areas on which questions will focus.
- **Observation**: the type of observation (e.g. overt or covert, participant or non-participant), how you will gain access to the group, the length of the study.
- **Secondary sources**: the type of source (e.g. official statistics, personal documents etc) and its availability, and how you will analyse the data.

When writing your description of your main research method, you should make use of the relevant section of Chapter 4. However, it is important to be selective and avoid simply copying out chunks of material.

Don't write about various different methods in this section. Stick to just the one method you have chosen.

Reasons for your choice

You need to explain in detail why you have chosen the method. This means you must focus on its strengths and explain why you think it is the best method for researching your proposed hypothesis or aim.

Reasons for your choice of method should include:

practical advantages

Is your chosen method likely to be quick or cheap? Will it be well suited to the subject matter? For example, unstructured interviews may be a good method of studying domestic violence because they establish rapport and allow the researcher to explore a sensitive issue.

theoretical advantages

For example, will your method produce valid, reliable and representative data? Note that any given method is unlikely to produce both valid *and* reliable data. You therefore need to decide whether your priority is to collect valid data, or reliable data. Then explain why your chosen method enables you to collect this type of data. You could also link the advantages of your method to an appropriate perspective. For example, you could explain that interpretivists prefer participant observation because it produces valid qualitative data.

ethical advantages

Does your method allow you to gain the informed consent of participants? Does it avoid harming them? For example, using overt participant observation avoids deceiving people or spying on them.

You must also explain how the advantages of your chosen method will help you study *your particular topic*. It is not enough simply to list the *general* advantages of the method. For example, if you were using participant observation to study the influence of peer groups on boys' achievement, you would need to explain how it enables you to see how peer groups affect boys' attitudes.

activity

1. Working in small groups, choose one of the following issues:
   (a) The impact of domestic violence on those who suffer it
   (b) Social class differences in the domestic division of labour
   (c) Primary school children and gender role socialisation
   (d) Truancy among secondary school pupils.
2. Decide what one main method you would use and give your reasons for choosing it to study this particular topic.
3. Describe how you would carry out the study using this method.

When giving your reasons for your choice of method, you should make use of the relevant section of Chapter 4 dealing with that method.

You also need to explain how you will 'operationalise' the key concepts in your hypothesis; that is, how you will actually measure them in your proposed research. For example, if you were testing the hypothesis that conjugal roles were becoming more equal, you might measure equality by finding out how often husbands do particular kinds of housework.

Don't write about the problems or disadvantages of your chosen method in this section, as you will not get any marks for doing so. Instead, save them for the next section.

Remember to go back and check your hypothesis or aim while you are working on this section of your coursework to make sure you are still focusing on it and to see if it needs adjusting in the light of what you have done.

What method would you use to study how the police deal with truancy?

Potential problems

This section of the coursework task carries 12 marks and has a maximum length of 300 words.

In this section you must identify and explain the potential problems that you would be likely to meet if you carried out your proposed research.

You must assess your chosen method to identify the problems that might arise when using it to study your particular topic. Why, and in what ways, might it prove difficult to research your topic using your chosen method?

For example, if you were using participant observation to study peer groups and boys' achievement, you might have problems gaining access because of age or gender differences. Similarly, because this method only allows you to study small groups, you might not be able to apply your findings to boys in general.

Don'ts

- *Don't* just reproduce a list of general disadvantages of your chosen method, for example from your notes or coursebook.
- *Don't* discuss the advantages of your chosen method. These belong in the previous section on 'main research method and reasons'.
- *Don't* write about how you would solve the potential problems you identify. You will gain no marks for doing so.
- *Don't* suggest alternatives to your chosen method. You will gain no marks for doing so. You are being asked to identify potential problems with your method, not to suggest other methods that might be used instead.

Types of problems

All research methods have potential problems. You need to explain the possible problems of using your chosen method to research your particular topic. To do this, you need to look at practical, theoretical and ethical (moral) problems.

practical problems

For example, is the method likely to be expensive and/or time-consuming? Will people co-operate with the research? Questionnaires often have low response rates, while some people may refuse to answer interview questions about personal matters. If you are using secondary sources, are the relevant statistics or documents available?

theoretical problems

Will there be problems in producing valid, reliable and representative data using your method? For example, structured interviews may not produce valid findings because of the artificiality of the interview situation and the use of closed-ended questions. Alternatively, unstructured interviews might not produce reliable data because they are hard to replicate.

You could also link the problems of your method to an appropriate perspective. For example, you could explain that positivists criticise participant observation for being unscientific and failing to produce quantitative data.

ethical problems

Will there be problems gaining the informed consent of your research subjects? Will the research put them at risk? For example, if you were conducting experiments in which children are shown violent videos, might this harm them? Will the researcher have to engage in criminal or immoral activities?

When explaining the potential problems of your chosen method, you should make use of the relevant section of Chapter 4 dealing with that method.

You also need to explain any potential problems you might face in operationalising (measuring) the concepts in your hypothesis. For example, if you were operationalising equality in conjugal roles in terms of how often husbands do particular kinds of housework, then this would not tell you whether the men saw themselves as responsible for housework, or as merely 'helping' their wives. It may thus not give you a true measure of equality.

Remember to go back and check your hypothesis or aim while you are working on this section to make sure you are still focusing on it and to see if it needs adjusting in the light of what you have done.

activity

Working in the same groups as for the previous activity on page 212 and using your answers to that activity:

1 Draw up a list of the problems you might encounter in carrying out the research using your chosen method. (These will vary according to the topic and method you have chosen.)

2 Explain clearly why each of them is a problem.

3 If you have time, swap your answers to the previous activity with another group in the class. Each group can then identify the potential problems in the other group's method and report back to them. Make sure that the other group has chosen a different topic or method from you.

QuickCheck Questions

1 If you do coursework for A2, does it have to be on the same topic as the one you did for AS coursework?

2 Do you have to be able to carry out your proposed research yourself
(a) for AS coursework
(b) for A2 coursework?

3 Explain the difference between an aim and a hypothesis.

4 How many of your pieces of context material should be from sociological sources?

5 True or false? It's better to use more than one method in your AS coursework.

6 In which section should you deal with the disadvantages of your chosen method?

7 True or false? You should try to suggest solutions to any problems you identify with your chosen method.

Answers are on page 275.

Coursework proposal

In this section, we look at an example of a piece of coursework written by Chloe, an AS level sociology student. As you will see, we have given comments in the margins as well as at the end of each of the four sections. At the end of the piece, we indicate how you could improve on Chloe's work and score a higher mark.

Section 1 Hypothesis or aim

My hypothesis is:

Schools with good exam results are more likely to attract middle-class children from outside the catchment area because of the advantages that middle-class families possess.

Relevant hypothesis, but unclear whether the focus is on schools with good results, or on the advantages that middle-class families possess.

I am interested in this because supporters of the 1988 Education Reform Act believed all pupils would benefit from greater choice of secondary school. However, sociologists have shown that middle-class pupils gain more.

I also have a personal interest. I attend a selective school in the next town. Although my parents are working-class, I have noticed that most pupils from outside the school's catchment area are from middle-class families.

Two appropriate reasons – one sociological and the other from personal experience.

(97 words)

5/8

Comments Chloe's hypothesis has a relevant sociological focus: class differences in education since the 1988 Act. Her reasons for choosing her hypothesis are appropriate.

However, there are two different questions within it and it is unclear which of these is the main focus. This may cause her problems in later sections.

Section 2 Context and concepts

An article that helps to put my hypothesis in context is "Comprehensive Education Revisited" by Clarke in Sociology Review (1999). She describes the purpose of comprehensive education as that of breaking down class barriers and creating a better and fairer society. However, Conservative governments from 1979 criticised comprehensives. They argued that standards and opportunities could only be improved by encouraging competition between schools and allowing parents and pupils more choice. The 1988 Act provided more choice of schools by introducing City Technology Colleges and Grant Maintained schools.

A relevant piece of context material summarised clearly and concisely.

My research will test the hypothesis that middle-class pupils have benefited most from these changes because of the advantages that middle-class families possess. Clarke quotes Ball's (1994) research, which shows that middle-class children, who are already advantaged in the system, are gaining while working-class children are losing out.

Useful to refer directly to your hypothesis when outlining the context, but Chloe only refers to the second part of hers.

Sharon Gewirtz (1995) provides evidence that class inequalities continue and are reinforced by allowing more parental choice. She argues that the 1988 Act created an 'education market' that benefits those with cultural capital. From a study of 14 schools, she identifies reasons why affluent, well-educated parents are able to take greater advantage of the choices open to them. They have the time and knowledge to explore the options and attend open evenings, the skills to complete application forms effectively, and can afford the costs of sending their children to schools further from home. These parents therefore have options denied to working-class parents.

Needs to briefly define 'cultural capital'.

Accurate and relevant context, but doesn't cover her whole hypothesis – it ignores whether 'good' schools attract middle-class pupils.

My concepts are 'marketisation' and 'privileged-skilled choosers'.

Marketisation is the process where market forces of supply and demand are introduced into areas that were previously run by the state. Marketisation has created an 'education market' in which pupils compete for places in the 'best' schools (measured by league tables). Both Clarke and Gewirtz examine the effects of marketisation and my study will test whether middle-class pupils have gained advantages from the education market because of their cultural capital.

Relevant concepts, but she needs to apply marketisation to schools competing to attract middle-class pupils.

Gewirtz uses the concept of privileged-skilled chooser to describe middle-class parents who gain most from the choices open to their children because they are affluent and well educated themselves. These parents know how the education system works and how to use their skills to get the most from it. This concept ties in with my hypothesis because such parents are more likely than other parents to send their children to selective schools outside their own areas.

(391 words)

12/20

Why 'selective schools'? This wasn't in her hypothesis. If Chloe is assuming 'selective' = 'best results', she needs to explain.

Comments **Chloe shows a very good knowledge of potentially relevant context material and concepts. However, in relation to her original hypothesis, the section is one-sided. She concentrates on the advantages middle-class families possess but fails to deal with the issue of schools with good results attracting middle-class pupils, so she only partly succeeds in providing an appropriate context.**

Section 3 Main research method and reasons

To test my hypothesis, I would use an anonymous postal questionnaire with pre-coded, closed-ended questions. These questions would be to find out about parental occupation and education, and how far choice of secondary school is influenced by exam results as against factors such as the cost of travel to the school, its 'image' (e.g. whether it is seen as rough), or the cost of housing in the catchment area. These questions would be tested on a small pilot sample of 20 parents to iron out any misunderstanding of questions.

Good outline of method and questions and suitable reason for a pilot study, all linked to her topic.

The sample will be taken from three schools, each at different levels in the league tables. The sampling frame will be the school roll. I shall seek the cooperation of the schools in selecting a stratified random sample of 100 parents from each school, divided equally between those living within and those living outside the school's catchment area.

How will she ensure that the schools are representative?

The hypothesis requires information from parents who are geographically dispersed and work during the day, so a postal questionnaire will be a good way to get it. A postal questionnaire would be ideal because it is mainly factual data that is needed for testing this hypothesis, such as parental occupation and education and reasons for choice of school. A postal questionnaire will be the best method to use because it will enable me to gain a large amount of quantitative data relatively cheaply and quickly. A large sample also adds weight to the findings and allows generalisations to be made on the basis of the findings.

Several good, convincing reasons for using a postal questionnaire.

Using this method will ensure reliability because all respondents will answer exactly the same questions, allowing comparisons to be made between them. The absence of interviewers and the guarantee of anonymity will encourage respondents to answer truthfully, especially potentially embarrassing questions about how they managed to get their children into selective schools.

Important point about anonymity. However, she could explain why these questions might be embarrassing.

Using three schools and a stratified sample allows for comparisons of the answers given by parents inside and outside the catchment area, to see if those outside the area are mainly middle-class and have chosen the school for its good exam results.

There would be no problem with ethical issues since we would be able to explain what the survey involves in the covering letter with the questionnaire and to gain the consent of those who take part. Also, by being anonymous, the questionnaire will ensure the privacy of the respondents is respected.

Chloe shows an awareness of relevant ethical issues.

(398 words)

Comments **Chloe shows a good understanding of her chosen method, gives appropriate reasons for choosing it and explains how she will use it in her particular study.**

However, while in the Context and Concepts section she provided a context for the issue of middle-class parents' advantages, she now neglects this in favour of the other half of her hypothesis – that of schools with good results attracting middle-class pupils from outside their area. She has applied the method to only part of her hypothesis, not the whole of it.

Chloe doesn't explain how she will ensure that the schools she chooses are representative or typical of schools in general. Without doing so, she won't know whether her findings can be generalised.

She doesn't explain how she will operationalise the two main concepts in her hypothesis – 'schools with good exam results' and 'midldle-class'.

Section 4 Potential problems

In doing this research, there may be problems of access to the schools and there could also be difficulties obtaining a sample of parents from outside the catchment area of the less popular schools, because these schools may not attract any pupils from outside their area. Also, some parents may have deliberately decided to move into the best school's catchment area so as to get their child into it. This is in fact exactly the kind of thing that privileged-skilled choosers would be likely to do, as they can afford to. If so, this would increase the number of middle-class parents inside the catchment area. The hypothesis does not take any account of this possibility.

Good point about access, but needs developing. And why choose schools with no pupils from outside the area in the first place?

300 parents and three schools is a relatively small and possibly untypical sample and it may not be enough to make generalisations from. For example, the schools chosen may be unusual, e.g. they may all be single sex.

Non-response could be a problem, given that there is no supervision of those who complete the questionnaires. Non-response could undermine the reliability of results because those who do not reply may be untypical (e.g. less educated parents may be less able to reply).

There may be problems with validity because with a postal questionnaire, the researcher decides the questions in advance. For example, some parents might have reasons for choosing a school that are not included in the questions, such as being impressed by a school's open evening. This is the main criticism interpretivists make of questionnaires, i.e. they don't give respondents the chance to say what they think is important.

These problems could undermine the reliability and validity of the data, making it difficult to decide whether the hypothesis is supported or rejected.

(287 words)

7/12

Unrepresentative schools shouldn't be offered as a problem. Chloe could avoid the problem by simply not choosing them.

Good to identify non-response as a potential problem, but it is one of representativeness, not reliability.

Good use of the interpretivist criticism.

Comments **Chloe identifies and explains some of the likely problems but without discussing them in relation to the hypothesis as a whole.**

She should explain why there might be problems of access. For example, schools might be reluctant to provide pupils' names and addresses, and schools with bad results might be unwilling to allow someone to research their poor performance.

Chloe doesn't identify the problems of operationalising the concepts 'schools with good exam results' and 'middle-class' in her research. For example, what difference might it make to use only the father's occupation rather than that of both parents to define a pupil's class? She also tends to confuse reliability, validity and representativeness.

Total mark: 36/60

How to improve this coursework

Overall, this is quite a good piece of work. However, it suffers from some important limitations and for this reason would probably not gain higher than a grade C.

To improve on Chloe's work, there are a number of steps you could take.

Begin with a clearer and more specific hypothesis. Chloe really had two hypotheses, not one, and she ran into problems because she was unable to deal with either of them fully.

It would be better if the hypothesis focused on either:

(a) whether schools with good exam results attract middle-class children; or

(b) the advantages middle-class families possess in gaining access to 'good' schools.

If you chose hypothesis (a), you could use **context** material on how high-achieving schools project an image to attract middle-class parents (e.g. studies by Fitz and by Walford). You could use the concept of 'marketisation', as Chloe does, but replace her **concept** of 'privileged-skilled choosers' with that of 'selection'.

For your **main method**, you could use, for example, a questionnaire to find out about a school's image as regards academic reputation, facilities etc.

Similarly, you could use a sample design that compares the class backgrounds of children in 'good' schools with those in low-achieving schools.

If you chose hypothesis (b), you could still use Chloe's existing **context and concepts.**

However, your **main method** should ask questions that focus in detail on class differences in parents' ability to deal with selection procedures, attend open days etc. These questions will help you make full use of your chosen concept of 'privileged-skilled choosers'.

Whichever hypothesis you choose, in your **potential problems** section, make sure you use key 'methods' terms such as reliability, validity and representativeness correctly. Explain problems fully, including how you would operationalise your key concepts.

Chapter summary

Choice of issue

You can choose any issue for your coursework proposal, but it makes sense to pick one you have already studied.

For AS, your proposal doesn't have to be something you could actually research yourself, but it will have to be if you want to continue with it for A2.

Hypothesis or aim

You can choose either an **aim** or a **hypothesis**, though a clear hypothesis will probably give your coursework a better focus.

An aim is an open-ended statement about what you hope to achieve.

A hypothesis is a more precise, testable statement that can be proved or disproved by evidence.

Choose a single hypothesis or aim. Give a couple of reasons for your choice. At least one should be a sociological reason.

Context and concepts

Your two **context** pieces set the scene for your proposal by linking it to relevant arguments or evidence. At least one piece should come from a sociological source.

Your two or three major **concepts** must be sociological ones. Define each one briefly but clearly.

Explain your reasons for including each concept. Do this by showing how they link to your context material. Ensure your concepts are relevant to your hypothesis/aim.

Main research method and reasons

Identify just *one* **main method** you propose to use. Describe it and how you would actually use it to study your topic.

Give **reasons** why it is the best method for studying your particular topic and hypothesis/aim. Consider its practical, ethical and theoretical advantages. Use the relevant section of Chapter 4 to research these, but apply them to your topic.

Make sure that you define and use key 'methods' terms such as reliability, validity and representativeness correctly.

Explain how you will operationalise the concepts in your hypothesis. Don't write about other methods. Don't write about problems or disadvantages in this section.

Potential problems

Identify and explain the **potential problems** you would be likely to meet if you carried out your proposed research. Consider the practical, ethical and theoretical problems involved in using your chosen method to study your particular topic. Use the relevant section of Chapter 4 to research these, but apply them to your topic.

Explain any problems operationalising the concepts in your hypothesis. Don't discuss your method's advantages in this section, or alternatives to it, or how you would solve the problems.

Throughout your coursework

Ensure that you keep within the word limit for each section. Treat your hypothesis/aim as a working or **provisional** one that you will probably modify later. When writing the later sections of your proposal, keep checking back to see they fit with your hypothesis. You will need to write several drafts of your coursework to get it right.

Chapter 6

Preparing for the exam

Revision

In this chapter, we look at how to succeed in the examination.

- The first section deals with how to revise and prepare effectively for the exam.
- The second section deals with the exam itself, including what the examiners are looking for, and how to go about making sense of and tackling the questions.
- The final section gives examples of exam questions you can try, together with students' answers and the examiner's marks, comments and advice on how to improve.

To maximise your chances of success, you should start to prepare early – in fact, from day one of your course. This doesn't mean you will be revising straight away, but it does mean that you need to get yourself and your work organised from the beginning. Try to start as you mean to go on!

Here are some of the important things you should be doing throughout your course.

- Keep up to date with your work. Attend your classes regularly and punctually, and do all the work you are set.
- Make sure there are no gaps in your notes. If you miss anything, copy up from a friend's notes as soon as possible and/or make notes from the relevant section of this coursebook, so you keep up with the class. If you're not sure whether you have missed something, check with your teacher and friends.
- Keep your file tidy and well organised so you can find relevant notes easily. Use dividers, colour coding or other ways of identifying notes on different topics.
- Review your notes regularly – every couple of weeks. If there is anything you don't understand, check it in your coursebook or with your teacher or friends.
- When doing homework assignments or coursework, look at any feedback given on previous work and avoid repeating your mistakes. Always write at least one draft of your work before your final version. File your marked work with the relevant topic notes.
- Read as much as possible. Make sure you read all the relevant chapters of this coursebook, and consult other sources as well where possible.

Materials you need for revision

- Your file of notes – including class notes and handouts, plus all the marked homework, timed questions, mock exams etc you have done
- Stationery: pens (several colours), pencils, eraser, highlighters, paper, index cards, dividers
- The AQA Specification; past exam papers; mark schemes; annual *Reports on the Examination* written by the Chief Examiner.

Your teacher or school/college library should have copies of these items. Copies of AQA publications can also be obtained from AQA, Publications Department, Stag Hill House, Guildford GU2 7XJ, telephone 01483 506506; or visit www.aqa.org.uk.

You will also find the specification for each AS topic at the beginning of Chapters 2, 3 and 4 in this coursebook.

Note on the OCR Specification: if you are studying the OCR specification, copies of publications can be obtained from: OCR, 1 Hills Road, Cambridge CB1 2EU, telephone 01223 553998; www.ocr.org.uk.

Getting organised

If you haven't already done so, now is the time to get your notes in order and fill in any gaps. When you have done this, these are the essential steps you need to take before you start revising:

- Study past exam papers to get an idea of the style of questions and the sorts of topics examiners ask about.
- Look at mark schemes. These are what examiners use to guide them when marking exam scripts. Studying them will give you insight into what the examiner is hoping to see in your answer.
- After each exam, the Chief Examiner writes a *Report on the Examination*. This tells you what students did well or badly on each question and gives useful advice. Read these reports alongside past papers.
- Study the 'Examining' questions at the end of chapters 2, 3 and 4 and the examples in this chapter.
- The specification gives details of what you have to study, what skills are being assessed, how many papers you have to do, their length, any coursework requirements and much more. Your teacher may already have given you a copy of the specification. You will also find a summary of the specified content for each topic at the start of chapters 2, 3 and 4 in this coursebook.

Your revision timetable

When should you start revising? It's impossible to be precise about how long you will need to revise for your sociology exams, as this will depend on how many other demands there are on your time (lesson times, part-time job, revising for other subjects etc), how much work you've done during your course and how many units you are sitting.

Obviously, though, the earlier you start revising the better. A reasonable revision period would be the six weeks before your exams.

To use your time effectively, you need to work to a revision timetable.

- Think hard about how much time you are really prepared to put into revising. Make allowance for other demands on your time.
- Build in some leisure and rest time. Use this as a reward for revising by giving yourself time to go out with friends or watch your favourite television programme. Allow for short breaks during your revision slots.
- The rest of your time is for revision. Divide this between the different subjects you are studying. When you have worked out how much time this gives you for sociology, divide it again between your topics.
- Make a large, detailed, day-by-day wall calendar for the period up to the dates of the exams. Write the exam slots (days and times) in red. Block out in black all the other times when you know you won't be revising. Then allocate the remaining slots to your revision topics. Leave a blank slot every so often – to allow you to catch up if you fall behind.
- Set yourself target tasks and target dates – e.g. 'by next Tuesday, finish gender and education'. Put these on your calendar.
- When you have drawn up your timetable, review it to see whether you have been realistic about what you can accomplish. You may need to amend your timetable as the weeks go by. But don't get into a pattern of re-writing it every other day – this means you're not being honest with yourself about what you can get done.

revision activity 1

For two people

1. Obtain a mark scheme for a past exam question from your teacher or AQA. Before reading the mark scheme, attempt question (e) or (f).
2. Now swap your answer with your friend. Study the mark scheme carefully, and then use it to mark each other's answer.
3. Using the mark scheme, write some feedback comments (as if you were the teacher) to explain why you gave it that mark, and some advice on how it could be improved.
4. Discuss your marks, comments and advice. You may want to amend them following discussion.
5. Re-write the answer together, taking account of the comments and advice.

Doing your revision

When and where?

- You need somewhere quiet where you won't be disturbed. Ideally you will have your own study area in a room at home where you can keep all your revision materials. If you can't study at home, remember there are school/college and public libraries, friends' homes etc.
- When revising, ask your family not to disturb you. Ask friends not to phone during these times – and switch off your mobile phone.
- Fit a little revision into those 'gaps' in the day – on the bus to school/college, in the lunch hour, while waiting for a friend. Carry some notes with you wherever you go. But don't cart your entire folder around: you risk losing your whole year's work if you leave it on the bus!

Be systematic

- Don't just keep going over the same topics. Make sure you revise everything that is in the specification and this coursebook because:
  - You don't have a choice of topics.
  - Each topic (e.g. Education; Families and Households) has six questions, so you're likely to be asked something about most main aspects of it.
- Therefore, you need to spend more time on aspects that you're less confident about. Don't move on to the next aspect until you feel you understand the current one.
- For each aspect of a topic, go through past papers looking for all the examples of questions on it. Make a list of them all. You will probably find there are both long and short questions. Practise answering both kinds.
- Write a summary each time you finish revising something before you start the next topic.

Be active, not passive

Obviously you will need to read your notes, but your revision will be more interesting and more successful the more you *act*. Psychologists have shown that we learn and remember more effectively when we actively process information rather than just passively read it. Here are some tips for more active revision:

- Always have a pen or highlighter to hand when reading.
- Highlight the key points in your notes.
- Make notes on your notes – either in the margin or on a separate sheet. Jot down any ideas, questions, comments, links to other topics etc that occur to you.
- Use abbreviations, icons, symbols, pictures etc – they save time and they make points more memorable.
- Write summaries of topics, studies, theories, concepts, facts etc on index cards.
- Re-organise your notes in different formats such as mind maps, spidergrams or tables with columns (good for comparing and contrasting two different views).
- How do you learn to tackle sociology exams? By doing as many past exam questions and 'Examining' questions from your coursebook as possible. Having a head full of sociology will be no good if you can't turn it into a suitable answer on the day. The best way to prepare for something is to practise doing it.

Bowles + Gintis (1976) 'Schooling in Capitalist America'

Marxist theory of role of education – two functions for capitalism:

1. reproduction of class inequality: correspondence principle + hidden curriculum – schooling mirrors work, e.g. managers/ teachers; extrinsic rewards (diplomas/wages)
2. legitimation of class inequality: myth of meritocracy – ideological function to persuade workers to accept exploitation

Criticisms: determinism – ignores pupil resistance; 'class first' approach – ignores gender, ethnicity etc.

Index cards are a good way of organising your revision notes.

Revise with friends

A good way of revising is to work with one or more friends. It's much more fun and, unless you just sit next to each other reading silently, it's bound to be more active. Some of the things you can do are:

- Test each other on what you have learnt.
- Play revision games together.
- Use each other as a source of information when you're unsure of something. Check facts together.
- Produce and share material: each summarise one study, theory etc, then share your summaries.
- Become the group's 'expert': take responsibility for understanding and explaining a topic to the others.
- Take turns explaining the same thing to each other. If you can explain it to a friend, you can probably explain it in the exam. Comment on each other's explanations: was any aspect not clear? Sort it out together.
- Mark and discuss each other's practice answers.

It's vital to be disciplined when you are revising with a friend – don't use it as an opportunity for idle chatter. Agree beforehand what you are going to do and how long you will spend on it. Allow yourself 10 minutes at the end for general conversation – this is your reward for your hard work.

Set yourself targets

Every time you start a revision session, begin by setting yourself a target: 'In the next hour I'm going to read and summarise my notes on Bowles and Gintis' view of the role of education'.

- Make sure your target is achievable within about an hour – you can't concentrate for much longer than this, and it will make you feel good when you hit it.
- Decide in advance what reward you will give yourself for achieving it. This helps increase your motivation.
- Take a short break to enjoy your reward; then set the next target.

revision activity 2

For large or small groups

1. As a class, draw up a list of studies on Families and Households or Education.
2. Next, divide into pairs and share out the studies. Each pair of students must then create a file card for each study they have been allocated.
3. On one side of the card, write the name of the authors and date of publication. On the other side, write three things about the study. In your pairs, decide which points are most important – e.g. key findings, perspective, criticisms, method etc.
4. When everyone has produced their cards, put them together into a 'pack' and deal them out, with the name of the authors face up. The recipient of a card must then state one or more important things about the study. They get a point for each one that appears on the reverse of the card.
5. If their answer doesn't appear, but they can convince the group that it should, they get a point. When everyone has had a turn, shuffle, re-deal and repeat.
6. You can make duplicate sets so that smaller groups can play with the full pack.

revision activity 3

'Concept cards' is a similar game.

- Choose the concepts you think are important. Write the concept on one side and its definition on the other.
- Produce a set and deal them out.
- Recipients have to give a definition, plus an example if you wish.
- You can also deal them definition-side up; recipients then have to say what the concept is.

Near the time of the exams

- As the exam gets nearer, you may find yourself suffering from exam nerves and feeling stressed. This is perfectly normal and you certainly won't be the only one. However, there are several simple practical steps you can take to reduce your stress levels:
    - Get into a regular daily routine.
    - Get enough sleep.
    - Eat regularly and sensibly – not too many chocolate rewards!
    - Exercise: physical activity is a great way to unwind and refresh yourself after you've been revising hard.
    - Relax: a good way to relax is listening to a relaxation tape (available from bookshops, libraries and health shops).
- A couple of days before the exam, check again that you know where and when it will be held. Ensure you have all the equipment you will need on the day: several pens in working order (black or dark blue biros or fountain pens – not felt tips); pencil, eraser and sharpener; your entry slip.

The night before

- Don't over-revise. Don't try to learn anything new – it will almost certainly panic you. If you do revise, limit it to going over things you know pretty well. For example, read through a few index card summaries or the practice answers you have written.
- Stop revising at least an hour before bedtime and do something relaxing.
- Make sure you pack all the necessary equipment (pens, pencil, eraser, sharpener); entry slip; revision notes, plus water and a snack to take with you.

On the day

- Get up in good time; have enough to eat.
- Take your equipment, water, snack, and any revision notes you want to look at before the exam (e.g. on the bus).
- Arrive early but not too early. Don't stand around allowing other people's anxiety to get to you; if possible, find somewhere quiet to relax.
- Some people find it useful to read through a few notes on something they already know well. This can boost confidence and help to get your brain in gear.
- Don't try to cram in anything new: trying to learn new material five minutes before an exam is ineffective and will undermine your self-confidence.

In the exam room

- Get settled quickly and set out your materials and entry slip. Take a few deep, slow breaths to calm yourself down.
- You should already know the instructions (how long, how many questions etc), but read them through to remind yourself.
- Read the Items and questions through carefully at least twice. Highlight key words and phrases in Items and questions. Underline any words or phrases in the Items that are referred to in the questions.
- Plan your answers before writing them by doing a brainstorm for each one, especially the longer questions.
- Leave a few minutes at the end to read through your answer and add anything you have missed out.
- Keep an eye on the clock. If you have only a few minutes left and you know you are going to run out of time, finish your last answer in note form.

After the exam

Don't stand around talking about what you did wrong; it just demoralises you for the next exam. Go and unwind for a little while, tick the exam off your list and start thinking about the next one – unless it was your last, in which case you can celebrate!

revision activity 4

For pairs or small groups

Each person chooses a different study, theory or method, and writes four or five sentences describing and evaluating it. When you have done this, go through and remove at least one key concept from each of your sentences.

Now take turns to read what others have written and insert the missing concepts. Finally, check whether the answers are correct.

Tackling the AS sociology exam

This section of the chapter focuses on the examination itself. It deals with:

- the knowledge and skills that you have to show to do well in your exams
- the format of the exam papers
- the different types of question and how to tackle them.

The Assessment Objectives

In AS sociology exams, your answers are assessed in terms of two aims or 'assessment objectives'. These are:

- Assessment Objective 1 (AO1): Knowledge and Understanding
- Assessment Objective 2 (AO2): the skills of Identification, Interpretation, Analysis and Evaluation.

Half the marks in the exam are for AO1 and half for AO2, so it's very important that you show evidence of both of them to the examiner. Let's take a closer look at the kind of knowledge, understanding and skills you need to demonstrate in your answers.

Knowledge and Understanding

You need to know about and understand some of the main theories, methods and concepts (ideas) that sociologists use in their work.

You also need to be familiar with some of the studies they have carried out and what these studies have found.

Identification

Identification involves being able to recognise something correctly. This could be a fact, idea, theory, explanation, viewpoint, reason, criticism or example.

In the exam, short questions often ask to you to 'identify' or 'identify and briefly explain' something.

Interpretation

Interpretation is about being able to select from what you know and apply it in a way that is relevant to the question you have been asked – instead of writing an 'all I know about everything' answer.

Interpretation includes:

- in essays, explaining what the question involves.
- using material from an Item when the question tells you to, linking it to your own knowledge and to the question.
- using relevant examples, e.g. from studies, news and current events, personal experience, other topics you have studied in sociology etc.
- showing how your examples are relevant to the question and to your sociological point.

Analysis

Analysis includes:

- breaking down an argument or explanation into the ideas that make it up and showing how they fit together.
- comparing and contrasting ideas to show their similarities and differences.
- organising your essays with a well-focused introduction and a clear, logical line of reasoning from paragraph to paragraph, leading to an appropriate conclusion.

Evaluation

Evaluation is about weighing things up, giving informed opinions or making balanced judgements about something. The 'something' could be different evidence, ideas, views, theories or methods. In exams, evaluation is often signalled by the word 'assess'.

Evaluation includes:

- looking at the arguments and evidence for and against a particular view.
- examining a theory's assumptions or linking it to a particular perspective.
- putting forward alternative views and perspectives.
- discussing the strengths (or advantages) and weaknesses (or disadvantages) of a research method.

In practice, the two assessment objectives often overlap. For example, in order to select and apply the right information (AO2), you first need to know some sociology and understand the set question (AO1).

The exam papers

For AS level Sociology, you must either take three written exams, or two exams plus coursework. Coursework is dealt with in chapter 5. The written exams take the format described below.

Each exam question consists of two Items of stimulus material – Item A and Item B – plus six questions labelled (a) to (f). Questions (a) to (d) are short questions, while questions (e) and (f) are mini-essays. Further details of the different questions are given below, with advice on how to tackle them.

the Items

The two Items are a very important source of help with the questions. In the exams, read the Items through carefully at least twice, underlining or highlighting any words or phrases that seem important. Use the line references given in the questions to find key terms in the Items. This will help you to answer the questions.

Item B usually provides material to help you with question (f), so read it carefully in the light of what the question asks you to do. When a question tells you to use material from the Item(s), make sure you do.

How long to spend on each question

First of all you should allow a few minutes to read the Items and questions. Then divide the remainder of your time roughly as follows: one third for answering (a) to (d), one third for (e) and one third for (f).

- For Units 1 and 2, this means about 20–25 minutes each for (e) and (f) and the same for the short questions.
- For Unit 3, you should allow five minutes less for each of these.

In practice, since (a) to (d) can be answered quite briefly, you may find you can complete these more quickly and give yourself a few minutes longer on (e) and (f).

Remember that these time allocations also include planning and checking time. You should spend a couple of minutes making a brief plan for (e) and (f), and you should leave a little time to read through each answer as you finish it and make any necessary alterations.

Structure of the exam papers

Unit 1

This paper is divided into three sections:

Section A: Families and Households

Section B: Health

Section C: Mass Media

You must choose one section and answer all six questions (a to f) in it.

Time allowed:
1 hour 15 minutes

Unit 2

This paper is divided into three sections:

Section A: Education

Section B: Wealth, Poverty and Welfare

Section C: Work and Leisure

You must choose one section and answer all six questions (a to f) in it.

Time allowed:
1 hour 15 minutes

Unit 3

This paper has only one section: Sociological Methods.

You must answer all six questions (a to f).

Time allowed:
1 hour

Unit values: Units 1 and 2 are each worth 35% of the total AS level marks (17.5% of the total A level marks). Unit 3 is worth 30% of the total AS level marks (15% of the A level).

Answering the short questions

The short questions (a), (b), (c) and (d) are together worth a third of the total marks, so a good performance on these will get you within range of a pass mark even before you tackle the longer questions. Don't spend too much time writing very long answers to questions (a) to (d). Long answers are often less clear and may end up scoring lower marks.

Question (a)

This question is worth 2 marks. It asks you to explain the meaning of a term or concept. For example:

Explain what is meant by 'meritocracy'.

This term will appear in one of the Items, so it's important to read these carefully. To get the 2 marks available, you must give a clear explanation or definition of the term.

points to remember

- Avoid repeating the word or phrase you're being asked about in your explanation – e.g. simply writing, 'Meritocracy is a system of rewards based on merit' doesn't show the examiner that you understand the term clearly. It would be better to write that 'It is a system of rewards based on the individual's effort and ability'. Put it in different words to make its meaning clear.
- Simply giving an example is not enough. You must explain the term properly.

Question (b)

This question is worth 4 marks. It usually asks you either to 'identify' or to 'suggest' two points, such as reasons, examples, criticisms, ways, functions, causes etc. For example:

Identify ***two*** *criticisms of the functionalist view of the family.*

Suggest ***two*** *functions that the extended family might perform today.*

'Identify' means 'state from your knowledge'. For example, two criticisms of the functionalist view are that it ignores conflict in the family and that it ignores diversity.

'Suggest' means that you can put forward *possible* functions, ways etc. There does not have to be definite evidence; nevertheless, your suggestions must be reasonably plausible (likely). For example, you could reasonably suggest, 'Helping out with the care of grandchildren while their mother goes out to work' as one function the extended family might perform today.

Sometimes, you may be asked to *explain the difference or similarity* between two things. For example:

Explain the difference between ascribed status and achieved status.

You need to define or explain each term so as to bring out the difference between them. For example, you could say, 'Ascribed status is a position fixed at birth that you can't alter, whereas achieved status is a position that you gain through your own efforts'.

Sometimes the question asks you to 'identify and briefly explain' one thing. In this case, you should answer in the way outlined for question (d) below.

Question (c)

This question is worth 6 marks. Like question (b), it asks you to 'identify' or 'suggest', but you have to make three points rather than two. For example:

Suggest ***three*** *advantages of using structured interviews in sociological research.*

You should write as much for each point here as for each point in (b) questions.

points to remember

- For (b) and (c) questions your answers can be quite short. One sentence for each point the question asks for will be enough.
- There will be a reference to an Item, so refer to it to get the context of the question.
- If you're not sure whether all your points are right but you can think of an extra one, put this down too; you won't be penalised. If you're asked for three reasons but give four, any three that are right will get the marks, even if the other one is wrong. But remember, the more points you give, the more time you use up.

Question (d)

This question is worth 8 marks. It asks you to 'identify and briefly explain' (or 'describe') two things. These 'things' might be two reasons, problems, criticisms, examples, ways, policies and so on. For example:

Identify and briefly describe ***two*** *policies that may have affected class differences in educational achievement.*

You gain 2 marks for each of the two points you identify (so 4 marks for the two identifications), plus a further 2 marks for each of these points that you go on to explain or describe (so 4 marks for the explanations or descriptions).

The best way to set out your answer is as follows. On the first line, briefly state the identification point. In the above example, you could simply say:

The introduction of comprehensive education affected class differences in achievement.

Now add another sentence (or two at most) to describe or explain the point you have identified. For example, you might say:

By abolishing grammar schools and making all children attend the same type of school, it made opportunities for a good education more equal for children of different classes.

Once you have done this, leave a line and repeat the process for your second point.

points to remember

- Set your answer out clearly, as described above.
- You only need a couple of sentences per point. Don't write a mini-essay: this often makes it harder for the examiner to find your identification points and therefore harder to give you marks.
- Make sure your two identified points are clearly different from each other and that you are not just repeating the same point in different terms.

Answering the longer questions

Questions (e) and (f) are both mini-essays. Each one carries a third of the total marks for the paper, so you should spend about a third of your time on each of them.

Question (e)

This question is worth 20 marks. It asks you to 'examine' something. For example:

Examine the extent of and reasons for family diversity in Britain today.

Examine the ways in which processes within schools may cause differences in educational achievement.

Examine the reasons why sociologists sometimes use written questionnaires in their research.

'Examine' means you need to look closely at something, to consider its different aspects or features in detail. You therefore need to show you have a good knowledge and understanding of relevant material and of the issues raised by the question.

Some questions ask you to examine one kind of thing (e.g. reasons, ways, factors, causes), but others may ask you to examine two kinds of thing (e.g. extent of *and* reasons for, causes *and* effects). Make sure you deal with both aspects if asked, even if you don't cover them equally.

Questions often ask for *the* reasons, *the* ways etc. You may well be able to think of many more reasons or ways than you could possibly write about in the time available. Don't worry; so long as you can write about a *range* of reasons, you don't have to cover every possible one under the sun.

Write a solid paragraph for each main point that you are examining, using your knowledge of studies, theories and examples as relevant to the question.

Question (e) is always 'free standing'. That is, it is not linked to the Items. This means that the knowledge you use to answer it needs to come from your own knowledge, rather than from the Items.

Of the 20 marks available for question (e), 14 are for AO1 Knowledge and Understanding and 6 for AO2. So, although the focus is on AO1, you still need to show some AO2 skills.

Question (f)

This question is worth 20 marks. It asks you to 'assess' something, often a view, theory, method or explanation. For example:

Using material from Item B and elsewhere, assess the view that husbands and wives are now more equal than in the past.

Using material from Item B and elsewhere, assess the Marxist view of the role of education.

Box 25: Using an Item

The Item and question below are from '*Examining* Childhood' on page 51. We have highlighted some of the key words and phrases in the Item that you could use as a starting point when answering the question. We have suggested some of the ways you could connect these ideas to other material on the topic and to the question. When using an Item, always try to find ways to link it to what you already know and to the question you have been asked.

Item A

According to some sociologists, children in today's supposedly child-centred society lead lives that are segregated and controlled, but childhood was not always like this. Nor is it yet the case for many children in the Third World.

For example, Ariès describes a medieval world in which, if children were not actually the equals of adults, they nevertheless mixed freely with adults in both work and leisure. Little distinction was drawn between adults and children.

According to this view, however, industrialisation brought major changes to the position of children. The development of industrial society meant that their lives were increasingly confined, disciplined and regulated by adults. This was done on the grounds that children were innocent, vulnerable and in need of protection from the dangers of adult society. The result is that in the west today, adults exercise a control over children's time, space and bodies that would have been unimaginable to medieval society. On this view, children today are the victims of adult oppression.

Not all sociologists share this view of modern childhood, however. Some argue that the distinction between childhood and adulthood is once again becoming blurred, and some even go so far as to argue that childhood is disappearing.

Question

Using material from **Item A** and elsewhere, assess the view that 'children today are the victims of adult oppression' (**Item A**, lines 12-13). (20 marks)

Here are some examples of how you could use the highlights to stimulate your thinking and make links to other material and to the question:

- What does 'supposedly child-centred society' mean? Why and in what ways are we child-centred? What examples can you give?
- What are the differences between the position of western and Third World children?
- What else do you know about Ariès' work? Medieval world … work and leisure. Little distinction … between adults and children. Why not? What evidence is there for this?
- Why and how might industrialisation have changed children's position? Mention laws, policies, new ideas about children and their rights, needs etc and why they came to be seen as innocent, vulnerable and in need of protection. Link this to the march of progress view.
- Give examples of how children are segregated and controlled … confined, disciplined and regulated…and of adults' control over children's time, space and bodies.
- Link the idea that children are victims of adult oppression to the concept of age patriarchy and the child liberationist view. Why are children in this position today? Is control really the same thing as oppression?
- Not all sociologists share this view … blurred ...disappearing. Use this to introduce contrasting views, e.g. Postman. Explain why he thinks the distinction is blurred or disappearing.

Using material from Item B and elsewhere, assess the usefulness of participant observation as a method of research.

'Assess' means the same as 'evaluate', so you need to focus on analysing and evaluating the material you use, rather than just describing or listing information. Of the 20 marks available for question (f), 14 are for the AO2 skills of Identification, Interpretation, Analysis and Evaluation. There are only 6 marks for AO1.

The other key feature of question (f) is that you need to use material from one (or occasionally both) of the Items. The question will usually say 'using material from Item B'.

This Item contains important information to help you answer the question. You will be rewarded for selecting and using material from it and it is a good idea to draw the examiner's attention to the fact that you have done so by using a phrase such as 'as Item B says'.

You can quote from the Item or put it in your own words, but always try to build on it by linking it to the question and your own knowledge.

Remember, too, that if you *don't* use the Item when told to, you won't be able to gain the higher marks. Box 25 gives an example of how you might use an Item.

You will also see that question (f) says 'material from ... *elsewhere*'. This is a signal that you must bring in your own knowledge as well. In other words, you won't find everything in the Item that you need to answer the question.

points to remember

- Read the question carefully until you understand it; then make a brief plan.
- Write a short introduction linking to key aspects of the question.
- Stick to the question. Don't write 'All I know about the family' (or education, or methods) answers.
- Discuss a range of concepts, explanations, theories/perspectives and/or methods. Use evidence from sociological studies.
- Use the Items, especially in question (f), and use examples.
- Write a brief conclusion following logically from the main points in your essay.
- For (e), most of the marks are for Knowledge and Understanding, but you still need to show some AO2 skills.
- For (f), focus on showing the AO2 skills, especially Analysis and Evaluation.

QuickCheck Questions

1 How much time do you have in the exam room to do:
(a) Unit 1 (Families and Households)
(b) Unit 2 (Education)
(c) Unit 3 (Sociological Methods)?

2 How many questions are there on Education:
(a) 4 (b) 5 (c) 6?

3 True or false? There are fewer questions on Sociological Methods than on other topics.

4 Which command word indicates that Evaluation will be a very important part of the answer:
(a) Examine (b) Explain
(c) Assess (d) Identify?

5 True or false? If the question asks for three reasons and you give four, the examiner will only mark the first three.

6 True or false? If a question asks you to 'explain what is meant by' a term, it's OK to just give an example of it.

7 True or false? Question (e) carries more marks for Knowledge and Understanding than for Identification, Interpretation, Analysis and Evaluation; for (f), it's the other way round.

8 Roughly how long should you spend on answering question (e) or (f) in Units 1 and 2?

Answers are on page 275.

Exam questions and answers

This section of the chapter looks at student answers to three typical exam questions, one for each Unit. For each answer, we give the Examiner's comments and marks, together with suggestions on how to improve on it.

activity

If you wish, you can use the three questions that follow as mock exams and then compare your answers with the examples given.

Unit 1 Families and Households

Item A The structure and composition of families and households has changed considerably over the last century. For example, the average household size has fallen by a half, and there has been a great increase in the number of households containing only one person. In 1901, only about one household in 20 was of this type, whereas today one-person households account for almost one in three of all households in Great Britain.

Recent years have also seen a decline in the proportion of 'traditional' households made up of a married couple and their own dependent children. For example, in the early 1960s, this type accounted for almost 40% of households, but by the end of the twentieth century this had fallen to less than a quarter of all British households. Such changes are partly the result of policies or laws introduced by government, but other social factors are also responsible.

Item B Functionalist sociologists argue that the family is a universal social institution found in all human societies. In their view, this is because of the beneficial functions that the family performs both for society and for all its members, such as the primary socialisation of individuals into society's norms and values and the stabilisation of adult personalities.

However, while the family is universal, the form it takes is not. Instead, its structure varies to fit the needs of the type of society in which it is found. For example, according to Talcott Parsons, in pre-industrial society we find that the extended family is predominant, while in industrial society the family is nuclear in form. These different family structures also perform different functions to some extent.

(a) Explain what is meant by a 'household' (**Item A,** line 2). (2 marks)

(b) Suggest **two** reasons for the increase in one-person households (**Item A,** line 3). (4 marks)

(c) Suggest **three** reasons for the 'decline in the proportion of "traditional" households made up of a married couple and their own dependent children' (**Item A,** lines 6-7). (6 marks)

(d) Identify **two** policies or laws **apart from** divorce that may affect family life, and briefly describe how they may do this (**Item A,** lines 9-10). (8 marks)

(e) Examine the reasons for changes in the patterns of marriage, cohabitation and divorce in Britain. (20 marks)

(f) Using material from **Item B** and elsewhere, assess the contribution of functionalist sociologists to our understanding of families and households. (20 marks)

Student answer by Meena

(a) Explain what is meant by a 'household' (**Item A**, line 2). (2 marks)

A household is a family that lives together under the same roof.

> Wrong – a household is a group of people living together, or one person living alone. They don't have to be a family. 0/2

(b) Suggest **two** reasons for the increase in one-person households (**Item A**, line 3). (4 marks)

Two reasons are first that people are getting married later, so some of them spend longer living as a single person alone. Secondly, there are more divorces, which means some people (usually the men) will move out and live alone.

> Both reasons are correct. 4/4

(c) Suggest **three** reasons for the 'decline in the proportion of "traditional" households made up of a married couple and their own dependent children' (**Item A**, lines 6-7). (6 marks)

The first reason is that not as many couples are getting married nowadays.

Secondly, more married couples are choosing not to have children at all.

Thirdly, due to increased divorce, there are more stepfamilies today, so in some families the children aren't the 'own' children of both partners.

> These are all valid reasons, so full marks. 6/6

(d) Identify **two** policies or laws **apart from** divorce that may affect family life, and briefly describe how they may do this (**Item A**, lines 9-10). (8 marks)

The first policy is the payment of child benefit, which is normally paid to the mother rather than the father. The effect of this is to give the woman at least some income (even if only a fairly small sum) that she directly has control over, which would make the financial relationship she has with her husband slightly more equal.

The second policy is that of more women going out to work. This gives women an income of their own and so makes the marriage more equal than if they had to depend entirely on their husbands for money.

> Meena's first policy is correct and she explains its effect clearly, so 4/4. However, more women going out to work is not a policy, so she scores 0/4 here. Other policies she could use include child protection laws, laws against rape in marriage, equal pay at work, adoption etc. 4/8

(e) Examine the reasons for changes in the patterns of marriage, cohabitation and divorce in Britain. (20 marks)

Thirty years ago people got married much earlier than they do today, couples did not live together before they got married and divorce was quite rare. Nowadays most people cohabit before they marry and a large number of those who marry end up getting divorced. These huge changes in marriage, cohabitation and divorce are due to many different reasons.

> A reasonable start, identifying some of the major patterns.

A major reason for the changes in the numbers of unmarried people cohabiting and the fall in the numbers marrying is due to the development of contraception. Scientific advances over the past 50 years have led to a much greater effectiveness in contraception and a lot more variety. As a result of these factors, people see contraception as convenient and readily acceptable.

Tries to use contraception to explain rise in cohabitation, but she isn't very successful.

Children being born 'out of wedlock' to unmarried mothers has also become a lot more widely acceptable than it was 30 years ago. Rights and support have been given to single parents. Both these factors, the acceptability of contraception and unmarried parents, have led to cohabitation being accepted. Single mothers have shown to society that a child does not necessarily need two parents, making divorce more acceptable to many.

Connects acceptability of single parenthood to rise in cohabitation, but still hasn't linked contraception clearly. A good point about divorce and single mothers at end.

Women have many more rights and are more accepted as being equal to men than they were 30 years ago. Women today are now able to go into the workplace and have a highly successful career in practically every line of work that men do. This change has led to major changes in marriage and the family.

Good point about women and work, but doesn't apply it to marriage, cohabitation and divorce.

Our society has changed over time and become one where we value freedom of choice. We are given an extremely wide choice on practically all aspects of our lives and the right to choose our partners, and whether or not to stay with the same person all our lives has become part of this. We see it as our right to choose to divorce if we wish.

Good point about freedom of choice and divorce. Could link greater choice to post-modern society.

Patterns of marriage, cohabitation and divorce have changed a great deal in the past 30 years and the main reasons are women's liberation and our feeling that we have the right to choose.

11/20

Relevant conclusion but too brief to add much.

Comments **Meena shows a reasonable knowledge of some potentially relevant material. However, firstly, she should say more about all three – marriage, cohabitation and divorce (e.g. other reasons for divorce include secularisation and changes in the law). Secondly, she needs to interpret what she knows more effectively, so it links clearly to the question – two good points, about contraception and women working, are poorly applied to the question. Thirdly, she could bring in some theories (e.g. feminism, postmodernism, the New Right) to make some evaluation points.**

(f) Using material from **Item B** and elsewhere, assess the contribution of functionalist sociologists to our understanding of families and households.
(20 marks)

I would agree that functionalist ideas are very useful in helping us understand the family. They see it as being like an organ in the body of society. This stresses its importance, because for many people the family is a place to turn to when other pressures in life become too great.

Good point about the organic analogy but could be explained further.

The functionalists Willmott and Young help us to understand the development of the family, as they see it as evolving over stages, beginning with the pre-industrial family as a unit of production, through to early industrial society where the family worked away from home in factories. This was followed by the modern symmetrical family, where housework is equally shared between men and women. This shows how the family has changed with industrialisation. However, another functionalist, Talcott Parsons, does not agree. He argues that the family moved from being a pre-industrial extended family to a nuclear one in modern society.

W&Y are not really function-alists. Better to start with Parsons, explain his views and then use W&Y to criticise him.

Parsons goes on to say that the two main functions of the family are the stabilisation of the adult personality and primary socialisation of the young, as Item B shows. This idea enables us to understand just how important the family is to modern life and makes us aware how different society would be if the family did not exist. If primary socialisation within the family did not take place in the early years of a child's life, society would be very different.

Relevant use of Item B, but these functions need fuller explanation.

The functionalist Murdock makes some important points about the family's role. He states four main functions of family life. These are Socialisation, Reproduction, Sexual and Economic. Without a sexual relationship in the family, reproduction could not occur and this would cause the family to die out. The family is also vital for economic functions. It acts as a means of economic support for all its members, and together they can work to earn a wage to support them as a family. Murdock argues that although other institutions could perform these functions, the sheer practicality of the nuclear family as a way of meeting these four needs is why it is found in all societies.

Quite a good account, but Murdock's views need evaluating.

Together the ideas of the different functionalists help us to understand the important things that make the family so essential for modern life. However, other sociologists such as feminists are very critical of their male bias in their view of family life.

Why wait until now to bring in feminism? It should appear earlier and be fully explained.

11/20

Comments Meena shows some sociological knowledge and makes limited use of Item B. However, although her interpretation of material is largely accurate and relevant, she doesn't analyse or evaluate it effectively. For example, she doesn't analyse Parsons' views on the modern nuclear family (e.g. its mobility, what its two functions actually mean). She misinterprets Willmott and Young as functionalists and doesn't use them to evaluate Parsons' views on industrialisation. Likewise, she could evaluate Murdock by using material on family diversity to challenge his 'universality' argument. Meena mentions the feminist critique in her final sentence and, if she developed it, this could make great evaluation of the functionalist view.

Total mark and overview Meena performed fairly well on the short questions, scoring 14/20. Her performance on the longer questions – 11/20 on each – was reasonable but a broader knowledge of theories would have been very useful in both. She needs to tie her material in clearly to the question and in part (f) she needs to focus on evaluating more. Meena's total mark is 36/60 – probably enough to earn her a grade C.

36/60

Unit 2 Education

Item A Sociologists have identified a wide range of factors responsible for educational differences between pupils of different social classes, ethnic groups and genders. For example, in the case of social class, some researchers have examined the negative effects of material deprivation on the educational chances of working-class children. Others argue that cultural deprivation is the main cause of their under-achievement.

However, there is a risk that focusing on material and cultural deprivation may lead us to neglect the impact of the education system itself and what takes place within it. For example, the educational policies of the government can help to widen or narrow the gap in achievement between the social classes, while the interactions that occur within school may also powerfully affect pupils' behaviour and achievement.

Item B According to functionalist sociologists, the education system performs two essential functions. Firstly, education selects and prepares individuals for their roles in the economy. Schools identify the talents and aptitudes of each pupil and equip them with the specific knowledge and skills they will need to perform their specialised occupational role.

Secondly, education performs the vital function of integrating individuals into wider society. In the view of functionalists, this is essential if we are to be able to work together to meet society's needs. By socialising children into the shared culture, the education system gives each individual a sense of being part of the wider society. If everyone has the same outlook, goals and values, they will work together harmoniously.

(a) Explain what is meant by 'material deprivation' (**Item A**, line 4). (2 marks)

(b) Identify **two** factors that may affect gender differences in education (**Item A**, lines 1–2). (4 marks)

(c) Identify **three** educational policies that may have affected social class differences in pupils' achievement (**Item A**, lines 8–9). (6 marks)

(d) Identify and briefly explain **two** ways in which interactions in school may affect pupils' behaviour and/or achievement. (**Item A**, lines 9–10) (8 marks)

(e) Examine the reasons for ethnic differences in educational achievement. (20 marks)

(f) Using material from **Item B** and elsewhere, assess the functionalist view of the role of the education system. (20 marks)

Student answer by Jack

(a) Explain what is meant by 'material deprivation' (**Item A**, line 4). (2 marks)

Material deprivation is deprivation of the norms and values needed to succeed, e.g. working-class pupils lack deferred gratification.

Jack has defined (and given an example of) cultural rather than material deprivation. Material deprivation refers to poverty and the lack of basic necessities. 0/2

(b) Identify **two** factors that may affect gender differences in education (**Item A**, lines 1–2). (4 marks)

One factor affecting gender differences in education is role models. Girls now have more career women as role models and this has improved their performance in school.

Another factor is early socialisation. Girls are encouraged to play with dolls etc and this may lead them to prefer nurturing subjects at school.

Two suitable factors identified – role models and early socialisation.

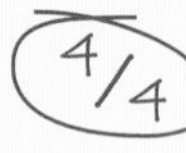

(c) Identify **three** educational policies that may have affected social class differences in pupils' achievement (**Item A**, lines 8–9). (6 marks)

One policy is comprehensive schooling. This made opportunities more equal for the working class.

Secondly, the way teachers treat pupils differently according to their class – the middle class are seen as 'ideal pupils'.

Thirdly, equal opportunities policies mean that girls are now doing much better than before in so-called 'boys' subjects' like science.

Jack's first point is correct, but his second isn't a policy and his third, although a policy, isn't about class. He could have used the tripartite system, maintenance grants, higher education fees etc. 2/6

(d) Identify and briefly explain **two** ways in which interactions in school may affect pupils' behaviour and/or achievement (**Item A**, lines 9–10). (8 marks)

One way is through labelling. This can affect a pupil's behaviour or achievement by the self-fulfilling prophecy, where pupils become what the teacher predicted – e.g. a working-class pupil labelled as stupid comes to see himself as stupid and so he fails.

A second way is through the forming of pupil subcultures. These too can be the result of pupils being labelled as good, bad, thick, clever etc by their teachers.

Both ways identified are correct. But only labelling is properly explained: Jack shows how it can lead to failure through the self-fulfilling prophecy. He needs to do something similar with subcultures – by explaining how they can reinforce the kind of behaviour (e.g. truanting) that leads to failure. 6/8

(e) Examine the reasons for ethnic differences in educational achievement. (20 marks)

There are many reasons why ethnic minorities under-achieve in education. Labelling theorists believe that the key is factors such as labelling and teachers' expectations, the self-fulfilling prophecy and the relationship between teachers and pupils.

> It would be better to point out that not all minorities do under-achieve. But labelling view is relevant.

Because most minorities come from working-class backgrounds, teachers often label them as 'slow'. Keddie found teachers favoured middle-class pupils and taught them more thoroughly. Ball found students were divided into two bands. In the top band were the more able students (middle-class) and in the bottom band were the less able (working-class). Once labelled, a child has two options, either live up to their label and it becomes a self-fulfilling prophecy, or fight against it to prove the teacher wrong.

> All accurate, but all about class – needs applying to ethnicity, using relevant studies.

According to Bernstein, many ethnic minorities also speak in a restricted code of short, unfinished sentences because their first language is not English. This then holds then back when at school, which uses the elaborated code.

> Not true – Bernstein's speech codes are based on class, not ethnicity. Speaking in a restricted code is not the same as speaking a different language.

However, there are other reasons why ethnic minorities fail in the education system. Driver and Ballard argue that one of the biggest factors is parents' emphasis on education. They argue that Asian students do better than Afro-Caribbeans because of the strong emphasis put on education by their parents, who are prepared to make sacrifices for their children to succeed.

> Relevant study, used appropriately. Good to distinguish between different minorities.

Also, poverty could contribute to the under-achievement of ethnic minorities. Afro-Caribbeans have worse housing, income and employment opportunities and this could explain why Afro-Caribbean students do very poorly in education. The Swann Report argues that this might have contributed to their failure.

> Another relevant factor.

Teachers often interpret the behaviour of ethnic minority pupils as being aggressive when they are only trying to develop their sense of ethnic identity as young black people. This can lead to confrontations and exclusions.

> Good point, but would go better with paragraph on labelling. Needs a conclusion, too.

10/20

Comments **Jack doesn't focus fully on the question. His material on Keddie and Ball is about class, not ethnicity, and he misinterprets Bernstein. However, he does show some awareness of differences between minorities and he describes three relevant reasons: parental support, poverty and teachers' interpretations. He needs a stronger knowledge of relevant studies (e.g. Wright, Fuller, Sewell, Mirza, Connolly), and differences between and within minorities (e.g. gender differences). He could organise his answer in terms of internal and external factors, using concepts such as teacher racism, the ethnocentric curriculum, cultural deprivation etc.**

(f) Using material from **Item B** and elsewhere, assess the functionalist view of the role of the education system. (20 marks)

Functionalism has a macro consensus view where individuals operate to meet society's needs. This can be applied to education, which performs functions that society requires to continue. As Item B says, functionalists see education as having several functions. The first is socialisation for wider society. Durkheim argues that education integrates us into society by teaching us society's shared culture. Parsons says it acts as a bridge moving us from the particularistic values of the family to the universalistic values of society (e.g. one law for everyone).

Good, clear account of functionalist views, using relevant concepts.

The other function is to allocate individuals to suitable jobs to keep the economy running smoothly. Davis and Moore say this is achieved meritocratically. Each pupil gets an equal opportunity to show their talents, which are measured by the exam system. Those who show most ability gain the best results. Qualifications are then used to allocate us to roles that match our talents, so the economy benefits by not having 'square pegs in round holes'. Everyone is motivated to try because the jobs that require most ability have the biggest rewards. Functionalists see this as fair – everyone has an equal opportunity.

Good analysis of Davis & Moore's views on role allocation, inequality and meritocracy.

Marxists see education differently. Marxism is also a macro theory, but based on conflict not consensus. Both approaches believe education prepares people for society, but functionalism sees individuals being socialised into society's norms and accepting the hierarchy as necessary for everyone's benefit, whereas Marxists see this as the oppression of the working class by the bourgeoisie, a way of the capitalist ruling class controlling the workers so they can be exploited.

Relevant analysis of similarities and differences between functionalism and Marxism.

Marxists Bowles and Gintis reject meritocracy as a 'myth' designed to get working-class pupils to accept working-class jobs by making them believe they failed through their own inadequacy. This legitimates capitalism, preventing revolution. They believe working-class pupils are denied equal opportunity. Those from wealthy backgrounds get the best education and the top jobs, thus reproducing the class system.

Accurate evaluation from a Marxist perspective, with good use of relevant concepts.

Others criticise functionalists for seeing education as the system shaping the pupils. Interactionists like Wrong see pupils as capable of resisting the socialisation that the system attempts. This is also a criticism of Bowles and Gintis made by Willis, who believes working-class pupils are not taken in by the myth of meritocracy. Another criticism is that functionalists ignore other functions, e.g. education provides a 'babysitting' service for parents, and a social control function, keeping young people off the streets. 17/20

Some good evaluation points – interactionist criticisms, and other functions that functionalists neglect. But needs a separate conclusion.

Comments Jack shows a sound knowledge of functionalist and other views on the role of education. He uses a good range of different concepts correctly (e.g. consensus, role allocation, myth of meritocracy etc). He interprets material accurately and uses it in ways relevant to the question, and he shows some good analysis of the different views, spelling them out in detail and comparing and contrasting them. He evaluates the functionalist view mainly from a Marxist perspective, but also refers to other approaches and functions. This is a very good answer, but could be further improved with a conclusion pulling the main arguments together and by further use of the Item and of other concepts such as the correspondence principle, hidden curriculum etc.

Total mark and overview Jack's performance is quite uneven. On the one hand, he achieves a very good mark on part (f), showing good skills of analysis and evaluation. On the other hand, he drops quite a lot of marks on the short questions, where he gained only 12/20. Similarly, on part (e) his lack of knowledge of relevant material on ethnicity and achievement meant he only scored half marks. A reasonable knowledge of a few of the main studies on ethnicity could have earned him the extra marks needed to turn this into a grade A. Equally, a better knowledge of policies on part (c) would have improved his grade. With a total mark of 39/60, Jack would probably achieve a grade B.

39/60

Unit 3 Sociological Methods

Item A In selecting a research method or source of data for analysis, the sociologist needs to consider how far the chosen method or source will produce reliable, valid and representative data. However, it is unlikely that any given method will be able to offer all three of these. In particular, it is often said that a single method cannot provide data that are both reliable and valid.

As well as these theoretical issues, the sociologist needs to be aware of practical considerations when selecting a method or source. These considerations may mean that the sociologist will opt to use a secondary source of data rather than use primary sources like structured or unstructured interviews and postal questionnaires. Secondary sources such as personal documents can sometimes offer great practical advantages to the researcher.

Item B The method I adopted for my research was covert participant observation. I began attending the Calvary church services on a regular basis, posing as a true believer. Despite my initial acceptance into the church, there was still some curiosity as to my real motive for joining. The reason I always gave was that although I was from a very religious background, my education had drawn me away from religion but now I just felt like going to church again.

However, I was very aware of the ethical problems with my covert approach and so I explained my research role to the church leader. He said he would do anything he could to help, and he concealed my research intentions from other church members. However, having made my research purpose overt to him, I found that he wanted something in return – my baptism and permanent membership of the church. Ultimately, I was baptised into the church. Baptism made a difference to my status and I was treated with a new openness by the members.

Source: adapted from Ken Pryce (1979)

(a) Explain what is meant by 'representative data' (**Item A**, line 3). (2 marks)

(b) Explain the difference between reliable data and valid data (**Item A**, lines 4-5). (4 marks)

(c) Suggest **three** disadvantages of using structured interviews in sociological research. (**Item A**, line 9). (6 marks)

(d) Identify and briefly explain **one** advantage and **one** disadvantage of using personal documents (**Item A**, line 10). (8 marks)

(e) Examine the advantages and disadvantages of using official statistics in sociological research. (20 marks)

(f) Using material from **Item B** and elsewhere, assess the usefulness of participant observation as a sociological research method. (20 marks)

Student answer by Simone

(a) Explain what is meant by 'representative data' (**Item A**, line 3). (2 marks)

If data is representative, it means that it is a typical cross-section of the group from which it is drawn.

> A clear and accurate explanation. 2/2

(b) Explain the difference between reliable data and valid data (**Item A**, lines 4-5). (4 marks)

Reliability means that the findings of a research can be replicated (repeated to get the same findings), whereas validity means that the data are a true or authentic picture of the topic.

> A clear explanation of the difference between the two terms. 4/4

(c) Suggest **three** disadvantages of using structured interviews in sociological research (**Item A**, line 9). (6 marks)

One disadvantage of structured interviews is that those who agree to be interviewed may be untypical, e.g. they may have more time on their hands compared to other people. This will make the sample unrepresentative.

Secondly, samples with structured interviews tend to be quite small, so this can lead to unrepresentative findings.

Thirdly, they are inflexible, as the questions have to be drawn up in advance and cannot be altered to follow up interesting points during the interview.

Fourthly, there is more risk of misunderstandings, as the interviewer has to stick to a set form of words. If the interviewee doesn't understand the question, the interviewer doesn't have much freedom to put it differently.

> Although the question asks for three disadvantages, Simone has given four – a wise move if you're not sure your first three are right. In Simone's case, this pays off, since her second reason is wrong: structured interviews usually have fairly large samples. Her other three reasons are correct. 6/6

(d) Identify and briefly explain **one** advantage and **one** disadvantage of using personal documents (**Item A**, line 10). (8 marks)

One advantage is that they are sometimes the only available source of information about a topic. For example, studying a time in the distant past when there is no-one still living today means primary methods cannot be used and there may not be any official documents either. People's letters and diaries may be the only sources surviving. Without them we would know nothing of that time.

One disadvantage is that personal documents such as diaries and letters may be unrepresentative. For example, if they come from a past time when only privileged people could read and write, their contents will probably not be representative of the experience of poorer illiterate people. They may also be unrepresentative because they are the only remaining documents, especially after a long time has passed. Many people's documents may be lost or destroyed, leaving only a few untypical ones.

> Two correct identifications, with very full and clear explanations of each. However, Simone has written more than necessary. In both paragraphs, she would still have gained full marks even if she had stopped after her second sentence. 8/8

(e) Examine the advantages and disadvantages of using official statistics in sociological research. (20 marks)

Positivists choose to use official statistics with numerical values, e.g. the numbers committing suicide in a given year, because they see quantitative data as more scientific. Examples of official statistics cover many topics, such as births, marriages, deaths, divorce, unemployment, crime, suicide and child abuse.

Relevant points, but might be better to briefly define official statistics (OS) first.

Sociologists often use official statistics as a source of secondary data because they cover the whole society and so are very representative. Using official statistics enables us to compare past and present data to find trends. It is a quick, cheap and easy way to obtain quantitative data, which is a big practical advantage in research. Another advantage of official statistics is that they are objective and have great reliability, as there is unlikely to be much researcher bias, if any.

Several advantages examined – representativeness, trends, practical issues – but should explain reliability fully.

However, one disadvantage is that researchers may be denied access to certain statistics. Also, statistics only provide a snapshot picture of one point in time, and since changes may have occurred between when the data was collected and when it is published, the figures in the statistics may be out of date.

Two relevant disadvantages here.

As already mentioned, positivists take an objective scientific approach and favour official statistics as they believe we can discover laws from them by establishing correlations between different variables. If two variables always go together, e.g. social class and educational achievement, then it may mean that one is the cause of the other and we have discovered a law of cause and effect. They therefore see official statistics as a stepping-stone to discovering social laws.

Good analysis of the link between OS and positivism, using concepts correctly.

Interpretivists reject the scientific approach. They claim official statistics lack depth and that there is no empathy with the person's feelings, so they favour participant observation or unstructured interviews instead. However, these methods are very time consuming and costly. The researcher must take this into account, as well as the theoretical and ethical considerations involved.

Some evaluation from interpretivist perspective, but 'theoretical and ethical considerations' needs linking to the question.

Durkheim used official statistics from many European countries to study suicide and discover sociological laws. However, it could be argued that the statistics were invalid because they were just the coroners' verdicts and interpretations, and not the individual's own situation.

Relevant evaluation of Durkheim, but could be developed further.

Official statistics might therefore be used if the researcher does not have much time and money or if they prefer quantitative data. However, it should be remembered that official statistics merely impose the theories of the people who collected them to begin with, such as the police or the government.

17/20

Appropriate conclusion with both advantages and disadvantages – but could link back to earlier point about coroners.

Comments **Simone shows a very good grasp of a range of issues, concepts and approaches. She examines a number of practical and theoretical advantages and disadvantages and uses relevant examples. She makes a good analysis of the relationship between official statistics and positivism, and provides some evaluation from an interpretivist perspective. She has a reasonable conclusion, but brings in a new point in the last sentence that needs further explanation (e.g. she could link it back to the point about coroners' interpretations). She might improve the structure of her answer by dealing with practical and theoretical issues in turn and then sum these up in the conclusion. A few points also need further development (e.g. reliability – an important advantage). She could also consider whether some statistics are more valid or reliable than others (e.g. birth, crime etc).**

(f) Using material from **Item B** and elsewhere, assess the usefulness of participant observation as a sociological research method. (20 marks)

The usefulness of participant observation (PO) depends partly on your perspective. It can provide knowledge of a group, but positivists believe that it produces invalid data. However social action theorists disagree. They see it as producing the most valid data.

Links PO to perspective and validity – but it would be a good idea to define PO first.

PO allows the sociologist to analyse a group by observing them. In Item B, Pryce participated in the group, allowing him to gain insight into them and share their feelings/emotions. This is seen as valid. He joined in their activities and routines and looked into their life experiences. Covert PO can also give accurate results, because if the subjects don't know someone is observing them then they will behave normally. PO can be done in a natural setting and not an artificial situation such as a laboratory experiment. This may help the sociologist to obtain more accurate information.

Uses Item. Understands covert PO but should define and distinguish it from overt. Identifies 'natural setting' as an advantage but should link it to validity.

Eileen Barker used PO in her study of a religious cult known as the Moonies. She observed them, read their publications, interviewed members and ex-members and asked them why they joined. She aimed to find out whether they were being brainwashed, as the press claimed. Barker disproved this, because they would not have left if they had been brainwashed. In fact, she found that to get people to stay, the Moonies were being nice to them.

Not well used. She describes Barker's aims and findings, but should discuss her use of PO instead.

Although PO can put the sociologist in an awkward or dangerous position, especially if it is covert, the results are highly valid. However, the sociologist then has to analyse and interpret the results, which may be unfair because the sociologist may be biased.

Good points about danger, validity and bias, but all need explanation.

PO is costly, time-consuming and unrepresentative because it only studies small groups and this prevents findings being generalised. For example, Parker's study in Liverpool of a gang of delinquent boys took him four years.

Identifies several disadvantages and gives an example – but again, all a bit brief.

PO provides good insight into the group members, the researcher may make friends, get to know people and reveal information. Social action theorists prefer this type of data.

Repeats points from first two paragraphs.

PO provides useful data which a researcher may go back to, to compare results or find any particular correlation with e.g. gender, age groups, classes. It is valid because it gives the sociologist first hand experienced data.

Not very convincing on 'correlation'. 'First hand experience' point needs developing. Fuller conclusion needed.

14/20

Comments **Simone shows a reasonably good knowledge of a range of material and gives both practical and theoretical aspects some attention. She is aware of different perspectives, but she should analyse their relationship to PO (e.g. explaining why action theorists prefer qualitative data). She makes a range of points but needs to develop some of them further (e.g. references to generalisation, danger). She should also discuss both overt and covert PO. There is some Evaluation, but she tends to state rather than discuss her points (e.g. *why* is a natural setting an advantage over a laboratory?). She refers to Item B, and has material from one or two studies, though she could develop this (e.g. Parker) or make it more relevant (e.g. give an account of Barker's methods rather than her findings). Overall, a good range of points, but she needs to deepen and develop them.**

Total mark and overview **Simone got off to an excellent start by scoring 20/20 on the shorter questions with clear and accurate answers. (Full marks on these questions will get you quite close to a pass mark even before you tackle the longer ones.) Although she wrote more than necessary at times on the short questions, she also wisely covered herself by including an extra point on part (c). Her answer to (e) was very thorough and well informed and, although (f) could have been better developed, she made a good range of points. With total mark of 51/60, Simone has achieved a very clear grade A.**

51/60

Chapter summary

Revision

Get organised before you start revising. Ensure your notes are in order. Get all your materials together: coursebook, notes, marked work, stationery, the specification etc. Study past papers to get an idea of what you can be asked and the style of the questions.

A realistic revision timetable is vital. Make allowance for other demands on your time. Include some leisure time as a reward for studying. Set yourself achievable targets with dates. When revising, build in short breaks and set yourself specific tasks.

Find somewhere quiet to study. Be systematic and cover everything. Make sure you understand each topic before moving on to the next one. Write summaries as you finish each topic.

Revise actively. Highlight key points, make notes on notes, use abbreviations, re-write your notes as mind maps etc. Do past exam questions and 'Examining' questions from your coursebook on every topic. Revise with friends. Test each other, explain ideas, play revision games, share summaries, mark each other's work. But be disciplined; don't waste time chatting.

As the exams get closer, **combat stress** by getting into a daily routine. Make sure you get enough sleep, food and exercise; try a relaxation exercise. Know when and where each exam will be held. Ensure you have all the necessary pens etc in working order, plus your entry slip.

The night before the exam, pack your equipment, entry slip, revision notes, plus water and a snack. Stick to revising things you know. Unwind for at least an hour before bedtime.

On the day of the exam, get up in good time, have enough to eat, dress comfortably. Take your equipment etc. Arrive early, but not too early. Find somewhere quiet to relax. Read through a few notes on something you already know well, to get your brain in gear. Don't try to learn anything new.

In the exam room, get settled quickly; take a few deep breaths. Read the instructions. Read the Items and questions at least twice, highlighting key words. Brainstorm a brief plan for the longer questions. Leave time to check through your answers. Keep an eye on the clock.

Tackling the AS sociology exam

The exam has two Assessment Objectives: AO1 and AO2. For AO1, you need to show **knowledge and understanding** of sociological theories, methods, concepts, studies and findings.

For AO2, you need to **identify** relevant information, and **interpret** and apply it in ways that help answer the set question. You need to **analyse**, e.g. by showing the steps in an argument and drawing conclusions. You need to **evaluate**, e.g. by weighing up arguments and evidence, discussing advantages and disadvantages and considering rival views.

You have to do an exam of one hour 15 minutes for Unit 1 (Families and Households) and Unit 2 (Education), plus either coursework or a one-hour exam for Unit 3 (Sociological Methods). Each exam has six questions worth 60 marks.

Don't write long answers to the **short questions (a) to (d)**. If asked to explain, give a clear explanation, not just an example. If asked to give two or three points, you can give more if you're unsure. Check the Item references in the questions for clues. Set out your answers clearly, with each point on a new line.

Spend about 20-25 minutes on questions (e) and (f). **Question (e)** will ask you to examine something (e.g. reasons, policies). The focus is on AO1 but you also need to show some AO2.

Question (f) focuses on AO2, so show plenty of analysis and evaluation. It also requires use of the **Item**, so study it carefully and include material from it.

Key Concepts

The following is an alphabetical list of some of the key concepts you need to know for AS level Sociology. You can use the list as:

- a handy reference to find a quick definition of a term you're not sure of
- a revision aid to ensure you know and understand important sociological ideas.

When you look up a concept in the list, you may find other terms in the explanation printed in *italics*. This means you will find a separate entry for these terms elsewhere in the list. You will also find that a lot of entries give you a 'see also' reference. Following these up will show you some of the links between concepts and broaden your understanding of them.

age patriarchy: see **patriarchy**

alienation: where an individual or group feels socially isolated and estranged because they lack the power to control their lives and realise their true potential. Marx describes workers in capitalist society as alienated because they are exploited and lack control of the production process. *See also* **Marxism**.

banding: a form of **streaming**.

birth rate: the number of live births per 1,000 of the population per year. *See also* **infant mortality rate**.

bourgeoisie: a Marxist term for the capitalist class, the owners of the means of production (factories, machinery, raw materials, land etc). Marx argues that the bourgeoisie's ownership of the means of production also gives them political and ideological power. *See also* **exploitation; ideology; Marxism; proletariat.**

capitalism: see **Marxism.**

case study: research that examines a single case or example, such as a single school, family or workplace, often using several methods or sources.

childhood: a socially defined age-status. There are major differences in how childhood is defined, both historically and between cultures. Western societies today define children as vulnerable and segregate them from the adult world, but in the past they were part of adult society from an early age. These differences show that childhood is a *social construction*. *See also* **patriarchy**.

closed-ended questions: questions used in a *social survey* that allow only a limited choice of answers from a pre-set list. They produce *quantitative data* and the answers are often pre-coded for ease of analysis. An example is 'Will you vote in the next election?' where the choices are Yes, No, Don't know. *See also* **open-ended questions.**

comparative method: a research method that compares two social groups that are alike apart from one factor. For example, Durkheim compared two groups that were identical apart from their religion in order to find out the effect of religion on suicide rates. The method is often used as an alternative to *experiments*.

compensatory education: government education policies such as Operation Headstart in the USA that seek to tackle the problem of under-achievement by providing extra support and funding to schools and families in deprived areas. *See also* **cultural deprivation.**

comprehensive system: a non-selective education system where all children attend the same type of secondary school. It was introduced in England and Wales from 1965. *See also* **tripartite system.**

conjugal roles: the roles played by husband and wife. Segregated conjugal roles are where the husband is breadwinner and the wife is homemaker, with leisure spent separately. In joint conjugal roles, husband and wife each perform both roles and spend their leisure time together. *See also* **symmetrical family.**

content analysis: a method of analysing the content of documents and media output to find out how often and in what ways different types of people or events appear. For example, the Glasgow University Media Group (1976) used content analysis to reveal bias in how television news reported strikes.

control group: in *experiments*, scientists compare a control group and an experimental group that are identical in all respects. Unlike the experimental group, the control group is not exposed to the variable under investigation and so provides a baseline against which any changes in the experimental group can be compared.

correlation: when two or more factors or *variables* vary together; e.g. there is a correlation between low social class and low educational achievement. However, the existence of a correlation between two variables does not necessarily prove that one causes the other. It may simply be coincidence. *See also* **experiments.**

correspondence principle: Bowles and Gintis' concept describing the way that the organisation and control of schools mirrors or 'corresponds to' the workplace in capitalist society. For example, the control teachers exert over pupils mirrors the control managers exert over workers. *See also* **reproduction.**

covert participant observation: see **participant observation.**

cultural capital: the knowledge, attitudes, values, language, tastes and abilities that the middle class transmit to their children. Bourdieu argues that educational success is largely based on possession of cultural capital, thus giving middle-class children an advantage. *See also* **reproduction; speech codes.**

cultural deprivation: the theory that many working-class and black children are inadequately socialised and therefore lack the 'right' *culture* needed for educational success; e.g. their families do not instil the value of *deferred gratification*. *See also* **compensatory education.**

culture: all those things that are learnt and shared by a society or group of people and transmitted from generation to generation through *socialisation*. It includes shared *norms*, *values*, knowledge, beliefs and skills. *See also* **subculture.**

curriculum: those things taught or learnt in educational institutions. The overt or official curriculum includes the subjects, courses etc offered (e.g. the National Curriculum), while the hidden curriculum includes all those things learnt without being formally taught and often acquired simply through the everyday workings of the school, such as attitudes of obedience, conformity and competitiveness. *See also* **ethnocentric.**

deferred gratification: postponing immediate rewards or pleasures, generally with the aim of producing a greater reward at a later date, e.g. staying in to revise rather than going out with friends, which will bring success in exams. It is seen as a characteristic of middle-class *culture*. *See also* **immediate gratification; values.**

dependency culture: where people assume that the state will support them, rather than relying on their own efforts and taking responsibility for their families. The *New Right* see the *welfare state* as over-generous, encouraging people to remain unemployed and dependent on benefits, and as responsible for the growing number of lone-parent families and rising crime rate. *See also* **underclass.**

deviance: behaviour that does not conform to the *norms* of a society or group. Deviance is a *social construction* (defined or created by social groups). Deviance is relative: what counts as deviant varies between groups and cultures and over time.

differentiation: distinguishing or creating differences between individuals or groups. In education, *streaming* is a form of differentiation that distinguishes between pupils on the basis of ability. In the study of *stratification*, differentiation refers to the process of distinguishing between people on the basis of class, gender, ethnic, age etc differences. *See also* **labelling.**

discrimination: treating people differently, whether negatively (disadvantaging them) or positively (advantaging them), usually because they are members of a particular social group. It can occur on grounds of *gender*, *ethnicity*, age, disability, *sexuality*, religion etc. See *also* **racism; sexism.**

domestic labour: work performed in the home, such as childcare, cooking, and cleaning. Functionalists see it as part of the expressive role performed by women, while feminists regard it as a major source of women's oppression. See *also* **dual burden.**

dual burden: when a person is responsible for two jobs. Usually applied to women who are in paid work but also responsible for *domestic labour*. See *also* **emotion work.**

emotion work: the work involved in meeting the emotional needs of other people, e.g. looking after a sick child involves responding to emotional as well as physical needs. Some sociologists argue that women carry a triple burden of housework, paid work and emotion work. See *also* **dual burden.**

empathy: an understanding of how another person thinks, feels or acts, achieved by putting oneself in their place. Interactionists advocate the use of qualitative methods such as *participant observation* as a way of achieving empathy and obtaining data high in *validity*. See *also* **interactionism; objectivity; subjectivity.**

empty shell marriage: a marriage in name only, where a couple continues to live under the same roof but as separate individuals. It may occur where divorce is difficult for legal, religious or financial reasons, or where a couple decides to stay together for the sake of the children.

ethics: issues of right and wrong; moral principles or guidelines. There are ethical objections to research that deceives or harms its subjects or fails to obtain subjects' *informed consent*.

ethnic group: people who share the same heritage, culture and identity, often including the same language and religion, and who see themselves as a distinct group, e.g. the Bangladeshi community in Britain. As well as having ethnic minority groups, societies such as Britain have an ethnic majority. See *also* **culture; racism; stratification.**

ethnocentric: seeing or judging things in a biased way from the viewpoint of one particular culture; e.g. the National Curriculum has been described as an ethnocentric *curriculum* since it tends to value white, western music, literature, languages, history, religion etc and disregards or does not value black and Asian cultures.

exchange theory: the idea that people create, maintain or break off relationships depending on the costs and benefits of doing so; e.g. a person may provide a relative with accommodation (cost) in return for help with childcare (benefit).

experiments: a laboratory experiment is a test carried out in controlled conditions in an artificial setting (a laboratory) to establish a cause-and-effect relationship between two or more variables. A field experiment has the same aim but is carried out in a natural setting (e.g. a street or workplace) not a laboratory. See *also* **control group; positivism.**

experimental group: see **control group.**

exploitation: paying workers less than the value of their labour. According to Marxists, it is the process whereby the *bourgeoisie* extract surplus value or profit from the labour of the *proletariat*. Feminists see men as exploiting the domestic labour of women. See *also* **Marxism; feminism.**

expressive role: the caring, nurturing, 'homemaker' role in the family. Functionalists argue that women are biologically suited to performing this role, but feminists reject this. See *also* **instrumental role.**

extended family: any group of kin (people related by blood, marriage or adoption) extended beyond the *nuclear family*. The family may be extended vertically (e.g. grandparents), horizontally (e.g. aunts, uncles, cousins), or both. See *also* **family structure.**

family structure: the composition of a group of people who live together as a family unit. Structures include the *nuclear family, extended family, reconstituted family*, lone-parent and same-sex families.

feminism: a sociological perspective and political movement that focuses on women's oppression and the struggle to end it. Feminists argue that sociology has traditionally taken a 'malestream' viewpoint that ignores women. Instead, they examine women's experiences and study society from a female perspective. There are different strands of feminism, including Marxist, radical, liberal and black feminism. *See also* **patriarchy.**

Fordism: a type of industrial production based on a detailed division of labour, using closely supervised, low-skilled workers and assembly-line technology to mass-produce standardised goods. Named after the car manufacturing techniques first introduced by the Ford Motor Company in the early 20th century. *See also* **alienation; post-Fordism.**

function: the contribution that a part of society makes to the stability or well-being of society as a whole. For example, according to Durkheim, one function of religion is to give individuals a sense of belonging to something greater than themselves and so integrate them into society. *See also* **functionalism.**

functional fit: Parsons' theory that, with *industrialisation*, the structure of the family becomes nuclear to fit the needs of industrial society for a geographically and socially mobile labour force. *See also* **functionalism; mobility.**

functionalism: a consensus perspective in sociology that sees society as based on shared values into which members are socialised. It sees society as like an organism, each part performing functions to maintain the system as a whole; e.g. the family and education system perform *socialisation* functions. *See also* **function; value consensus.**

gender: the social and cultural characteristics of men and women. Unlike sex differences, which are biological and inborn, gender differences in behaviour are cultural in origin and learned through gender role *socialisation*. Definitions of masculinity and femininity are socially constructed and vary between cultures and social groups. *See also* **feminism; patriarchy.**

geographical mobility: *see* **mobility.**

Hawthorne Effect: where the subjects of a research study know they are being studied and begin to behave differently as a result, thereby undermining the study's *validity*. The term comes from Elton Mayo's studies at the Hawthorne electrical plant.

hidden curriculum: *see* **curriculum.**

hierarchy: an organisation or social structure based on a 'pyramid' of senior and junior positions and top-down control; e.g. an army with its different ranks and command from above. *See also* **stratification.**

household: a group of people who live together and share things such as meals, bills, facilities or chores, or one person living alone.

hypothesis: an untested theory or explanation, expressed as a statement. Sociologists seek to prove or disprove hypotheses by testing them against the evidence. *See also* **experiments.**

identity: the individual's sense of self, influenced by *socialisation* and interactions with others; a sense of belonging to a community. Postmodernists see identity as a choice that individuals make from among different sources of identity, such as *gender, ethnic group*, religion, *sexuality*, leisure interests, nationality etc. *See also* **postmodernism.**

ideology: originally a Marxist idea meaning a set of beliefs that serve the interests of a dominant social group by justifying their privileged position. The term usually implies that the beliefs are false or only partially true; e.g. Bowles and Gintis argue that meritocracy is a 'myth', i.e. untrue. *See also* **legitimation; Marxism.**

immediate gratification: a preference for immediate pleasure or reward, without regard for the longer-term consequences; e.g. going out with friends instead of doing one's homework. *Cultural deprivation* theorists argue that working-class children are socialised into the value of immediate gratification and that this explains their educational failure. *See also* **deferred gratification; values.**

industrialisation: the shift from an agricultural economy to one based on factory production. In Britain, industrialisation occurred from about the late 18th to the mid-19th centuries. Industrialisation often occurs along with *urbanisation.*

individualism: the belief that the individual is more important than the group or community. In modern and postmodern society, individualism becomes more important than in traditional society and individuals' actions are influenced more by calculations of their own self-interest than by a sense of obligation to others.

infant mortality rate: the number of infants who die before their first birthday, per 1,000 live births per year. *See also* **birth rate.**

informed consent: where those taking part in a study have agreed to do so and understand the purpose of the study, the uses to which its findings may be put, and its possible effects. *See also* **ethics.**

instrumental role: the breadwinner or provider role in the family. Functionalists argue that this role is performed by men. *See also* **expressive role.**

interactionism: a sociological perspective that focuses on small-scale (micro-level) interactions between individuals and groups rather than the large-scale workings of society. Interactionists seek to understand the meanings that social actors give to actions and situations, usually by using qualitative research methods. *See also* **interpretivism; labelling; self-fulfilling prophecy.**

interpretivism: a term covering a range of perspectives including *interactionism*. Interpretivists focus on how we construct our social worlds through the meanings we create and attach to events, actions and situations. They favour qualitative methods and see human beings as fundamentally different from the natural phenomena studied by scientists, in that we have free will, consciousness and choice. *See also* **positivism; subjectivity.**

interview schedule: the list of questions to be asked in an interview. It is useful because it allows some standardisation of the interviewing process, since all interviewers will use the same schedule of questions.

interviews: a method of gathering information by asking questions orally, either face-to-face or by telephone. Structured (or formal) interviews use pre-set, standardised, usually *closed-ended questions* producing *quantitative data*. Unstructured (informal or depth) interviews are more like a guided conversation and use *open-ended questions* producing *qualitative data*. Semi-structured interviews include both types of question. *See also* **questionnaires.**

labelling: the process of attaching a definition or meaning to an individual or group; e.g. teachers may label a pupil as a 'trouble maker'. Often the label is a *stereotype* that defines all members of a group in the same way. The concept is widely used in the study of *deviance*, mental illness and education. *See also* **self-fulfilling prophecy.**

legitimation: justifying something by making it seem fair and natural. This is the main function of *ideology*. Marxists argue that institutions in capitalist society such as education, the media and religion are 'ideological state apparatuses' whose function is to legitimate inequality. *See also* **meritocracy.**

life chances: the chances that different social groups have of obtaining those things society regards as desirable (e.g. educational qualifications) or of suffering those things regarded as undesirable (e.g. low income). Statistics on education, health, income etc show that such opportunities vary by class, gender and ethnic group. See *also* **stratification.**

longitudinal study: study of a *sample* of people (sometimes called a panel) in which information is collected at regular intervals over an extended period of time; e.g. the National Child Development Study has been running since 1958. These studies usually use questionnaires or interviews, but other methods may also be employed.

macro-level: theories such as *functionalism* and *Marxism* that focus on the large scale, i.e. on the social structure as a whole or on the relationships between social institutions like the education system and the economy. These theories see the individual as shaped by society. See *also* **micro-level; positivism.**

marketisation: the policy of introducing market forces of supply and demand into areas run by the state, such as education and the National Health Service. The 1988 Education Reform Act began the marketisation of education by encouraging competition between schools and choice for parents. See *also* **New Right.**

Marxism: a conflict perspective based on the ideas of Karl Marx (1818–83). It sees society as divided into two opposed classes, one of which exploits the labour of the other. In capitalist society, the *bourgeoisie* exploits the *proletariat*. Marx predicted the proletariat would unite to overthrow capitalism and create a classless society. Marxist sociologists argue that institutions such as education and the media function to maintain capitalism. See *also* **alienation; exploitation; ideology; modernism; polarisation; reproduction.**

material deprivation: poverty; a lack of basic necessities such as adequate diet, housing, clothing or the money to buy these things. In education, material deprivation theory explains working-class under-achievement as the result of the lack of such resources; e.g. parents are unable to afford educational aids, overcrowding deprives children of a quiet study area etc.

means of production: see **bourgeoisie.**

meritocracy: an educational or social system where everyone has an equal opportunity to succeed and where individuals' rewards and *status* are achieved by their own efforts rather than ascribed by their *gender*, class or ethnic origins. See *also* **myth of meritocracy.**

micro-level: theories such as *interactionism* that focus on small-scale, face-to-face interaction, e.g. between teacher and pupils in a classroom. These theories see individuals constructing society through their interactions. See *also* **interpretivism; macro-level.**

mobility: movement; change of position. Sociologists distinguish between geographical mobility, in which people move from one place to another (e.g. in search of work), and social mobility, in which they change position or *status* in a *hierarchy* or *stratification* system. Functionalists argue that the geographical and social mobility of the *nuclear family* enable it to meet the needs of industrial society. See *also* **industrialisation.**

modernism: modernist perspectives (e.g. *functionalism, Marxism* and *positivism*) believe that society has a fairly clear-cut, predictable structure and that it is possible to gain true and certain scientific knowledge of how society functions. This knowledge can be used to achieve progress to a better society. See *also* **postmodernism.**

multicultural: a society or institution that recognises and gives value to different cultures and/or ethnic groups; e.g. multi-cultural education teaches children about the cultures of other groups, not just the dominant or majority culture.

myth of meritocracy: Functionalists argue that the education system is meritocratic, but Bowles and Gintis claim that meritocracy is an *ideology* legitimating inequality by falsely claiming that everyone has equal opportunity and that unequal rewards are the 'natural' result of unequal ability. *See also* **legitimation; meritocracy.**

New Right: a conservative political perspective whose supporters believe in self-reliance and individual choice, rather than dependence on the state. They believe in applying free market principles, e.g. the *marketisation* of education, and argue that generous welfare benefits encourage the growth of an *underclass*.

new vocationalism: the idea that education should be primarily about meeting the needs of the economy, especially by equipping young people with the knowledge, skills, attitudes and values needed to prepare them for work. Since the 1970s it has given rise to educational initiatives such as the Youth Training Scheme, vocational GCSEs, GNVQ and AVCE.

non-participant observation: a primary research method where the observer records events without taking part in them; e.g. a sociologist might observe and record how gender roles influence children's play without taking part. In sociology, *participant observation* is used much more often.

norms: social rules, expectations or standards that govern the behaviour expected in particular situations. Norms may be formal (e.g. written laws or rules) or informal (e.g. rules of politeness). Each *culture* has detailed norms governing every aspect of behaviour. *See also* **values.**

nuclear family: a two-generation family of a man and woman and their dependent children, own or adopted. *See also* **family structure.**

objectivity: the absence of bias or preconceived ideas. It implies that we can look at things as they really are, without our opinions or values getting in the way (and thus we can get at the truth). Positivists believe sociology can achieve objectivity by modelling itself on the natural sciences, using methods that keep sociologists detached from their research subjects. *See also* **positivism; subjectivity.**

official statistics: *quantitative data* collected by the government. They can be gathered either by registration (e.g. the law requires parents to register births) or by official surveys (e.g. the ten-yearly Census of the entire population).

open-ended questions: questions in a *social survey* that allow respondents to answer as they wish, in their own words (e.g. 'How did you feel about being excluded from school?'). Answers are harder to analyse because they cannot be pre-coded. *See also* **closed-ended questions.**

operationalisation: the process of turning a sociological concept or theory into something measurable. For example, a sociologist studying the effect of social class on educational achievement might use parental occupation to measure the concept *'social class'*.

overt participant observation: *see* **participant observation.**

participant observation: a primary research method in which the sociologist studies a group by taking a role within it and participating in its activities. It may be overt, where other participants are aware of the researcher's true identity and motive. Alternatively, it may be covert ('undercover'), where the sociologist's identity and purpose are kept secret.

patriarchy: literally, rule by the father. Feminists use the term to describe a society based on male domination; a system or ideology of male power over women. Child liberationists argue that children are victims of 'age patriarchy' – the domination of fathers, or adults generally. *See also* **feminism.**

personal documents: secondary data in the form of diaries, letters, autobiographies, wills, photographs etc, normally created by or belonging to an individual and providing first-person accounts of events and experiences.

pilot study: a small-scale trial run, usually of a *social survey*, conducted before the main study. Its basic aim is to iron out any problems, clarify questions and their wording, give interviewers practice etc, so that any necessary changes can be made before the main study is carried out.

polarisation: a process that results in the creation of two opposite extremes, e.g. pupils' responses to *labelling* and *streaming* in schools can create a pro-school and an anti-school pupil *subculture*. In the study of stratification, Marx describes how in capitalist society, the class structure becomes polarised into a wealthy *bourgeoisie* and impoverished *proletariat*. *See also* **differentiation; self-fulfilling prophecy; Marxism.**

population: in a *social survey*, the population (sometimes called the 'survey population') is all the members of the group that the researcher is interested in; e.g. in a study of political opinions, the population may be the entire electorate. *See also* **sampling frame.**

positivism: the belief that society is made up of 'social facts' that can be studied scientifically to discover laws of cause and effect. Durkheim took *official statistics* on suicide as social facts and tried to produce a law explaining why suicide rates vary between groups. With such knowledge, sociologists would be able to find solutions to social problems. *See also* **comparative method; experiments; interpretivism; objectivity.**

post-Fordism: a type of industrial production. A highly skilled, adaptable workforce, combined with computerised technology, means that production takes the form of 'flexible specialisation', able to respond swiftly to changing consumer demands and to produce for a variety of small, customised 'niche' markets. *See also* **Fordism**.

postmodernism: a perspective that rejects the modernists' belief in progress and their view that we can have certain, true knowledge of society that will enable us to improve it. Society has become so unstable and diverse that it is now impossible to produce any absolute explanations. No one theory is 'truer' than any other; theories such as *Marxism* and *functionalism* are merely viewpoints. Instead, sociology should concentrate on reflecting and celebrating social diversity. *See also* **modernism.**

primary data: information collected first hand by sociologists themselves for their own research purposes. Methods such as *participant observation, social surveys* and *experiments* are sources of primary data. *See also* **secondary data.**

primary socialisation: *see* **socialisation.**

privatised family: a *nuclear family* whose lifestyle and leisure patterns centre on the home rather than the *extended family*, workmates or wider community. In Young and Willmott's study, many families who moved out of Bethnal Green to the suburbs became privatised.

proletariat: the working class in capitalist society. They own no means of production and are 'wage slaves', forced to sell their labour-power to the *bourgeoisie* in order to survive. *See also* **exploitation; Marxism.**

qualitative data: information, usually expressed in words, about people's thoughts, feelings, motivations, attitudes, values etc. It is obtained from qualitative methods and sources such as *participant observation*, unstructured *interviews*, diaries and letters. It aims to give an insight into what it is like to be in another person's 'shoes'. *See also* **empathy; interactionism.**

quantitative data: information in numerical form (percentages, tables, graphs etc). *Official statistics* and the results of *social surveys* are two important sources of quantitative data. *See also* **closed-ended questions; positivism.**

questionnaires: lists of questions. Written or self-completion questionnaires are widely used in large-scale *social surveys*, where they may be sent out and returned by post. Questionnaires tend to use mainly *closed-ended questions* with pre-coded answers for ease of analysis. *See also* **quantitative data; response rate.**

racism: a system of beliefs that defines people as superior or inferior, and justifies their unequal treatment, on the basis of biological differences such as skin colour. Individual racism refers to the prejudiced views and discriminatory behaviour of individuals. Institutional racism exists when the routine ways an organisation operates have racist outcomes regardless of the intentions of the individuals within it.

reconstituted family: a stepfamily, in which one or both partners has children from a previous relationship. *See also* **family structure.**

reliability: a piece of research is reliable if it produces exactly the same results (a replica) when repeated using identical methods and procedures. In general, quantitative methods such as *experiments* and *questionnaires* are more reliable than qualitative methods because they use standardised procedures that are easier to replicate; e.g. a questionnaire asking all respondents the same set of questions.

representative: typical; a cross-section. A researcher may choose to study a *sample* of a larger group. If the sample is representative, those in it will be typical of the larger group. This will allow the findings to be generalised, i.e. applied to all members of the group, not just those in the sample.

reproduction: the re-creation or continuation of something into future generations; e.g. Marxists argue that schooling reproduces the class structure by failing working-class pupils so that they take working-class jobs. *See also* **correspondence principle; Marxism.**

response rate: the proportion of those people included in a *social survey* who actually reply or respond to the questions asked. A high response rate is important to help ensure that findings are *representative*.

role: how someone who occupies a particular *status* is expected to act; e.g. someone playing the role of bus driver is expected to drive safely, stop for passengers, charge the correct fare etc.

sample: a smaller group selected from the larger survey *population* to take part in a study. It may be too costly or time-consuming to study the whole population in which we are interested, so we choose a sample to study instead. *See also* **sampling; sampling frame.**

sampling: the process of selecting a *sample*. The aim of sampling is usually to select a sample that is *representative* of the wider survey *population*, so as to allow the study's findings to be generalised. There are several types of sampling, e.g. random, stratified random, quota and snowball sampling. *See also* **sampling frame.**

sampling frame: the list of people from which a *sample* for a *social survey* is selected, e.g. a school roll could be the sampling frame for a survey of pupils. It should list all the members of the survey *population* that the sociologist is interested in studying, though this is not always possible; e.g. there is no complete list of all criminals (since some are not caught).

sanctions: see **social control.**

secondary data: information collected not by sociologists themselves for their own research purposes, but by other people or organisations for non-sociological purposes. Sociologists make extensive use of this 'secondhand' information because it is often free or cheap, readily available and covers large numbers. Secondary sources of data include *official statistics*, the media and *personal documents*. *See also* **primary data.**

secondary socialisation: see **socialisation.**

secularisation: the decline of religion; the process whereby religious beliefs, practices and institutions lose their importance or influence; e.g. fewer couples now marry in church and many people disregard religious teachings on issues like divorce, homosexuality etc.

self-fulfilling prophecy: where a prediction made about a person or group comes true simply because it has been made. For example, in predicting that some pupils will do badly, teachers treat them in line with these lower expectations. This will discourage the pupils from trying and make the prediction come true. The prediction is a form of *labelling*. It works by changing the individual's self-image to bring it in line with the expectations that others have of him/her. See *also* **interactionism; streaming.**

sexism: prejudice and discrimination on the grounds of sex; e.g. seeing girls as better suited for courses in 'caring' subjects. See *also* **patriarchy.**

sexuality: sexual orientation; a person's sexual preference; e.g. heterosexual, homosexual (gay or lesbian).

social class: social groupings or *hierarchy* based on differences in wealth, income or occupation. Marx identified two opposed classes in capitalist society, the *bourgeoisie* and *proletariat*. Many sociologists use occupation to distinguish between a manual working class and a non-manual middle class. Some also identify an *underclass* beneath the working class. See *also* **life chances; Marxism.**

social construction: where something is created by social processes, rather than simply occurring naturally. For example, interpretivists argue that official crime statistics are socially constructed through the interactions of police and suspects. When something is socially constructed, it is likely to vary historically and between cultures. Sociologists see *childhood, gender, identity* etc as social constructs.

social control: the means by which society tries to ensure that its members behave as others expect them to. Control can be formal (e.g. the law) or informal (e.g. peer pressure). Negative sanctions (punishments) may be threatened or positive sanctions (rewards) offered to encourage individuals to conform to society's *norms* and *values*.

social mobility: see **mobility.**

social policy: the actions, plans and programmes of government bodies and agencies that aim to deal with a problem or achieve a goal, e.g. raising levels of educational attainment. Policies are often based on laws that provide the framework within which these agencies operate. See *also* **welfare state.**

social survey: any research method that involves systematically collecting information from a group of people (either a *sample* or the whole target *population*, e.g. the Census) by asking them questions. Usually, this involves using written *questionnaires* or structured *interviews* and the questions are standardised.

socialisation: the process by which an individual learns or internalises the *culture* of society. Primary socialisation occurs largely within the family and involves acquiring basic skills and values, while much secondary socialisation takes place within educational institutions and includes acquisition of knowledge and skills needed for work. Other agencies of socialisation include peer groups, the mass media and religion.

speech codes: patterns or ways of using language. Bernstein argues that the working class use only the context-bound restricted code, with short, grammatically simple sentences and limited vocabulary. The middle class use the context-free elaborated code, with complex sentences and able to describe abstract ideas. This code is used in education, giving middle-class children an advantage. See *also* **cultural capital.**

status: a position in society. Ascribed status occurs where our position in society is determined by fixed characteristics that we are born with and cannot normally change, e.g. *gender*, ethnicity or family of origin. Achieved status occurs where an individual's position is the result of their effort and ability, e.g. getting into university. See *also* **meritocracy.**

stereotype: a simplified, one-sided and often negative image of a group or individual which assumes that all members of that group share the same characteristics; e.g. the image that all black boys are disruptive and unruly. See *also* **labelling.**

stigma: a negative label or mark of disapproval, discredit or shame attached to a person, group or characteristic. The stigma is used to justify the exclusion of the individual from normal social interaction; e.g. in the past, divorcees were often stigmatised and excluded from 'respectable' company. *See also* **labelling.**

stratification: the division of society into a *hierarchy* of unequal groups. The inequalities may be of wealth, power and/or status. Stratification systems may be based on differences in *social class, ethnic group,* age, *gender,* religion etc. Members of different groups usually have different *life chances*.

stratified diffusion: the spread of beliefs and practices from one social class to another; e.g. Young and Willmott claim that the *symmetrical family* developed first among the middle class and then spread down the class structure eventually to become the norm for the working class as well.

streaming: where children are separated into different ability groups or classes ('streams') and then each ability group is taught separately from the others for all subjects; the opposite of mixed-ability teaching. *See also* **differentiation; self-fulfilling prophecy.**

subculture: a group of people within society who share *norms, values,* beliefs and attitudes that are in some ways different from or opposed to the mainstream *culture*; e.g. an anti-school subculture formed by pupils in lower streams.

subjectivity: bias, lack of *objectivity*, where the individual's own viewpoint influences their perception or judgement. Interpretivists believe sociology is inevitably subjective, since it involves understanding other humans by seeing the world through their eyes. *See also* **empathy; interpretivism.**

survey: *see* **social survey.**

symmetrical family: Young and Willmott's 'stage three' privatised *nuclear family* with more equal and joint *conjugal roles*, in which husbands participate in domestic labour as well as being breadwinners, and wives go out to work as well as being homemakers. The couple spend their leisure time together and are more home-centred.

triangulation: the use of two or more different methods or sources of data so that they complement each other, the strengths of one countering the weaknesses of the other and vice versa; e.g. using both a qualitative method such as *participant observation* and a quantitative method such as structured *interviews*.

tripartite system: the system of secondary education created by the 1944 Education Act, based on three types of school. The 11+ exam was used to identify pupils' aptitudes and abilities. Those identified as having academic ability (mainly middle-class) went to grammar schools; most working-class children went to secondary modern schools. Although replaced in most areas after 1965, the tripartite system still continues in some. *See also* **comprehensive system.**

triple shift, triple burden: *see* **emotion work.**

underclass: those at the lowest level of the class structure; a class below the working class with a separate, deviant *subculture* and lifestyle, including a high rate of lone-parent families, male unemployment and criminality. *See also* **dependency culture; New Right.**

unit of consumption: unlike the pre-industrial family, the modern family no longer works together, but still consumes together as a single unit or group the income that its members earn, e.g. on food, housing and leisure activities. *See also* **unit of production.**

unit of production: where family members work together as economic producers, said to be more common in pre-industrial society; e.g. an extended family that works together on a farm. *See also* **unit of consumption.**

urbanisation: the process of change from a rural society where the majority of the population lives in the countryside to an urban society where most people live in towns and cities. It often occurs along with *industrialisation*.

validity: the capacity of a research method to measure what it sets out to measure; a true or genuine picture of what something is really like. A valid method is thus one that gives a truthful picture. Methods such as *participant observation* that produce *qualitative data* are usually seen as high in validity. *See also* **empathy; interactionism.**

value consensus: agreement among society's members about what values are important; a shared culture. According to functionalists, it integrates individuals into society by giving them a sense of solidarity or 'fellow feeling' with others and enables them to agree on goals and cooperate harmoniously. *See also* **functionalism.**

values: ideas or beliefs about general principles or goals. They tell society's members what is good or important in life and what to aim for, and they underlie more detailed *norms* of conduct. Functionalists see shared values as vital in holding society together. *See also* **functionalism; value consensus.**

variables: any factor that can change or vary, such as age, *gender*, occupation or income. Sociologists seek to discover correlations between variables; e.g. between social class and educational achievement. Laboratory *experiments* are occasionally used to control variables and measure their effect.

vocational: connected to a career. Vocational education and training transmits knowledge, skills and attitudes needed to pursue particular careers, e.g. courses in engineering, health and social care, IT or hairdressing. *See also* **new vocationalism.**

welfare state: where the government or state takes responsibility for people's well being, especially their basic minimum needs. In Britain, today's welfare state was created largely in the late 1940s. It includes various benefits to provide a minimum income, as well as the NHS, state education and council housing. *See also* **dependency culture; underclass.**

Bibliography

Adonis A and Pollard S (1998) *A Class Act*, Penguin

Allan G (1985) *Family Life*, Blackwell

Allan G (1996) *Kinship and Friendship in Modern Britain*, Oxford University Press

Althusser L (1971) *Lenin and Philosophy and Other Essays*, New Left Books

Anderson M (1980) *Approaches to the History of the Western Family*, Macmillan

Ansley F (1972) cited in Bernard J (1976) *The Future of Marriage*, Penguin

Arber S and Ginn J (1995) 'The Mirage of Gender Equality', *British Journal of Sociology*

Ariès P (1960) *Centuries of Childhood*, Penguin

Arnot C (2004) 'Where White Liberals Fear to Tread', *The Guardian*

Askew S and Ross C (1988) *Boys Don't Cry*, Open University

Atkinson M (1971) 'Societal Reactions to Suicide' in Cohen S (ed) *Images of Deviance*, Penguin

Ball S (1981) *Beachside Comprehensive*, Open University

Ball S (1994) *Education Reform*, Open University

Ballard R (1982) 'South Asian Families' in Rapoport R and Rapoport R (ed) *Families in Britain*, RKP

Barrett M and McIntosh M (1991) *The Anti-Social Family*, Verso

Bartlett W (1993) 'Quasi-Markets and Educational Reform' in LeGrand et al (ed) *Quasi-Markets and Social Policy*, Macmillan

Beck U (1992) *Risk Society*, Sage

Beck U and Beck-Gernsheim E (1995) *The Normal Chaos of Love*, Polity

Becker H et al (1961) *Boys in White*, University of Chicago Press

Becker H (1971) 'Social Class Variations in the Teacher–Pupil Relationship' in Cosin B et al (ed) *Education Structure and Society*, Penguin

Bejin A (1985) *Western Sexuality*, Blackwell

Bell C (1968) *Middle Class Families*, RKP

Benedict R (1934) *Patterns of Culture*, Houghton Mifflin

Bereiter C and Engelmann S (1966) *Teaching Disadvantaged Children in Pre-school*, Prentice Hall

Bernard J (1976) *The Future of Marriage*, Penguin

Bernstein B and Young D (1967) 'Differences in Conceptions on the Use of Toys', *Sociology*

Bernstein B (1975) *Class, Codes and Control*, Schocken

Bernstein B (1976) 'Education Cannot Compensate for Society' in Butterworth E et al (ed) *The Sociology of Modern Britain*, Fontana

Bilton T et al (1987) *Introductory Sociology*, Macmillan

Black D et al (1980; 1992) 'The Black Report' in Whitehead M et al (ed) *Inequalities in Health*, Penguin

Blau P and Duncan O (1978) *The American Occupational Structure*, Free Press

Blauner R (1964) *Alienation and Freedom*, University of Chicago Press

Blundell J and Griffiths J (2003) *Sociology Since 1995*, Connect

Boaler J (1998) 'Mathematical Equity' in Epstein D et al (ed) *Failing Boys?* Open University

Bott E (1957) *Family and Social Network*, Tavistock

Boulton M (1983) *On Being a Mother*, Tavistock

Bourdieu P (1984) *Distinction*, RKP

Bourne J (1994) *Outcast England*, Institute of Race Relations

Bowker G (1968) *The Education of Coloured Immigrants*, Longman

Bowles S and Gintis S (1976) *Schooling in Capitalist America*, RKP

Brannen J et al (1994) *Young People, Health and Family Life*, Open University

British Crime Survey (2000; 2002) www.homeoffice.gov.uk

British Household Panel Survey (1998) www.iser.essex.ac.uk/bhps

British Social Attitudes (2000) www.esds.ac.uk

Browne N and Ross C (1991) 'Girls' Stuff, Boys' Stuff', in Browne N (ed) *Science and Technology in the Early Years*, Open University

Bull D (1980) *What Price Free Education?* Child Poverty Action Group

Burn E (2001) 'Battling Through The System', *International Journal of Inclusive Education*

Byrne E (1979) *Women and Education*, Routledge

Cameron M (1964) *The Booster and the Snitch*, Free Press

Cashmore E (1985) *Having to. The World of One Parent Families*, Allen and Unwin

Chamberlain M (1999) 'Brothers and Sisters, Uncles and Aunts' in Silva et al (ed) *The New Family?* Sage

Chapman K (1986) *The Sociology of Schools*, Tavistock

Cheal D (1991) *Family and the State of Theory*, Harvester

Cheal D (1993) 'Unity and Difference in Postmodern Families', *Journal of Family Issues*

Chester R (1985) 'The Rise of the Neo-Conventional Family', *New Society*

Chubb J and Moe T (1990) *Politics, Markets and America's Schools*, Brookings

Cicourel A and Kitsuse J (1963) *The Education Decision-Makers*, Bobbs Merill

Cicourel A (1968) *The Social Organisation of Juvenile Justice*, Wiley

Coard B (1971) *How the West Indian Child is Made Educationally Subnormal in the British School System*, New Beacon

Cockburn C (1987) *Two Track Training*, Macmillan

Colley A (1998) 'Gender and Subject Choice in Secondary Education', in Radford J (ed) *Gender and Choice in Education and Occupation*, Routledge

Commission for Racial Equality (1992) *Set to Fail*, CRE

Commission for Racial Equality (1993) *Draft Circular on Admission Arrangements*, CRE

Connolly P (1988) *Racism, Gender Identities and Young Children*, Routledge

Connor H and Dewson S (2001) *Social Class and HE*, DfES Research Report

Crompton R (1997) *Women and Work in Modern Britain*, Oxford University Press

Crystal D (1997) *The Cambridge Encyclopaedia of Language*, Cambridge University Press

Cumberbatch G and Negrine R (1992) *Images of Disability on Television*, Routledge

David M (1993) *Parents, Gender and Education Reform*, Polity

Davis K and Moore W (1945; 1967) 'Some Principles of Social Stratification' in Bendix and Lipset (ed) *Class Status and Power*, RKP

Dean H and Taylor-Gooby P (1992) *Dependency Culture*, Wheatsheaf

Devine F and Heath S (1999) *Sociological Research Methods in Context*, Macmillan

Dewar A (1990) 'Oppression and Privilege in Physical Education', in Kirk D et al (ed) *Physical Education, Curriculum and Culture*, Falmer

Ditton J (1977) *Part-time Crime*, Macmillan

Dobash R and Dobash R (1979) *Violence against Wives*, Open Books

Donzelot J (1977) *The Policing of Families*, Hutchinson

Douglas J (1964) *The Home and the School*, Penguin

Downes D and Rock P (1989) *Understanding Deviance*, Oxford University Press

Drew E et al (1995) *Families, Labour Markets and Gender Roles*, www.eurofound.eu.int

Driver G (1977) *Cultural Power, Social Power and School Achievement*, New Community

Duncombe J and Marsden D (1995) 'Women's Triple Shift', *Sociology Review*

Dunne G (1999) 'A Passion for Sameness', in Silva E et al (ed) *The New Family?* Sage

Durkheim E (1893; 1985) *The Division of Labour in Society*, Penguin

Durkheim E (1897; 2002) *Suicide*, Routledge

Durkheim E (1903; 2002) *Moral Education*, Dover

Edgell S (1980) *Middle Class Couples*, Allen and Unwin

Elwood P and Murphy J (1998) 'Gendered Learning Outside and Inside School', in Epstein D et al (ed) *Failing Boys?* Open University

Epstein D et al (1998) 'Boys' Underachievement in Context', in Epstein D et al (ed) *Failing Boys?* Open University

Fairhurst E (1977) 'On Being a Patient in an Orthopaedic Ward', in Horobin G et al (ed) *Medical Encounters*, Croom Helm

Feinstein L (1998) 'Which Children Succeed and Why?', *New Economy*

Ferri E and Smith K (1996) *Parenting in the 1990s*, Family Policy Studies Centre

Ferri E and Smith K (1998) *Step-parenting in the 1990s*, Family Policy Studies Centre

Festinger L et al (1956) *When Prophecy Fails*, Harper and Row

Finch J (1983) *Married to the Job*, Allen and Unwin

Finch J and Mason J (1989) *Family Obligations and Social Change*, Polity

Finch J and Mason J (1993) *Negotiating Family Responsibilities*, Routledge

Finn D (1984) 'Leaving School and Growing Up', in Bates I et al (ed) *Schooling for the Dole*, Macmillan

Firestone S (1970) *The Dialectics of Sex*, Paladin

Firestone S (1979) 'Down with Childhood', in Hoyles M (ed) *Changing Childhood*, Writers and Readers

Firth R (1970) *Rank and Religion in Tikopia*, Routledge

Fitz J et al (1997) 'Opting into the Past?', in Glatter P et al (ed) *Choice and Diversity in Schooling*, Routledge

Fletcher R (1966) *The Family and Marriage in Britain*, Penguin

Flew A (1984) *Education, Race and Revolution*, Centre for Policy Studies

Foster P (1990) *Policy and Practice in Multicultural and Anti-Racist Education*, Routledge

Foucault M (1976) *The Birth of the Clinic*, Routledge

Frank A (1965) *The Diary of Anne Frank*, Pan

French J and French P (1993) 'Gender Imbalances in the Primary Classroom', in Woods P et al (ed) *Gender and Ethnicity in Schools*, Routledge

Fuller M (1984) 'Black Girls in a London Comprehensive School', in Deem R (ed) *Schooling for Women's Work*, RKP

Furlong J (1984) 'Interaction Sets in the Classroom', in Hammersley M et al (ed) *Life in Schools*, Open University

Gauntlett D and Hill A (1999) *TV Living*, Routledge

Gershuny J et al (1994) 'The Domestic Labour Revolution', in Anderson M et al (ed) *The Social and Political Economy of the Household*, Oxford University Pres

Gewirtz S et al (1995) *Markets, Choice and Equity in Education*, Open University

Giddens A (1992) *The Transformation of Intimacy*, Polity

Gill R (1988) 'Altered Images', *Social Studies Review*

Gillborn D (1990) *Race, Ethnicity and Education*, Unwin Hyman

Gillborn D (1997) 'Race and Ethnicity in Education 14–19', in Tomlinson S (ed) Education *14–19 Critical Perspectives*, Athorne

Gittins D (1998) *The Child in Question*, Macmillan

Glasgow University Media Group (1976) *Bad News*, RKP

Goldthorpe J and Lockwood D et al (1969) *The Affluent Worker in the Class Structure*, Cambridge University Press

Goode W (1964) *The Family*, Prentice Hall

Graham H (1983) 'Do Her Answers Fit His Questions?', in Gamarnikow E et al (ed) *The Public and the Private*, Heinemann

Graham H (1984) *Women, Health and the Family*, Prentice Hall

Gregson N and Lowe M (1994) *Servicing the Middle Classes*, Routledge

Griffin J (1962) *Black Like Me*, Collins

Hardill I et al (1997) 'Who Decides What?', *Work, Employment and Society*

Hareven T (1999) *Families, History and Social Change*, Westview

Hargreaves D (1967) *Social Relations in a Secondary School*, RKP

Hatcher R et al (1996) *Racial Equality and the Local Management of Schools*, Warwick Papers on Education Policy

Haywood C and Mac an Ghaill M (1996) 'Schooling Masculinities', in Mac an Ghaill M (ed) *Understanding Masculinities*, Open University

Hillman M (1993) *Children, Transport and the Quality of Life*, Policy Studies Institute

Hitchcock G (1995) 'Writing Lives', *Sociology Review*

Hite S (1991) *The Hite Report on Love, Passion and Emotional Violence*, Penguin

Hochschild A (1983) *The Managed Heart*, University of California Press

Hochschild A (1997) *The Time Bind*, Metropolitan Books

Hockey J and James A (1993) *Growing Up and Growing Old*, Sage

Holmes L (1974) *Samoan Village*, Thompson

Holt J (1974) *Escape from Childhood*, Penguin

Howard M et al (2001) *Poverty the Facts*, Child Poverty Action Group

Hugo R (1982) *The Hitler Diaries*, William Morrow

Humphreys L (1970) *The Tea Room Trade*, Duckworth

Hyman H (1967) 'The Value Systems of Different Classes', in Bendix R and Lipset S (ed) *Class, Status and Power*, RKP

Irvine J (1987) *Demystifying Social Statistics*, Pluto

Jackson D (1998) 'Breaking the Binary Trap', in Epstein et al (ed) *Failing Boys?* Open University

Jenkins R (1986) *Racism and Recruitment*, Cambridge University Press

Katz C (1993) 'Growing Girls', in Katz C et al (ed) *Full Circles*, Routledge

Keddie N (1971) 'Classroom Knowledge', in Young M (ed) *Knowledge and Control*, Macmillan

Keddie N (1973) *Tinker, Tailor: the Myth of Cultural Deprivation*, Penguin

Kelly A (1987) *Science for Girls*, Open University

Kempson E et al (1994) *Hard Times?*, Family Policy Studies Centre

Kendal Project (2004) www.lancs.ac.uk

Khan V (1979) *Minority Families in Britain*, Macmillan

Kinsey A et al (1953) *Sexual Behaviour in the Human Female*, WB Saunders

Labov W (1973) 'The Logic of Nonstandard English', in Keddie N (ed) *Tinker, Tailor: the Myth of Cultural Deprivation*, Penguin

Lacey C (1970) *Hightown Grammar*, Manchester University Press

Lancet (2002) www.thelancet.com

Land H (1978) 'Who Cares for the Family?' *Journal of Social Policy*

Lane T and Roberts K (1971) *Strike at Pilkingtons*, Fontana

Laslett P (1972) *Household and Family in Past Time*, Cambridge University Press

Lawrence E (1982) 'The Sociology of Black Pathology', in CCCS (ed) *The Empire Strikes Back*, Hutchinson

Lawson T and Garrod J (2000) *The Complete A to Z Sociology Handbook*, Hodder

Leach E (1967) *Runaway World?* BBC

Lees S (1986) *Losing Out*, Hutchinson

Lees S (1993) *Sugar and Spice*, Penguin

Leonard D (1978) 'The Regulation of Marriage', in Littlejohn G et al (ed) *Power and the State*, Croom Helm

Liebow E (1967) *Tally's Corner*, Little Brown

Litwak E (1960) 'Occupational Mobility and Extended Family Cohesion', *American Sociological Review*

Lobban G (1974) 'Data Report on British Reading Schemes', *Times Educational Supplement*

Lyotard J (1984) *The Postmodern Condition*, Manchester University Press

Mac an Ghaill M (1994) *The Making of Men*, Open University

MacDonald M (1980) 'Socio-cultural Reproduction and Women's Education', in Deem R (ed) *Schooling for Women's Work*, RKP

Macklin E (1980) 'Non-Marital Heterosexual Cohabitation', in Skolnick A et al (ed) *The Intimate Environment*, Little Brown

Macrae S et al (1997) 'Competition, Choice and Hierarchy in the post-16 Market', in Tomlinson S (ed) *Education 14–19 Critical Perspectives*, Athorne

Malinowski B (1957) *The Sexual Life of Savages*, RKP

Marshall G (1988) *Social Class in Modern Britain*, Harper Collins

Marx K (1848; 2002) *The Communist Manifesto*, Penguin

Mason D (1995) *Race and Ethnicity in Modern Britain*, Oxford University Press

Mayo E (1927; 2003) *Human Problems of an Industrial Civilisation*, Routledge

McKee L and O'Brien M (1983) 'Interviewing Men', in Gamarnikow E et al (ed) *The Public and the Private*, Heinemann

McRobbie A (1978) 'Working Class Girls and the Culture of Femininity', in Hall S et al (ed) *Resistance Through Ritual*, Hutchison

McRobbie A (1994) *Postmodernism and Popular Culture*, Routledge

McVeigh T (2001) 'Boys Lagging in Class for Years', *The Observer*

Mead M (1943) *Coming of Age in Samoa*, Penguin

Merton R (1949) *Social Theory and Social Structure*, Free Press

Milgram S (1974) *Obedience and Authority*, Harper Collins

Millett K (1970) *Sexual Politics*, Doubleday

Mirrlees-Black C (1999) *Domestic Violence*, The Home Office

Mirza H (1992) *Young, Female and Black*, Routledge

Mirza H (1997) *Black British Feminism*, Routledge

Mitchell J and Goody J (1997) 'Feminism, Fatherhood and the Family in Britain', in Oakley A and Mitchell J (ed) *Who's Afraid of Feminism*, Penguin

Mitsos E and Browne K (1998) 'Gender Differences in Education', *Sociology Review*

Moore D and Davenport S (1990) 'Choice: the New Improved Sorting Machine', in Boyd W et al (ed) *Choice in Education*, McCutchan

Morgan D (1996) *Family Connections*, Polity

Morgan D (1997) 'Risk and Family Practices', in Silva E et al (ed) *The New Family*, Sage

Morris L (1990) *The Workings of the Household*, Polity

Morrow R and Torres C (1998) 'Education and the Reproduction of Class, Gender and Race', in Torres C et al (ed) *Sociology of Education: Emerging Perspectives*, University of New York Press

Mortimore P and Whitty G (1997) *Can School Improvement Overcome the Effects of Disadvantage?*, Institute of Education

Moynihan D (1965) *The Negro Family*, US Department of Labor

Murphy P (1991) 'Gender Differences in Pupils' Reactions to Practical Work', in Woolnough B (ed) *Practical Science*, Open University

Murphy P and Elwood J (1998) 'Gendered Learning Outside and Inside School', in Epstein D et al (ed) *Failing Boys?* Open University

Murray C (1984) *Losing Ground*, Basic Books

National Audit Office (2002) www.nao.gov.uk

Nazroo J (1997) *The Health of Britain's Ethnic Minorities*, Policy Studies Institute

Newby H (1977) *The Deferential Worker*, Allen and Unwin

Noon M (1993) 'Racial Discrimination in Speculative Applications', *Human Resources Management Journal*

Norman F et al (1988) 'Look, Jane, Look', in Weiner G (ed) *Just a Bunch of Girls*, Open University

O'Brien M and Jones D (1996) 'Revisiting Family and Kinship', *Sociology Review*

Oakley A (1973) *Sex, Gender and Society*, Temple Smith

Oakley A (1974) *The Sociology of Housework*, Martin Robertson

Oakley A (1982) *Subject Women*, Penguin

Oakley A (1997) 'A Brief History of Gender', in Oakley A and Mitchell J (ed) *Who's Afraid of Feminism*, Penguin

Opie I (1993) *The People in the Playground*, Oxford University Press

Paetcher C (1998) *Educating the Other*, Falmer

Pahl J and Vogler C (1993) 'Social and Economic Change and the Organisation of Money within Marriage', *Work, Employment and Society*

Papworth J (2000) 'Millions of Children Work: Most are Exploited', *The Guardian*

Parker A (1996) 'Sporting Masculinities', in Mac an Ghaill M (ed) *Understanding Masculinities*, Open University

Parker H (1974) *View From the Boys*, David and Charles

Parker H et al (1998) *Illegal Leisure*, Routledge

Parsons T (1951; 1991) *The Social System*, Routledge

Parsons T (1955) 'The American Family', in Parsons T and Bales R (ed) *Family Socialisation and Interaction Process*, Free Press

Parsons T (1961) 'The School Class as a Social System', in Halsey A et al (ed) *Education, Economy and Society*, Free Press

Patrick J (1973) *A Glasgow Gang Observed*, Methuen

Pilcher J (1995) *Age and Generation in Modern Britain*, Oxford University Press

Pirie M (2000) 'How Exams are Fixed in Favour of Girls', *The Spectator*

Pollock L (1983) *Forgotten Children*, Cambridge University Press

Polsky N (1971) *Hustlers, Beats and Others*, Penguin

Postman N (1994) *The Disappearance of Childhood*, Vintage

Pryce K (1979) *Endless Pressure*, Penguin

Punch M (1979) *Policing the Inner City*, Macmillan

Qualifications and Curriculum Authority (1999) www.qca.org.uk

Qvortrup J (1990) *Childhood a Social Problem*, Centre for Study of Adult Life

Rapoport R and Rapoport R (1971) *Dual Career Families*, Penguin

Rapoport R and Rapoport R (1982) *Families in Britain*, RKP

Redman P and Mac an Ghaill M (1997) 'Educating Peter', in Steinberg D et al (ed) *Border Patrols*, Cassell

Renvoize J (1985) *Going Solo*, Routledge

Rex J (1986) *Race and Ethnicity*, Open University

Reynolds T (1997) 'Mis-representing the Black Super-woman', in Mirza S (ed) *Black British Feminism*, Routledge

Rich J (1968) *Interviewing Children and Adolescents*, Macmillan

Rist R (1970) *Student Social Class and Teacher Expectations*, Harvard Educational Review

Robertson Elliot F (1996) *Gender, Family and Society*, Macmillan

Robinson P (1997) *Literacy, Numeracy and Economic Performance*, London School of Economics

Rosenhan D (1973) 'On Being Sane in Insane Places', *Science*

Rosenthal R and Jacobson L (1968) *Pygmalion in the Classroom*, Holt Rinehart and Winston

Roulstone A (1998) 'Researching a Disabling Society', in Shakespeare T (ed) *The Disability Reader*, Cassell

Schofield M (1965) *The Sexual Behaviour of Young People*, Longman

Schor J (1993) *The Overworked American*, Basic Books

Scott J (1990) *A Matter of Record*, Polity

Scruton R (1986) 'The Myth of Cultural Relativism', in O'Keefe D (ed) *Anti-Racism: an Assault on Education and Value*, Sherwood

Sewell T (1998) 'Loose Cannons', in Epstein D et al (ed) *Failing Boys?* Open University

Sharp R and Green A (1975) *Education and Social Control*, RKP

Sharpe S (1994) *Just Like a Girl*, Penguin

Shaw C (1930) *The Jack-Roller*, University of Chicago Press

Shelton B and John D (1993) 'Does Marital Status Make a Difference?', *Journal of Family Issues*

Shipman M (1997) *Limitations of Social Research*, Longman

Shorter E (1975) *The Making of the Modern Family*, Fontana

Silver H (1987) 'Only So Many Hours in a Day', *Service Industries Journal*

Sissons M (1970) *The Psychology of Social Class*, Open University

Skeggs B (1997) *Formations of Class and Gender*, Sage

Slee R (1998) 'High Reliability Organisations and Liability Students', in Slee R et al (ed) *School Effectiveness for Whom?* Falmer

Smithers R (2001) 'Today's Special', *The Guardian*

Spender D (1983) *Invisible Women*, Women's Press

Stables A and Wikeley F (1996) 'Pupil Approaches to Subject Option Choices', Conference Papers cited in Epstein D et al

Stacey J (1998) *Brave New Families*, University of California Press

Steel L and Kidd W (2001) *The Family*, Palgrave

Stein P (1976) *Single*, Prentice-Hall

Stone M (1981) *The Education of the Black Child in Britain*, Fontana

Sugarman B (1970) 'Social Class Values and Behaviour in Schools', in Craft M (ed) *Family Class and Education*, Longman

Swann J and Graddol D (1994) 'Gender inequalities in classroom talk', in Graddol et al (ed) *Researching Language and Literacy in Social Contexts*, Clevedon

Swann J (1998) 'Language and Gender', in Epstein D et al (ed) *Failing Boys?* Open University

Swann Report (1985) *Education For All*, HMSO

Thomas W and Znaniecki F (1919; 1995) *The Polish Peasant in Europe and America*, University of Illinois Press

Thompson K (1992) 'Social Pluralism and Postmodernity', in Hall S et al (ed) *Modernity and its Futures*, Polity

Thornton S (1995) *Club Cultures*, Polity

Townsend P (1979) *Poverty in the United Kingdom*, Penguin

Troyna B and Williams J (1986) *Racism, Education and the State*, Croom Helm

Tuchman G (1978) *Hearth and Home*, Oxford University Press

Tuckett D (2001) *An Introduction to Medical Sociology*, Routledge

Tumin M (1967) *Social Stratification*, Prentice Hall

Usher R et al (1997) *Adult Education and the Postmodern Challenge*, Routledge

Vogler C (1994) 'Money in the Household', in Anderson M et al (ed) *The Social and Political Economy of the Household*, Oxford University Press

Wagg S (1992) 'I Blame the Parents', *Sociology Review*

Walford G et al (1991) *City Technology College*, Open University

Warde A and Hetherington K (1993) *A Changing Domestic Division of Labour?*, Work, Economy and Society

Weber M (1905; 2002) *The Protestant Ethic and the Spirit of Capitalism*, Routledge

Weeks J et al (1999) 'Everyday Experiments', in Silva E et al (ed) *The New Family?* Sage

Weeks J (2000) *Making Sexual History*, Polity

Weiner G (1993) 'Shell-shock or Sisterhood', in Arnot M et al (ed) *Feminism and Social Justice in Education*, Falmer

Weiner G et al (1995) *Equal Opportunities in Colleges and Universities*, Open University

Weston K (1992) 'The Politics of Gay Families', in Thorne B and Yallom M (ed) *Rethinking the Family*, Northeastern University Press

Westwood S and Bhachu P (1988) *Images and Realities*, New Society

Whitty G et al (1998) *Devolution and Choice in Education*, Open University

Whyte W (1955) *Street Corner Society*, University of Chicago Press

Wilkinson R (1996) *Unhealthy Societies*, Routledge

Willis P (1977) *Learning to Labour*, Saxon House

Willmott P (1988) *The Evolution of a Community*, Routledge

Wilson A (1985) *Family*, Routledge

Women's Aid Federation (1999; 2003) www.womensaid.org.uk

Woodroffe C et al (1993) *Children, Teenagers and Health*, Open University

Woods P (1979) *The Divided School*, RKP

Wright C (1992) 'Early Education', in Gill D et al (ed) *Racism in Education*, Sage

Wrong D (1961) 'The Oversocialised Conception of Man', *American Sociological Review*

Yablonsky L (1973) *The Violent Gang*, Penguin

Yearnshire S (1997) 'Analysis of Cohort', in Bewley et al (ed) *Violence Against Women*, RCOG Press

Young M and Willmott P (1962) *Family and Kinship in East London*, Penguin

Young M and Willmott P (1973) *The Symmetrical Family*, Penguin

Answers to QuickCheck Questions

Chapter 1 Introduction to Sociology

Answers to questions on page 11

1 A programme or plan by government that aims to achieve a particular goal.

2 It is learnt through nurture or contact with others.

3 (a) All those things learnt and shared by a society or group and transmitted from generation to generation, including norms, values, language, beliefs etc.

(b) Specific rules governing behaviour.

(c) The process of transmitting, learning or internalising culture.

4 Ascribed: based on fixed characteristics we are born with. Achieved: gained through our own efforts.

5 False.

6 False.

7 Agreement among society's members about basic values.

8 It enables members to agree on goals and cooperate to achieve them.

9 Male-dominated society.

10 Urbanisation: the shift from a society where people live in the countryside to one where they live in towns. Industrialisation: where the workforce moves out of agriculture and into factory production.

11 (a) Modern; (b) traditional; (c) postmodern.

12 False.

Answers to questions on page 14

1 Three.

2 (a) False; (b) false.

3 Any from: work with others; ask questions; use your coursebook; apply what you learn to the real world; be critical, don't take things at face value; take ideas apart; answer the question when doing written work.

4 (a) Interpretation; (b) Evaluation; (c) Analysis.

Chapter 2 Families and Households

Answers to questions on page 30

1 False.

2 Joint.

3 (a) Working full-time.

4 Freezers, microwave ovens, ready meals.

5 The different roles that men and women in heterosexual couples are expected to play.

6 Marxist feminism sees capitalism as the source of women's oppression (e.g. women reproduce the workforce for capitalism). Radical feminism sees men as the source of women's oppression (e.g. men benefit from women's unpaid domestic labour).

7 Kempson; Barrett and McIntosh; Graham.

8 They earn more.

9 It is too widespread; it follows particular social patterns (e.g. its perpetrators are usually men).

10 Children; the lowest social classes; those in rented accommodation; those on low incomes; drug/alcohol users.

Answers to questions on page 39

1 Fixed by birth.

2 True.

3 Geographical mobility: movement between different places. Social mobility: movement between social positions (e.g. from farm labourer to doctor).

4 Because of social changes (e.g. geographical mobility, higher living standards, more married women working, the welfare state, better housing, labour-saving technology in the home).

5 Household size was small, marriage and childbearing were late and people died young, so most households only contained two generations.

6 Because conditions were harsh, there was no welfare state and the extended family provided mutual aid.

7 O'Brien and Jones; Litwak; Willmott; Bell; Allan; Finch and Mason; Ballard; Chamberlain.

Answers to questions on page 50

1 False.

2 Children take responsibility at an earlier age; less value is placed on them showing obedience; their sexual behaviour is often viewed differently.

3 Giving a newborn baby the same name as a dead sibling; referring to the baby as 'it'; forgetting how many children they had.

4 False.

5 Among poorer children, these are more likely: low birth weight, delayed development, higher infant mortality rates, longstanding illness, hyperactivity and conduct disorders, falling behind at school, being on the child protection register.

6 Adult domination/control and child dependency.

7 Because television is destroying the information hierarchy between adults and children and giving children access to knowledge that hitherto only adults possessed.

8 The spread of western ideas of childhood as vulnerable etc to the rest of the world, e.g. via aid agencies.

Answers to questions on page 70

1 Increases in the number of couples cohabiting, people remaining single, divorces, lone-parent families, same-sex couples and births outside marriage.

2 False.

3 The decline in the influence of religion in society.

4 Women are having fewer children; they are having them later; more are remaining childless; more births are outside marriage.

5 The higher value placed on the extended family; the need for support and assistance when migrating; the higher proportion of people of childbearing age in British Asian communities.

6 False.

7 True.

8 Organisational; life stage; generational.

9 True.

10 Feminism; greater opportunities for women in education and in work; availability of contraception.

11 Because its members enter the relationship on an equal basis and are free to leave if their needs are not met.

12 A group of people connected by divorce (e.g. former in-laws, ex-husband's new partner), whose key members are usually female.

Answers to questions on page 79

1 False.

2 Because they reward irresponsible or anti-social behaviour (e.g. encouraging fathers to abandon their families in the knowledge that the welfare state will provide for them).

3 Child benefit; maternity leave.

4 Familistic: policies assume that there is a traditional division of labour and little state welfare/childcare. Individualistic: policies assume couples are equally responsible both for breadwinning and domestic labour, and there is extensive state welfare/childcare provision.

5 Individualistic.

6 False.

Chapter 3 Education

Answers to questions on page 104

1 (a) Deferred: making sacrifices now for greater rewards later. Immediate: seeking pleasure now rather than making sacrifices to gain future rewards.

(b) Elaborated: context-free; communicates abstract ideas; wider vocabulary; grammatically complex sentences. Restricted: context-bound; descriptive; limited vocabulary; short, often unfinished, grammatically simple sentences.

(c) Cultural capital is the culture of the middle class. Economic capital is wealth.

2 Overcrowding means nowhere to study; poor diet leading to illness and absence from school; have to leave school early to get a job; unable to afford study materials.

3 The introduction of market forces of supply and demand into areas that were previously run by the state.

4 The Education Reform Act; the Parents' Charter.

5 Labelling involves attaching a meaning or definition to someone, e.g. 'thick'. The self-fulfilling prophecy is a prediction that comes true simply by virtue of it having been made, e.g. the pupil labelled 'thick' internalises the label and under-achieves.

6 Labelling theory is deterministic and wrongly assumes that once labelled, pupils have no choice but to fulfil the prophecy and fail. It ignores the wider structures of power within which labeling takes place.

7 True.

8 As a response to being put in a low stream; as a means of obtaining status among those labelled as failures.

Answers to questions on page 116

1 Whites, Bangladeshis, blacks.

2 True.

3 Cultural deprivation theory ignores the positive effects of ethnicity on achievement, e.g. of black girls. Black pupils under-achieve because of racism, not cultural deprivation. Black pupils are culturally different, not culturally deprived, but schools are ethnocentric.

4 Sociologists include Gillborn, Bourne, Foster, Fuller, Sewell.

5 By accepting the label and fulfilling the prophecy; by ignoring it; by seeking to disprove it, e.g. by working harder.

6 A curriculum that gives priority to one culture or ethnic group and ignores others, e.g. teaching only European languages, not Asian ones.

Answers to questions on page 130

1 False.

2 The impact of feminist ideas; changes in the family, e.g. more divorce; more job opportunities for women; changes in girls' ambitions or priorities.

3 Laddish anti-school subcultures; parents spend less time with sons reading; boys have more behavioural problems and are more likely to be excluded; boys see education as feminine; over-confidence means they do less revision; the decline of traditional men's jobs.

4 True.

5 Science teachers are more likely to be men; examples used are often from boys' interests; boys monopolise apparatus.

6 By teasing boys for doing less well than girls; by ignoring or encouraging verbal abuse of girls; by intervening in female teachers' lessons to restore order.

Answers to questions on page 150

1 Ascribed status: fixed at birth. Achieved status: gained through the individual's own effort and ability.

2 Achieved.

3 False.

4 Repressive: police; courts; army. Ideological: education; mass media; religion.

5 Reproduction: transmitting inequality from generation to generation, e.g. by failing working-class pupils in each generation. Legitimation: justifying it as fair and natural, e.g. the myth of meritocracy.

6 Parallels or similarities between school and workplace, e.g. hierarchy of teachers and pupils mirrors hierarchy of bosses and workers.

7 A production system based on flexible specialisation, using advanced technology and adaptable, skilled workers, where production is customised for niche markets.

8 (a) It argues that the reproduction of inequality by the education system remains important.

(b) It argues that reproduction of non-class forms of inequality is important.

9 By ensuring that successful schools will be in greater demand, allowing them to be more selective in recruiting higher-achieving middle-class pupils.

Chapter 4 Sociological Methods

Answers to questions on page 159

1 (a) Quantitative data are information in a numerical form. Qualitative give a 'feel' for what something is like.

(b) Primary: collected by sociologists themselves for their own purposes. Secondary: collected or created by someone else for their own purposes, but which the sociologist can then use.

2 (a) Questionnaires; structured interviews.

(b) Letters; diaries.

3 Conducting covert observation; deceiving people in order to study them; breaking the law so as to study criminals; doing research that might harm the participants; publishing findings about a group without their consent.

4 True.

5 A true or genuine picture of what something is really like.

6 Time; money; funding bodies' requirements; researcher's personal skills and characteristics; the nature of the subject matter or group being studied.

7 (a) True; (b) false.

Answers to questions on page 163

1 Environment (or situation); manipulate (or control); variables (or factors).

2 (a) Society is so complex it is impossible to identify and control all possible variables; experiments cannot be used to study the past.

(b) Difficulties obtaining informed consent from groups (e.g. children) who are unable to understand what is being proposed; the experiment may harm the subjects.

3 The problem of the subjects reacting to the fact that they are being observed by behaving differently.

4 False.

5 It avoids artificiality; can be used to study past events; poses no ethical problems such as harming or deceiving subjects.

Answers to questions on page 168

1 True.

2 Closed: respondents must choose their answer from a limited range of possible answers that the researcher has decided upon in advance. Open: respondents are free to give whatever answer they wish.

3 True.

4 It gives direction to the research and a focus to the questions asked.

5 The process of defining a concept in such a way that it can be measured.

6 A trial run carried out on a small sample before the actual survey to iron out problems, clarify questions, give interviewers practice etc.

7 True.

Answers to questions on page 172

1 The ten-yearly survey of the whole UK population, in the form of a written questionnaire.

2 A person who completes and returns a questionnaire or takes part in a survey.

3 Because they need to be fairly brief (most respondents will not complete long ones), thus limiting the amount of information that can be gathered.

4 Because those who respond may be different from those who don't.

5 Because once finalised, the researcher is stuck with the questions they have decided to ask and cannot explore any new areas of interest that may come up during the research.

6 They are snapshots; they are too detached; it is not possible to clarify misunderstandings; respondents may lie, forget, not know; closed-ended questions restrict respondents' ability to express their meanings.

Answers to questions on page 181

1 Structured: (b), (d), (e), (h) and (i).
Unstructured: (a), (c), (f) and (g).

2 A group interview, where the researcher asks the group to discuss certain topics and records their views.

3 (a) Both are cheap and quick; can survey large numbers; are suitable for collecting factual information; can quantify results easily; are reliable.

(b) In interviews, questions are read out and answers filled in by the interviewer, not the respondent; interview response rates are higher.

4 False.

5 By asking 'leading' questions; by their facial expression, body language or tone of voice.

6 Where the respondent seeks to win approval by giving answers that present them in a favourable light.

Answers to questions on page 190

1 Empathy (understanding that comes from putting yourself in another person's place).

2 It allows the sociologist to start with an open mind, rather than with a fixed hypothesis or questions. As new situations are encountered, new explanations can be formulated and followed up there and then.

3 Re-entering one's normal world can be difficult; loyalty may prevent the researcher from disclosing what they have learnt in case this harms the group.

4 It avoids ethical problems of deception and of having to join in illegal activities. It allows the observer to use interviews, ask naïve but important questions and take notes openly.

5 (a) The group studied is usually small and the sample often selected haphazardly.

(b) It is a 'unique' method where much depends on the personal characteristics of the individual researcher, making it difficult for others to replicate; it produces qualitative data, making comparisons with other studies difficult.

6 We can see for ourselves what people actually do, rather than what they say they do; we can experience their way of life first hand and so gain a true insight.

Answers to questions on page 198

1 Data that others have already created or gathered for their own purposes but which sociologists can use in their research.

2 By registration and through official surveys.

3 Births, deaths, marriages, divorces, crime, suicide, exam results, school exclusions, unemployment, health etc.

4 Trade unions, businesses, churches, pressure groups.

5 They are a free source of information, save time, allow comparisons, show trends and are representative and reliable.

6 (a) A true or genuine picture of what something is really like; a valid method is one that measures the thing it claims to measure.

(b) Because of under-reporting, under-recording, misclassifying cases (e.g. crimes); because they are social constructs.

7 Data may not be collected or available on some topics; official definitions may be different from the sociologist's or may change over time; statistics may contain recording errors.

8 Diaries, letters, photo albums, autobiographies.

9 Laslett; Anderson; Hareven; Ariès.

Answers to questions on page 202

1 False.

2 Burn; Lane and Roberts; Weber; Townsend; the Kendal Project.

3 True.

4 False.

5 Douglas; the National Child Development Study; Lacey; Gauntlett and Hill; Parker.

6 Losing some of the original sample during the course of the study.

7 They can trace developments over a period of time; they allow a detailed picture to be built up; by comparing groups over time, we can identify causes.

8 The weaknesses of each one can be countered by the strengths of the other.

Chapter 5 The Coursework Guide

Answers to questions on page 214

1 No.

2 (a) No; (b) yes.

3 Aim: a statement about what you propose to study and hope to achieve. Hypothesis: a statement that can be tested against the evidence and proved true or false.

4 At least one, but can be both.

5 False.

6 'Potential problems'.

7 False.

Chapter 6 Preparing for the exam

Answers to questions on page 233

1 (a) One hour 15 minutes.

(b) One hour 15 minutes.

(c) One hour.

2 (c) 6.

3 False.

4 (c) Assess.

5 False.

6 False.

7 True.

8 About 20–25 minutes.

Index